THE
ECONOMIC AND POLITICAL
IMPACT OF
GENERAL REVENUE SHARING

F. Thomas Juster, Editor

Michigan. Univ.

Contributors:

Thomas J. Anton	James Fossett	Gail R. Wilensky
Robin Barlow	Edie Goldenberg	Richard E. Barfield
Harvey E. Brazer	F. Thomas Juster	Robert Snider

Survey Research Center • Institute for Social Research • The University of Michigan • Ann Arbor, Michigan

ISR Code No. 3909

HJ
275
.M49
1977

This report was originally prepared for the National Science
Foundation under National Science Foundation/Research
Applied to National Needs Grant APR-75-17473.

Any opinions, findings, conclusions, or recommendations
expressed in this publication are those of the author(s) and
do not necessarily reflect the views of the National Science
Foundation.

Library of Congress Catalog Card No. 76-620083
ISBN 0-87944-217-4 clothbound

Published by the Institute for Social Research
The University of Michigan, Ann Arbor, Michigan 48106

First Published 1977
Manufactured in the United States of America

FOREWORD

This study, made possible by a grant to the Survey Research Center from the Research Applied to National Needs Directorate of the National Science Foundation, is designed to aid policymakers in their evaluation of the General Revenue Sharing Program (The State and Local Government Fiscal Assistance Act of 1972). Needless to say, the National Science Foundation bears no responsibility for its content or conclusions.

Any study of this magnitude owes a great deal to its research support staff, as well as to its listed contributors. Given the tight time schedule imposed by the needs of the public policy purposes that it was designed to serve, it is more true here than is usually the case. The staff of the Revenue Sharing Study worked long and hard, especially during the summer of 1974 (when the basic survey instrument was being designed) and during the spring and summer of 1975 (when the monograph was in the process of preparation). During the preparation stage of the survey itself, Tracy Berckmans of the Field Division of the Survey Research Center contributed enormously to the solution of problems ranging from design of the basic field instrument to the successful completion of interviews. A response rate in excess of 96 percent is testimony to some of these efforts. During the same period, Irene Hess and Jean Harter of the Survey Research Center's sampling staff managed to produce a sample design which can only be described as spectacularly successful. Survey researchers have had long and bitter experience with the failure of survey responses to aggregate up to known external totals. That this is the fault of the survey instrument, or of the inability of respondents to provide accurate data, is usually assumed. But here it can be clearly demonstrated, since the adequacy of the SRC sample of local government units can be ascertained by reference to a known external reference group—the population of all U.S. general government jurisdictions at the local level. Since our sample estimates of the total local government revenue sharing allocation come to within one percent of the known external total, it can be assumed that the sample can hardly be improved on.

During the early stages of the project, including instrument design, thanks are due to Kent Jennings and Richard Hofferbert of the Center for Political Studies at the Institute for Social Research, to members of the Advisory Committee for the Revenue Sharing Project, and for research support to Michael Conte, Toni Kramer, Greg Protasel, and John Wilman.

During the analysis and final report stage, the study benefited greatly from the enthusiasm and determination of a considerable stable of research support personnel. These include Regina Guptill, Pamela Hartmann, Robert Johnson, Daphne Kenyon, Fred Leech, Mary Ann Ritter, Amaury de Souza and Anne Thompson, as well as James Fossett and Robert Snider who are listed as contributors. Robert Snider not only managed the data base and organized the support staff activities, but provided help on the analysis side as well. The mammouth job of typing the monograph, completed within a remarkably short span of time, is due to the skills and energy of Kristin Westrum, aided by whatever assistance could be borrowed from the Economic Behavior Program staff and from others, including Priscilla Hildebrandt, Nancy McAllister, Alice

Snider, Ted Thompson, and Kathy Yale. It is fair to say that the project could not have been completed without this support staff, who literally worked evenings and weekends to get the job done.

The Advisory Committee to the Revenue Sharing Project fulfilled a useful and indeed essential role. They provided us with reaction both to the questionnaire itself and to preliminary analyses and analysis plans, often gave us very useful insights into substantive issues, and generally functioned as an Advisory Committee should. Members of the Committee include: Michael D. Bird, David A. Caputo, Richard I. Cole, Priscilla Crane, Maurice Criz, Jane Fenderson, Delphis C. Goldberg, Carol Goldfarb, Walter Heller, Tim Honey, Trudi Lucas, Milton Moss, Will S. Myers, Jr., Richard P. Nathan, Robert D. Reischauer, Morton H. Sklar, Lawrence Susskind, Ralph L. Tabor, Richard Thompson, and Eugene B. Tryck.

Helpful comments on an earlier draft of the monograph were received from Ralph J. Perotta, as part of review by the National Clearinghouse on Revenue Sharing; from Robert Pearl, as part of an evaluation of National Science Foundation research on Revenue Sharing conducted by a committee of the American Statistical Association; from Charles W. Binford, Andre Blum and James E. Gunderson, as part of a review conducted by the Municipal Finance Officers Association; and from Richard P. Nathan of the Brookings Institution.

Finally, the project would not have been conducted at all except for the perceptive insight of Dr. Trudi Lucas, of the RANN Directorate of the National Science Foundation, who conceived the need for the study and provided encouragement and support throughout.

F. Thomas Juster
The University of Michigan
Ann Arbor, Michigan
April 1976

THE ECONOMIC AND POLITICAL IMPACT OF GENERAL REVENUE SHARING

Contents

PART I

Overview

PART II

Economic Impact

PART III

Political Impact

PART IV

Appendices

CHAPTER 1

Introduction and Summary

F. Thomas Juster* and Thomas J. Anton

INTRODUCTION

This monograph provides an assessment of the State and Local Fiscal Assistance Act of 1972—the General Revenue Sharing legislation under which States and general purpose local governments in the United States received a total of some $30 billion from the Federal Government over a period of five years beginning in January 1972 and extending through December of 1976. The Act provided for the distribution of approximately $6 billion each year over the period,[1] with roughly one-third of the total being distributed among the States and the remaining two-thirds being divided among municipalities, towns, townships, and counties.[2]

BACKGROUND

The State and Local Fiscal Assistance Act resulted from the coalescing of both liberal and conservative political forces. Liberal proponents of the revenue-sharing idea were concerned about the "fiscal mismatch" between the Federal Government and State and local governments, resulting primarily from the responsiveness of Federal

revenues to income growth and the relative lack of responsiveness of State and local revenues. The differential response arose out of the tax structure: Federal revenues were dominantly income taxes, and tax yields rose as income rose; but State and local revenues were dominantly property or sales taxes, and the increase in revenue was either smaller than income growth or dependent on property reassessment. On the conservative side, support for revenue sharing arose from concern over the growth of Federal power and Federal bureaucracy. Transfer of resources from the Federal Government to State and local governments was viewed as a way of transferring decision-making power over expenditure programs to jurisdictions that were viewed as more responsive to the needs of individual citizens.[3]

These very different strands of support produced a welter of inconsistent expectations regarding the objectives of the program. The Act itself speaks rather generally of strengthening State and local governments and enabling them to better meet the needs of their constituents. But objectives as diverse as providing assistance to financially hard-pressed cities, reducing the power of the Federal Government, tailoring public services to community needs, reducing the burdens of regressive local property taxes, etc., were all consistent with what at least some political decision-makers thought the program ought to accomplish.

As part of the mechanism for determining whether or not any particular objective was being met, the revenue-sharing legislation required States and local governments to file Official Use Reports, indicating the purposes for which

*Juster is Professor, Department of Economics and Program Director, Survey Research Center, The University of Michigan; Anton is Professor, Department of Political Science and Research Scientist, Institute of Public Policy Studies, The University of Michigan.

[1]The actual amounts were less than $6 billion in the early years, more than that in the later ones.

[2]Allocation of the funds was determined by a complex formula involving population, tax effort, and per capita income (and sometimes degree of urbanization and income tax effort): recipient jurisdictions were simply sent payments in accordance with the formula. This study concentrates on analysis of the economic and political impact of revenue sharing: technical issues concerning the allocation formula are almost entirely ignored.

[3]See Richard P. Nathan, Allen D. Manvel, Susannah E. Calkins and Associates, *Monitoring Revenue Sharing*, Washington, DC, The Brookings Institution, 1975; and Paul Dommel, *The Politics of Revenue Sharing*, Bloomington: Indiana University Press, 1974, for extensive discussion of the origins of the revenue sharing program.

revenue-sharing monies had been spent.[4] Some restrictions were imposed on the use of revenue-sharing funds for local governments, but these restrictions were quite loose in keeping with the general spirit of the Act—that revenue sharing funds were designed to be general purpose monies whose use was best determined by local governments and not by Federal authorities. Thus eight priority categories were established; the only clear-cut exclusions were local operating expenditures for education and public welfare spending in the form of cash payments. The legislation also prohibited revenue-sharing funds from being used as the local share of matching funds for other Federal programs (Block or Categorical Grants).

In understanding and interpreting the results reported in this study, it is important to recognize both the policy focus of the research and the relatively short time horizon of the project. An important objective of the study was to provide data that would aid policy makers in the decision about whether and on what terms to extend the revenue-sharing program. The present revenue-sharing legislation porvides funds up through the end of calendar 1976, and discussion about its continuation began in the spring of 1975. To provide meaningful guidance to policy, research had to be completed by the middle of 1975, since it was originally anticipated that the key decisions would be made by or around that date. Thus the project, which was begun in May 1974, aimed at a completion date of summer 1975. For a major research study, this is an extremely short time horizon, which is the principal reason we focus almost entirely on the results of a survey of State and local government officials.

RESEARCH DESIGN

The data and analyses contained in this monograph are based in large part on the results of a survey conducted among a sample of some 2,000 State and local government officials who have the basic responsibility for administering the general revenue sharing program. All fifty State governments are included in the analysis. The basic local government sample comprises 149 counties and 668 municipalities, including towns and townships. The municipality and county sample consists of randomly selected governmental units drawn from the Survey Research Center's national probability sampling frame, with some augmentation in areas where too few of the appropriate types of municipal government were within the SRC sampling frame.[5] Some cities and counties are included

in the sample with certainty because of their size, while others are included with probability of selection proportionate to size.

As Appendix B indicates, the resulting sample of governmental units is quite representative of all U.S. local governments, as reflected by such measures as per capita tax efforts, per capita revenue sharing allocation, total revenue-sharing allocation, per capital income, and so forth. Estimates derived from sample distributions of the four major U.S. regions are also quite close to the population estimates, although the sampling errors are obviously much greater for regional than for national aggregates.

For each jurisdiction in this sample of governmental units, we selected two, three or four respondents to interview. In all State governments, four interviews were scheduled: these included the governor (chief executive officer), the chief finance officer, and the respective heads of the appropriations committees in the upper and lower chambers. In municipalities of 25,000 or more population, three interviews were scheduled: these included the mayor (chief executive officer), the chief finance officer, and the chief administrative officer. The same interview schedule applied to all county governments in the sample. For municipal governments under 25,000 population, two interviews were scheduled: these included the mayor (executive officer) and the chief finance or budget officer.

The actual number of interviews scheduled and completed is shown in Table 8 of Appendix B, which summarizes the sample distributions by size class and type of governmental units. Response rates are extremely high: the only unsatisfactory response rates are among governors and mayors of cities with over 300,000 population. Otherwise, all response rates are in the high 90's, with several being 99 percent. In particular, response rates are always over 96 percent for the chief finance officers in every category of State and local government, averaging over 97 percent in the sample as a whole. Thus, the data obtained from the survey have the substantial merit of being totally representative of all U.S. State and local governments, especially if one is concerned with the analysis of the responses from chief finance officers.[6]

---

[6]Because the results reported in this monograph are based on data obtained from a fully representative national sample of U.S. local governments, it is the only study of the revenue sharing program that permits generalizations about the program as a whole. All other studies of the impact of revenue sharing have dealt with the experiences of particular local areas (mainly states), of small numbers of cities (mainly large ones) or of a diverse collection of communities designed to reflect the fact that the revenue sharing program applied to all types of governments. This is the only study that reflects a probability sampling of U.S. communities.

A compendium of research on revenue sharing is contained in Volume 5 of *General Revenue Sharing: Research Utilization Project,*"Ancilla to Revenue Sharing Research, National Science Foundation, Research Applied to National Needs, December 1975.

---

[4]In part, the Use Reports appear to have been designed simply to discourage irresponsible use of the funds—to pave the road where the mayor's house was located, for example.

[5]The sample characteristics are outlined in detail in Appendix B, "Sample Design, Respondent Selection and Response Rates for the Study of General Revenue Sharing."

The interviews themselves took an average of close of one hour to complete and covered topics of both economic and political import. On the economic side, we attempted to assess in a generally qualitative way the impact of the program on expenditures and taxes. In essence, we asked respondents how their budget situation would have been different if the Revenue Sharing program had not existed. That seemed to us the right question to ask, since it attempts to get at the true net effects of the program on expenditures and taxes, rather than asking how revenue-sharing funds were officially allocated to eligible (priority) uses. It should be recognized that the question we asked is extremely difficult to answer. Although we attempted to provide step-by-step guidance to respondents in the form of question sequences which asked about particular kinds of program areas (current expenditures, capital expenditures, taxes, borrowing, changes in surplus), it is still true that it is difficult for anyone to say what would have happened in the absence of the program. Nonetheless, it is our view that these responses are the best single measure that we have of the national impact of the revenue-sharing program on U.S. municipalities, counties and States.

In addition to overall programmatic impacts of GRS, we also attempted to get judgments about specific programs that would have been eliminated if GRS had not existed, and to assess which population groups would have been most affected if the programs supported by revenue-sharing funds had not been undertaken. Again, for assessing impact, these are clearly the right questions to ask, although as with the overall programmatic evaluations they are difficult (and politically sensitive) questions to answer. Finally, we asked a number of questions dealing with innovation: respondents were asked to specify programs which they regarded as innovative, to indicate the cost of these programs, whether or not they would have been undertaken without GRS, and so forth.

Two points need to be asked in the discussion of economic impact. First, it is often argued, with some justification, that the political sensitivity of the revenue-sharing program is such that people charged with administering the program cannot be expected to provide entirely candid responses to questions of the sort asked in the survey. While we recognize that there is some merit in that general criticism, we also think it is important to note that this concern is likely to be exaggerated. An interview is, after all, an extended interaction between respondent and interviewer. In an interview situation lasting for about an hour, it is unreasonable to expect any but the most skilled respondent to carefully disentangle impressions of what really happened from perceptions of answers likely to be

politically palatable to readers of the results. Our judgement is that after an initial period of caution, most respondents were providing answers which represented their best assessments of the program, rather than giving views that were inaccurate but perceived to be politically palatable.[7]

Second, most of what we attempted to do in the survey in measuring economic impact was necessarily qualitative. It was our initial view that a survey could not be effectively used to get details of budget decisions from respondents. Nonetheless, it turns out that our basically qualitative data permit enough quantitative inferences to make it possible to construct rough quantitative estimates of the overall fiscal impact of the revenue-sharing program.

On the political issues, we asked about the impact of the revenue-sharing program on decision making processes and structure—whether it affected the budget process, whether it affected the community's ability to plan, whether it was likely to affect the number or types of functions performed by local governments, and so on. Both local and State government officials were asked about the allocation formula—whether they thought it gave too much weight to big cities or too little weight, too much or too little weight to tax effort, too much or too little weight to need, and so forth. We inquired at length about the extent of public participation in the budget process associated with the GRS program—whether hearings were held, whether and which community groups attended, whether these were new groups or groups that had always attended budget hearings, and so forth. Finally, we asked a number of general opinion questions about the program, and questioned State and local government officials about the kinds of problems faced by their communities, and whether the revenue-sharing program had helped in the resolution of these problems.

OUTLINE OF THE STUDY

The monograph contains four sections: I, Introduction, Summary of Findings, and Policy Implications; II, Economic Impact; III, Political Impact; IV, Basic Data Appendices. The introduction, summary of findings and policy implications section represents a joint product of the revenue-sharing research staff, with primary responsibility resting with F. Thomas Juster and Thomas J. Anton. Section II contains five chapters. Chapters 2 and 3 contain a basic description and analysis of the

---

[7]That does not of course mean that the perceptions of officials are accurate. That issue is discussed at greater length in Chapter 2.

survey estimates of fiscal impact, both overall (Chapter 2) and in terms of particular expenditure categories and programs (Chapter 3). The analysis here concerns only local governments (municipalities, towns, townships and counties) and is the basic responsibility of Juster. Chapter 4 models the fiscal impact estimates of Chapter 2, and provides an explanation and interpretation of the reasons why revenue-sharing funds were allocated to the uses indicated by the survey. This chapter is the primary responsibility of Gail Wilensky. Chapter 5 analyzes the fiscal information forms obtained from a sample of local government jurisdictions in the study. Here, expenditure and tax data are used in an attempt to assess the impact of revenue-sharing funds on both overall fiscal allocations and allocations to particular programs. This chapter is the primary responsibility of Robin Barlow. Chapter 6 is concerned with fiscal impact on the states. It covers the attitudes of State officials, their estimates of fiscal impact, and analysis of factors associated with both attitudes and fiscal impact. This chapter is the primary responsibility of Harvey Brazer.

Section III is concerned with the impact of revenue sharing on political processes and structure. Chapter 7 is an overview of attitudes of public officials, mainly but not entirely local government officials, about the impact of the program on governmental structure, and is the primary responsibility of Thomas J. Anton. Chapter 8 deals with revenue sharing and local decisionmaking, focusing primarily on planning, the relation between revenue sharing and perceived local government problems, and innovation. This chapter is the principal responsibility of James Fossett. The final chapter, Chapter 9, is concerned with revenue sharing and public participation. It examines the extent of participation in the GRS decision process, and compares and contrasts it with participation in budget decision-making generally among U.S. local government jurisdictions. This chapter is the primary responsibility of Edie Goldenberg.

The study contains three appendices. Appendix A describes the basic data obtained from the survey of State and local government officials. The basic data are not themselves incorporated in the mongraph, primarily because of space and length limitations, but can be obtained on request to the Survey Research Center of The University of Michigan. The Data Appendix is the responsibility of Richard Barfield. Appendix B analyzes the SRC sample of local government jurisdictions, prepared under the direction of Irene Hess and Jean Harter of the sampling section at the Survey Research Center. The sampling appendix is the joint responsibility of Juster, Hess and Amaury de Souza. Ap-pendix C reproduces the survey instruments used for local government officials and State officials.

SUMMARY OF FINDINGS

Economic Impact

The basic issues on the economic impact of revenue sharing have to do with the uses of revenue-sharing funds in States and local governments. To what degree were revenue-sharing funds used to provide new services to the public? To what degree did they permit State or local taxes and borrowing to be reduced or stabilized? What kinds of programs did revenue sharing facilitate—public safety, social services, highway construction? Which population groups appear to have benefited most from the expenditure of revenue-sharing monies, or from the impact of revenue-sharing funds on local taxes? Do the Official Use Reports, which local governments are required to file with the Office of Revenue Sharing, provide an accurate indication of the net fiscal impact of revenue-sharing monies on local budgets? These are the questions that this section of the study is designed to answer.

The one thing on which all revenue-sharing studies agree is that fiscal impact is hard to measure because money is "fungible." Concretely, that means it is important to distinguish the apparent or earmarked uses of revenue-sharing funds from the eventual uses. If a community "uses" its revenue-sharing funds for public safety, in that it earmarks these funds for the payment of salaries or the purchase of equipment in the police or fire departments, but in fact the public safety budget is the same as it would have been in the absence of the revenue-sharing program, then the real effect of revenue sharing cannot have been on public safety but must be sought elsewhere. The key question is: if revenue-sharing funds had not been available, what would have been different about State and local government budgets. Which programs would have been smaller in size, which taxes would have been higher, etc.

A number of different approaches are used to examine these issues. For the most part, we rely on data obtained from survey questions which ask State and local government officials how their budgets would have been different in the absence of revenue sharing. We also examine time-series data on local expenditures and taxes, in an attempt to assess the impact of revenue sharing as the difference between actual spending or taxes and the level of spending or taxes that might have been expected in the absence of revenue sharing. And we compare the results of the fiscal impact estimates derived from the survey with a number of other studies that use different techniques.

Uses of Revenue Sharing Funds

The weight of the evidence in Section II of the monograph suggests a number of conclusions regarding the impact of the revenue-sharing program on State and local government budgets:

1. The principal impact of the program was to expand the capital outlays of local governments, and to expand the transfer payments of State governments.

2. More revenue-sharing funds were used to maintain or expand operating programs than to reduce or stabilize taxes.

3. Other uses of revenue-sharing funds—reduction or stabilization of borrowing, additions to fund balances—were relatively unimportant.

4. The overall patterns of revenue-sharing fund use mask a great deal of diversity among municipalities of different sizes, among States with different levels of income, and among comparably sized communities in different geographic regions of the United States.

   a) In the largest U.S. cities, those with populations of 300,000 or more, revenue-sharing funds were used predominantly for the maintenance of existing operating programs: in large U.S. cities more than two-thirds of the local government revenue sharing allocation was used to maintain operating outlays.

   b) In muncipalities with less than 100,000 population, the expansion of capital outlays was far and away the most important use of revenue-sharing monies, typically accounting for half or more of the local government total. The same emphasis on capital outlays also tended to be found in county governments of all size classes.

   c) In moderate-sized U.S. cities, those with populations between 100,000 and 299,000, tax reduction or stabilization was the most important use of local government revenue-sharing funds (about 40 percent), with the remainder divided about evenly between maintenance of operating outlays and expansion of capital outlays.

   d) Among State governments, tax reduction or stabilization was an important use in States with below average income, but not in other States.

   e) Among geographic regions, cities in the Northeast tend to show a relatively heavier use of revenue-sharing funds for the maintenance of operating outlays (large cities), and for tax stabilization (moderate and small cities), than cities in other parts of the country. Cities in the West, in contrast, show much more emphasis on capital outlays, much less on operating outlays or tax stabilization.

   f) Not only was tax stabilization a much more important use of revenue sharing funds in Northeast cities than elsewhere, it was the dominant use of such funds in Northeast cities over 25,000 population and accounted for over 70 percent of the revenue-sharing money in Northeast cities between 100,000 and 299,999 population.

5. Both at the local and State level, GRS funds appear to have been used primarily to support ongoing activities, with only modest amounts of revenue-sharing monies going to activities that would be appropriately characterized as innovative. For both local governments and States, the principal barriers to innovative use of GRS funds appear to have been the limited (5-year) duration of the program and the fiscal pressure produced by a combination of rising costs of government services and sluggish revenue growth.

6. The major uncertainties about measurement of the impact of revenue sharing on State and local governments concerns the size of tax effects. Alternative methodologies, especially econometric modeling of local government budgets, suggests a stronger tax abatement (reduction or stabilization) effect than the quite modest overall effect suggested by the survey. On balance, however, the weight of the evidence suggests that tax abatement accounted for something like 20-25 percent of revenue-sharing funds in 1974 and perhaps 30-35 percent in 1975, and that tax abatement uses of GRS funds were less important than capital outlay uses during both of those years.

Comparisons with Other Studies

The survey estimates of fiscal impact are compared with estimates from other studies, as well as with estimates obtained from the analysis of budget data from a subset of communities in the SRC sample. Most of the studies agree with the emphasis found in the survey data on the capital outlay uses of revenue-sharing funds, and with the generally less important roles of operating outlay or tax abatement uses. These results give added validity to the differences shown by the survey in the relative importance of capital and operating outlay uses in communities of different size classes and in different geographic regions. Overall, however, evidence on the relative importance of tax abatement is less clear. Most of the evidence suggests that, as the survey finds, tax abatement was a relatively modest overall use of revenue-sharing funds. In most other studies that report larger tax abatement effects than the survey, the differences tend to disappear once account is taken of the types of communities included in the other studies. And to the extent that differences in the survey estimates and other estimates continue to exist, they suggest that the survey estimates of tax abatement are biased on the low side, but that the bias is small.

Program Impacts of Revenue-Sharing Funds

The survey data suggest that the principal program beneficiaries of revenue-sharing monies were public safety, transportation, amenities and environmental control. The public safety functions turn out to be principally fire services in the municipalities, almost entirely police services in the counties. The survey estimates tend to be inconsistent with the program impact estimates shown by the Official Use Reports, but the inconsistencies are largely, if not entirely, due to differences between the survey and Use Report estimates for large cities—those with over 100,000 population—and large counties. In small communities the survey and Use Report estimates are quite close. And the analysis of budgetary data from the subset of sample communities comes to just about the same conclusion as does the survey with regard to program impact—significant effects of revenue sharing on expenditures are found for fire services, highways, and sewerage—three of the four categories identified in the survey as being principally impacted by revenue-sharing funds in moderate sized cities.

Interpretation of Fiscal Impact Results

Evidence bearing on the reasons that State and local governments allocated their revenue-sharing funds in the manner indicated is found in both the economic and political sections of the study. Overall, the survey data convey some clear-cut impressions about the reasons why large cities used most of their revenue-sharing funds for the maintenance

of existing programs and/or tax abatement, while smaller communities tended to use most of their revenue-sharing funds for capital outlays.

The picture that emerges from the data is one of financially hard-pressed large cities using revenue-sharing monies to maintain services perceived to be vital or to reduce what are perceived to be the heavy burden of local property taxation. Other cities see themselves as financially much less constrained, but as being concerned about the temporary nature of the revenue-sharing program.

The capital outlay pattern in moderate to smaller-sized communities and in counties is easiest to understand. These communities see as their major problems what might be called housekeeping functions—the provision of police and fire services, transportation services, recreation services, etc. The revenue-sharing program was apparently viewed as an opportunity to upgrade capital stocks in these areas, thus serving to speed up existing capital programs without incurring any future liabilities for the provision of new services. These communities typically do not seem to be under any pressure to reduce or even stabilize local taxes, except in parts of the country (the Northeast) where a combination of stagnant or declining population growth, a population mix that brings with it heavy demands for public services, and a burdensome local property tax structure seems to have resulted in the use of much of the revenue-sharing money to reduce local taxes while continuing existing service levels.

In large municipalities, the data suggest a persistent mismatch between fiscal capacity and need. Many such cities face strong demands for services, and appear to have insufficient capacity to meet those demands. Large cities see fiscal and economic problems as the major ones they face, strongly favor a substantial increase in the size of the revenue-sharing program, and report that the existing program has barely enabled them to "stay afloat" financially. They also tend to face strong public pressure for stabilization of local taxes, and as a result tended to put their revenue-sharing funds into the maintentance of existing services or into tax abatement. In short, the contrast between the fiscal situation perceived by local officials in large cities and that perceived by their counterparts in moderate to smaller-sized communities is stark indeed, and accounts for a good bit of the variation in the uses of revenue-sharing funds.

Political Impact

Approximately half of the survey of State and local officials was devoted to an examination of the various political issues raised by General Revenue Sharing. We were especially interested in the extent to which State and local government officials supported or opposed the program, in their assessment of the impact of revenue sharing on local politics and decisionmaking, in their views about the consequences of revenue sharing for intergovernmental relations, and their preferences for adjusting the revenue sharing program in the years ahead. Because the study includes a number of variables relating to each of these broad issues, we are in a position to provide a detailed evaluation of the political consequences of General Revenue Sharing, as perceived by municipal, county and state officials.

Support

First of all, it is quite clear that the overwhelming majority of local officials support General Revenue Sharing and are strongly in favor of its continuation: more than 94 percent of the officials we interviewed expressed this opinion. Moreover, 73 percent of mayors and 77 percent of local finance officers believe that the funds available through the revenue-sharing program should be increased. Among officials who report losses in other Federal assistance programs there is less inclination to support increases in revenue sharing, but apart from that group, support for an extension of revenue sharing is widespread and strong.

Allocation Formula

Both local and state officials expressed widespread support for changing the allocation formula to provide more funds to poor communities, but neither group was favorably inclined towards increasing GRS support for large cities per se. In addition, state officials generally favored changing the allocation formula to modify the within-state distribution of GRS funds to reflect the relative importance of state governments and local jurisdictions as tax collectors. Finally, substantial support can be found among both local and state officials for changes in the allocation formula designed to include at least some user charges in the definition of tax base, to encourage consolidation of the smallest units of local government, and to remove the "priority" expenditure restrictions currently imposed on local governments.

Impact on Process

In general, revenue sharing appears to have had very little impact on local political processes. Less than 40 percent of local officials reported that they held hearings on the first revenue-sharing entitlement, and fewer than 15 percent report such hearings for the second fiscal period. Since virtually all (75-100 percent) respondents report that they had already adopted the practice of holding public

hearings on their budgets, the decline in reported hearings for revenue-sharing funds does not suggest a reluctance to make fiscal information public; rather it suggests that, after an initial increase in publicity caused by the first entitlement, revenue-sharing monies have gradually been folded into normal processes of decisionmaking. Instead of changing local practices with regard to hearings, revenue sharing appears to have been absorbed by those practices.

Responses to questions regarding groups and group conflict reveal a similar pattern. Officials report that very few new groups have been formed because of revenue sharing. Groups reported to have been active are groups already established prior to revenue sharing, and their activity has been largely nonthreatening: very few officials report any group criticism over revenue-sharing decisions, and very few perceive any increase in conflict between themselves and other such groups or the public at large. These perceptions of relatively benign environments may help to explain the reluctance of local officials to endorse proposals that might change existing relationships. When asked how they felt about changing revenue sharing "to require the formation of citizen advisory committees to decide how to use revenue-sharing money," some 80 percent of city and county executives indicated that they were opposed—most of them strongly opposed.

It is very important to understand that none of these conclusions apply to large cities. Just as fiscal conditions in large U.S. cities are different than those in smaller municipalities, so too are the estimates of political impacts given by officials from those cities. In large cities, hearings are reported more frequently, group activity is reported to have increased, the level of conflict appears to have increased, and officials—particularly mayors—are quite sensitive to criticism over revenue-sharing allocations. Since these officials are more likely to perceive a net loss in Federal assistance because of reductions in other grant programs, their perceptions that increases in activity as a result of revenue sharing have come primarily from social service groups (economic opportunity, welfare) suggest that disputes over social service programs have also been folded into normal budget processes. Given the level of fiscal pressure experienced by large municipalities, it is hardly surprising that demands to assume obligations previously supported by special federal funds would produce perceptions of increased conflict.

Local Decisionmaking

Our data suggest that GRS has had little or no impact on the processes through which local over a period of years might therefore represent an improvement in the efficiency and equity of the program. Similarly, the evidence suggests that many large U.S. cities are under extreme fiscal pressure, and have been unable to use revenue-sharing funds for more than a continuation of existing services that otherwise might have had to be cut. Some of these jurisdictions have been affected by the 145 percent ceiling in the revenue-sharing formula, and a lifting of that ceiling, again phased over several years would, by inference, represent an improvement in the effectiveness and equity of revenue-sharing fund uses. Finally, virtually all officials—more than 95 percent—feel that some mechanism should be found to bring greater certainty to the payments they receive. Year-to-year variation in GRS allotments clearly causes problems for local officials in preparing their budgets, and some way should be found to reduce that variability.

Duration of Funding

The present revenue-sharing program has a five-year funding period. One of the clearest and least arguable findings from this study, and one supported by most other studies of the revenue-sharing program, is that the impermanence of revenue sharing has had a major impact on the way in which local governments used GRS funds. Specifically, the heavy emphasis on the use of revenue-sharing funds to finance capital outlays appears to be due in significant part to a concern among local governments that new operating programs might eventually have to be funded from local sources if revenue sharing were to be discontinued. It may be that our results reflect only the fact that the program was new, and that local officials were cautious in responding to it. But the evidence we have suggests that the limited horizon of the program did have an impact on the way in which funds were used, and that the heavy capital outlay emphasis on revenue-sharing fund uses was not an optimal allocation of these funds. If local governments use their own sources of revenue in a ratio of 3 or 4 to 1 for operating versus capital outlays, it is hard to see why an optimal use of revenue-sharing funds involves a significantly different allocation, as appears to have been the case. Thus our findings imply that permanence has desirable features, although that is not incompatible with a revenue-sharing program which has some fraction of funding on a permanent basis and another fraction which is variable and subject to annual appropriation.

Level of Funding

Most officials we surveyed support extension of GRS. However, local officials are far from unanimous in supporting a large expansion in the program. While more than 70 percent of mayors and finance officers would prefer an increase in the GRS program, only 42 percent of the mayors and 54 percent of the finance officers indicate a preference for increasing the program "a lot." This suggests that local officials across the country view GRS as one among many federal assistance programs and not as a program to be expanded into *the* major source of federal aid.

Eligibility

A majority of State officials interviewed in this survey believe that GRS encourages "the continued existence of inefficient units of local government." That belief is strongest in the North Central and Southern States, where a majority of State officials would prefer to eliminate very small local units from the GRS program. Although support for small-unit elimination is not as strong in other regions, very substantial proportions of local, as well as State, officials are in favor of using GRS to "encourage" the consolidation of small units. Thus, the belief that revenue sharing props up functionless governments, and a willingness to impose stricter eligibility requirements, both appear to be widespread.

Similarly, most local and State officials feel that the revenue-sharing formula should be changed to give more weight to need: some two-thirds of mayors and finance officers favor allocating more GRS money "to poorer communities." This does not necessarily imply that big cities should receive more favored treatment—only a few officials believe that. But widespread support for weighting need more heavily in the allocation formula, coupled with equally widespread willingness to reduce the number of small governments, suggests a broad base of support for a modification of the eligibility criteria.

Accountability

The survey data tend to confirm results from other studies that are by now widely accepted: Official Use Reports cannot be regarded as uniformly reliable indicators of the uses to which revenue-sharing funds are put. Although survey estimates and Use Reports are resonably congruent for units of 100,000 or less, there is considerable divergence between survey and Use Report data for units of over 100,000. If the survey data are regarded as roughly accurate, this must mean that Use Reports are unreliable for units that account for between one-third and one-half of all all GRS local government funds. If meaningful accountability is to be achieved, these results suggest it will have to be achieved through some mechanism other than the Planned and Actual Use Reports.

The problem, of course, is fungibility. Recipient units can easily substitute locally generated dollars for GRS dollars in order to finance programs not entitled to GRS support. Because permitted uses (the so-called "priority" categories) are so broad, GRS dollars can then be channeled into accounts from which local dollars have been withdrawn, thus obscuring the ultimate uses of Federal dollars. One solution to this problem would be to require more detailed accounting reports, covering all funds available to recipient jurisdictions in a fashion that would prevent the confusion caused by fund transfers. Survey respondents are strongly (70 percent) opposed to this idea, in part because it conjures up images of the "red tape" that GRS was designed to eliminate. Yet it is difficult to imagine a workable alternative. The survey data reveal that GRS funds are being gradually absorbed into existing decision routines and accounts. If so, meaningful accountability can only be achieved by a comprehensive perspective on all existing fiscal processes. As much as any other issue, this one raises the question of fundamental purpose in an uncompromising way: decisionmakers can choose accountability or unit freedom, but not both.

Income Distribution

Both advocates and opponents of revenue sharing have expressed concern over the effectiveness of the revenue-sharing program in meeting the needs of the disadvantaged—the poor, the elderly, the powerless, etc. The data that we have examined shed very little light on the subject, and much of that indirect and inferential. We too have found that very little revenue-sharing funds have gone for social services to disadvantaged groups. But it is impossible to tell from that information whether revenue sharing has been a help or a hindrance in income redistribution generally, since the uses to which revenue-sharing funds have been put tend to be quite broad, and to affect the well-being of rich and poor alike. Perhaps the principal message that comes from the study is that a program designed to provide aid with relatively few or no strings attached is simply not a good vehicle for focusing on disadvantaged population segments or on income distribution issues generally. In our view, those who think that income distribution policies have the highest possible priority will have a difficult time in shaping a revenue-sharing program designed to achieve that aim.

Restrictions or "strings"

Our data suggest a number of areas where the revenue-sharing program might be improved by a liberalization of restrictions. The most important of these is probably the prohibtion against the use of revenue-sharing funds as the local "matching" contribution in certain Federal programs. The survey evidence suggests that local jurisdictions have been inhibited in their use of revenue-sharing funds by this provision, that one casualty of the no-match provision has been the area of social services where other federal programs presently exist, and that most local officials favor elimination of this provision. It is true that the no-match provision is hard to enforce and evaluate. Nevertheless many local officials appear to have been extremely cautious in their use of funds for activities already supported by other Federal grants, where use of revenue-sharing funds might possibly be considered as a violation of the no-match provision. In a program with a no-strings-attached philosophy, the no-match provision appears to be unproductive.

Participation

Although the evidence on citizen participation is difficult to interpret, we think it is important. Survey data on public hearing activity suggests that the initial GRS entitlement caused a noticeable increase in hearing activity but that this activity was reduced to normal levels in succeeding periods as GRS was folded into standard procedures. Overall, group participation in hearings appears to have been limited to organizations already in existence prior to GRS. The domination of standard procedures and established groups suggests that GRS has had a mild but significant impact on citizen participation. Where special hearings were held (mostly in large cities) they appear to have had a modest impact: more "new" groups participated and more alternatives appear to have been considered. In short, hearings can affect participation and should be encouraged, although major participatory changes would probably have to be implemented through hearings procedures associated with regular budgetary processes.

Civil Rights

At the time of our survey—Fall 1974—the Office of Revenue Sharing had not yet circulated instructions on the civil rights implications of GRS. Whether for this or some other reason, most (85 percent) recipient jurisdictions believed the civil rights section of the State and Local Fiscal Assistance Act (122a) to be neither more nor less restrictive than existing civil rights legislation. Moreover, of those who thought section 122a to be different, most thought it was *less* restrictive, thus overlooking the inclusion of a prohibition against sexual, as well as racial or religious discrimination in the use of revenue-sharing funds. In view of the absence of contact between ORS and recipient units regarding revenue sharing, these views are not surprising. The absence of such contact, some two years after initiation of the program, suggests that ORS itself did not regard civil rights enforcement as a high priority issue. This is a largely negative conclusion, but it is surely relevant to a consideration of future civil right enforcement activity.

The above summary of policy implications should not be taken to reflect the views of all of the researchers who have worked on the study. Rather, it presents conclusions that, in the view of its authors, can legitimately be drawn from the survey data. Others, of course, may challenge our judgments. Indeed, we welcome such challenges and invite all who are interested in the future of General Revenue Sharing to consider the following chapters and inspect the data arrayed there or in the various appendices. In the long run, the adequacy of our conclusions is less important than the contribution we hope to have made to the public dialogue. That contribution, in the form of argument and supporting evidence, is now rightly in the public domain.

CHAPTER 2

Fiscal Impact on Local Governments

F. Thomas Juster

SUMMARY

The weight of the evidence on fiscal impact suggests a number of clear-cut conclusions, and others that are more in question. Findings that receive consistently strong support both from the survey and from other studies using other methodologies are that:

1. The dominant impact of revenue sharing in large cities (those over 300,000 population) was to maintain operating outlays; both capital outlay and tax abatement (stabilization or reduction) uses of revenue-sharing funds were relatively modest in those cities.

2. The most important use of revenue-sharing funds in moderate-sized cities (between 100,000 and 299,999 population) was to stabilize or reduce (abate) local taxes, with capital outlay uses being next in order of importance.

3. In all cities with less than 100,000 population and in counties, the dominant effect of revenue sharing was to facilitate new capital outlays—usually, to speed up existing capital outlay programs rather than to encourage completely new ventures.

4. The fiscal impact of revenue sharing varied significantly by geographic region; in particular, tax abatement impacts were relatively stronger in the Northeast part of the country than elsewhere.

The conclusion that is most in doubt relates to the overall tax abatement impact of revenue sharing. The weight of the evidence, in my judgment, is that the overall tax abatement impact of revenue sharing was relatively modest—perhaps 20-25 percent of fiscal year 1974 revenue-sharing funds went for tax abatement, and perhaps 30-35 percent of fiscal year 1975 revenue-sharing funds went for that purpose. But there are studies which appear to show a significantly larger tax abatement impact; these studies all tend to be econometric analyses of budget data.

Other conclusions from the survey, which lack corroboration from other studies because the questions could not be examined, relate to the impact of GRS on counties, to the differences in the impact of revenue sharing between various fiscal years, and to the detailed characteristics of regional differences in revenue-sharing impact.

By and large, the survey data indicate that the impact of revenue sharing on counties was about the same as its impact on moderate to small-sized cities.

Interestingly enough, the detailed data suggest that revenue sharing impacts in different-sized counties were not all that different from each other, in sharp contrast to the marked differences found among different-sized municipalities. Regional differences among counties were evident, and they tended generally to follow the pattern found in municipalities with under 100,000 population. However, it should be kept in mind that the fiscal impact estimates for counties are less reliable than for municipalities.

The principal differences between the impact of revenue sharing in fiscal year 1974 and fiscal year 1975, as measured by the survey, were that tax abatement effects were substantially larger in fiscal year 1975 and capital outlay effects were somewhat smaller. Operating outlay impacts tended generally to be larger in fiscal year 1975, with the exception of operating impacts in very large cities—these were very large in fiscal year 1974 and fell slightly in fiscal year 1975.

Finally, it is important to highlight the survey findings regarding regional differences in revenue-sharing impacts. These differences can fairly be described as enormous. The general pattern of regional impacts was for operating and capital expenditure adjustments to be quite small in the Northeast, successively larger as one proceeds through the North Central, South and West. In contrast, the tax abatement impact was very large in the Northeast, especially in cities between 100,000 and 300,000 population, and small in other parts of the United States. The exception to these regional patterns lies in the behavior of very large cities, where the survey indicates that fiscal year 1974 operating outlay adjustments tended to be very large generally and largest in the Northeast; tax abatement was absent in the Northeast and small elsewhere. During fiscal year 1975, however, the survey data suggest that very large cities began to move toward the regional pattern shown by moderate and smaller-sized cities in fiscal year 1974—relatively smaller expenditure adjustments in the Northeast and larger ones elsewhere, with larger tax abatement effects in the Northeast as the offset.

INTRODUCTION

One of the questions of most concern to both policymakers and social scientists involves the uses of General Revenue Sharing (GRS) funds by the recipient governmental units. How did the recipient governments use the funds? How much of the GRS money went to maintain existing programs, how much went to begin new programs, how much to reduce or stabilize local taxes, how much to reduce or stabilize local borrowing, etc.?

It should be recognized that analysis of the fiscal impact of revenue sharing is actually a good deal more complex than analysis of what happened to GRS money in the States and local governments to whom the funds were allocated. In the broadest perspective, the GRS program can be thought of as representing a substitution of Federal tax and/or expenditure programs for some combination of State and local government taxes and/or expenditure programs. After all, the funds appropriated by Congress for the GRS program must have left a trail at the Federal level as well as at the State and local government level.

Thus the question raised in this study is really only part of the issue. We ignore entirely the fact that the GRS program had fiscal impacts at the Federal level, and concentrate only on measurement of impacts at the State and local government level where GRS funds were a source of additional revenue. To gain a complete picture of the impact of this program, any conclusions that we might come to about what happened at the State and local government level would have to be supplemented by counterpart analysis of how Federal taxes and expenditure programs would have been affected by the absence of GRS.

In a general way, it is useful to think through conceptually the implications of various possible outcomes. Suppose for example we find that GRS went predominantly for tax abatement at the State and local government level. What that means is that the effect of the GRS program at the State and local level was to substitute private for public consumption. If it were also true that GRS monies represented a higher level of Federal spending than would otherwise have obtained, the ultimate effect is to substitute Federal taxes for State and local government taxes, with the end result being a redistribution of income away from people who pay Federal taxes and towards people who pay State and local government taxes. If, on the other hand, the impact on State and local governments turned out to be entirely in the maintenance or expansion of expenditure programs, and at the Federal level, GRS monies came out of other Federal programs that would otherwise have taken their place, the ultimate effect is to substitute State and local government services for Federal Government services, with no change between total public and private consumption at all. In this study, we can merely note the existence of these problems, and proceed to examine a subset of them.

As noted in Chapter 1, the intent of the GRS legislation is far from clear so far as fiscal impact is concerned. The legislation established "priority categories" for the expenditure of GRS monies, but these categories were extremely broad; and the lack of monitoring and enforcement machinery suggests that the categories were thought of as providing rather general guidelines. Hence one possible answer to the question is that the legislation was not really concerned with how the funds were allocated, and reflected the view that one of the purposes of GRS was to provide funds with relatively unrestricted uses to State and local government units.

Even so, it is still interesting and important to ask what actually appears to have happened to expenditures, taxes and borrowing at the State level as a consequence of the GRS program. This chapter describes estimates of fiscal impact derived mainly from a survey of governmental officials at the State and local levels, supplemented in some cases by fiscal data derived from external sources. The analysis is basically descriptive, and is designed to represent the best estimates one can make from the survey data about how GRS funds were actually used. We do present extensive comparisons of the survey estimates of fiscal impact with other estimates, primarily in order to judge the probable reliability of the survey data. Analysis of the apparent rationale for the uses of GRS funds, as estimated from the survey, is contained in Chapter 4 below.

FISCAL IMPACT ESTIMATES

Although it is clear enough that people are interested in the question of how GRS funds were used, it is equally clear that no simple answer can be forthcoming to that question. The basic difficulty with measuring fiscal impact is the general "fungibility" of money. A community could report that it earmarked GRS funds for, say, police and fire protection, and then take roughly the same amount of local tax receipts out of the police and fire budget and proceed to use those funds for entirely different programs. Analysis is really concerned with ultimate rather than earmarked uses, and the relevant question always is: how would the budget picture in a given community be different if GRS funds had not existed? In short, we wish to ascertain how the "purple dollars" represented by GRS monies worked their way through the expenditure and tax systems of State and local government and eventually came to rest; operationally, we want to know what final difference would have existed in State and local government budgets in the absence of GRS funds.

One can think of at least three alternative ways in which the appropriate fiscal impact measures might be obtained. The traditional route that would be followed by public finance economists involves first, creation of a model of explain State and local government expenditures and receipts; second, prediction of State and local government expenditures and tax rates, using the model, for the environment in which GRS funds appeared; and third, estimation of the impact of GRS as the difference between what the model predicts and what actually happened. This approach requires the development of a properly specified model of expenditures and taxes at the State and local

government level. If such a model existed, the best estimate of GRS impact would be represented by the difference between actual expenditure and taxes and what the model says would have happened in their absence. But the specification problem is not simple, and the econometric problems are no simpler here than elsewhere.[1]

An alternative approach, used by the Brookings Institution in the "Monitoring Revenue Sharing" study, is to rely on a combination of personal observation and expert judgments to make decisions about where GRS monies appear to have wound up. The Brookings "model" essentially says that one has to study fiscal processes and become intimately involved with decision-making in order to form a judgment as to what might have happened if GRS funds had not become available. Hence Brookings used some 20 odd "observers" to monitor the way in which GRS funds worked their way into State and local government budgets, and these observers were asked to supply estimates of fiscal impact in a number of categories. The implicit logic of the Brookings approach is that econometric modeling is subject to serious specification and measurement problems, and is by no means guaranteed to yield reasonable results.

A third alternative, and the one described in this chapter, uses survey methods to measure fiscal impact. As indicated in Chapter 1, an important part of the survey of State and local government officials conducted by the Survey Research Center (SRC) was concerned with an attempt to measure fiscal impact. In essence, we asked chief executives, chief finance officers and chief administrative officers in State and local government units how their budget situation would have been different if GRS monies had not become available. The implicit logic of the survey approach is that those concerned with administering the GRS program, being closely associated with and involved in the budgetary decisionmaking process, should be able to supply estimates of net fiscal impacts that are at least as accurate as those obtainable from analysis of budgetary data, since the respondents are able to take account of features of their own governmental

---

[1]In addition, such an analysis would, as a minimum, require data on fiscal year 1974 expenditures and taxes for state and local governments, as well as for a sufficient number of previous years to permit construction of an explanatory model for various classes of State and local governments. To be useful for analysis of the impact of GRS, the fiscal year 74 data would be crucial since that is the first year during which one could reasonably expect GRS monies to have impacted on the budget-making process. Fiscal year 73 data would be heavily influenced by the windfall characteristics of a grant received in the middle of a budget period. The fiscal year 74 data would not have been available in time for a study with the timetable we were attempting to meet.

unit that are often quite difficult to handle in statistical models. While the survey approach is, in principle, likely to be less accurate than the Brookings "professional observer" model, it is able to be applied across a much wider and representative range of governmental units at reasonable cost.

It is important to note that these alternative ways of measuring fiscal impact are not competitive so much as complementary. Our choice of the survey method was not based on the presumption that it constituted the best possible way to measure fiscal impact—it is unlikely that the relatively simple measures obtained via a survey of government officials would be superior to, for example, the Brookings method comparing communities on a 1-for-1 basis. And the conventional wisdom of public finance economists would surely be that econometric estimates of total budgets for State and local governments is conceptually the method of estimating fiscal impact most likely to yield accurate and unbiased estimates. Those judgments may well be correct, but as indicated earlier, neither could be effectively applied to a large and fully representative sample of local governments without incurring either prohibitively high costs or unacceptable delays. Thus we opted for the survey methodology, because (a) it could be readily applied to a fully representative sample of U. S. **governments at reasonable costs; (b) it could be** used to measure fiscal year 1974 and fiscal year 1975 fiscal impact; and (c) the results would be available in time to impact the decision on the future of the GRS program. But the relative novelty of this approach, as well as the abundant skepticism of many regarding the usefulness of survey data, require that our estimates be compared against those derived from comparative methodologies to the maximum degree possible, with the view that the reliability of the survey findings would be judged, at least in part, by its consistency with results of other methodologies.[2]

---

[2]Although we had no advance indication that our estimates of fiscal impact would show very large differences among different city sizes and geographic regions, it turns out that such differences appear to exist. That simply underscores the importance of estimating the fiscal impact of GRS from a fully representative sample of U.S. communities. If it had turned out that the GRS impact was about the same in different kinds of communities, then one could argue that studying a small number of communities intensively would produce a fairly accurate picture of what was happening in the United States as a whole. But if the experience of different communities with GRS funds varies widely, there is no way to estimate the impact for the United States as a whole without the use of a fully representative sample of local government jurisdictions.

SURVEY METHODOLOGY

To understand and evaluate the survey estimates of fiscal impact, it is important to understand the model which underlies the survey methodology. As indicated earlier, a conceptually correct estimate of the GRS fiscal impact can only be obtained by measuring the difference between expenditures and local taxes when GRS funds were available with an estimate of what expenditures and local taxes would otherwise have been. The possible differences between the actual budget situation with GRS and what it would have been without it can be classified into five types of adjustments. Without GRS funds:

1. Local operating expenditures might have been lower than they were;

2. Local capital expenditures might have been lower than they were;

3. Local taxes might have been higher than they were;

4. Local borrowings might have been higher than they were;

5. Local reserves (surplus) might have been lower than they were

It is logically necessary that the algebraic sum of these five adjustments be equal to the amount of GRS funds for each State and local government jurisdiction. Put most simply, something had to change as a consequence of GRS funds, and the five categories specified above are a mutually exclusive and fully exhaustive set of changes that might have taken place.[3] Thus we started off by asking a series of question: "Would you have reduced operating expenditures if GRS funds had not been available? Would you have reduced capital expenditures if GRS funds had not been available? Would local tax rates have been higher if GRS funds had not been available? Would local borrowing have been higher if GRS funds had not been available? Would your surplus position have been affected if GRS funds had not been available?" Each of these questions was followed by detailed information on the degree to which expenditures, taxes, or borrowing would have been affected, although the specific

---

[3]The Brookings fiscal impact categories are somewhat more detailed than these, although they have the same characteristics of being mutually exclusive and fully exhaustive. Brookings distinguished nine types of fiscal impact, distinguishing between GRS funds used to maintain operating outlays and those used for new operating programs, etc. For a description of the Brookings fiscal impact categories, see *Monitoring Revenue Sharing*, Nathan *et al.*, Chapter 7.

questions depend on the answer to earlier questions and differ somewhat with respect to the treatment of expenditures and taxes.[4]

It was our initial expectation that the survey would be able to give a general *qualitative* picture of the fiscal impact of GRS funds, but that it was unlikely to produce very much in the way of useful *quantitative* answers. It turned out that the results greatly exceeded our initial expectations. Not only were we able to obtain data of a qualitative sort, but the majority of respondents provided answers that could be given an unambiguous quantitative interpretation. In part, this appears to have been due to the fact that we questioned respondents only about very broad categories, and did not attempt to get the kind of refined details that, for example, show up in the Brookings study.

At this point, we do not wish to judge the accuracy of the responses obtained in the survey, as judged by comparison with, for example, what econometric modeling might show or what the Brookings—trained professionals—approach might show. Rather, we will describe how the data were obtained, what they show and what some of their apparent biases are, then proceed to discuss the accuracy issue.

It is important to understand that some of the estimates that we asked officials to make are really very difficult ones, and sometimes turn on judgments about what others might have done.

In particular, the distinction between maintenance of operating expenditures and avoidance of tax increases, or between maintenance/expansion of capital outlays and borrowing avoidance, is extremely difficult to judge.

The problem can be illustrated with two types of situations. Assume that a city is faced with the alternative of eliminating highly desirable public services or maintaining those services and financing them through an increase in local taxes. Whether or not a public official will indicate that the impact of GRS was on the maintenance/expansion of operating outlay or on the stabilization of local taxes depends on a political judgment: if in the absence of revenue-sharing funds the service would have been retained and the tax increase voted, the impact of GRS in our accounting framework should be placed in the tax stabilization category—operating outlays would have been the same in the absence of GRS, and revenue-sharing funds have simply replaced what would otherwise have been a tax increase. But, if the same official judged that a tax increase would not have been legislated, either because the local governing body would not have voted for it or because the public would not have voted for it in

communities where a referendum is required, then the right answer for our impact categories is that operating expenditures would have been lower and local taxes would not have been affected. But that constitutes a very delicate judgment about how a political decision would have come out.

The situation is just as troublesome if not more so for the contrast between maintenance/expansion of capital outlays and avoidance of local borrowing. In many communities, capital programs are financed via bond issues, and those bond issues must be placed on referendum and be approved by the public before the funds can be spent. Thus whether GRS enabled a higher level of capital outlays or resulted in a reduction of local borrowing depends entirely on a judgment as to whether the vote on a hypothetical bond issue would have been yes or no: if the public would have voted yes, the capital program would have been done whether or not GRS funds had been obtained, and the impact of GRS should be on borrowing avoidance. But if the public would have voted no, the capital program would not have been undertaken in the absence of GRS, and the correct answer is that capital outlays would have been lower and local borrowing would not have been affected.

In such circumstances, it is attractive to pass the buck to the econometricians, and take the view that the only way to find out what really happened is to analyze trends in expenditure and revenue data to determine whether local expenditures or local sources of funds appear to have been impacted by the GRS program. But, the difficulties here are equally formidable. Econometric analysis, after all, must work on the basis of historical relationships. The results produced by such models depend on the degree to which relationships which existed in the past can be extrapolated, and the degree to which that is successful depends entirely on the absence of exogeneous factors that could not be captured in past experience because they did not exist. But revenue sharing came into being at just about the same time as a major escalation in the rate of inflation in the United States, and it has had its entire existence during a period when either rapid inflation or the most serious recession since the 1930's constituted the external environment in which State and local governments were making budget decisions. Certainly it can be argued that the world of State and local government finance has more continuity than change, and that the world in which revenue sharing first appeared was not all that different than the world that existed before. But it is unfortunately true, for analysis of revenue-sharing impacts via econometric modeling, that major differences in external circumstances characterize the State/local government environment, and that specification of a model for

---

[4]A copy of the questionnaire is reprinted as Appendix C.

local expenditures or local taxes is subject to more than the usual collection of hazards.

ESTIMATION PROCEDURES

As indicated above, respondents were basically asked about the difference between their actual budgets and what their budgets would have been in the absence of GRS funds, initially in a qualitative way and then, for specific types of qualitative responses, in a precise quantitative way. We started out by asking respondents whether their operating expenditures would have been lower in the absence of GRS. No distinction was made between the use of GRS funds to maintain existing operating programs or to start new ones—we simply asked whether fiscal year 1974 operating programs, which might or might not have included new programs, would have been lower if GRS had not been there. For respondents who indicated yes, we then asked whether operating programs would have been reduced by the full amount of GRS funds or by less than that amount. If the respondent answered "by the full amount," we have an unambiguous statement that the full impact of GRS would have been on operating programs. If the respondent said "less than," we asked "how much less," getting responses either in the form of dollars, percentages, or sometimes qualitative statements "a lot less." The same sequence was followed for capital expenditures. For taxes and borrowing we initially asked whether local tax rates or local borrowing would have been higher in the absence of GRS, and for respondents who said yes, we then asked how much higher. Responses to the quantitative tax and borrowing sequence came also in the form of dollar or percentage figures; in the case of taxes, responses were typically in the form of millages or mills—"tax rates would have been 9 mills higher," etc.

As the appendix of this chapter indicates, we combined this array of qualitative and quantitative answers into a complete allocation of GRS funds, using a complex program of estimation and decision rules. The appendix also indicates our judgment as to the apparent quality of the data so generated. As Appendix Tables 2A-3 and 2A-4 indicate, we judge that about 50 percent of the total GRS allocation to local governments can be accounted for unambiguously, given the survey responses we obtained. The remaining 50 percent contains more ambiguity, and we were often forced to make assignments that were, to a greater or lesser degree, arbitrary.

BIAS IN SURVEY RESPONSES

Before presenting and discussing the estimates, it would be well to examine the question of bias. One can think of three sources of possible bias:

1) Bias due to deliberate misrepresentation by the respondent.

2) Bias due to lack of information by the respondent.

3) Bias due to the design of the survey.

The survey asked chief executive officers, chief finance officers, and chief administrators what they thought had been the fiscal impact of GRS. These are, of course, the people responsible for administering the GRS program. Hence it might be argued that our respondents had incentives to provide answers that they thought might be more palatable to Congress or to the Administration, who would be concerned with whether or not, and on what terms, the GRS program would be renewed. It is easy to see that potential bias of this sort exists, since our respondents were politically sensitive people who must have been aware of the fact that their answers would (or might) have an impact on the future of the program. Nonetheless, it is our view, and the view of the interviewers conducting the study, that it is extremely difficult for a respondent in the course of a one-hour-plus interview to provide a consistent, coherent, and artificial account of GRS when he/she is being asked a very long series of questions about the impact of GRS. It is somewhat similar to keeping two sets of books—one for the public and one for the stockholders and the management. While it is certainly possible to do that, it seems to us unlikely that many of our respondents would have been able to sustain a politically palatable fiction about the uses of GRS funds in a way that would not have allowed significant elements of what they really thought had happened to show up in the survey responses. Thus our judgment is that the possible bias in survey responses due to the political palatability issue is one that clearly exists but is likely to be of second-order magnitude.

The second source of bias is much more serious—if the respondent does not really know what the ultimate impact of GRS funds was, he or she can hardly tell the interviewer. It should be recognized that the question that was asked, while it is clearly the right question, is very difficult to answer. Money is in fact fungible, decision processes are not always clear in retrospect, and it is a real issue whether any survey of any group of respondents can be free from possible serious biases: for example, apparent earmarking of funds might be mistaken for ultimate uses, judgments about what would otherwise have happened are difficult for many people to make and may be biased against tax impacts, capital expenditures may be more visible than operating expenditures and may often come to be mentioned with too high a frequency, etc. We recognize the possible bias from this source, and are hard put to do more than suggest that the reader interpret the results with considerable caution. It is not easy to quantify this type of bias; it is our judgment that it is probably important, but we do not clearly know how it affected the results.

The third source of bias, due to the design of the survey, is one that would probably exist even in an instrument perfectly designed to do its job; responses to one question may to some degree be influenced by previous questions. For example, it may make a difference to estimates of fiscal impact whether respondents are asked first about expenditure impacts and second about tax impacts, or vice versa. There is nothing that could be done about that, except to conduct an experiment where half the sample is done one way and the other half the other way. From the SRC survey, we know of one clear-cut bias that almost certainly exists in the measures of fiscal impact, and this bias is due to the way the questionnaire was designed and could in principle have been avoided.

The problem arises from the fact that the survey measures of fiscal impact were designed to provide a way of allocating the fiscal year 1974 and fiscal year 1975 revenue sharing monies, and once we had achieved a complete allocation of those funds, additional questions about fiscal impact were not asked. But many communities had hold-over GRS funds at the beginning of fiscal year 1974, and presumably also at the beginning of fiscal year 1975. Hence the uses of GRS funds during fiscal year 1974, and fiscal year 1975, especially during the former year, might well have exceeded the fiscal year 1974 (fiscal year 1975) GRS allocation—with the difference being made up by drawing down fiscal year 1973 hold-over balances. Thus, when we asked respondents whether operating expenditures would have been lower in the absence of GRS, and then whether they would have been lower by the full amount of revenue-sharing funds or by less than that amount, we did not ask questions about tax or borrowing impacts if respondents indicated that expenditure adjustments had fully exhausted the fiscal year GRS allocation. But it is of course entirely possible for respondents to have reported that operating expenditures would have been lower by the full amount of fiscal year 1974 GRS monies, and in addition there would have been a tax impact because the total fiscal year 1974 impact would have been greater than the fiscal year 1974 allocation.

The effect of this bias is clear in direction, and reasonable judgments can be made about its size. In general terms, it must have the effect of causing our fiscal impact estimates to understate somewhat both the tax and borrowing impacts; there is no reason why it should have any effect on the expenditure estimates. As to size, it is our view that the bias is relatively small—it depends entirely on the degree to which holdover funds from fiscal year 1973 might have been used during fiscal year 1974 and fiscal year 1975 to reduce or stabilize local tax rates and to reduce or stabilize local borrowing. The reader can make his own judgments about this, but we would be surprised if the bias amounts were more than 5 or 10 percentage points of the total GRS allocation. Some empirical evidence in support of this judgment is provided below when we discuss the official Use Report data.

QUALITY OF THE SURVEY ESTIMATE

The quality of the survey data is discussed at length in the appendix to this chapter. Here, we wish to note a few general characteristics. "Quality" has a quite special meaning in this discussion. It simply refers to the degree to which the survey provided "unambiguous," as opposed to "arbitrary" estimates of fiscal impact. It does *not* make any judgment about the *accuracy* of unambiguous responses, as measured by what might be shown via alternate research strategies or as measured by some ultimate standard of truth. Thus quality as used here simply refers to the degree of arbitrariness needed to produce fiscal impact estimates from the survey materials.

In general terms, we have three different quality groups, with some differentiation within them. Overall, roughly half the total dollar amount of revenue-sharing funds can be unambiguously allocated on the basis of the survey responses; the design of the survey was such that these tend to be predominantly situations where the impact of revenue sharing was on expenditures. These unambiguous expenditure assignments result mainly from respondents who indicated that either operating or capital or both types of expenditures would have been lower in the absence of revenue sharing funds, and that the expenditure reduction would have been equal to the full amount of GRS funds. The other category where an unambiguous assignment was possible comprises respondents who indicated that there was no expenditure, tax or borrowing adjustment from revenue-sharing funds, hence by implication the revenue-sharing funds must have ended up as additions to fund balances and had not yet been spent.

The second general quality category consists of cases (representing approximately 30 percent of the dollar total) where some hard quantitative data were obtained from the survey, but where additional and essentially arbitrary assumptions had to be made in order to produce consistent estimates of fiscal impact. Some of these cases are not necessarily lower quality than those in the first category, since they include cases where respondents reported a substantial number of different types of adjustments, provided quantitative measures of all adjustments they reported, and where the reported adjustments were not exactly equal to the externally derived dollar total of revenue-sharing money. Thus some of our best data fall into this category, although other cases in the same general group contain a good bit of essentially qualitative data where more or less arbitrary assignments had to be made. In estimating fiscal impacts for respondents in this category, we made extensive use of externally derived data, primarily in connection with the reported impacts of revenue sharing on local taxes. Respondents reporting a tax impact of revenue sharing either reported a dollar impact, a percentage (presumably of the local tax base) impact, or most frequently, an impact reported in terms of mills. For the latter two cases, we resorted to external information on either local tax base or local assessed valuation base.

The final category consists of cases where all our data are basically qualitative, either because respondents could not provide any quantitative data, or because the quantitative data that was provided turned out to be of sufficiently poor quality so that it could not be used. The basically qualitative (and essentially arbitrary) cases amount to about 15 percent of the total dollar amount of revenue-sharing funds at the local government level.

It turns out that there are considerable differences among cities and counties with respect to the distribution of estimated quality, and also between different types of respondents. By our measures, cities provided higher quality data than counties, and chief finance officers provided higher quality data than chief executives. For example, almost a quarter of the revenue-sharing allocation for counties had to be derived from essentially arbitrary qualitative assignments, while only a bit more than 10 percent of the total for municipalities had to be assigned in that way. Similarly, less than a third of the revenue-sharing funds could be unambiguously assigned for chief executive officers, compared to about half for chief finance officers.

The principle difference however, between chief finance officers and chief executive officers with respect to the estimated quality of the fiscal impact estimates lies in the very substantial difference in nonresponse: very few chief executive officers of major cities responded to the survey. Thus about 20 percent of the fiscal year 1974 total revenue-sharing dollar allocation could not be assigned because of nonresponse for chief executive officers, compared to only about 3 percent for chief finance officers; and an additional 6 percent of the chief executive officer data turned out to be totally unusable because of poor quality, compared to only about 1.5 percent for chief finance officers. On the basis of this kind of evidence, it is our view that the best measures of fiscal impact from the survey were obtained from chief finance officers, and we generally tend to place more weight on those responses than on the ones from chief executive officers.

BASIC FINDINGS—QUALITATIVE DATA

Tables 2-1–2-4 contain the basic survey findings on fiscal impact, using only the qualitative information obtained from the survey. We display data for fiscal year 1974 and fiscal year 1975 reported by the finance officers of local government jurisdictions in the sample. The fiscal impact measures are all derived from the survey variables described above—would expenditures, taxes or borrowing have been different if GRS funds had not been available? Four fiscal impact measures are shown: the use of GRS monies to prevent reductions (below what would otherwise have been the case) in operating expenditures, similarly defined reductions in capital expenditures, the use of GRS funds to prevent increases (above what would otherwise have been the case) in local taxes, and similarly defined impacts on borrowing. Thus the data reflect what finance officers thought had been the impact of GRS funds on helping to keep up or expand operating or capital expenditures, and to hold down or reduce local taxes and borrowing. Obviously, more than one of these impacts could be, and often was, reported in any given community, hence the impacts will not add to 100 percent. Tables 2-1 and 2-2 are weighted by population, and should be interpreted as the proportion of the population living in communities where the specified types of impacts were reported for fiscal year 1974 (Table 2-1) and fiscal year 1975 (Table 2-2). Tables 2-3 and 2-4 use a somewhat different weighting scheme, designed to reflect the *number* of particular types of communities in which the specified fiscal impacts were reported by finance officers. In Tables 2-3 and 2-4 both the number of communities affected by the various impacts, and the percentage of all communities of that size, are

Table 2-1

Weighted Percent of Local Governments Reporting Some Impact of GRS in Specified Fiscal Category, Finance Officer Responses, FY74

		Fiscal Impact Categories			
Type of Unit	Number of Cases	Maintained or Increased Operating Expenditures	Maintained or Increased Capital Expenditures	Stabilized or Reduced Local Taxes	Stabilized or Reduced Local Borrowing
Municipalities					
300,000 + ...	27	72.7	40.2	14.1	1.1
100,000-299,999.	40	58.3	56.4	60.9	18.8
25,000-99,999	215	36.2	76.4	35.4	17.1
10,000-24,999	92	26.9	71.9	28.7	12.7
2,500-9,999	85	21.6	70.2	34.1	23.0
Under 2,500	120	40.9	69.0	22.1	14.4
Townships: 9,000 + ...	42	45.0	65.4	33.2	19.4
Townships: < 9,000	30	36.2	70.1	13.1	13.5
Counties					
500,000 + ...	35	37.4	62.3	32.7	25.2
100,000-499,999.	48	44.7	70.4	29.6	20.4
Under 100,000	59	55.6	86.0	20.3	9.2
Total	793	44.4	64.5	29.3	14.2

Table 2-2

Weighted Percent of Local Governments Reporting Some Impact of GRS in Specified Fiscal Category, Finance Officer Responses, FY75

		Fiscal Impact Categories			
Type of Unit	Number of Cases	Maintained or Increased Operating Expenditures	Maintained or Increased Capital Expenditures	Stabilized or Reduced Local Taxes	Stabilized or Reduced Local Borrowing
Municipalities					
300,000 + ...	27	79.6	42.4	46.4	6.3
100,000-299,999.	40	69.9	64.9	60.2	13.9
25,000-99,999	215	38.0	74.2	31.8	15.8
10,000-24,999	92	33.6	68.8	33.8	7.9
2,500-9,999	85	35.0	74.9	37.0	22.1
Under 2,500	120	40.9	67.7	16.5	9.2
Townships: 9,000 + ...	42	36.4	65.5	32.7	10.5
Townships: < 9,000	30	42.8	66.5	13.0	13.7
Counties					
500,000 + ...	35	52.4	66.7	46.4	37.6
100,000-499,999.	48	47.7	71.3	52.2	27.9
Under 100,000	59	50.7	83.1	26.2	13.3
Total	793	49.2	65.1	36.5	13.5

Table 2-3

Estimated Number and Percent of Local Governments Reporting Some Impact of GRS in Specified Fiscal Category, Finance Officer Responses, FY74

Type of Unit	Estimated Total Number	Maintained or Increased Operating Expenditures		Maintained or Increased Capital Expenditures		Stabilized or Reduced Local Taxes		Stabilized or Reduced Local Borrowing		Sample Size
		N	%	N	%	N	%	N	%	
Municipalities										
300,000 + ...	45	27	59.5	26	58.9	10	21.4	1	2.2	27
100,00-299,999....	97	61	62.1	58	59.3	57	58.6	16	16.1	40
25,000-99,999	837	301	36.0	649	77.5	310	37.0	139	16.6	215
10,000-24,999	1,401	347	24.8	1,009	72.0	406	29.0	193	13.8	92
2,500-9,999	3,961	883	22.3	2,813	71.0	1,238	31.3	864	21.8	85
Under 2,500	14,871	5,608	37.7	9,532	64.1	3,299	22.2	2,166	14.6	120
Townships: 9,000 +	571	269	47.2	412	72.1	106	18.5	54	9.4	42
Townships: < 9,000	8,525	4,626	54.3	4,076	47.8	686	8.0	712	8.4	30
Counties										
500,000 + ...	50	17	34.9	29	59.1	23	45.9	16	32.0	35
100,000-499,999...	251	100	40.0	167	66.6	80	31.8	56	22.2	48
Under 100,000	3,122	1,754	56.2	2,712	86.8	957	30.6	443	14.2	59
Total	33,733	13,994	41.5	21,483	63.7	7,171	21.3	4,659	13.8	793

Table 2-4

Estimated Number and Percent of Local Governments Reporting Some Impact of GRS in Specified Fiscal Category, Finance Officer Responses, FY75

Type of Unit	Estimated Total Number	Maintained or Increased Operating Expenditures		Maintained or Increased Capital Expenditures		Stabilized or Reduced Local Taxes		Stabilized or Reduced Local Borrowing		Sample Size
		N	%	N	%	N	%	N	%	
Municipalities										
300,000 + ...	45	32	71.4	26	57.1	12	27.6	5	10.1	27
100,000-299,999...	97	73	74.4	68	69.7	57	58.1	11	11.7	40
25,000-99,999	837	347	41.5	626	74.8	250	29.8	131	15.6	215
10,000-24,999	1,401	437	31.2	967	69.0	481	34.3	106	7.6	92
2,500-9,999	3,961	1,396	35.2	2,882	72.7	1,432	36.2	834	21.1	85
Under 2,500	14,871	5,292	35.6	8,590	57.8	2,064	13.9	1,193	8.0	120
Townships: 9,000 +	571	219	38.4	435	76.2	88	15.5	29	5.1	42
Townships: < 9,000	8,525	4,952	58.1	4,245	49.8	1,015	11.9	631	7.4	30
Counties										
500,000 + ...	50	21	41.7	30	59.6	23	47.3	17	34.4	35
100,000-499,999...	251	104	41.5	168	66.8	137	54.7	86	34.3	48
Under 100,000	3,122	1,639	52.5	2,645	84.7	1,598	51.2	815	26.1	59
Total	33,733	14,511	43.0	20,680	61.3	7,158	21.2	3,859	11.4	793

reported, so that readers can get an idea of the absolute numbers of communities affected by each kind of fiscal impact.

Our basic classification of local government jurisdictions is by function and date. We distinguish six size classes of municipalities, and include as municipalities towns or townships in New England that perform exactly the same function as those performed elsewhere by cities. We include two sizes classes of townships (by definition, limited to townships in the North Central region of the United States and in New York State), and three size classes of counties.[5]

According to Table 2-1, the most common fiscal impact of GRS funds was to maintain or expand capital outlays, followed by the maintenance or expansion of operating expenditures, then by tax abatement, with borrowing abatement bringing up the rear. Overall, almost two-thirds of the U. S. population lived in communities reporting a capital expenditure impact of GRS, while less than 30 percent lived in communities reporting tax abatement. For fiscal year 1975, the frequency of the various fiscal impacts is roughly the same, although there is some evidence that more communities used GRS funds to maintain operating outlays than in fiscal year 1974, and similarly that tax abatement was a more important use of GRS funds in fiscal year 1975.

There exist substantial differences in these fiscal impact measures by type and size of local government. For example, virtually all cities with populations over 300,000 reported that GRS funds had helped to maintain or expand operating expenditures, and this type of fiscal impact is much less likely to be reported by finance officers in smaller cities or in townships and counties. In contrast, capital expenditure impacts are reported by finance officers representing close to three-quarters of the population in most classes of cities, counties and townships, with the single exception of finance officers from very large cities—here, only about 40 percent reported that GRS funds had an impact on capital outlays. Tax impacts were quite small in the largest cities, much larger in cities between 100,000 and 300,000 population, and generally tend to decline as city size declines—with the exception, as noted, of the largest cities. Borrowing impacts were much less frequently reported and the data here are erratic, although they tend to follow somewhat the same general pattern of tax abatement. The fiscal year 1975 data generally follow the same pattern as that for fiscal year 1975, except that tax adjustments generally tend to be larger and, with the exception of very large cities, the frequency of operating expenditure adjustments also tends to be larger.

—————————————
[5]See Appendix B for a description of the sample.

A somewhat different way of measuring the same phenomenon, which many readers will find more understandable and of greater interest, is contained in Tables 2-3 and 2-4, which display estimates of the number of different types of communities in which each of these fiscal impact estimates were reported by finance officers. Overall, the same basic pattern is indicated in terms of numbers of communities rather than communities weighted by population. Capital expenditure impacts are reported most frequently (in over 21,000 of the 34,000 odd communities represented by our sample, or in about 64 percent of all local governments), operating expenditure adjustments are next most frequent, tax abatement effects are third most frequent, and borrowing abatement is least frequent. Again, capital expenditure impacts are reported more frequently by finance officers in cities under 100,000 population than in larger cities, while operating expenditure impacts are reported more frequently by big city finance officers than by those in smaller communities or in counties. The tax impact pattern is also similar to that discussed above; tax impacts are most frequent in cities between 100,000 and 300,000, and generally decline as cities become smaller. The very large cities do not fit the pattern—here, tax abatement is relatively modest, reported by only 10 of the estimated 45 cities with populations over 300,000. The data for fiscal year 1975 is again similar to that for fiscal year 1974, with tax and operating expenditure impacts reported a bit more frequently, and both capital expenditure and borrowing impacts a bit less frequently. The largest borrowing impacts, incidentally, seem to be in counties, especially the larger ones.

BASIC FINDINGS—QUANTITATIVE DATA

The survey findings just discussed reflect qualitative measures of fiscal impact, and serve to indicate the incidence of various types of fiscal impact.[6] While incidence would certainly be expected to be related to dollar impact, there is not necessarily a close relation between them. This section details the survey estimates of fiscal impact in quantitative terms, using the complex estimation method described briefly in the first part of the chapter and discussed at length in the appendix.

For the quantitative analysis of fiscal impact, we specify a somewhat more refined set of fiscal impact categories. These have been discussed

—————————————
[6]The estimates in Tables 2-1 and 2-2 can also serve to provide upper bounds to the survey measures of fiscal impact, as discussed below.

generally above, but will be recapitulated here. The first two categories relate to the impact of GRS funds on expenditures—they measure the use of GRS funds either to maintain or increase operating expenditures (column 1 in each of the following tables) or to maintain or increase capital expenditures (column 2). No distinction is made between the use of funds to maintain existing programs or to begin new ones. The third column measures the use of GRS funds either to stabilize or to reduce local taxes, while column 4 reports the use of these funds to stabilize or reduce local borrowing. The next two categories reflect fund balance or surplus uses of GRS funds. Column 5 reports the amount of revenue-sharing dollars allocated to communities who specifically reported that there was no expenditure, tax or borrowing adjustment attributable to the receipt of GRS funds. If those reports are correct, the funds must still be unused and hence were assigned as additions to local government surplus. The sixth column is simply a residual—it represents the difference between the adjustments that we could quantify or knew existed, and the externally derived revenue-sharing allocation. Thus in communities where expenditure, tax or borrowing impacts added up to more than the GRS allocation for a given fiscal year, column 6 would be negative, since the responses imply that previously accumulated GRS balances must have been drawn down during that particular year. For communities who reported adjustments adding up to less than the amount of revenue-sharing funds, column 6 would be positive.[7] The seventh column contains nonresponse, and consists of three kinds—nonresponse due to data of such poor quality that we could make no sense of the survey responses, nonresponse due to the fact that we did not obtain an interview from the chief executive officer or chief finance officer of the local government jurisdiction in question, and nonresponse due to the fact that some respondents did not answer the fiscal impact questions.

The description above indicates that our estimates of surplus or reserve funds uses of GRS monies are derived entirely by residual, rather than measured directly in the survey. As indicated earlier, we did ask respondents about the impact of GRS on their surplus or reserve position, but it became clear from examination of the survey responses that many if not most of our respondents (understandably) misunderstood the question;

hence we judged that the answers were essentially worthless and had to be discarded. The difficulty arose with respect to the relevant time frame. We asked respondents whether their surplus or reserve position at the end of fiscal year 1974 was higher than it would otherwise have been as a consequence of the availability of GRS monies. Our frame of reference in asking the question was ''higher than it would otherwise have been relative to its beginning fiscal year 1974 level,'' since we were interested in identifying the additions or subtractions to surplus during fiscal year 1974.

Almost all respondents indicated that their surplus position was higher as a consequence of the GRS program. A few follow-up telephone calls made it perfectly clear that what this meant was that the surplus position of most communities was better at the end of fiscal year 1974 than it had been before the GRS program started, not that it was better than it would have been relative to the end of fiscal year 1973. The confusion is entirely understandable, since the time frame was implicit rather than explicit in the question. In retrospect, we should simply have asked whether more (less) GRS monies were used during fiscal year 1974 than were received during fiscal year 1974, rather than trying to measure changes in surplus directly. But the data as they stand are essentially worthless, and all of our analysis concerning the impact of GRS on the surplus positions of State or local governments is derived via a residual from other known adjustments and the externally derived fiscal year 1974 revenue-sharing allocation.

SAMPLE VS. UNIVERSE COMPARISONS OF GRS FUNDS

Before proceeding to describe the survey findings on the fiscal impact of GRS funds, it is useful to look briefly at the question: How well does the Survey Research Center's sample of U.S. local government jurisdictions represent the universe of all U.S. local government jurisdictions? The answer to this question is shown by Tables 2-5 and 2-5A as well as by the counterpart tables in the Appendix to this chapter. Table 2-5 contains detailed estimates of the fiscal impact of GRS for the various classes of municipalities, townships and counties, with the survey estimates based on responses by the finance officers of sample jurisdictions. Table 2-5A contains the same data, expressed in percent distribution form.

The last column of Table 2-5 contains an estimate, derived from the SRC's sample of local government jurisdictions, of the total amount of revenue sharing dollars allocated to municipalities, townships and counties in the various size classes.

---

[7]In general, it is our expectation that an accurate measure of fiscal year 1974 or fiscal year 1975 revenue sharing impacts would show column 6 predominantly negative, since we know from external data that a substantial amount of revenue sharing funds from the first three entitlement periods (ending June 30, 1973 or before fiscal year 1974 began for most communities) had not been spent and therefore were still available to be used.

Table 2-5

Estimated Fiscal Impact of GRS during FY74, Finance Officer Responses,
SRC Sample of Municipalities, Townships and Counties
(millions of dollars)

		Fiscal Impact Categories							
Type of Unit	Number of Cases	Maintained or Increased Operating Expenditures	Maintained or Increased Capital Expenditures	Stabilized or Reduced Local Taxes	Stabilized or Reduced Local Borrowing	Additions to Surplus	Residual	Non-Re-sponse	Total Revenue Sharing Allocation
Municipalities									
300,000 + ...	27	528.9	100.8	85.6	6.2	33.7	16.5	70.2	841.9
100,000-299,999....	40	82.5	78.3	121.8	45.6	0.0	-38.7	2.7	292.2
25,000-99,999	215	71.5	268.9	108.5	43.3	19.6	5.1	6.1	523.0
10,000-24,999	92	26.7	161.3	40.9	26.8	8.9	5.2	6.8	276.6
2,500-9,999.........	85	18.3	137.2	40.5	25.8	9.5	4.8	52.3	288.4
Under 2,500........	120	26.0	60.2	14.2	6.1	9.6	7.1	1.5	124.7
Townships: 9,000 + .	42	10.6	26.0	11.8	6.3	0.5	3.1	0.7	59.0
Townships: < 9,000 .	30	8.6	28.1	1.8	6.8	15.0	0.5	1.4	62.2
Subtotal	651	773.1	860.8	425.1	166.9	96.8	3.6	141.7	2468.0
Counties									
500,000 + ...	35	93.0	199.9	53.3	64.8	0.0	24.1	19.9	455.0
100,000-499,999....	48	84.9	194.0	52.9	54.3	10.2	4.0	24.1	424.4
Under 100,000	59	164.0	369.1	110.3	34.1	4.4	49.8	0.0	732.1
Subtotal	142	341.9	763.0	216.5	153.2	14.6	77.9	44.0	1611.5
Grand Total .	793	1115.0	1623.8	641.6	320.1	111.4	81.5	185.7	4079.5

Table 2-5A

Estimated Fiscal impact of GRS during FY74, Finance Officer Responses,
SRC Sample of Municipalities, Townships and Counties
(percentages)

		Fiscal Impact Categories							
Type of Unit	Number of Cases	Maintained or Increased Operating Expenditures	Maintained or Increased Capital Expenditures	Stabilized or Reduced Local Taxes	Stabilized or Reduced Local Borrowing	Additions to Surplus	Residual	Non-Re-sponse	Total Revenue Sharing Allocation
Municipalities									
300,000 + ...	27	62.8	12.0	10.2	0.7	4.0	2.0	8.3	100.0
100,000-299,999....	40	28.2	26.8	41.7	15.6	-	-13.2	0.9	100.0
25,000-99,999	215	13.7	51.4	20.7	8.3	3.7	1.0	1.2	100.0
10,000-24,999	92	9.7	58.3	14.8	9.7	3.2	1.9	2.5	100.0
2,500-9,999.........	85	6.3	47.6	14.0	8.9	3.3	1.7	18.1	100.0
Under 2,500........	120	20.9	48.3	11.4	4.9	7.7	5.7	1.2	100.0
Townships: 9,000 +..	42	18.0	44.0	20.0	10.7	0.8	5.3	1.2	100.0
Townships: < 9,000 .	30	13.8	45.2	2.9	10.9	24.1	0.8	2.3	100.0
Subtotal	651	31.3	34.9	17.2	6.8	3.9	0.1	5.7	100.0
Counties									
500,000 + ...	35	20.4	43.9	11.7	14.2	-	5.3	4.4	100.0
100,000-499,999....	48	20.0	45.7	12.5	12.8	2.4	0.9	5.7	100.0
Under 100,000	60	22.4	50.4	15.1	4.7	0.6	5.9	1.0	100.0
Subtotal	143	21.2	47.3	13.4	9.5	0.9	4.4	3.2	100.0
Grand Total .	794	27.3	39.8	15.7	7.8	2.7	1.8	4.7	100.0

Sources: Derived from Table 5.

The overall total, shown in the lower right hand corner of the table, comes to 4.079 billion dollars for fiscal year 1974. An externally derived total for the amount of GRS funds allocated to local governments during fiscal year 1975 comes to 4.030 billion dollars—an estimate that differs from our sample estimate by about 1 percent.

This comparison simply demonstrates what we noted briefly above in Chapter 1—that the SRC sample of local government jurisdictions is a very accurate representation of the total U.S. universe of local government jurisdictions. The crucial point is simply that estimates of the allocation of revenue sharing funds derived from the SRC's sample would permit fully valid generalizations about the allocation of GRS funds in the U.S. as a whole. In short, our sample of 817 local government jurisdictions is a remarkably accurate microcosm of the U.S. universe of some 34,000 local government jurisdictions.[8]

Examination of the nonresponse category in Table 2-5 is also highly reassuring. Less than 200 million dollars (out of 4 billion) of GRS funds was allocated to communities for which we have no estimates of fiscal impact, either because of nonresponse to the survey itself or because the fiscal data were of such poor quality that they could not be used. Most of this nonresponse represents communities where interviews were not obtained or where the fiscal impact questions were skipped.[9]

The appendix to this chapter displays detailed estimates of fiscal impact comparable to the information in Tables 2-5 and 2-5A. Data in the appendix are shown for finance officer responses for both fiscal year 1974 and 1975, for chief executive officer responses in both fiscal year 1974 and 1975, and for chief administrative officer responses in both fiscal year 1974 and 1975. Summaries of the detailed tables are included in the text as the basic findings are discussed.

---

[8]The actual number of general government units in the U.S. is a bit over 38,000, the vast bulk of which are relatively small. Our sample is designed to represent all except for those with populations under 100, and except for Indian tribes and Alaskan villages.

[9]Nonresponse is a much more serious problem for fiscal impact responses obtained from chief executive officers, as indicated earlier. Appendix Tables 2A-3 and 2A-4 show that about 25 percent of the total revenue-sharing funds going to local governments could not be allocated because of nonresponse among chief executive officers. Roughly two-thirds of this total is attributable to the fact that we were unable to obtain survey responses from any of the mayors of very large U.S. cities. Thus, aside from municipalities with over 300,000 population, the fiscal impact responses from chief executive officers in local government jurisdictions were not too different in terms of nonresponse than the data for finance officers shown in Table 2-5, although nonresponse is typically a more serious problem for the chief executive officer data than for the finance officer data.

CHIEF FINANCE OFFICERS—FISCAL YEAR 1974

For local governments as a whole, our data for chief finance officers indicate that slightly more than a quarter of the total GRS funds were used to maintain or increase operating expenditures in fiscal year 1974, about 40 percent were used to maintain or increase capital expenditures, a bit more than 15 percent went for tax abatement, about 8 percent for borrowing abatement, and about 5 percent was (on balance) added to surplus. As indicated above, less than 5 percent is represented by non-response (Tables 2-5 and 2-5A).

These overall patterns mask very substantial differences in the allocation of GRS funds among different types of communities. According to the survey results, the predominant use of fiscal year 1974 GRS funds in very large cities was to maintain or increase operating expenditures: almost 70 percent went for that purpose, while a-bit over 10 percent was to stabilize or reduce local taxes and about the same proportion was used for the maintenance or expansion of capital outlays. In sharp contrast, no other type of government jurisdiction used as much as 30 percent of GRS funds for the maintenance or expansion of operating outlays; for most local government communities, less than 20 percent of GRS funds went into operating expenditures (Table 2-6).[10]

For local government jurisdictions other than big cities, the dominant use of fiscal year 1974 GRS funds is reported to have been the maintenance or expansion of capital expenditures: in all cities with less than 100,000 population, as well as in townships and counties, at least 40 percent of GRS funds were reported to have gone for that purpose, and the allocations are close to or above 50 percent in a number of size classes. Only in cities between 100,000 and 300,000 was the capital allocation smaller—here, it was a shade less than the allocation to operating outlays, and both were a bit under 30 percent of the total. There appears to be little differentiation among cities under 100,000 population, in townships or in counties in the proportion of GRS funds going to capital outlays

The tax and borrowing impacts also differ sharply as a function of community type and size. Tax abatement is reported to be the most important single use of GRS funds in cities between 100,000 and 299,999 population, accounting for over 40 percent of the total. For no other type of community was tax abatement as much as half that

---

[10]Table 2-6 and its counterpart tables differ from Table 2-5 and its counterparts in two ways. First, it allocates nonresponse to the various fiscal impact categories (in proportion to the impacts). Second, it represents a summary with some size classes and types of impacts combined.

Table 2-6
Summary of Estimated Fiscal Impact of GRS, Finance Officer Responses
(percentages)

Type of Unit	Number of Cases	FISCAL IMPACT CATEGORY[a]				
		Maintained or Increased Operating Expenditures	Maintained or Increased Capital Expenditures	Stabilized or Reduced Local Taxes	Other	Total Revenue Sharing Allocation
		A: Fiscal Year 1974				
Municipalities						
Over 300,000	27	68.5	13.1	11.1	7.3	100.0
100,000-299,999.	40	28.4	27.0	42.1	2.4	100.0
100-99,999	512	12.5	54.8	17.8	15.0	100.0
Townships	72	16.1	45.4	11.4	27.0	100.0
Counties.	142	21.9	49.0	13.9	15.3	100.0
Grand Total	793	28.7	41.8	16.6	13.0	100.0
		B: Fiscal Year 1975				
Municipalities						
Over 300,000	27	51.9	13.4	34.1	0.5	100.0
100,000-299,999.	40	30.3	33.7	37.6	-0.2	100.0
100-99,999	512	18.9	50.9	22.1	8.1	100.0
Townships	72	21.3	42.7	12.2	23.8	100.0
Counties.	142	21.9	42.7	21.5	14.0	100.0
Grand Total	793	27.5	38.8	25.0	8.7	100.0

[a]Derived from Tables 2A-5 and 2A-7: non-response allocated.

proportion, and typically it is reported to be around 15 percent of GRS funds. The smallest tax abatement allocations are found in the very large cities and in the very small townships. Borrowing impacts tend to be relatively unimportant overall except in the counties, where they are about the same as tax abatement effects in two of the three classes. Finally, additions to surplus turn out to be important only in the smaller communities—municipalities under 2,500 and rural townships. They represent almost a quarter of the total GRS allocation in rural townships, for example (Table 2-5A).

As a broad descriptive generalization, the survey responses for chief finance officers in fiscal year 1974 indicate that the dominant use of GRS funds in very large cities was to maintain or increase (principally maintain, for reasons discussed below) operating expenditures, the dominant use in most other communities was the maintenance or expansion of capital outlays, while tax abatement effects

were modest except in one size class—cities between 100,000 and 299,999 population

CHIEF FINANCE OFFICER DATA, FISCAL YEAR 1975

The estimates of fiscal impact based on the survey responses of finance officers shows some interesting differences between fiscal year 1974 and fiscal year 1975. Overall, there is evidence of a stronger impact of GRS on local taxes in fiscal year 1975, a slightly weaker impact on capital outlays, and less impact on additions to surplus. The biggest difference is in the tax impact category. Tax impacts are not only stronger overall in fiscal year 1975, as measured by the survey, but the pattern is also different: very large cities now show a significant impact of GRS on local taxes, second only to the continued strong impact of cities in the

100,000-299,999 size class, and all the other communities show larger fiscal year 1975 impact on tax stabilization.[11]

Moreover, detailed examination of the data clearly suggests a stronger impact on operating expenditures in fiscal year 1975 for most communities. What happens is that the very heavy fiscal year 1974 operating expenditure impacts in big cities are considerably reduced, although still very large, and in most other size classes the fiscal year 1975 estimates of operating expenditure impact are higher than fiscal year 1974 counterparts. The heavy emphasis on capital outlays is clear in both years, but it is systematically a little lower in 1975. And for tax abatement, as indicated, big cities show a pronounced use of GRS funds for tax abatement in fiscal year 1975 compared to their very low estimates in 1974, and most other communities show somewhat higher estimates of tax abatements in fiscal year 1975. Finally, additions to surplus are typically a bit smaller in fiscal year 1975; the very large additions to surplus estimated for rural townships in fiscal year 1974 are much modified in the fiscal year 1975 data.

Thus the finance officer data show some modest but perceptible trends between these two years: uses of GRS funds for operating programs are generally higher, and uses for tax abatement are generally higher. The offsets are a slightly less (though still very heavy) use of GRS funds for capital expenditures, and less evidence of increased fund balances as represented by additions to surplus.

CHIEF EXECUTIVE OFFICER ESTIMATES

As noted above, the most striking difference between the chief executive officer estimates of fiscal impact and the finance officer estimates is in the virtual absence of meaningful data on fiscal impact for chief executive officers from cities with 300,000 or more population. If one ignores that difference, the fiscal impact patterns are broadly similar (Table 2-7). Both show a relatively modest impact of GRS funds on the maintenance or expansion of operating expenditures, a much heavier impact on the maintenance or expansion of capital outlays, and

---

[11]The sharp jump in the reported impact of GRS on tax stabilization for very large cities is not due to one or more very large cities showing a significant tax impact in fiscal year 1975 against none in fiscal year 1974—rather, it is a pervasive phenomenon among a large number of the cities in this size class. The reader should be warned, however, that it is possible in that size class for one very large city (NYC) to cause significant change in the entire category. NYC accounts for approximately 25 percent of the weight in cities over 300,000 population in the SRC sample.

tax and borrowing stabilization effects smaller than those found for operating expenditures. The distribution of fiscal impact among size class is somewhat different in these data than in that for finance officers. For example, tax abatement impacts are more evenly spread among cities: there is little difference in tax abatement impacts for the three classes of cities between 10,000 and 299,999 population in the chief executive officer data, in contrast to the marked differential in tax impact shown by the finance officer responses for communities in the 100,000-299,999 size class. Finally, the chief executive officer data do not indicate any increase in tax abatement in fiscal year 1975 over fiscal year 1974, although they show the same tendency as noted in the finance officer data for the GRS impact on operating expenditures to be greater in fiscal year 1975.

CHIEF ADMINISTRATIVE OFFICER ESTIMATES

For some size classes of municipalities, and for counties, we also conducted an interview with the chief administrative officer of the jurisdiction. By definition, this official could not have been the chief finance officer as well. Interviews were originally scheduled in cities with populations of 25,000 and above, and in all counties, for chief administrative officers. As noted in Appendix B, not all the scheduled interviews were attempted, since interviewers often found that there was no individual with the requisite responsibilities and the number of interviews was cut from three to two.

Looking at comparable communities, the principal impression one gets from the chief administrative officer data on fiscal impact is that by and large they are consistent with the finance officer data. The main exception to that generalization is in the responses of chief administrative officers in very large cities. Administrators indicate a much weaker impact than reported by finance officers on the use of GRS funds for the maintenance or expansion of operating expenditures, and a considerably stronger impact of GRS funds on tax abatement. But that impression may well be misleading, since it is apparent from the dollar totals (Appendix Table 2A-13) that many of the very largest cities are not represented in the chief administrative officer responses. Adjusting for that difference, the pattern of the responses is, on the whole, quite similar. While administrative officers report proportionally more tax abatement overall than finance officers, that is due solely to the fact that cities of 25,000 and over are the only ones represented in the administrator data: the tax abatement impact reported by administrative

Table 2-7
Estimated Fiscal Impact of GRS, Chief Executive Officer Responses
(percentages)

Type of Unit	Number of Cases	Maintained or Increased Operating Expenditures	Maintained or Increased Capital Expenditures	Stabilized or Reduced Local Taxes	Other	Total Revenue Sharing Allocation
			FISCAL IMPACT CATEGORY[a]			
			A.: Fiscal Year 1974			
Municipalities						
Over 300,000	18	*	*	*	*	100.0
100,000-299,999	36	22.1	49.9	25.9	2.1	100.0
Under 2,500-99,999 . .	505	14.6	48.6	19.8	16.9	100.0
Townships	70	17.6	41.3	18.8	22.4	100.0
Counties.	133	24.2	45.7	15.2	14.9	100.0
Grand Total	762	20.8	47.1	17.9	14.2	100.0
			B: Fiscal Year 1975			
Municipalities						
Over 300,000	18	*	*	*	*	100.0
100,000-299,999	36	28.5	41.6	23.8	6.1	100.0
Under 2,500-99,999 . .	505	20.4	54.6	19.0	6.0	100.0
Townships	70	21.5	43.2	13.5	21.8	100.0
Counties.	133	28.1	48.1	13.2	10.5	100.5
Grand Total	762	26.1	49.3	16.2	8.3	100.0

Sources: Derived from Appendix Tables 2A-9 and 2A-11. Non-response allocated.
*Estimates unreliable due to non-response.

officers are about the same as those reported by finance officers, given the same city size classes.

As with the finance officer and chief executive data, administrative officers report a consistently heavier impact of GRS funds on the maintenance or expansion of capital expenditures compared to uses of these funds for operating expenditures. For counties, the administrative officer data suggest more tax abatement than either of the other two sets of responses, and except for the largest counties, a smaller impact on operating outlays than that suggested by the finance officer data. Interestingly enough, although the data on the use of GRS funds to stabilize or reduce local borrowing tend to be very erratic, there is a strong consistency between the estimates of borrowing impact by chief administrative officers and chief finance officers at the municipality level, but there is almost no consistency between the two for counties.

FISCAL IMPACT OVERVIEW

Taking account of differences due to non-response, the fiscal impact estimates derived from the survey of local government officials suggests several patterns that seem to be quite unambiguous, and others where there is more room for disagreement. The most straightforward finding, which turns up in all of the data with only minor variations, is that the dominant impact of GRS funds on local government expenditures was on capital rather than current outlays. That generalization holds for every size class of municipality, township and county, with a single exception: municipalities with 300,000 or more population show exactly the reverse pattern, with the dominant use of GRS funds being to maintain or expand operating programs. The more

Table 2-8
Summary of Estimated Fiscal Impact of GRS, Chief Administrative Officer Responses
(percentages)

Type of Unit	Number of Cases	FISCAL IMPACT CATEGORY				
		Maintained or Increased Operating Expenditures	Maintained or Increased Capital Expenditures	Stabilized or Reduced Local Taxes	Other	Total Revenue Sharing Allocation
A: Fiscal Year 1974						
Municipalities						
Over 300,000	21	28.5	24.1	29.8	17.6	100.0
100,000-299,999.....	32	27.4	39.1	39.5	-6.0	100.0
25,000-99,999	174	24.1	45.5	21.8	8.7	100.0
Townships	227	26.5	35.9	28.7	8.9	100.0
Counties................	91	21.9	38.8	18.8	20.5	100.0
Grand Total	318	24.3	37.3	24.1	14.3	100.0
B: Fiscal Year 1975						
Municipalities						
Over 300,000	21	24.4	24.3	37.4	13.9	100.0
100,000-299,999.....	32	26.6	21.4	34.6	17.4	100.0
25,000-99,000	174	25.4	39.7	22.1	12.8	100.0
Townships	227	25.2	29.0	31.4	14.4	100.0
Counties................	91	19.3	48.3	16.8	15.6	100.0
Grand Total	318	22.4	38.3	24.4	14.9	100.0

Sources: Derived from Appendix Tables 2A-13 and 2A-15.

problematical finding relates to the impact of GRS on tax abatement. Most of the evidence suggests that the tax impact was modest, and much of it suggests that the impact was stronger in fiscal year 1975 than in fiscal year 1974.

But there is considerable room for disagreement about just how "modest" tax abatement effects were. None of the groups of officials we interviewed felt that tax abatement was as important a use of GRS funds as expenditure maintenance or expansion. Within size classes, most of the evidence suggests that tax abatement was much more important in moderate size cities (between 10,000 and 299,999) than either in very large or very small cities, or in townships and counties. Finally, the data suggest that tax abatement uses of GRS funds were much stronger in large cities in fiscal year 1975 than they were in fiscal year 1974.

Although a detailed examination of the probable reliability of these survey estimates is provided below, a brief note is in order here. It is by no means clear that one can get reliable measures from surveys of the relative importance of, for example, capital outlay uses of GRS funds versus tax abate-

ment uses. We noted earlier that the question asked in the survey is difficult to answer, since it depends on judgments that are neither simple nor easy to make. Thus deciding whether local taxes would have been higher, or local expenditures lower, in the absence of GRS is not a judgment that necessarily has a high degree of reliability and is without potentially serious bias. But other kinds of judgments seem, in principle, to be much more free of potential bias. For example, judgments about the relative importance of capital vs. operating uses may be subject to less bias than judgments about expenditure uses as a whole vs. other uses, even though the relatively high visibility of capital expenditures is clearly a possible source of bias.

In a similar vein, judgments about the uses of GRS funds in different years, where data for both years are obtained via the survey, ought not to be subject to many of the biases that might affect an expenditure vs. tax judgment. Finally, and most importantly, survey estimates of GRS impact in different types of communities, say for example, relating to the relative importance of operating outlays adjustments in large and small communities, ought not to be subject to many of the potential biases discussed above; whatever bias attaches to statements about expenditure impacts generally presumably attaches equally to expenditure impact estimates obtained from officials in both large and small communities. The same would be true of survey estimates relating to regional differences.

In sum, while the use of surveys to measure fiscal impact may well be subject to unknown and possibly serious bias when the question relates to the relative importance of different types of adjustments (expenditure vs. tax vs. borrowing, for example), we see no persuasive reason why differences in the same kind of adjustment across various size classes of communities or among regions, or between years, is necessarily subject to the same bias, and we expect the survey to be a reliable instrument for the analysis of such differences. In short, we feel a good deal more confident that, whatever the importance of expenditure adjustments might have been, operating expenditures were a much more important use of GRS funds in big cities, and capital expenditures a

much more important use in other cities. Similarly, we feel confident that tax abatement effects are much more important in moderate size cities than in either very large or very small ones, and so forth.

REGIONAL IMPACTS

It is by no means clear that one would expect to find differences in the fiscal impact of GRS funds among geographic regions of the U. S., comparing similar types and sizes of local governments, except as such differences can be explained by factors like income, governmental function, etc. that vary systematically by region. In Chapter 4 we attempt to model the survey measures of fiscal impact, and try to explain some of the differences described above. Here, we examine regional differences for comparably sized units, simply noting the differences that seem to exist without making any systematic attempt to explain them. Tables 2-9 and 2-10 summarize fiscal impacts by region for groups

Table 2-9
Estimated Fiscal Impact of GRS by Region, Finance Officer Responses,
FY74
(percentages)

Local Government Unit	N	Fiscal Impact Category				
		Operating Expenditures	Capital Expenditures	Local Taxes	Other	Total Revenue Sharing Allocation
A. Municipalities: 300,000 and Over Population						
Northeast	5	93.4	0.0	4.8	1.7	100.0
North Central	7	79.6	8.7	14.4	-2.6	100.0
South	8	32.3	27.5	22.8	17.4	100.0
West	7	31.5	37.5	9.6	21.3	100.0
B. Municipalities: 100,000 to 299,000 Population						
Northeast	11	12.7	2.1	71.8	13.4	100.0
North Central	10	41.2	35.5	33.9	-10.6	100.0
South	8	32.1	37.5	27.5	0.9	100.0
West	11	41.7	46.8	12.8	-1.3	100.0
C. Municipalities: 100 to 99,000 Population						
Northeast	178	7.4	38.7	38.0	15.8	100.0
North Central	167	13.4	57.5	11.3	17.8	100.0
South	85	12.6	67.9	9.5	15.8	100.0
West	82	19.1	66.2	6.5	8.5	100.0
D. Counties						
Northeast	28	25.4	35.3	24.2	15.1	100.0
North Central	44	32.9	46.4	10.5	10.6	100.0
South	49	22.8	47.6	10.4	19.3	100.0
West	22	9.8	60.0	12.4	13.1	100.0

Local Government Unit	N	Fiscal Impact Category				
		Operating Expenditures	Capital Expenditures	Local Taxes	Other	Total Revenue Sharing Allocation
A. Municipalities: 300,000 and Over Population						
Northeast	5	52.5	0.0	47.1	0.0	100.0
North Central	7	91.0	9.0	0.0	0.0	100.0
South	8	28.3	45.6	32.5	-6.4	100.0
West	7	39.4	13.1	34.8	12.7	100.0
B. Municipalities: 100,000 to 299,000 Population						
Northeast	11	18.2	20.9	81.6	-20.7	100.0
North Central	10	39.6	46.3	14.2	0.0	100.0
South	8	31.4	36.1	19.3	13.2	100.0
West	11	49.1	41.4	10.0	-0.4	100.0
C. Municipalities: 100 to 99,000 Population						
Northeast	178	10.0	39.5	48.3	2.2	100.0
North Central	167	18.1	51.8	14.6	15.2	100.0
South	85	24.6	54.4	11.0	10.0	100.0
West	82	25.5	63.1	7.1	4.8	100.0
D. Counties						
Northeast	28	17.7	33.9	33.6	14.7	100.0
North Central	44	24.4	48.1	21.4	5.6	100.0
South	49	29.0	43.8	14.0	13.4	100.0
West	22	12.2	43.8	28.9	15.1	100.0

of local governments defined by size and function, for fiscal year 1974 and fiscal year 1975, using finance officer responses. Basically, these tables are simply a rearrangement of the fiscal impact estimates shown in Table 2-6 and in Appendix Tables 2A-5 and 2A-7.

The regional differences can only be described as startling and striking. In particular, they show a marked difference in the fiscal impact of GRS funds in the Northeast region compared to the rest of the country. For very large cities, the operating expenditure uses of GRS funds, while relatively heavy overall, vary from over 90 percent of the revenue-sharing total in the Northeast to just over 30 percent in the West, while the capital expenditure uses vary from a zero proportion in the Northeast to almost 40 percent in the West. Tax abatement effects are modest overall for large cities, being somewhat heavier in the South (Panel A).

But for other municipalities, including those ranging all the way from populations of 100 to those of 299,000, the pattern is entirely different. Here, operating expenditure uses are relatively lower in the Northeast, rising as one proceeds through the North Central and South regions, and are highest in the West. Capital outlay uses follow exactly the same pattern—lowest in the Northeast, highest in the West. The obvious implication is that tax abatement and/or borrowing abatement must follow a reverse pattern. As Panels B and C indicate quite clearly, it is tax abatement that makes up the bulk of the differential. Tax abatement impacts are very high in the Northeast, tend to decline proceeding through the North Central and South, and end up being negligible for the West.

Although tax abatement effects overall are modest in the survey, as noted earlier, almost three-quarters of the total GRS funds went for that purpose in Northeast cities between 100,000 and 299,000 population. In municipalities between 100 and 99,999 population, almost 40 percent of GRS funds went for tax abatement uses. For the West, in contrast, tax abatement impacts for the same size classes are about 12 percent and 6 percent, respectively. As argued above where the issue of bias is discussed, there is no reason to believe that these regional differences in the survey measures of fiscal impact do not reflect real differences.

Regional differences are not so marked for counties, although they tend generally to follow the pattern found for small or moderate size municipalities—more capital expenditure adjustments in the West and fewer in the Northeast, tax abatement heaviest in the Northeast and relatively modest in the West.

Although there are some marked differences in the fiscal year 1975 data compared to those just discussed for fiscal year 1974, the same general pattern still exists. The principal difference between the two years is that tax abatement in the very large cities now follows the 1974 pattern for moderate or small municipalities—heaviest in the Northeast and lighter in the rest of the country. The striking difference between moderate-size (100,000-299,-999) cities in the Northeast and elsewhere is just as striking in 1975 as it was in 1974: more than 80 percent of the GRS funds went for tax abatement in moderate-sized Northeast cities, and no other region showed as much as 20 percent for cities of the same size class. For smaller municipalities, the same pattern shows up: almost half the GRS funds went for tax abatement in small (100-99,999) cities in the Northeast, and no other region showed as much as 15 percent going to tax abatement in the same size class. The offsets to the tax abatement pattern continued to be predominantly the capital outlay pattern, although operating outlays also tended to be the lowest in the Northeast and highest in the West.

These regional differences are so marked that one wonders if there is an obvious explanation for them. Although there are some differences that one could point to in the Northeast compared to the remainder of the U. S. (the Northeast is older, growing more slowly, tends to have relatively high local property tax levels) none of the differences seem to be sufficiently striking to account, in a statistical way, for the extreme differences in the estimated uses of GRS funds. By far the most striking feature of the regional data are the tax abatement differences. The political folklore speaks loosely of

a "tax revolt" in the U. S. The estimates in Tables 2-9 and 2-10 of the fiscal impact of GRS funds suggest that the tax revolt is a much more virilent phenomenon in the Northeast part of the U. S. than anywhere else, and that this is especially so in moderate-sized Northeast cities (100,000-299,-999).[12]

COMPARISONS WITH OTHER ESTIMATES

As indicated earlier, we think it important to compare fiscal impact estimates obtained from the survey with estimates derived from other methodologies. The survey contains some inherent limitations, especially in situations where it is used to measure what is essentially a hypothetical difference between the local jurisdictions' budget situation as it was and as it would have been in the absence of GRS funds. In addition, most other studies of the impact of the GRS program address themselves to the question of fiscal impact. Since all the other studies concern themselves with fragments of the relevant population of all U.S. local government jurisdictions, and since most of the other studies involve a much more detailed investigation of a particular set of communities, comparison of estimates from the survey with those found in other studies is extremely useful. If it turns out, for example, that for comparable communities in the SRC sample, the survey estimates of fiscal impact are about the same as those found by other investigators using different (and either more intensive or more conventional) methodologies, our confidence in the survey estimates would be enhanced. Moreover, it would then be possible to use the survey estimates to make judgments about the overall fiscal impact of the GRS program, something that is simply not possible with any of the other studies because of the fragmented universe of municipalities or states that they represent.

On the other hand, it may be that such comparisons will show that the survey estimates appear to be systematically biased. If that were to be the case, we would at least know the nature and extent of the bias, and could therefore make overall judgments about the fiscal impact of GRS by adjusting for known biases in the survey estimates.

Since the estimates discussed above are quantitative, in that they report the dollar distribution of GRS funds among various types of local government jurisdictions, the most useful comparisons

[12]Again, we remind the reader that whatever bias may exist in the estimates of fiscal impact derived from the survey, it is hard to see any reason why differences among regions in the extent of tax abatement should be biased. And the data speak clearly to a striking difference among regions.

are with other studies that have a similar data orientation.

Of the various studies that might be compared with the survey data, three stand out as warranting systematic investigation. These are the Brookings Institution study, "Monitoring Revenue Sharing," by Nathan, *et al.* the study done by Anton, Larkey, *et al.* published by the Institute for Public Policy Studies at The University of Michigan, and the study published by Lovell, *et al.* published by the Drylands Research Institute. The Brookings study uses the "expert observer" technique and examines fiscal impacts in 65 communities including both states and local governments. The Anton-Larkey *et al.* study is a very careful examination, using historical budget data, of five moderate-sized U.S. cities. The Lovell *et al.* study includes estimates of fiscal impact using the "expert observer" approach as well as a time-series econometric analysis. In addition, we compare the survey estimates with data from the Official Use Reports. We also produce a comparison of the survey estimates with the econometric modeling efforts reported above in Chapter 5 of this study.

Official Use Reports

The simplest, most straightforward and most comprehensive comparison that can be made is that of survey estimates vis-a-vis those contained in the Official Use Reports, which must be filed by all jurisdictions receiving GRS funds. At the aggregate level, the only comparison that is analytically relevant involves the tax and borrowing abatement effects of GRS. The Use Reports contain a good deal of data on program impact, but there is no way to use these data for analysis of overall expenditure impacts:[13] By definition, Use Reports assign all GRS funds to some expenditure category. However, officials filing these reports are asked to indicate whether or not GRS funds were used to limit tax increases, to permit tax reductions, or to avoid new taxes, and are also asked whether GRS funds enabled them to avoid borrowing or to reduce borrowing. These estimates are entirely qualitative, and can be compared directly with similar qualitative estimates derived from the survey. Table 2-11 compares Use Report estimates of the proportion of communities in each size class reporting tax or borrowing abatement effects of GRS with estimates derived from the finance officer responses in the survey. Both sets of estimates are based entirely on the SRC's sample of local government jurisdictions, for which Use Report data were extracted from the Office of Revenue Sharing basic data tape.

Results of this comparison are unambiguous. The Official Use Reports show substantially higher

_____

[13]The Use Report estimates of program impact are compared with the survey data in Chapter 3.

Table 2-11
Fiscal Impact Estimates from Survey Responses
Compared to Official Use Reports, FY 1974

	Weighted Percent Reporting Some:			
	Tax Stabilization		Borrowing Stabilization	
Type of Unit	Survey (Finance Officers)	Use Reports[a]	Survey (Finance Officers)	Use Reports
Municipalities				
300,000 + ...	14.1	63.4	1.1	9.9
100,000-299,999	60.9	90.8	18.8	12.0
25,000-99,999	35.4	72.2	17.1	26.6
10,000-24,999	28.7	67.0	12.7	39.7
2,500-9,999	34.1	68.7	23.0	40.5
Under 2,500.................	22.1	65.4	14.4	38.5
Townships: 9,000 + ...	33.2	74.7	19.3	42.3
Townships: < 9,000	13.1	58.2	13.5	23.6
Counties				
500,000 + ...	32.7	70.1	25.2	18.1
100,000-499,999	29.6	78.8	20.4	41.2
Under 100,000	20.3	57.0	9.2	36.3
Total	29.3	69.8	14.2	27.8

[a]Official Use Report data were obtained from the Office of Revenue Sharing tape.

estimates of both tax and borrowing abatement than does the survey: on the average, more than twice as many communities indicated some degree of tax abatement on the Use Reports than was true for estimates derived from the survey, and about the same relationship holds for evidence of borrowing abatement. Interestingly enough, although the *levels* are quite different the patterns by size of community are remarkably similar. Municipalities in the 100,000-299,999 size class show the strongest tax abatement impact on both the Official Use Reports and in the survey, and both show the least tax abatement in the big cities and in the rural counties and townships. (The Spearman rank correlation coefficient between survey and Use Report estimates of tax abatement is +0.84). The data on borrowing abatement are much less similarly patterned, and show essentially no relationship between the Use Reports and the survey.

Aside from the difference in level, the closeness of the association between Use Report and survey measures of tax abatement can be seen from Table 2-12, which classifies Use Report estimates of tax abatement against survey estimates in a 2 × 2 contingency table. The upper left-hand corner of these tables shows the proportion of communities in which both the Use Reports and the survey report some degree of tax abatement, the lower right-hand corner shows the proportion of communities in which neither Use Reports nor the survey report tax abatement, the upper right-hand corner has cases where the Use Reports show tax abatement but the survey does not, while the lower left-hand corner shows communities where the survey reports tax abatement but the Use Reports do not.

These data document the proposition that, although the levels of tax abatement reported on the Use Reports and the survey are very different, the correlation between them is very high. The great majority of communities reporting tax abatement on the survey also report the same thing on the official Use Reports, while the great majority of communities reporting no tax abatement on the Use Report also report no tax abatement on the survey. The lower left hand cell is very small in almost all cases, while the upper right hand cell is very large—a pattern that necessarily follows from the difference in levels and the high proportion of matching cases.[14]

The obvious question to ask is, does the Use Report data or the survey data give a more accurate

---

[14]The small differences between the data in Table 2-11 and these data, for any given type and size of community, are due to the fact that the sample here must be matched, and thus contains a few less cases. We found some 30 communities with no Use Report on the ORS tape, and there are some 20 communities with a Use Report but no survey response.

Table 2-12
Comparison of Survey and Use Report Estimates of Tax Abatement, Weighted Percentages

Survey Tax Abatement	Use Reports Tax Abatement		
	No	Yes	All
A. Municipalities: Over 300,000			
No	35.4	49.3	84.7
Yes	1.1	14.1	15.2
All	36.5	63.4	100.0
B. Municipalities: 100,000-299,999			
No	8.5	30.9	39.4
Yes	0.7	59.8	60.5
All	9.2	90.8	100.0
C. Municipalities: 10,000-99,999			
No	18.1	45.9	64.0
Yes	9.7	26.2	35.9
All	27.8	72.2	100.0
D. Municipalities: 2,500-9,999			
No	27.0	43.8	70.8
Yes	6.0	23.2	29.2
All	33.0	67.0	100.0
E. Townships: Over 9,000			
No	20.7	45.4	66.0
Yes	4.6	29.3	33.9
All	25.3	74.7	100.0
F. Counties: 100,000-499,999			
No	19.8	50.2	70.0
Yes	1.4	28.6	30.0
All	21.2	78.8	100.0

assessment of tax abatement? We discuss that question later when all the comparisons and evidence have been presented, but for the moment it will suffice to note that there is no a priori evidence in favor of either from the data presented above. It is not even clear that the Use Reports and the survey represent in some sense upper and lower bounds to the possible size of the tax abatement effect, although we have noted above reasons why we suspect the survey measures of tax abatement to be somewhat, though not greatly, understated.

Surplus Fund Uses

One interesting sidelight from the Use Reports is that they provide an estimate of the degree to which local governments drew down accumulated revenue-sharing balances during fiscal year 1974. The Use Reports basically ask for allocation of GRS funds to "priority" expenditure categories. But the Use Reports for fiscal year 1974 do not simply simply indicate the uses of the fiscal year 1974 GRS allocation, but report uses of all GRS funds, whether allocated currently or previously, during fiscal year 1974. From the SRC sample of local government jurisdictions, we estimate that total uses of revenue-sharing funds during fiscal year 1974 came to roughly $200 million more than the 1974 revenue sharing allocation, implying that fund balances were drawn down by about that amount. This figure can be taken as a rough guide for the degree to which the survey responses might have underestimated tax and/or borrowing abatement effects by our failure to ask about tax or borrowing impacts of GRS in situations where the respondent had already reported that the full amount of fiscal year 1974 GRS funds had been allocated to an expenditure category or categories. If the Use Report estimate is accurate, it suggests that the degree of underestimation is quite modest, and could not be responsible for the relatively modest amount of tax abatement reported in the survey.

IPPS Study

As part of the NSF-RANN sponsored research on General Revenue Sharing, a group of researchers headed by Thomas Anton and affiliated with the Institute of Public Policy Studies (IPPS) undertook an extensive study of five moderate or large-sized U.S. cities. Their procedure was to look at long-term trend data to model the expenditure and revenue patterns for each of the cities, and at the same time to explore particular aspects of the development of these cities in an attempt to build a more precisely specified model of their budgetary decisions.

The Anton group studied Albuquerque, New Mexico; Ann Arbor, Michigan; Detroit, Michigan; Cincinnati, Ohio; and Worcester, Massachusetts. These are all moderate to large-sized cities (the smallest, Ann Arbor, has just about 100,000 people) which have somewhat different background and different patterns of development. Two of them are also included in the Survey Research Center's sample of local government jurisdictions. It is thus possible to compare exactly the survey estimates of fiscal impact with roughly comparable estimates of fiscal impact from the Anton *et al.* study.

The methodologies employed in these two studies differ about as much as one could imagine. Anton *et al.* applied statistical modeling techniques to data covering a very long time span, and estimated revenue-sharing impacts from the difference between predictions of the model and the actual fiscal behavior of the respective cities. The survey interviewed key officials in local government jurisdictions, and asked them how their budget would have been different if revenue-sharing money had not been available. Direct comparisons between the two studies are possible with respect to the estimate of GRS impacts on total expenditures, local taxes, and local borrowing. Both studies allocated the fiscal year 1974 GRS funds to either expenditure, tax or borrowing categories, and the survey in principle also provided for an allocation to surplus.

Table 2-13 summarizes the estimates of fiscal impact for the two cities which overlap between the Anton *et al.* study and the survey. In one of the two cities, we interviewed both the chief executive and the chief finance officer, while in the other we obtained an interview only from the finance officer.

The similarity between the IPPS results and the survey is remarkably close for both cities using the finance officer responses, less close for the one city where we have a chief executive response. In city A, the finance officer we interviewed as well as the IPPS study concluded that the principal impact of GRS was on tax stabilization (81 vs. 73 percent of GRS funds), with the difference being in expenditure maintenance or expansion (19 vs. 27 percent). In contrast, the chief executive officer of city A estimated that a bit less than half of GRS funds went for tax stabilization, about 80 percent went into expenditures, and surpluses were drawn down by about 25 percent of the GRS fiscal year 1974 allocation. For the other city, both studies show precisely the same thing—all the funds went to expenditure maintenance or expansion.

One should not make too much of the fact that two cities happen to show a very close match between fiscal impact estimates using statistical modeling techniques and those used by the survey. Still, it is impressive that the survey shows a very large tax stabilization impact in city A, especially since overall the survey shows a quite modest impact of GRS on tax abatement. And even in the case of the survey responses that differ somewhat from the findings of the IPPS study (the chief executive officer response), our data indicate a very large tax abatement effect, although less than estimated by IPPS.

	Percent of Revenue Sharing Funds Allocated to:				
	Expenditure Maintenance or Expansion	Tax Stabilization or Reduction	Borrowing Stabilization or Reduction	Other	Total
City A					
Survey					
Chief Executive..........	79.2	45.2	—	-24.4	100.0
Finance Officer..........	18.7	81.3	—	—	100.0
Anton et al.	26.6	73.4	—	—	100.0
City B					
Survey					
Finance Officer..........	100.0	—	—	—	100.0
Anton et al.	100.0	—	—	—	100.0

Sources: SRC survey of local government officials, and *Understanding the Fiscal Impact of General Revenue Sharing*, Institute of Public Policy Studies, The University of Michigan, June 1975, Thomas J. Anton, principal author.

Brookings "Monitoring Revenue Sharing" Study

One of the earliest and most comprehensive of the revenue-sharing studies is the one in process at the Brookings Institution. The first of what is planned as a series of volumes was published in 1975, authored by Nathan, Manvel, Calkins and associates, entitled *Monitoring Revenue Sharing*. Brookings examined some 65-odd state and local governments, using professional observers to make an in-depth study of the effects of GRS on budgets. Observers were expected to use whatever resources were available—data on the jurisdictions' past expenditures or receipts, conversations with officials, observations at public meetings, Use Reports, etc., to provide estimates of fiscal impact. The Brookings fiscal impact categories are somewhat more detailed and defined than the ones used in the survey: for example, they distinguish the use of GRS funds to expand operating outlays as opposed to simply maintaining existing ones, and they estimate separately tax reduction and tax stabilization effects. But the Brookings categories can be defined to be exactly comparable to the ones used in this chapter.

Although Brookings examined 65 jurisdictions, these were not designed to represent any but a "convenient" sample. The communities studied did include large ones and small ones, States as well as local governments, and one Indian tribe. But the data as presented simply report either the total amount of revenue-sharing dollars estimated for the 9 fiscal impact categories in the 65 jurisdictions in the sample, without any attempt to weight responses for the probability that they would appear in a sample selected by conventional probability sampling methods, or the unweighted means of the fiscal impact proportions reported by the Brookings communities for each of the nine adjustment categories.

The most relevant comparison involves the distribution of total revenue-sharing dollars among fiscal impact categories for the local governments in the Brookings study. These are roughly comparable to the survey estimates, which show the allocation of revenue-sharing dollars by fiscal impact categories in sample communities, weighted by population and the probability of selection. The Brookings estimates of unweighted means, which treat cities like New York exactly the same as rural townships, appear to be less useful for purposes of comparison.

The fact that the Brookings sample includes New York City means that the aggregate data as reported gives a misleading impression of overall fiscal impact, since New York comprises something like 40 percent of the total revenue-sharing dollar allocation in the Brookings collection of local governments. Thus, for example, the aggregate dollar tabulation in the Brookings study estimates tax reduction or tax stabilization effects as amounting to slightly over 40 percent of the total revenue-sharing allocation. But these data are dominated by the inclusion of New York City, where Brookings estimates a very large impact of the revenue-sharing program on tax stabilization. The estimated 40 percent of revenue-sharing funds used for tax stabilization turns out to be more like 20 percent if one simply excludes New York City from the calculation. The alternative estimate from the Brookings data, the unweighted mean proportion of all communities, is about 13 percent for tax effects.

A similar problem shows up in estimates of borrowing avoidance, where the Brookings aggregate dollar figures show about 14 percent (compared to about 3 percent for the unweighted means). But this again is due almost entirely to the estimated impact of revenue sharing on borrowing avoidance in New York City. Simply eliminating New York City from the tabulation drops aggregate estimates of borrowing avoidance to about 3 percent.

Although there is no acceptable way to convert the Brookings data so as to produce comparisons that are fully appropriate vis-a-vis the survey, the best compromise appears to be to recalculate the aggregate dollar totals and exclude New York City from those totals. That tabulation is shown in Table 2-14, where the two left-hand columns simply reproduce the fiscal impact table for local governments from the Brookings study, and the two right-hand columns recalculate the Brookings data excluding New York City from the local government sample.[15]

With the adjustment of excluding New York City, the overall estimates of fiscal impact shown in the Brookings study are not very different from those shown by the survey—Brookings shows roughly 20 percent for fiscal year 1973 compared to about 16 percent for fiscal year 1974 and 25 percent for fiscal year 1975 for the survey. But the Brookings sample is in no sense a probability sample and there is no way to convert it into one. All one can say is that fiscal impact as estimated by professional observers is a good bit more like 20 percent than 40 percent of the local government total, and it is hard to know whether the 20 percent would be high or low if the Brookings procedure were applied to a representative sample. The presumption is that 20 percent is too high; the Brookings dollar figures are almost certainly overweighted with relatively large cities (even excluding New York City), and the survey data indicate that cities in the 100,000-299,999 size class show a good deal more tax abatement than either very large or very small communities. On the other hand, all the Brookings data are for allocations of GRS funds made up to July 1 of 1973, and tax abatement is likely to have been higher in the later years of the GRS program than in the earliest one.

Besides the tax adjustment and borrowing avoidance calculations discussed above, the Brookings data show a very heavy impact of GRS on new capital—close to half the total—and the implied distribution between capital and operating outlays is quite close to the relationships shown above for the survey data—capital vs. operating is roughly 44 percent vs. 28 percent in the Brookings study, about 42 vs. 29 percent for the survey. And it is probably true that the differences between fiscal year 1973 and fiscal year 1974 fiscal impacts would tend to suggest not only more tax stabilization and borrowing avoidance impacts in fiscal year 1974, but probably less capital outlay impact and more

---

[15] A further comment on the Brookings vs. survey comparisons, in terms of the sampling issue, is worth noting. The SRC sample is a fully representative probability sample of the population of U.S. local government jurisdictions. Communities in that sample are assigned weights, which depend both on their probability of selection and on the absolute size of their population. Thus each SRC community "stands" for the appropriate number of other communities in the United States which, in a sampling sense, can be thought of as being exactly like the communities included in the sample. The success of the probability sampling scheme is amply demonstrated by the comparisons shown above in Tables 2-5 and 2-5A.

For the Brookings study, in contrast, there is no explicit sampling frame. A number of divergent types of communities are included in the study, since the objective was to measure GRS impacts in communities of different sizes, types, regions, etc. But there is no way in which the Brookings collection of local government communities can be converted to a sample that represents anything but itself.

This is not so much a criticism of the Brookings procedure as a reflection of different research strategy. Brookings opted for a

very intensive examination of a quite small number of local government jurisdictions, while SRC opted for a much less intensive examination of a larger and fully representative sample of local government jurisdictions. Even if the Brookings sample were drawn on a probability basis, the sample size (57 local government jurisdictions) would have made it virtually impossible to draw reliable conclusions about the universe. Hence adopting random probability sampling methods would not have really gotten around the problem, since the sample size would have been far too small to keep variances within tolerable limits. And the Brookings sample size could not have been increased without proportional increases in costs which we can assume could not have been supported. Nonetheless, it is still true that neither the aggregate fiscal impact estimates presented in the Brookings study, nor the unweighted mean estimates, can be thought of as representing anything more than estimates that are applicable to the 57 jurisdictions included in the Brookings study: there is no way in which either of these statements of fiscal impact can be generalized beyond the communities actually included in the Brookings study.

Table 2-14
Fiscal Impact Estimates Derived from Brookings'
"Monitoring Revenue Sharing" Study

	Brookings Data—Fiscal Impact			
	Local Governments		Local Governments Excluding New York City	
FISCAL IMPACT CATEGORIES	$	%	$	%
New Spending	250.3	31.4	250.3	52.4
New Capital	211.4	26.5	211.4	44.3
Expanded Operations	22.7	2.9	22.7	4.7
Increased Pay	16.2	2.0	16.2	3.4
Unallocated	0.0	0.0	0.0	0.0
Substitutions	546.4	68.6	227.3	47.6
Restoration of Aid	7.0	0.9	1.5	
Tax Reduction	56.2	7.1	56.2	11.8
Tax Stabilization	265.6	33.3	46.4	9.7
Program Maintenance	94.2	11.8	94.2	19.7
Borrowing Avoidance	114.9	14.4	14.9	3.1
Increased Balances	8.5	1.1	8.5	1.8
Unallocated	0.0	0.0	0.0	0.0
TOTAL	796.8	100.0	477.6	100.0

Sources: *Monitoring Revenue Sharing*, Richard P. Nathan, Allen D. Manvel, Susannah E. Calkins and Associates, The Brookings Institution, Washington, DC, 1975.

operating outlay impact. Thus the overall comparisons, all things considered, are really quite close provided one excludes New York City from the Brookings estimates.[16]

Drylands Study of Southern California

The next comparison that can be made is between the survey and the results of a detailed examination of 97 cities in Southern California, conducted by a group of researchers at the Drylands Institute headed by Catherine Lovell. Alternative methodologies were used in the Drylands study, since both time-series extrapolation and professional observer approaches were tried. The former, using budgetary data on expenditures and revenues, estimating the impact of GRS by includ-

[16]A direct comparison between the survey estimates of fiscal impact and the Brookings estimates can of course be made for New York City—as well as for a few other specific cities. For New York, the two estimates are quite different. The survey shows no tax abatement impact in New York City for fiscal year 1974, although tax impacts do show up in fiscal year 1975. The Brookings study shows of course very large tax abatement effects in fiscal year 1973, and presumably equally large or larger effects in fiscal year 1974. It does not seem useful to speculate on which estimate is more likely to be correct.

ing a "dummy" variable for GRS in the time-series regressions for years when GRS was in effect. The professional observer technique was actually an extensive and unstructured interview using the Brookings fiscal impact categories.

The professional observer estimates from Lovell's study can be compared directly with the survey estimates, and they appear to agree quite closely. Lovell's data and the survey data are shown in the top and bottom panels of Table 2-15, with Lovell's fiscal impact categories combined so as to be consistent with the survey ones. To make the comparisons as close as possible, the survey estimates shown above use only cities in Orange County, California. As far as we can tell, there is a great deal of overlap between the 25 odd cities in the SRC Orange County sample and the cities in the Lovell study. The survey estimates are limited to cities between 25,000 and 299,999 population, which are the size classes most comparable to the ones examined by Lovell.

Excluding Lovell's big city category, both her data and the survey data suggest that the dominant impact of revenue sharing was on new capital spending, with much weaker impacts on operating outlays, tax abatement and borrowing abatement. The general order of magnitude of fiscal impacts in the Lovell data and the survey data seem quite close although the Lovell data may show a bit more emphasis on operating outlays, a bit less on capital. Both sets of data indicate that capital impacts were something like five times as large as tax impacts—a result which is also consistent with the data for the West region as a whole, shown above in Table 2-9.

However, the Lovell *et al.* study de-emphasizes the professional observer data shown in Table 2-15, arguing that those estimates of fiscal impact are not really much different from the Use Report estimate, and that both are seriously biased. As an alternative, Lovell presents estimates of fiscal impact based on analysis of historical expenditure and tax data. This analysis finds significant impacts of revenue sharing on several forms of local taxes and on capital outlays, but not on operating outlays. The regression coefficients of the revenue-sharing variables are such that tax effects appear to be about the same order of magnitude as capital outlay effects—a finding in sharp contrast with the data in Table 2-15.

ECONOMETRIC ANALYSIS OF BUDGET DATA

The final comparison involves the survey results and the econometric analysis of budgetary data discussed above in Chapter 5, which is based on a small subset of the SRC sample of municipalities. These results, at least as far as overall fiscal impact is concerned, are also sharply at variance with the survey estimates.[17] The econometric analysis shows some evidence that revenue-sharing impacted on local tax rates, but no evidence of an impact either on operating or on capital expenditures. The latter is particularly surprising, since no other study that I am aware of fails to find a significant impact of revenue sharing on capital outlays. The explanation is probably one of very small sample size and serious problems with the data: the econometric analysis in Chapter 5 is based on budgetary information obtained directly from sample municipalities, and we were unable to check the accuracy of the data for more than its overall reasonableness compared to external (Census of Governments) sources. But the sample is quite small, especially for analysis of capital outlays; many cities do not report capital and operating outlays separately but simply combine the two into functional categories like public safety, highways, etc. Moreover, the program areas where the Chapter 5 analysis shows significant impacts of revenue sharing tend to be ones in which capital outlays are more likely to be involved than operating outlays (fire services, highways, sewerage); hence we tend to regard the findings on capital outlay effects as unreliable.

---

[17]Interestingly enough, the Chapter 5 analysis of program impacts is remarkably consistent with the survey estimates of program impact. These comparisons are discussed in Chapter 3.

Table 2-15
Fiscal Impact Estimates for Southern California
Local Governments
Percent of Total Revenue Sharing

	Maintained or Increased Capital Expenditures	Maintained or Increased Operating Expenditures	Stabilized or Reduced Local Taxes	Stabilized or Reduced Local Borrowing	Other	Total
A. City Type (Lovell Data)						
City Type						
Middle Class-Suburban...........	62.6	20.6	8.9	5.2	2.7	100.0
Median.........................	48.6	24.4	17.4	6.7	2.9	100.0
Wealthy-Conservative...........	54.7	27.1	9.8	0.3	8.2	100.0
Poor Non-Black Working Class ...	48.4	16.9	15.7	7.9	11.0	100.0
Older-Urban.....................	47.1	22.0	15.0	9.5	6.3	100.0
Big City........................	24.4	40.3	25.0	0.2	10.1	100.0
Rapid Growth-Conservative.......						
Suburban......................	97.9	2.1	0.0	0.0	0.0	100.0
Commercial Enclave	76.2	23.8	0.0	0.0	0.0	100.0
Deprived-Dependent-Black	25.4	41.6	0.0	0.0	0.0	100.0
Working Class-Homeowners......	54.8	25.2	5.7	14.3	0.1	100.0
B. Size Class (SRC Data)						
Size Class						
100,000-299,999................	67.4	9.7	26.8	0.0	-4.8	100.0
25,000-99,000	58.4	10.9	5.1	4.7	20.0	100.0
10,000-24,999	0.0	0.0	0.0	0.0	100.0	100.0
Total.....................	59.3	10.2	11.3	3.2	15.9	100.0

Appendix to Chapter 2
Estimates of Fiscal Impact

The basic fiscal impact data from the survey of State and local government officials comes from a sequence of questions designed to elicit judgments from respondents about the way in which local expenditures, local taxes, and local borrowing would have been different in the absence of the GRS program. Respondents were channeled into one of four question sequences depending on their answers to the questions:

1) In the absence of GRS, would operating expenditures have been lower during fiscal year 1974(75) [in this jurisdiction]?

2) In the absence of GRS, would capital expenditures have been lower during fiscal year 1974(75) [in this jurisdiction]?

Respondents answering yes to both questions fell into question sequence I; those answering yes to the first but no to the second fell into question sequence II; no to the first but yes to the second into question sequence III; and no to both questions, into question sequence IV.

Sequence I respondents were then asked whether the reduction in operating and capital expenditures combined would have been equal to the amount of revenue-sharing funds or less than that amount (or greater). If they said "less than," they were asked how much less, then asked whether local taxes and/or local borrowing would have been higher in the absence of GRS.

In addition, sequence I respondents were asked whether the reduction in operating outlays would have been equal to, less than, or greater than the reduction in capital outlays.

Sequence II respondents were asked whether the reduction in operating expenditures would have been equal to the amount of GRS funds or less than that amount, or greater, and if they said less than, how much less, then whether local taxes and/or local borrowing would have been higher in the absence of GRS.

Sequence III respondents were asked whether the reduction in capital outlays would have been equal to or less than the amount of GRS funds (or greater), and if they said less than, whether they would have made up the difference primarily by taxes or by borrowing.

Finally, sequence IV respondents were asked whether local taxes would have been higher in the absence of GRS, whether local borrowing would have been higher, and if yes to either, how much higher. The entire question sequence was repeated for fiscal year 1975.

The logic of the fiscal impact question sequence is that the allocation of GRS funds must be fully accounted for either by expenditure, tax or borrowing adjustments, or else the funds have not yet been included in budgets and are still available to be used. In the latter case, the funds are presumably in unspent fund balances of one sort or another. But GRS funds must have left a trail which can ultimately be identified as representing either an impact on operating or capital expenditures, on local taxes, on local borrowing or on locally held surpluses. Thus a logical identity requires that the sum of all these impacts be equal to the revenue-sharing allocation.

The distribution of respondents among the four basic categories (sequences I-IV) is shown in Table 2A-1 for both fiscal year 1974 and fiscal year 1975, with respondents classified by size and type of local governments. More respondents (specifically, respondents representing a greater population) fell into sequence III generally, although most big city respondents fell into sequence I or II.

Table 2A-2 shows the incidence of various kinds of fiscal impacts as recorded by the qualitative variables just discussed. Not all respondents could have indicated all four (operating expenditures, capital expenditures, tax or borrowing) impacts, since respondents who reported expenditure impacts of GRS and also indicated that these impacts accounted for the full amount of the GRS allocation were not asked about local tax or local borrowing impacts. Thus operating expenditure impacts could be found only in sequences I and II, capital expenditure impacts in sequence I and III, tax impacts in all four sequences in principle (but not when respondents reporting expenditure impacts also indicated that expenditures fully accounted for the GRS allocation), and similarly for borrowing impacts. The data in Table 2A-2 is quite comparable to the data reported above in Tables 2-1 and 2-2, since our basic estimates of quantitative fiscal impact started out with these qualitative judgments. The data here are not exactly the same, however, because of

Table 2A-1

Summary of Expenditure Impact of Revenue Sharing

Weighted Percent of Chief Fiscal Officers
Reporting that, in Absence of Revenue Sharing

Government Type and Size	Operating & Capital Expenditures Both Would Have Been Lower		Operating Expenditures Would Have Been Lower		Capital Expenditures Would Have Been Lower		There Would Have Been No Expenditure Adjustment		Expenditure Adjustment Not Ascertained		Total	
	FY74	FY75	FY74	FY75	FY74	FY75	FY74	FY75	FY74	FY75	FY74	FY75
Municipalities												
300,000 or more population	33.5	34.6	42.9	48.7	10.3	11.5	13.3	5.2	–	–	100.0	100.0
100,000-299,999 population	41.3	57.2	17.0	12.7	15.1	7.7	26.6	22.4	–	–	100.0	100.0
25,000-99,999 population	31.7	36.4	4.9	3.3	45.1	39.5	17.6	18.2	0.7	2.6	100.0	100.0
10,000-24,999 population	23.6	25.3	3.4	8.3	48.4	43.5	23.9	22.9	0.8	–	100.0	100.0
2,500-9,999 population	22.5	35.0	–	0.9	48.2	40.8	22.4	22.3	6.7	0.9	100.0	100.0
Less than 2,500 population	32.4	31.5	8.5	9.4	36.5	36.3	21.3	21.4	1.2	1.5	100.0	100.0
Townships	32.8	26.3	10.0	13.9	35.7	40.9	21.5	18.9	–	–	100.0	100.0
Total (Cities and Townships)	31.1	34.2	14.4	16.2	33.5	31.4	19.8	17.3	1.1	0.8	100.0	100.0
Counties												
100,000 or more population	27.4	45.1	10.0	7.3	34.9	21.6	25.2	23.6	2.5	2.5	100.0	100.0
25,000-99,999 population	38.4	39.9	6.4	7.8	32.0	31.4	22.1	20.9	1.2	—	100.0	100.0
Less than 25,000 population	48.9	50.7	6.6	–	37.0	32.3	4.6	10.7	2.9	6.2	100.0	100.0
Total (Counties)	38.5	45.5	7.7	4.8	34.8	28.5	16.8	18.1	2.2	3.1	100.0	100.0
Number of Cases (unweighted)	242	273	63	71	297	269	181	173	10	9	793	793

Table 2A-2

**Percent Reporting That Indicated Fiscal Adjustment
Would Have Been Made in Absence of Revenue Sharing**

(Chief Fiscal Officers)

Government Type and Size	Lower Operating Expenditures		Lower Capital Expenditures		Higher Taxes		Higher Borrowing	
	FY74	FY75	FY74	FY75	FY74	FY75	FY74	FY75
Municipalities								
300,000 or more population	76.4	83.3	43.8	46.1	14.1	46.4	1.1	6.3
100,000-299,999 population	58.3	69.9	56.4	64.9	60.8	61.3	25.3	19.9
25,000-99,999 population	36.6	39.7	76.5	75.9	37.8	36.4	17.4	19.5
10,000-24,999 population	27.1	33.0	71.7	69.4	34.8	39.3	19.3	9.3
2,500-9,999 population	22.7	35.3	70.9	75.6	37.1	39.0	24.3	23.6
Less than 2,500 population	40.6	40.6	68.5	67.3	27.4	18.1	15.8	9.2
Townships	42.8	40.2	69.8	67.2	28.0	29.0	19.9	13.0
Total (Cities and Townships)	45.5	50.4	64.8	65.6	31.9	38.9	16.0	14.1
Counties								
100,000 or more population	41.3	49.4	65.7	68.0	45.8	56.0	23.5	35.9
25,000-99,999 population	45.2	37.9	87.9	78.9	23.0	12.4	3.4	6.5
Less than 25,000 population	61.0	60.7	83.9	83.6	23.9	50.1	20.1	26.4
Total (Counties)	44.8	48.3	73.2	72.6	37.7	45.2	17.7	27.8
Number of Cases (unweighted)	305	344	539	542	285	307	141	130

various modifications made in the process of editing responses that, for one reason or another, appeared to be inconsistent or questionable. Such editing would be reflected in Tables 2-1 and 2-2, but would not be reflected in the basic survey response data shown in Tables 2A-1 and 2A-2.

The survey estimates of fiscal impact do contain one additional and extensive type of editing, which characterizes all of the fiscal impact data in this monograph. The survey schedule contained a tightly structured series of questions regarding the fiscal impact of GRS. A number of other places in the survey, however, contain questions that relate to fiscal impact, and many of the survey schedules contain comments made by respondents, in reaction to other questions, that bear directly on fiscal impact. Shortly after the field work had been completed and the returned survey schedules were in the process of coding, we decided that it was worthwhile to undertake a complete reediting and recoding job on the structured fiscal impact part of the questionnaire, using information both from within the fiscal impact sequence and from a number of other places in the questionnaire.

In some cases, this reediting and recoding placed respondents in different question sequences than the ones they had actually been asked. For example, a respondent might have originally been in sequence IV, implying that there were no expenditure impacts but at most only tax and/or borrowing impacts. But other information on the survey schedule might clearly suggest that there were expenditure impacts that had not been reported in the structured fiscal impact section of the questionnaire. In cases of that sort we transferred the respondent from sequence IV to the appropriate alternative sequence, recoded what the responses should have been taking account of all the information on the survey schedule, and effectively equipped the respondent with a different set of fiscal impacts that had originally been reported. In other cases, the respondent might have reported no tax or borrowing effects originally, but data reported elsewhere on the survey might clearly suggest that either taxes or borrowing had been affected. In that case, we would again have reedited and recoded the original fiscal impact information to take account of all of the data contained in the survey.

An important difference between this reediting and recoding operation and the original (and conventional) editing and coding of survey responses is in the characteristics of the people who did the recoding. The Survey Research Center typically conducts its coding operations with a staff of professional coders under strict supervision and guidelines: the object of the game is to capture what the respondent said, not for the coder to try to guess what the respondent might have meant. But

for the fiscal impact data, the issue is not to interpret what the respondent said on a particular question, but to try to make sense of a wide range of data on fiscal impact. Consequently, the reediting and recoding were done by members of the professional staff of the Revenue Sharing Project, assisted by graduate students from the Economics Department at The University of Michigan. Hence the "coders" were not typical coders but professional economists, and it is our view that the resulting restructured fiscal impact data more closely approximates what the respondent actually meant than does the original fiscal impact data.

In part, the reason we decided to reedit and recode the entire fiscal impact section was the recognition that the tightly structured sequence of questions worked well only if the respondent gave accurate answers to the first one or two questions asked in the sequence. Once a respondent got into the "wrong" question sequence there was no way for the interviewer to go back and recast the questions in order to include questions that clearly ought to have been asked and to exclude ones that, in retrospect, clearly ought not to have been asked. Respondents did wind up in the wrong sequence, in our judgment, in something like 10 percent of the cases. Finally, to avoid a situation where other researchers are forced to use our judgmental recodes, the basic data tapes include both the original responses and the recoded ones.

To get from the qualitative responses in the survey to the quantitative estimates of fiscal impact in Chapter 2 involves a long and sometimes tortuous process. After looking through the basic responses to these survey questions, it became clear to us that quantitative answers could be produced for a large proportion of the total responses if we could find a way of estimating tax effects from responses given either in terms of percentages (of the tax base) or in millages. It was also clear that many of the quantitative responses given on the expenditure impact side could also be translated into dollar estimates, and that this translation did not require the addition of any external data.

In general terms, the quantitative estimation procedure was as follows:

1) For a great many cases—almost half the total dollar allocation—a quantitative assignment could be made unambiguously on the basis of the survey responses. These were cases where the respondent indicated, first, that operating or capital expenditures would have been lower in the absence of GRS, and second, that the reduction in operating or capital outlays would have been

equal to the amount of the GRS allocation. Here, the respondent is essentially saying that all GRS funds went into operating or capital outlays. And as discussed earlier, we did not ask about further GRS impacts on the tax abatement or borrowing abatement side, since we had already achieved a complete allocation of the funds. In retrospect, that was a mistake: communities could clearly have used (during fiscal year 1974) more than the fiscal year 1974 GRS allocation, and we thus have an underestimate of tax or borrowing effects.

2) For respondents who indicated that operating or capital outlays would have been affected and that the reduction in expenditures would have been less than the amount of the GRS allocation, we asked how much less. Responses came in various forms: dollar amounts, percentage amounts, or rather general qualitative statements. Both the dollar and percentage amount have a straightforward interpretation. If the respondent said that expenditures would have been reduced by less than the allocation, and then said by "$100,000 less," that can be interpreted to mean that $100,000 of the GRS allocation were accounted for in other ways and the expenditure allocation could be estimated as (revenue-sharing allocation minus $100,000). If the respondent indicated that expenditures would have been 25 percent less (than the revenue-sharing allocation) in the absence of GRS, that can be interpreted to mean that 25 percent of the allocation has yet to be accounted for, and the expenditure allocation can be estimated as revenue-sharing allocation X (1.00-0.25).

3) Where respondents indicated that both operating and capital expenditures would have been affected, a qualitative question was asked—would operating or capital adjustments have been larger? These could either be respondents who also said the expenditure adjustment accounted for the full amount of the allocation, or who indicated otherwise. In either case, we arbitrarily assigned a two-thirds-one-third allocation to whichever adjustment (capital or operating) had been indicated to be larger.

4) Respondents who either indicated no expenditure adjustment, or who reported an expenditure adjustment less than the revenue-sharing allocation, were asked about tax and borrowing effects. If they indicated either, they were asked (depending on the particular sequence) how much higher taxes or borrowing would have been, or whether tax or borrowing effects would have been larger. For respondents asked about the amount of tax or borrowing adjustments, responses also came in various forms—percentages, dollar figures, or most commonly in the case of taxes, millages. The dollar figures were handled in a straightforward manner: if a respondent said that local taxes would have been $100,000 higher (in the absence of GRS) that was taken to be the estimate of revenue sharing tax abatement. If a respondent said that taxes would have been 10 percent higher, we estimated the amount of tax abatement by applying the 10-percent figure to the local tax base, derived from the Office of Revenue Sharing tape. And if the respondent provided an answer in mills, we applied the millage answer to an estimate of local assessed valuation, obtained from Moody's Governments Manual.

For borrowing impacts, responses came in the form of dollars or percentages. For dollar amounts, the same procedure was followed as for taxes—respondents indicating that borrowing would have been $2 million higher were assigned a borrowing impact of $2 million. But respondents indicating borrowing impacts in terms of percentages could not be handled in any satisfactory way, since the cost of extracting the base (local outstanding debt) were extremely high, and the number of cases involved was quite small. Hence we ignored the "percent change" data on borrowing impacts.

5) A number of respondents indicated that there were no expenditure, tax or borrowing impacts of GRS in their community. Taking those responses at face value, we assigned the GRS allocation to surplus, which implies that the funds had not yet been spent. Most such cases turned out to be in rather small communities, and examination of the survey schedules suggested that this interpretation was entirely plausible—most of these cases were in fact communities that were accumulating GRS funds for a

specific outlay (usually capital), and were waiting until the funds got to be of sufficient size that the outlay could be made.

6) Many of the qualitative responses were not accompanied by useful quantitative data. For example, respondents might indicate an expenditure adjustment, but when asked whether it would be equal to or less than the revenue-sharing allocation would reply that they didn't know. Or the respondent might indicate that local taxes would have been higher, but when asked how much, indicate that they would be "quite a lot higher" or that they "couldn't tell." And similarly for borrowing impacts. We adopted arbitrary rules for allocating the revenue-sharing monies in cases of this sort. Generally, we divided adjustments into operating and/or capital expenditure impacts on the one hand, and tax and/or borrowing impacts on the other. If both types of adjustments were reported, we divided the GRS funds 50-50 between them. For respondents reporting both operating and capital adjustments as well as either a tax or borrowing adjustment, we assigned half the funds to expenditures and half to tax or borrowing, further dividing the operating/capital funds depending on which the respondent had indicated to be higher along the lines discussed above in #3. Similarly, if respondents indicated a capital or an operating adjustment, and both a tax and borrowing adjustment, we assigned half the funds to expenditures and divided the remainder between tax and borrowing impacts. And if the respondent reported an expenditure impact, indicated that the impact was less than the revenue-sharing allocation, and did not report either a tax or borrowing impact, we assigned 75 percent of the funds to the indicated expenditure category and the remaining 25 percent to additions to surplus.

7) In a few cases, respondents indicated in a qualitative ways that either taxes or borrowing would have been affected, did not indicate any amount, and indicated no expenditure adjustment. In these cases we assigned the entire amount to either taxes or borrowing. As indicated earlier, if both tax and borrowing impacts were indicated, the amount was divided evenly between them.

8) In one of the question sequences, respondents were not asked specifically about the amount of tax or borrowing impacts, but were asked whether the tax or borrowing impact needed to make up the difference (between the revenue-sharing allocation and the adjustment previously indicated) would have been larger. A two-thirds-one-third allocation was made for whichever category was indicated to be the larger adjustment.

These decision rules cover all the possible cases, given the basic data obtained in the survey. It is obvious that a large number of arbitrary adjustments were made. But these have surprisingly little impact, in our view, on the basic structure of the fiscal impact estimates, for the simple reason that most cases could be handled without the need for any of the arbitrary adjustments described above. This can be seen from an examination of Tables 2A-3 and 2A-4, which classify the fiscal impact data into various data quality categories. As indicated in the text, by data quality we do not mean the accuracy of these estimates as reflected by the degree to which they represent the true allocation of GRS funds. We simply mean the degree to which the basic data permitted unambiguous and nonarbitrary assignments, as compared to ambiguous and basically arbitrary ones. These tables contain eight different categories of data quality, defined as follows:

1. All estimates represent expenditure impacts, and all reflect a complete assignment of GRS funds to either capital or operating expenditures, or both. These are cases where the respondent indicated an expenditure adjustment, and indicated that the adjustment accounted for the full amount of GRS funds. The only arbitrary element is a division between operating and capital (two-thirds-one-third) in cases where the respondent indicated that both types of adjustments have taken place and that one was larger than the other.

2. All adjustments were assigned to surplus, as respondents indicated that there was no impact of GRS on operating expenditures, capital expenditures, local taxes, or local borrowing.

Table 2A-3

Estimated Distribution of Data Quality, FY74, Chief Fiscal Officers: SRC Sample of Municipalities, Townships and Counties (percent)

Type of Unit	Point Estimate, All Expenditures	Point Estimate, All Surplus	All Quantitative Estimates Surplus Residuals	One Qualitative Adjustment Only	Some Quantitative, Two Qualitative	All Qualitative	Look Up	No Useful Survey Data	Non-Response	Total
Municipalities										
300,000 +	62.7	6.6	8.8	5.2	—	16.8	—	—	—	100.0
100,000-299,999	37.6	—	28.9	12.3	14.6	5.4	1.3	—	—	100.0
25,000-99,999	42.2	4.6	13.3	20.3	6.2	9.1	3.6	0.7	—	100.0
10,000-24,999	42.8	6.6	13.7	8.6	6.0	14.2	7.2	0.8	—	100.0
2,500-9,999	36.6	6.9	4.6	15.4	14.9	12.6	2.5	6.5	—	100.0
Under 2,500	42.4	9.9	8.6	13.9	6.6	14.5	3.0	1.2	—	100.0
Townships: 9,000+	47.3	2.1	11.0	17.8	10.9	10.9	—	—	—	100.0
Townships: <9,000	52.9	16.9	6.7	13.0	—	7.0	3.4	—	—	100.0
Counties										
500,000+	36.4	—	13.3	8.5	9.8	26.9	2.8	2.5	—	100.0
100,000-499,999	39.6	6.5	17.2	11.1	11.1	9.7	3.7	1.2	—	100.0
Under 100,000	43.7	1.2	12.4	10.9	11.1	17.5	0.4	2.9	—	100.0
Grand Total	46.1	5.7	12.0	12.8	7.1	12.5	2.5	1.2	—	100.0

Table 2A-4

Estimated Distribution of Data Quality, FY75, Chief Fiscal Officers: SRC Sample of Municipalities, Townships and Counties (percent)

Type of Unit	Point Estimate, All Expenditures	Point Estimate, All Surplus	All Quantitative Estimates Surplus Residuals	One Qualitative Adjustment Only	Some Quantitative, Two Qualitative	All Qualitative	Look Up	No Useful Survey Data	Non-Response	Total
Municipalities										
300,000+	45.0	—	9.9	3.3	6.3	35.5	—	—	—	100.0
100,000-299,999	37.1	—	31.6	18.3	8.1	5.0	—	—	—	100.0
25,000-99,999	40.8	0.9	25.7	9.0	9.8	11.1	—	2.6	—	100.0
10,000-24,999	41.9	2.4	18.6	11.5	9.5	16.1	—	—	—	100.0
2,500-9,999	44.7	3.2	8.1	23.9	8.0	11.1	—	0.9	—	100.0
Under 2,500	51.0	11.0	7.5	6.7	5.2	17.0	—	1.5	—	100.0
Townships: 9,000+	47.7	4.5	15.1	9.1	15.0	8.6	—	—	—	100.0
Townships: <9,000	66.2	7.0	3.4	9.7	3.7	10.1	—	—	—	100.0
Counties										
500,000+	25.5	—	20.5	11.9	10.7	29.0	—	2.5	—	100.0
100,000-499,999	29.8	—	13.9	12.1	11.2	33.0	—	—	—	100.0
Under 100,000	46.4	7.3	11.0	9.3	8.4	11.4	—	6.2	—	100.0
Grand Total	44.0	2.6	16.0	10.6	8.6	17.2	—	1.0	—	100.0

3. All data were basically quantitative, derived from various kinds of "how much" responses. This category must contain cases where respondents indicated both expenditure and tax and/or borrowing adjustments. As would be expected, summing up the indicated adjustments never comes out precisely to the known revenue-sharing allocation, and we calculated a residual defined as the difference between the sum of the indicated fiscal impacts and the externally derived revenue-sharing allocation. The residual could be either positive or negative, depending on whether the sum of the impacts added up to less than the revenue sharing allocation or more than that amount.

4. This category includes those cases in which one qualitative adjustment (of necessity taxes or borrowing) was indicated, and no quantitative data were provided. The full amount of the revenue-sharing allocation was assigned to the single indicated adjustment.

5. This category contains multiple adjustments, at least one of which must be quantitative, and one or more of which must be qualitative, and includes a wide variety of possible cases. For example, a respondent might have indicated an expenditure adjustment, provided a quantitive estimate of the adjustment, and also indicated a tax adjustment for which no quantitative data were given. In that case the tax adjustment would be estimated as the difference between the revenue-sharing allocation and the specified expenditure adjustment. If both tax and borrowing adjustments had been indicated in this case, the residual would have been divided evenly between them. Alternatively, the respondent might have indicated an expenditure adjustment of some sort, indicated that the adjustment was less than revenue sharing but provided no usable quantitative data on how much less, and also provided a tax impact estimate of a quantitative nature. In that case the expenditure adjustment would be estimated as the residual, and if both operating and capital adjustments were indicated, the residual would have been divided according to the survey data about which adjustment was larger.

6. This category contains all of the entirely qualitative and basically arbitrary estimates that we made. No quantitative data were available for cases in category 6, and assignments were made in accordance with the type of qualitative adjustment indicated. The general guidelines were that any expenditure adjustment was assigned 50 percent of the total, with the remainder assigned to either taxes or borrowing or divided equally between them. In many of these cases, the assignment between operating and capital expenditures, or between taxes and borrowing, was unequal because the respondent had indicated that one or the other was greater. Proportions of two-thirds-one-third were used where we knew qualitatively which type of adjustment was larger or smaller.

7. This category applies only to the responses for finance officers, in fiscal year 1974 (plus a handful of cases in fiscal year 1974 for chief executive officer responses). It represents cases where, for one reason or other, we decided to go back and look at the basic survey schedules. It was often the case that apparent major inconsistencies could be resolved in this way, and the data were then edited and entered on the basic data tape. Although we judged that most apparent inconsistencies could easily be resolved by recourse to the basic survey schedule, we decided not to pursue this course for fiscal year 1975 data because the basic estimates of fiscal impact derived from the survey were hardly affected at all by the substantial number of cases where this procedure was applied for fiscal year 1974. In short, the gain was not worth the cost.

8. This category is used to represent cases where no useful information on fiscal impact was available from the survey. Typically, respondents did not answer any of the questions, and it was impossible to make any assignments of fiscal impact. As indicated in the text, we treated this category as identical to non-response on the survey itself.

The procedures described above apply to the data for finance officers in fiscal year 1974 and fiscal year 1975, for chief executive officers in both years, for chief administrative officers in both years, and for the chief finance officers and the heads of the respective appropriations committees in the State legislatures. The only general exception to these rules is with regard to the fiscal year 1974 finance officer responses at the local government level—on which we spent a great deal more time than on any other set of information. Here, we made one further adjustment between quality categories 3 and 6. As the above discussion indicates, quality category 3 is the only one where the estimates sum of fiscal impacts could be different from the revenue-sharing allocation. In all other categories, the estimation procedure was such that the sum of the adjustments necessarily had to equal the known revenue-sharing allocation. But this was not true in quality category 3, and the residuals could have been positive or negative. We judged that cases in which the sum of the reported adjustments was less than half the known revenue sharing allocation, or more than twice the known allocation, represented data of questionable validity. In those cases, we ignored all of the quantitative data provided by respondents and treated them in exactly the same way as if only qualitative data were available. The same procedure was not followed for other respondents sets or for fiscal year 1975, for the same reason as described above with respect to cases that we reexamined the basic survey schedule in order to clear up inconsistency—the gain as reflected by the difference in fiscal impact estimates did not appear to be worth the cost.

Given the extensive manipulation of the fiscal impact data and the essential arbitrariness of many of our allocations, the reader may well ask: How much reliability can be placed on the fiscal estimates discussed in Chapter 2? The best answer to this question is a careful perusal of Tables 2A-3 and 2A-4. It is quite true that we did make a large number of arbitrary assumptions in making assignments for particular cases. But fully half the total revenue-sharing allocation was estimated on the basis of completely unambiguous responses, and an additional 30 percent contained at least some quantitative data. For finance officers in fiscal year 1974, only about 11 percent of the total revenue-sharing dollar allocation for municipalities, and a little more than 20 percent for counties, was assigned on the basis of the arbitrary quantitative assumption underlying quality category 6. It is our judgment that the general pattern of the results described in Chapter 2 will hold irrespective of the specific assumptions made about cases in which no quantitative data could be obtained or where only partially quantitative data were obtained. That is to say, the qualitative adjustements comprise a sufficiently small part of the total dollar allocation of revenue-sharing money so that the broad pattern of results is comparatively insensitive to alternative assumptions. This statement is less true of the chief executive officer responses than of the chief finance officer responses: the element of arbitrary assignment is substantially greater for the former, and it is partly for that reason that we place a good deal more reliance on the finance officer responses for the analysis in Chapter 2.

A final note of caution on the issue of data quality. We have argued that the fiscal impact estimates in Chapter 2 are basically dominated by unambiguous and nonarbitrary assignments, and that the results would not be much affected by alternative assumptions. But this is not the same thing as saying that the fiscal impact estimates represent truth. They reflect the perceptions and judgments of State and local government officials who had the basic responsibility for carrying out the revenue-sharing program. But they can be no better or more accurate than those perceptions and judgments, and the lack of ambiguity and arbitrariness in the assignment procedure cannot be taken as a guarantee that the basic perceptions and judgments of our respondents were without serious biases of various sorts.

FISCAL IMPACT ESTIMATES

Chapter 2 contains summaries of the fiscal impact estimates for various categories of respondents and various years. In this appendix, we provide detailed estimates of both dollar amounts and percent distribution for all of the various respondent categories, for both fiscal year 1974 and fiscal year 1975. Tables 2A-5 and 2A-6 are identical to Tables 2-5 and 2-5A in this chapter—they contain the basic fiscal impact estimates for the chief finance officers of local governments in fiscal year 1974, in terms of dollars (Table 2A-5) and percent distribution (Table 2A-6). Tables 2A-7 and 2A-8 show chief finance officer fiscal impact estimates for fiscal year 1975, in dollar (Table 2A-7) and percent distribution (Table 2A-8). Tables 2A-9 and 2A-10 show fiscal impact estimates of chief executive officer responses in fiscal year 1974, and Tables 2A-11 and 2A-12 contain the same data for fiscal year 1975. Tables 2A-13 and 2A-14 show responses for chief administrative officers in fiscal year 1974, and 2A-15 and 2A-16 show these data for fiscal year 1975.

Table 2A-5

Estimated Fiscal Impact of GRS during FY74, Finance Officer Responses,
SRC Sample of Municipalities, Townships and Counties
(millions of dollars)

Type of Unit	Number of Cases	Maintained or Increased Operating Expenditures	Maintained or Increased Capital Expenditures	Stabilized or Reduced Local Taxes	Stabilized or Reduced Local Borrowing	Additions to Surplus	Residual	Non-Response	Total Revenue Sharing Allocation
Municipalities									
300,000+	27	528.9	100.8	85.6	6.2	33.7	16.5	70.2	841.9
100,000-299,999......	40	82.5	78.3	121.8	45.6	0.0	-38.7	2.7	292.2
25,000-99,999	215	71.5	268.9	108.5	43.3	19.6	5.1	6.1	523.0
10,000-24,999	92	26.7	161.3	40.9	26.8	8.9	5.2	6.8	276.6
2,500-9,999..........	85	18.3	137.2	40.5	25.8	9.5	4.8	52.3	288.4
Under 2,500..........	120	26.0	60.2	14.2	6.1	9.6	7.1	1.5	124.7
Townships: 9,000+....	42	10.6	26.0	11.8	6.3	0.5	3.1	0.7	59.0
Townships: <9,000....	30	8.6	28.1	1.8	6.8	15.0	0.5	1.4	62.2
Subtotal	651	773.1	860.8	425.1	166.9	96.8	3.6	141.7	2468.0
Counties									
500,000+	35	93.0	199.9	53.3	64.8	0.0	24.1	19.9	455.0
100,000-499,999......	48	84.9	194.0	52.9	54.3	10.2	4.0	24.1	424.4
Under 100,000	59	164.0	369.1	110.3	34.1	4.4	49.8	0.0	732.1
Subtotal	142	341.9	763.0	216.5	153.2	14.6	77.9	44.0	1611.5
Grand Total	793	1115.0	1623.8	641.6	320.1	111.4	81.5	185.7	4079.5

Table 2A-6

Estimated Fiscal Impact of GRS during FY74, Finance Officer Responses,
SRC Sample of Municipalities, Townships and Counties
(percentages)

Type of Unit	Number of Cases	Maintained or Increased Operating Expenditures	Maintained or Increased Capital Expenditures	Stabilized or Reduced Local Taxes	Stabilized or Reduced Local Borrowing	Additions to Surplus	Residual	Non-Response	Total Revenue Sharing Allocation
Municipalities									
300,000+	27	62.8	12.0	10.2	0.7	4.0	2.0	8.3	100.0
100,000-299,999......	40	28.2	26.8	41.7	15.6	—	-13.2	0.9	100.0
25,000-99,999	215	13.7	51.4	20.7	8.3	3.7	1.0	1.2	100.0
10,000-24,999	92	9.7	58.3	14.8	9.7	3.2	1.9	2.5	100.0
2,500-9,999..........	85	6.3	47.6	14.0	8.9	3.3	1.7	18.1	100.0
Under 2,500..........	120	20.9	48.3	11.4	4.9	7.7	5.7	1.2	100.0
Townships: 9,000+....	42	18.0	44.0	20.0	10.7	0.8	5.3	1.2	100.0
Townships: <9,000....	30	13.8	45.2	2.9	10.9	24.1	0.8	2.3	100.0
Subtotal	651	31.3	34.9	17.2	6.8	3.9	0.1	5.7	100.0
Counties									
500,000 + ...	35	20.4	43.9	11.7	14.2	—	5.3	4.4	100.0
100,000-499,999......	48	20.0	45.7	12.5	12.8	2.4	0.9	5.7	100.0
Under 100,000	60	22.4	50.4	15.1	4.7	0.6	5.9	1.0	100.0
Subtotal	143	21.2	47.3	13.4	9.5	0.9	4.4	3.2	100.0
Grand Total	794	27.3	39.8	15.7	7.8	2.7	1.8	4.7	100.0

Table 2A-7

Estimated Fiscal Impact of GRS during FY75, Finance Officer Responses,
SRC Sample of Municipalities, Townships and Counties
(millions of dollars)

		Fiscal Impact Categories							
Type of Unit	Number of Cases	Maintained or Increased Operating Expenditures	Maintained or Increased Capital Expenditures	Stabilized or Reduced Local Taxes	Stabilized or Reduced Local Borrowing	Additions to Surplus	Residual	Non-Re-sponse	Total Revenue Sharing Allocation
Municipalities									
300,000+	27	410.9	106.0	269.6	3.6	0.0	0.6	72.0	862.7
100,000-299,999	40	89.6	99.8	111.4	20.6	0.0	-25.6	3.6	299.4
25,000-99,999	215	110.2	247.3	122.7	48.8	2.0	-10.2	15.1	535.9
10,000-24,999	92	38.5	151.3	63.7	19.3	2.5	6.3	1.8	283.4
2,500-9,999	85	50.8	146.4	67.4	20.0	6.2	-16.4	21.1	295.5
Under 2,500	120	27.5	66.9	11.6	6.1	9.1	3.6	3.0	127.8
Townships: 9,000+ ...	42	9.7	25.8	12.3	6.9	1.9	3.1	0.7	60.4
Townships: <9,000	30	16.2	26.3	2.6	8.0	6.3	2.9	1.4	63.7
Subtotal	651	753.4	869.8	661.3	133.3	28.0	-35.7	118.7	2528.8
Counties									
500,000+	35	110.3	157.8	125.6	82.4	0.0	-21.0	11.2	466.3
100,000-499,999	48	65.7	186.8	98.5	56.9	0.0	18.8	8.2	434.9
Under 100,000	59	179.7	350.0	124.4	36.3	36.8	23.0	0.0	750.2
Subtotal	142	355.7	694.6	348.5	175.6	36.8	20.8	19.4	1651.4
Grand Total	793	1109.1	1564.4	1009.8	308.9	64.8	-14.9	138.3	4180.4

Table 2A-8

Estimated Fiscal Impact of GRS during FY75, Finance Officer Responses,
SRC Sample of Municipalities, Townships and Counties
(percentages)

		Fiscal Impact Categories							
Type of Unit	Number of Cases	Maintained or Increased Operating Expenditures	Maintained or Increased Capital Expenditures	Stabilized or Reduced Local Taxes	Stabilized or Reduced Local Borrowing	Additions to Surplus	Residual	Non-Re-sponse	Total Revenue Sharing Allocation
Municipalities									
300,000+	27	47.6	12.3	31.3	0.4	—	0.0	8.3	100.0
100,000-299,999	40	29.9	33.3	37.2	6.9	—	-8.6	1.2	100.0
25,000-99,999	215	20.6	46.1	22.9	9.1	0.4	-1.9	2.8	100.0
10,000-24,999	92	13.6	53.4	22.5	6.8	0.9	2.2	0.6	100.0
2,500-9,999	85	17.2	49.5	22.8	6.8	2.1	-5.5	7.1	100.0
Under 2,500	120	21.5	52.3	9.1	4.8	7.1	2.8	2.3	100.0
Townships: 9,000+	42	16.1	42.7	20.4	11.4	3.1	5.1	1.2	100.0
Townships: <9,000	30	25.4	41.3	4.1	12.6	9.9	4.6	2.2	100.0
Subtotal	651	29.8	34.4	26.2	5.3	1.1	-1.4	4.7	100.0
Counties									
500,000+	35	23.7	33.8	26.9	17.7	—	-4.5	2.4	100.0
100,000-499,999	48	15.1	43.0	22.6	13.1	—	4.3	1.9	100.0
Under 100,000	59	24.2	47.1	16.7	4.9	5.0	2.3	0.1	100.0
Subtotal	142	21.6	42.2	21.2	10.7	2.2	0.9	1.2	100.0
Grand Total	793	26.6	37.5	24.2	7.4	1.6	-0.5	2.3	100.0

Estimated Fiscal Impact of GRS During FY74, Chief Executive Officer Responses,
SRC Sample of Municipalities, Townships and Counties
(millions of dollars)

| | | Fiscal Impact Categories | | | | | | |
Type of Unit	Number of Cases	Maintained or Increased Operating Expenditures	Maintained or Increased Capital Expenditures	Stabilized or Reduced Local Taxes	Stabilized or Reduced Local Borrowing	Additions to Surplus	Residual	Non-Response	Total Revenue Sharing Allocation
Municipalities									
300,000+	18	58.8	76.1	21.4	—	—	-2.9	688.5	841.9
100,000-299,999......	36	55.0	123.9	64.3	8.2	—	-1.4	42.2	292.2
25,000-99,999	208	71.8	249.7	112.1	25.2	5.4	40.6	18.2	523.0
10,000-24,999	91	32.9	112.9	79.8	46.5	6.0	-8.0	6.5	276.6
2,500-9,999	87	38.7	129.5	26.3	14.1	6.4	36.7	36.7	288.4
Under 2,500	119	24.4	64.0	9.0	10.7	4.9	5.2	6.5	124.7
Townships: 9,000+....	40	13.1	21.2	16.9	2.6	0.4	0.9	3.9	59.0
Townships: <9,000 ...	30	7.3	26.7	4.9	6.1	15.4	0.5	1.3	62.2
Subtotal	629	302.0	804.0	334.7	113.4	38.5	71.6	803.8	2468.0
Counties									
500,000 + ...	29	97.5	96.6	59.5	17.5	—	20.7	163.2	455.0
100,000-499,999......	47	70.7	194.0	59.3	36.8	18.4	6.8	38.4	424.4
Under 100,000	57	163.0	333.8	87.6	75.9	10.1	23.9	37.8	732.1
Subtotal	133	331.2	624.4	206.4	130.2	28.5	51.4	239.4	1611.5
Grand Total	762	633.2	1428.3	541.0	243.6	67.1	123.1	1043.3	4079.5

Estimated Fiscal Impact of GRS During FY74, Chief Executive Officer Responses,
SRC Sample of Municipalities, Townships and Counties
(percentages)

| | | Fiscal Impact Categories | | | | | | |
Type of Unit	Number of Cases	Maintained or Increased Operating Expenditures	Maintained or Increased Capital Expenditures	Stabilized or Reduced Local Taxes	Stabilized or Reduced Local Borrowing	Additions to Surplus	Residual	Non-Response	Total Revenue Sharing Allocation
Municipalities									
300,000+	18	7.0	9.0	2.5	—	—	-0.3	81.8	100.0
100,000-299,999......	36	18.8	42.4	22.0	2.8	—	-0.5	14.4	100.0
25,000-99,999	208	13.7	47.7	21.4	4.8	1.0	7.8	3.5	100.0
10,000-24,999	91	11.9	40.8	28.9	16.9	2.2	-2.9	23.5	100.0
2,500-9,999	87	13.4	44.9	9.1	4.9	2.2	12.7	12.7	100.0
Under 2,500	119	19.6	51.3	7.2	8.6	3.9	4.2	5.2	100.0
Townships: 9,000+....	40	22.2	35.9	28.6	4.4	0.7	1.5	6.6	100.0
Townships: <9,000....	30	11.7	42.9	7.9	9.8	24.8	0.8	2.1	100.0
Subtotal	629	14.4	34.3	13.4	5.6	1.6	2.9	27.9	100.0
Counties									
500,000+	29	21.4	21.2	13.1	3.9	—	4.5	35.9	100.0
100,000-499,999......	47	16.7	45.7	14.0	8.7	4.3	1.6	9.0	100.0
Under 100,000	57	22.5	46.0	12.1	10.5	1.4	2.3	5.2	100.0
Subtotal	133	20.6	38.9	12.9	8.1	1.8	2.8	14.9	100.0
Grand Total	762	15.5	35.1	13.3	6.0	1.6	2.9	25.6	100.0

Table 2A-11

Estimated Fiscal Impact of GRS During FY75, Chief Executive Officer Responses, SRC Sample of Municipalities, Townships and Counties

(millions of dollars)

Type of Unit	Number of Cases	Maintained or Increased Operating Expenditures	Maintained or Increased Capital Expenditures	Stabilized or Reduced Local Taxes	Stabilized or Reduced Local Borrowing	Additions to Surplus	Residual	Non-Response	Total Revenue Sharing Allocation
Municipalities									
300,000+	18	79.3	56.3	16.0	—	—	—	711.1	862.7
100,000-299,999	36	73.0	106.6	61.0	17.8	3.6	-5.9	43.3	299.4
25,000-99,999	208	107.2	292.2	118.8	16.9	4.1	-21.1	17.8	535.9
10,000-24,999	91	53.7	129.4	63.1	45.5	4.5	-16.8	4.0	283.4
2,500-9,999	87	60.2	168.1	37.9	20.6	7.8	-0.5	1.4	295.5
Under 2,500	119	26.3	72.5	11.9	7.3	5.5	-0.5	4.8	127.8
Townships: 9,000+	40	12.2	24.8	12.1	4.7	0.2	1.4	5.0	60.4
Townships: <9,000	30	13.1	26.1	3.8	7.7	8.5	3.2	1.3	63.7
Subtotal	629	425.0	876.0	324.6	120.5	34.2	-40.0	788.5	2528.8
Counties									
500,000+	29	95.2	111.3	45.3	8.4	—	13.6	192.5	466.3
100,000-499,999	47	104.0	166.7	81.3	87.2	3.5	-47.5	39.7	434.9
Under 100,000	57	194.3	393.3	58.2	60.7	11.8	9.3	22.6	750.2
Subtotal	133	393.5	671.3	184.8	156.3	15.3	-24.7	254.9	1651.4
Grand Total	762	818.6	1547.3	509.5	276.7	49.5	-64.8	1043.6	4180.4

Table 2A-12

Estimated Fiscal Impact of GRS during FY75, Chief Executive Officer Responses, SRC Sample of Municipalities, Townships and Counties

(percentages)

Type of Unit	Number of Cases	Maintained or Increased Operating Expenditures	Maintained or Increased Capital Expenditures	Stabilized or Reduced Local Taxes	Stabilized or Reduced Local Borrowing	Additions to Surplus	Residual	Non-Response	Total Revenue Sharing Allocation
Municipalities									
300,000+	18	9.2	6.5	1.9	—	—	—	82.4	100.0
100,000-299,999	36	24.4	35.6	20.4	5.9	1.2	-2.0	14.5	100.0
25,000-99,999	208	20.0	54.5	22.2	3.2	0.8	-3.9	3.3	100.0
10,000-24,999	91	18.9	45.7	22.3	16.7	1.6	-5.9	1.4	100.0
2,500-9,999	87	20.4	56.9	12.8	7.0	2.6	-0.2	0.5	100.0
Under 2,500	119	20.6	56.7	9.3	5.7	4.3	-0.4	3.8	100.0
Townships: 9,000+	40	20.2	41.1	20.0	7.8	0.3	2.3	8.3	100.0
Townships: <9,000	30	20.6	41.0	6.0	12.1	13.3	5.0	2.0	100.0
Subtotal	629	16.8	34.6	12.8	4.8	1.4	-1.6	31.2	100.0
Counties									
500,000+	29	20.4	23.9	9.7	1.8	—	2.9	41.3	100.0
100,000-499,999	47	23.9	38.3	18.7	20.1	0.8	-10.9	9.1	100.0
Under 100,000	57	25.9	52.4	7.8	8.1	1.6	1.2	3.0	100.0
Subtotal	133	23.8	40.7	11.2	9.5	0.9	-1.5	15.4	100.0
Grand Total	762	19.6	37.0	12.2	6.6	1.2	-1.6	25.0	100.0

Estimated Fiscal Impact of GRS during FY74, Chief Administrative Officer Responses,
SRC Sample of Municipalities, Townships and Counties
(millions of dollars)

Type of Unit	Number of Cases	Fiscal Impact Categories						Total Revenue Sharing Allocations
		Maintained or Increased Operating Expenditures	Maintained or Increased Capital Expenditures	Stabilized or Reduced Local Taxes	Stabilized or Reduced Local Borrowing	Additions to Surplus	Residual	
Municipalities								
300,000+	21	106.9	90.7	112.1	24.0	15.3	26.5	375.5
100,000-299,999......	32	57.5	82.2	83.0	36.0	—	-48.6	210.1
25,000-99,999	174	93.1	175.9	84.5	22.8	4.7	6.0	387.0
10,000-24,999								
2,500-9,999...........			*NO DATA AVAILABLE*					
Under 2,500...........								
Townships: 9,000+....								
Townships: <9,000....								
Subtotal	227	257.5	348.8	279.6	82.8	20.0	-16.1	972.6
Counties								
500,000+	32	122.8	132.1	88.2	27.4	12.6	38.0	421.1
100,000-499,999......	30	40.7	128.9	65.7	16.5	7.8	16.3	275.9
Under 100,000	29	27.1	177.2	79.6	8.2	8.8	52.5	353.4
Subtotal	91	190.6	388.2	163.5	52.1	19.2	106.8	870.4
Grand Total	318	448.1	687.0	443.1	134.9	39.2	90.7	1,843.0

Estimated Fiscal Impact of GRS during FY74, Chief Administrative Officer Responses,
SRC Sample of Municipalities, Townships and Counties
(percentages)

Type of Unit	Number of Cases	Fiscal Impact Categories						Total Revenue Sharing Allocation
		Maintained or Increased Operating Expenditures	Maintained or Increased Capital Expenditures	Stabilized or Reduced Local Taxes	Stabilized or Reduced Local Borrowing	Additions to Surplus	Residual	
Municipalities								
300,000+	21	28.5	24.1	29.8	6.4	4.1	7.1	100.0
100,000-299,999......	32	27.4	39.1	39.5	17.1	—	-23.1	100.0
25,000-99,999	174	24.1	45.5	21.8	5.9	1.2	1.6	100.0
10,000-24,999								
2,500-9,999...........			*NO DATA AVAILABLE*					
Under 2,500...........								
Townships: 9,000+....								
Townships: <9,000....								
Subtotal	227	26.5	35.9	28.7	8.5	2.1	-1.7	100.0
Counties								
500,000+	32	29.2	31.4	20.9	6.5	3.0	9.0	100.0
100,000-499,999......	30	14.8	46.7	23.8	6.0	2.8	5.9	100.0
Under 100,000	29	7.7	50.1	22.5	2.3	2.5	14.9	100.0
Subtotal	91	21.9	38.8	18.8	6.0	2.2	12.3	100.0
Grand Total	318	24.3	37.3	24.1	7.3	2.1	4.9	100.0

Table 2A-15

**Estimated Fiscal Impact of GRS during FY75, Chief Administrative Office Responses,
SRC Sample of Municipalities, Townships and Counties
(millions of dollars)**

Type of Unit	Number of Cases	Maintained or Increased Operating Expenditures	Maintained or Increased Capital Expenditures	Stabilized or Reduced Local Taxes	Stabilized or Reduced Local Borrowing	Additions to Surplus	Residual	Total Revenue Sharing Allocation
				Fiscal Impact Categories				
Municipalities								
300,000+	21	126.0	125.6	193.6	5.2	—	66.7	517.1
100,000-299,999......	32	75.8	61.0	98.4	22.5	—	27.1	284.8
25,000-99,999	174	110.2	172.1	95.9	35.3	2.3	18.1	433.9
10,000-24,999								
2,500-9,999..........								
Under 2,500..........								
Townships: 9,000+....								
Townships: <9,000....								
Subtotal	227	312.0	358.7	387.9	63.0	2.3	111.9	1,235.8
Counties								
500,000+	32	130.4	162.7	86.5	25.3	11.3	17.1	433.3
100,000-499,999......	30	62.2	149.6	47.6	26.3	—	2.8	288.5
Under 100,000	29	29.6	243.6	59.5	74.8	1.1	20.8	429.4
Subtotal	91	222.2	556.9	193.6	126.4	12.4	40.7	1,152.2
Grand Total	318	534.2	915.6	581.5	189.4	14.7	152.6	2,388.0

Table 2A-16

**Estimated Fiscal Impact of GRS during FY75, Chief Administrative Officer Responses,
SRC Sample of Municipalities, Townships and Counties
(percentages)**

Type of Unit	Number of Cases	Maintained or Increased Operating Expenditures	Maintained or Increased Capital Expenditures	Stabilized or Reduced Local Taxes	Stabilized or Reduced Local Borrowing	Additions to Surplus	Residual	Total Revenue Sharing Allocation
				Fiscal Impact Categories				
Municipalities								
300,000+	21	24.4	24.3	37.4	1.0	—	12.9	100.0
100,000-299,999......	32	26.6	21.4	34.6	7.9	—	9.5	100.0
25,000-99,999	174	25.4	39.7	22.1	8.1	0.5	4.2	100.0
10,000-24,999								
2,500-9,999..........								
Under 2,500..........								
Townships: 9,000+....								
Townships: <9,000....								
Subtotal	227	25.2	29.0	31.4	5.1	0.2	9.1	100.0
Counties								
500,000+	32	30.1	37.6	20.0	5.8	2.6	3.9	100.0
100,000-499,999......	30	21.6	51.9	16.5	9.1	—	1.0	100.0
Under 100,000	29	6.9	56.7	13.9	17.4	0.3	4.8	100.0
Subtotal	91	19.3	48.3	16.8	11.0	1.1	3.5	100.0
Grand Total	318	22.4	38.3	24.4	7.9	0.6	6.4	100.0

CHAPTER 3

Program Impact of Revenue Sharing on Local Governments

F. Thomas Juster

INTRODUCTION

One of the questions of principle interest to those concerned with the fiscal impact of revenue sharing on States and local governments relates to the program impact of GRS funds. To the extent that GRS supported existing activities or permitted new ones to begin, what sort of activities were they? Were the funds used predominantly to maintain existing programs or to begin new and innovative ones? Were they fairly allocated as between various claimants in the community? Did they go into police and fire protection, or into health and hospitals? Did the poor, the young, and the elderly get a disproportionate share, or less than their "fair" share? Does the allocation of GRS funds reported on the official "Use Reports" accurately reflect how the funds were really used, or do these reports provide a misleading picture? We turn to these questions in this chapter.

SURVEY MEASUREMENTS OF PROGRAM IMPACT

As indicated in earlier chapters, we expected to be able to get a general qualitative picture of both the overall fiscal impact and the specific program impact of GRS funds, but not to be able to provide very precise quantitative answers to fiscal impact questions. The survey data do shed a good bit of light on what types of programs were facilitated by GRS, but it is more true here than in the analysis of overall fiscal impact that the insights obtained from the survey are much more on the qualitative than the quantitative side. Basically, we obtained program impact data within the same general framework used to obtain estimates of overall fiscal

impact. Respondents were asked whether operating or capital outlays or both would have been lower if the GRS program had not existed, as discussed extensively in Chapter 2. Respondents who indicated that either operating or capital expenditures would have been lower were then asked what specific programs would have been reduced or eliminated if GRS funds had not been available. We also asked what specific population groups would have been affected by these program reductions, in an attempt to get at the distributional impact of GRS of various population groups.

For the most part, we were comparatively successful in getting program impacts of GRS in terms of functional types of expenditures, such as police, fire, health, recreation, etc., but comparatively unsuccessful in getting estimates of population groups that would have been differentially affected if GRS funds had not been available. Our procedure was to ask first which program would have been reduced or eliminated, and code the subsequent answers into what was basically an expenditure classification. Most respondents who indicated that expenditures would have been affected also indicated specific program or types of programs that would have been reduced or eliminated, although some simply indicated that "all programs" would have been affected and they could not distinguish among them. We attempted to get the same type of data with respect to impact on particular population groups. But here the dominant response was that "everybody" would have been affected, and we were unable to get most respondents to be more specific than that. Hence for impacts on population groups, we have no useful data at all for the most part.

To put these qualitative data on program impacts into a quantitative mode requires assumptions about the size and cost of programs affected by GRS. The survey did not ask for quantitative data, hence it is necessary to make assumptions about the relative size of different programs except in the case where only one program area (e.g. public safety) was indicated to have been affected.

Two alternative assumptions are used, and results are presented for both. The first assumption says that all programs affected by GRS were of equal size in terms of dollars. The second says that the relative dollar size of programs affected by GRS, as reported by the respondent, is in the same proportion as are total expenditures for the respective program categories as reported in the Census of Governments. To illustrate: if a respondent reported that both public safety and health programs would have been reduced or eliminated if GRS funds had not been available, we calculate program impacts on the assumptions that, (1) the dollar impact of both programs would have been the same, or (2) that the dollar impact would be in proportion to expenditures by communities of that type on public safety and health. We do not suggest that these alternative assumptions bound the range of possible outcomes—they simply represent two specific assumptions that are not clearly unreasonable.

The legislation under which GRS came into being required all participating general government jurisdictions to file Actual Use Reports, indicating the way in which each community's GRS funds were allocated according to the various "priority" categories. The Use Report data have been analyzed by a number of researchers, and most have come to the conclusion that the data cannot be used for a serious examination of the program impact of GRS. The reason is simple enough. The Use Reports seem to represent a way

of designating categories for which GRS funds can be said to be earmarked. But money is fungible, and it is clear that a community can earmark GRS funds for one purpose and actually end up using them for a totally different purpose. The relevant question always is: If GRS funds had not been available, what would the community have done instead, and that is simply a different question than the one addressed by the Use Reports.

The fact that money is fungible does not of course guarantee that the Use Reports are invalid for analysis of program impacts, but it does suggest that one should use these data very carefully and only after their validity has been demonstrated. In addition, many researchers who have looked into this question, after talking with officials responsible for administering the program and/or filing Use Reports, have come to the conclusion that Use Reports are viewed as political documents in which uses thought to be politically palatable were apt to be reported, and that the Use Reports were not viewed as a vehicle whose purpose was to trace the "ultimate" effects of revenue sharing.[1]

Table 3-1–3-5 contain the basic data for the analysis of program impact. Table 3-1 shows the distribution of local government expenditures by

---

[1]The Use Report format is clearly not designed to provide a reasonable estimate of fiscal impacts. All jurisdictions are required to specify how all of their revenue sharing funds were allocated to the various priority expenditure categories; in addition, communities are then asked whether GRS funds were used to reduce or stabilize local taxes or local borrowing. Thus Use Reports technically overallocate GRS funds, since *all* money must be designated as having been used for some priority category of expenditures, and in addition communities are asked whether the funds are used for tax or borrowing abatement.

Table 3-1
Estimates of GRS Program Impact on Local Governments
During FY 1974, Official Use Reports
(Percent of GRS Funds Allocated to Indicated Category)

Government type and size class	Public Safety	Environment	Land Use	Transportation	Amenities	Education	Health	Social Service	Admin. & Finance	Other	Residual	Total
Municipalities												
300,000 and over	57.6	14.9	0.2	9.2	4.3	0.3	2.0	1.7	2.5	—	7.3	100.0
100,000-299,999	42.5	17.1	4.3	6.8	8.8	1.1	6.0	2.3	10.5	0.1	0.6	100.0
25,000-99,999	31.0	12.2	1.1	19.0	12.8	0.3	3.3	1.1	14.2	1.8	3.0	100.0
10,000-24,999	33.7	15.6	2.6	26.0	6.3	1.1	5.3	0.5	8.2	0.3	0.5	100.0
2,500-9,999	27.1	5.3	2.7	16.5	8.3	0.9	12.4	0.5	10.1	0.1	16.1	100.0
Less than 2,500	24.1	7.5	1.6	34.9	4.8	—	8.1	0.1	14.5	0.4	4.0	100.0
Townships, 9000 and over	16.8	23.6	—	23.2	13.9	—	2.5	3.5	15.7	—	0.8	100.0
Townships, less than 9000	17.1	0.2	—	42.5	6.8	—	0.2	—	12.3	—	20.9	100.0
Counties												
500,000 and over	41.8	3.4	0.1	7.5	8.9	0.2	17.6	5.1	15.3	0.1	—	100.0
100,000-499,999	26.9	1.8	0.1	16.9	10.1	1.1	8.2	4.7	30.2	—	—	100.0
Less than 100,000	14.7	1.0	0.5	38.7	4.1	6.5	9.1	1.6	23.6	0.1	0.2	100.0
All	35.3	8.9	1.0	18.8	7.4	1.6	7.0	2.1	14.0	0.3	3.5	100.0

Table 3-2

**Estimates of GRS Program Impact on Local Governments
During FY1974, Survey Data Using Equal Dollar Weights
(Percent of GRS Funds Allocated to Indicated Category)**

Government type and size class	Public Safety	Environ- ment	Land Use	Trans- portation	Amen- ities	Educa- tion	Health	Social Service	Admin. & Finance	Other	Residual	Total
Municipalities												
300,000 and over......	16.7	10.1	3.2	14.8	16.4	8.1	13.1	0.1	5.2	5.7	6.7	100.0
100,000-299,999	37.1	11.9	14.8	9.3	10.1	3.5	2.2	4.2	3.9	2.0	1.1	100.0
25,000-99,999.........	24.0	15.4	4.1	20.0	14.4	2.0	3.1	0.7	10.6	1.4	4.3	100.0
10,000-24,999.........	33.6	27.2	0.3	22.0	6.3	1.0	1.0	0.0	3.4	1.2	3.9	100.0
2,500-9,999	21.5	22.3	3.3	28.6	13.8	1.1	0.3	0.1	2.9	0.7	5.3	100.0
Less than 2,500........	21.6	16.7	1.7	32.1	13.1	0.5	0.0	0.6	5.1	5.6	3.0	100.0
Townships, 9000 and over	17.5	6.0	5.7	29.8	19.9	0.0	1.6	6.6	1.1	—	11.7	100.0
Townships, less than 9000	10.3	6.8	2.7	50.0	4.6	0.1	0.0	1.6	10.6	1.1	12.8	100.0
Counties												
500,000 and over......	12.9	2.5	3.9	8.3	8.7	4.5	7.6	4.9	2.3	2.2	42.0	100.0
100,000-499,999	20.8	2.2	7.5	29.5	9.8	4.3	7.7	4.6	6.9	0.6	6.0	100.0
Less than 100,000	27.4	7.2	15.1	13.2	7.6	10.1	4.7	3.6	6.2	0.5	4.3	100.0
All	22.6	10.8	6.7	17.5	11.5	5.5	6.1	2.1	5.6	2.4	9.2	100.0

Table 3-3

**Estimates of GRS Program Impact on Local Governments
During FY 1974, Survey Data Using Census Expenditure Weights
(Percent of GRS Funds Allocated to Indicated Category)**

Government type and size class	Public Safety	Environ- ment	Land Use	Trans- portation	Amen- ities	Educa- tion	Health	Social Service	Admin. & Finance	Other	Residual	Total
Municipalities												
300,000 and over......	15.1	13.8	1.2	9.6	19.9	6.2	11.6	0.2	4.9	4.3	13.2	100.0
100,000-299,999	31.6	8.7	6.2	5.5	18.7	2.2	7.1	2.7	6.3	1.5	9.3	100.0
25,000-99,999.........	18.4	19.1	3.0	19.3	20.9	2.4	3.2	1.5	8.1	1.8	2.3	100.0
10,000-24,999.........	26.2	21.3	0.4	25.8	8.1	2.0	0.3	0.3	4.6	0.8	10.2	100.0
2,500-9,999	25.1	29.2	3.0	26.1	8.2	0.4	0.2	0.1	1.4	0.8	5.5	100.0
Less than 2,500........	16.9	14.9	1.0	26.6	18.9	0.2	0.3	0.2	8.2	2.6	10.1	100.0
Townships, 9000 and over	21.7	7.3	10.1	18.9	12.4	1.7	6.5	8.2	6.5	1.1	5.6	100.0
Townships, less than 9000	5.4	11.3	0.7	52.7	9.2	0.2	—	—	2.1	10.4	8.0	100.0
Counties												
500,000 and over......	19.6	1.2	4.3	5.7	7.6	3.8	7.4	9.1	5.5	1.2	34.4	100.0
100,000-499,999	16.9	4.1	3.8	18.6	7.8	3.7	9.4	5.7	9.5	1.6	18.7	100.0
Less than 100,000	29.9	0.9	6.6	18.7	12.5	5.7	9.1	2.8	8.4	1.7	3.6	100.0
All	20.8	9.7	4.2	16.6	14.4	3.7	6.8	3.8	6.7	2.2	11.0	100.0

program for fiscal year 1974, taken from the official Use Reports. The program categories are not the "priority" categories, but are ones that appear to be sensible given the distribution of the survey data on program impact. The categories are quite close to priority categories, and are also close to Census Bureau reporting categories for local government jurisdictions.[2] As indicated earlier, the Use Report data in Table 3-1 distribute all the GRS monies used by local governments in fiscal year 1974. Actually,

the total amount of funds distributed in this table is slightly more than the fiscal year 1974 allocation, suggesting that communities on balance drew on accumulated GRS fund balances during that year. Use Report estimates are shown for the 11 size classes and types of communities that have been used in previous chapters.

The next four tables contain the basic survey data on program impact for both fiscal year 1974 and fiscal year 1975. Tables 3-2 and 3-3 show the percent distribution of program uses according to the survey, using the two alternative ways of weighting specific expenditure programs reported as having been made possible by GRS. Table 3-2

[2]The appendix to this chapter details how priority categories and Census categories were adjusted to fit the list of categories used for Tables 3-1 to 3-5.

uses equal dollar weights, and Table 3-3 uses Census weights. Tables 3-4 and 3-5 contain the same data for fiscal year 1975.

The Use Reports and the survey estimates of program impact do not have a precisely comparable base. For the Use Reports, as indicated, we simply tabulated the dollar expenditures indicated by communities in the SRC sample of local government jurisdictions. These amounted to slightly over $4.2 billion—an amount somewhat in excess of the fiscal year 1974 GRS local government allocation. But the program impact estimates obtained from the survey are based on the Chapter 2 estimates of overall fiscal impact: hence the amount of funds being allocated in these tables is about $2.5 billion—the amount indicated in Chapter 2 as representing the total dollar amount of operating and capital outlays made possible by GRS.

The survey estimates of program impact assign what are essentially Census of Governments expenditure weights to those GRS funds designated by respondents as having gone for "all programs." Many respondents, especially in very large cities, indicated that it was not possible to specify program impact, since if GRS funds had not been available, all programs operated by the jurisdiction would have been affected. We took that to mean that all programs would have been affected in proportion to their size, and allocated the funds in accordance with expenditure weights from Census of

Table 3-4

**Estimates of GRS Program Impact on Local Governments
During FY 1975, Survey Data Using Equal Dollar Weights
(Percent of GRS Funds Allocated to Indicated Category)**

Government type and size class	Public Safety	Environment	Land Use	Transportation	Amenities	Education	Health	Social Service	Admin. & Finance	Other	Residual	Total
Municipalities												
300,000 and over	20.5	10.9	2.1	14.3	13.8	8.1	13.5	0.1	4.3	5.7	6.6	100.0
100,000-299,999	45.7	15.0	13.2	6.1	8.1	3.7	0.9	0.9	3.2	1.0	2.0	100.0
25,000-99,999	31.7	17.8	1.5	17.8	12.3	2.0	2.4	0.0	8.9	1.4	4.3	100.0
10,000-24,999	37.5	32.6	0.1	17.5	3.1	1.0	0.6	0.0	2.3	1.2	3.9	100.0
2,500-9,999	12.9	11.6	11.5	26.0	11.4	0.2	0.3	16.6	5.9	0.5	3.2	100.0
Less than 2,500	26.5	15.4	0.0	35.1	8.4	0.5	0.0	0.0	5.3	5.6	3.2	100.0
Townships, 9000 and over	37.4	30.0	—	16.9	2.4	—	—	—	1.4	—	11.7	100.0
Townships, less than 9000	25.0	14.4	—	33.7	8.7	—	—	—	4.3	1.1	12.8	100.0
Counties												
500,000 and over	14.4	2.7	3.1	11.1	3.3	7.8	5.6	3.1	4.3	2.2	42.0	100.0
100,000-499,999	28.1	4.6	7.7	20.8	6.6	9.5	7.0	3.3	5.6	0.6	6.0	100.0
Less than 100,000	28.8	4.8	7.9	21.3	6.8	9.6	7.0	3.3	5.6	0.5	4.3	100.0
All	27.0	12.3	4.3	17.8	8.6	6.1	6.2	1.4	4.9	2.3	9.2	100.0

Table 3-5

**Estimates of GRS Program Impact on Local Governments
During FY 1975, Survey Data Using Census Expenditure Weights
(percent of GRS Funds Allocated to Indicated Category)**

Government type and size class	Public Safety	Environment	Land Use	Transportation	Amenities	Education	Health	Social Service	Admin. & Finance	Other	Residual	Total
Municipalities												
300,000 and over	18.4	14.8	1.2	9.6	16.0	6.2	12.5	0.1	3.7	4.3	13.2	100.0
100,000-299,999	44.0	11.1	5.0	4.5	14.2	2.2	2.0	0.8	5.2	1.5	9.4	100.0
25,000-99,999	23.0	26.5	1.0	16.2	17.5	2.4	1.7	0.3	7.2	1.8	2.3	100.0
10,000-24,999	28.0	29.4	0.4	21.5	4.4	1.3	0.3	0.0	3.5	0.8	10.2	100.0
2,500-9,999	16.6	16.0	8.4	24.7	9.4	0.2	0.2	16.6	4.2	0.4	3.3	100.0
Less than 2,500	19.9	15.4	1.0	31.5	12.7	0.2	0.0	0.0	6.7	2.6	10.0	100.0
Townships, 9000 and over	29.2	31.2	0.3	22.4	4.5	1.4	0.6	—	3.7	1.1	5.6	100.0
Townships, less than 9000	20.5	15.8	0.9	32.7	13.4	—	—	—	6.8	1.4	8.0	100.0
Counties												
500,000 and over	20.0	0.5	1.8	15.7	5.9	3.4	7.8	3.8	5.5	0.8	34.7	100.0
100,000-499,999	23.4	1.7	2.0	18.4	6.9	5.4	9.8	5.0	0.9	1.7	18.6	100.0
Less than 100,000	28.4	1.5	2.5	22.3	8.5	5.8	11.6	5.8	8.2	1.7	3.6	100.0
All	24.2	12.2	2.3	17.3	11.1	3.8	6.8	3.3	5.8	2.0	11.0	100.0

Governments data. This procedure mainly affects cities with populations of 300,000 or more, where it accounts for close to half the total dollar value of programs in both fiscal year 1974 and fiscal year 1975.

Several questions can be asked of the program impact data displayed above. First, what appears to be the overall pattern of program use of GRS funds as reflected by the survey? Second, do the actual Use Reports show a pattern of program impacts that are the same as or different from that shown by the survey? Third, do GRS funds appear to have been used in the same way as local governments "typically" use funds (as reflected by the Census of Governments expenditures patterns) or have revenue sharing funds been used differently?

AGGREGATE FINDINGS

The most important overall use shown both by the actual Use Reports and the survey for fiscal year 1974, according to Tables 3-1—3-5, is public safety. More than a third of GRS funds went for public safety according to the Use Reports, about one-fifth according to the survey. Next most important on both the Use Reports and the survey is transportation (highways and roads, mainly). Administration and finance expenditures (mainly public buildings) is third most important on the Use Reports but much less important on the survey, where amenities (recreational programs and facilities, libraries, etc.), and environmental control (mainly sewerage and sanitation) are next in order of importance.

Within size classes, the Use Reports indicate that public safety is far and away the most important category for both big cities and large urban counties. The survey estimates differ sharply: here, small to moderate-sized communities report relatively larger public safety outlays than either very large or very small ones. On both the Use Reports and the survey, transportation is a more important use of GRS funds in moderate to small-sized communities than in larger ones, again a pattern which hold both for municipalities and for counties. As noted earlier, administration and finance uses of GRS monies are much less important in the survey estimates than in the Use Reports, while amenities are somewhat more important on the survey. Land use is substantially more important in the survey: for the most part this appears to reflect the purchase of land for future development. Other categories tend to show little systematic difference in relative importance, comparing estimates from the use Reports with those from the survey.

There appears to be relatively little difference between the equal dollar weight and Census weight estimates of program impact derived from the survey. Public safety is a bit less important when equal dollar weights are used, and amenities are a bit more important. But the data clearly indicate that it makes little difference to estimates of program impact which weighting scheme is used. Since the alternative weighting schemes are very different, the implication is that survey estimates of program impact are relatively insensitive to even large differences in the relative dollar importance of particular programs reported by respondents as having been impacted by GRS. It is a plausible inference that the results would be insensitive to virtually any weighting scheme that might be devised.

Between fiscal year 1974 and fiscal year 1975, the survey shows a decline in the relative importance of public safety, a decline in the importance of land use, a rise in the importance of amenities and of social services, and a decline in education. The patterns among differently sized communities are about the same in fiscal year 1975 as they were in fiscal year 1974.

The analysis above has been concerned with comparisons of the GRS program impact as reported on the survey and as measured by the official Use Reports. A quite different question concerns the relation between the estimated uses of revenue-sharing funds and the typical uses of all local government funds. That is, do communities appear to have used revenue-sharing funds in the same way that they use funds generally? The answer to this question is obtained by comparing the data on the program impact of GRS (Table 3-1, Use Report estimate, and Table 3-3, survey estimate) with the data shown in Table 3-6 on the expenditure pattern for local governments obtained from the U.S. Census of Governments. Although the years are not quite comparable, the expenditure patterns shown in Table 3-6 are not sensitive to the choice of particular fiscal years, since these patterns change only very slowly.

The data clearly show that neither the Use Reports nor the survey estimates of program impact for GRS funds are at all similar to the typical uses of local government funds as reflected by Census of Government expenditure data, with the exception of comparisons involving the survey estimates and the Census of Governments estimates for cities with over 300,000 population. And the latter is a simple artifact of the way in which the survey program impact estimates were constructed: as indicated earlier, close to half the total weight for cities with populations over 300,000 were derived directly from the Census expenditure weights, since respondents had indicated that "all

Table 3-6

Table 3-6
Percent of Local Government Budgets Spent on Indicated Category,
by Size and Type of Government, FY 1971

Local Government type and size Class	Total Expenditures (in Millions of $'s)	Public Safety	Environ-mental Control	Land Use	Trans-portation	Ameni-ties	Educa-tion	Health	Services	Financial	Other	Total
Municipalities												
300,000 and over	19,720.6	19.9	16.1	3.6	9.6	4.7	18.2	8.0	0.2	6.8	12.9	100
100,000-299,999......	5,008.3	19.6	22.6	3.5	8.0	6.5	17.3	2.8	1.2	7.4	11.1	100
25,000-99,999	7,537.2	20.4	25.2	1.9	9.7	6.5	14.2	3.8	0.3	7.3	10.7	100
10,000-24,999	3,334.2	19.8	34.9	0.7	12.0	5.3	7.2	3.6	0.1	7.6	8.8	100
2,500-9,999	2,738.2	17.7	39.5	0.6	13.6	4.1	3.4	3.4	0.1	8.2	9.4	100
Less than 2,500	973.0	19.1	11.4	0.0	20.0	1.0	3.3	0.05	0.3	9.7	35.2	100
Counties................	19,743.8	15.6	4.3	0.0	13.8	3.2	20.2	14.1	9.1	10.1	9.6	100
Total..........................		18.4	15.9	1.8	11.4	4.5	16.7	8.5	3.3	8.2	11.0	

Source: Census of Governments and Appendix to Chapter 3

programs" would have been affected by the absence of revenue-sharing funds.

The Use Reports estimates indicate that public safety, transportation, amenities, and administration and financial services were more important uses of GRS funds than of local government funds generally. Environmental control, education, and residual (unspecified) uses were less important uses of GRS funds than of regular funds. The survey estimates of program impact show roughly the same comparison against Census estimates, except that administrative and financial services were not, according to the survey, purchased with greater frequency out of GRS funds than from regular local government sources of funds.

More definitive comparisons of program impact are facilitated by calculation of a statistic reflecting the amount of difference between the various estimates. Given the characteristics of the data, there is no technically correct statistic that one can compute from which inferences can be made about significant difference. The closest one can come is calculation of the Chi-square statistic, treating one of the distributions, say the program impact estimates from the survey, as the expected value and one of the others, either the Use Reports or the Census of Governments expenditure data, as the actual data.

The Chi-square statistics are summarized in Table 3-7, with comparisons shown between Actual Use Reports and the survey estimates for fiscal year 1974, between the two types of survey estimates for 1974 (equal dollar weights and Census weights) and between the survey estimates and Census of Government expenditures. Although one must be cautious about drawing inferences relating to sig-

Table 3-7
Chi-Square Statistics for Selected Comparisons of Program Impact in Municipalities and Counties

Government Type and Size	Survey Estimates vs. Use Reports Estimates[1]	Survey Estimates vs. Census Expendi-tures[2]	Alternative Weights for Survey Estimates[3]
Municipality			
300,000 and over	402.8	22.1	1.7
100,000-299,999.....	44.4	139.1	17.4
25,000-99,999.	13.2	97.0	8.2
10,000-24,999.	24.7	60.4	7.0
2,500-9,999 ...	90.4	47.4	7.6
Less than 2,500	60.3	145.8	4.4
County			
500,000 and over	1,740.0	NA	14.0
100,000-499,999.....	105.2	NA	12.3
Less than 100,000.....	298.2	NA	12.4

[1]Use Report estimate treated as expected, survey as actual.

[2]Survey estimate treated as expected, Census expenditures as actual.

[3]Equal dollar weights treated as expected, Census weights treated as actual.

nificant differences, the general pattern of the results is clear. In cities of more than 300,000 population, the Use Reports and the survey estimates of program impact are very different and the Chi-square statistics are very large. The same phenomena show up in large urban counties. A few other size classes also show very large chi-squares statistics, but these are all size classes in which there are very substantial sampling errors, over and above any differences that might arise due to the way in which program impact is measured via Use Reports or via the survey. Except for the large urban cities and counties, the only size classes with very large chi-square statistics are those where a relatively small sample is being used to represent a larger number of comparable communities and where one or two communities reporting a particular kind of program impact can generate an enormous difference between the survey estimates and the Use Report estimates.[3] Aside from these cases, all the other municipality size classes tend to show relatively small chi-square statistics, indicating moderate—and perhaps non-significant—differences between Use Report and survey estimates of program impact.

The comparison of program impact estimates from the survey using equal dollar weights or Census expenditure weights suggests that there is little difference between program impact estimates obtained either way. None of the chi-squares are very large, and the estimates of program impacts appear to be quite insensitive to alternative weighting schemes, as noted above.

Finally, the data clearly indicate that the survey estimates of program impact are very different from the typical use of funds by local governments in various size classes, again with the exception of large cities where the two are alike for reasons already noted.

MICRO-LEVEL COMPARISONS

The data just discussed present what are essentially comparisons of averages or aggregates from the Use Reports and the survey, and suggest that the Use Reports are, at least on average, not necessarily misleading as to actual uses of GRS funds for moderate to small-sized local governments. This finding is in marked contrast to that of most other investigators of the revenue-sharing program. Since the usefulness and reliability of the Use Reports is an important issue, a closer comparison on an individual community level is clearly warranted.

---

[3]The sampling error problem can be illustrated by one rather spectacular case. In the 2,500-9,999 size class, the SRC sample contains one community with a GRS allotment of close to $200,000, a "weight" of close to 200 (meaning that it stands for 200 other similar places, and a survey report indicating that *all* the GRS funds were used for social services. That one case would be sufficient to produce a very large chi-square statistic unless the Use Report said exactly the same thing.

Two additional types of comparisons are possible with the data at hand, both being essentially internal consistency checks. For a subsample of the communities in the SRC sample, we have independent responses from both the finance officers and chief executives of local government jurisdictions. Both officials were asked the same questions about fiscal impact generally and program impact specifically, and one can test to see whether the two sets of responses provide the same picture of program impact. Secondly, we can compare survey responses with Use Report responses for identical communities. For the Use Reports to have validity it has to be the case that they show the same general pattern as the survey, comparing individual communities with each other, and that the two types of survey estimates show a reasonable degree of internal consistency. Neither is of course a sufficient condition for concluding that the Use Reports have validity, since both Use Report and survey data could be reflecting the same phenomenon and both could be systematically biased in the same way. Thus a further (external) consistency check is needed, but the internal consistency check is clearly the first order of business.

Tables 3-8 and 3-9 show a number of 2 x 2 contingency tables, reflecting the indicated presence or absence of a program impact in four expenditure areas that tend to show relatively frequent program impacts on both the Use Reports and the survey: public safety, environmental control, transportation and amenities. Table 3-8 compares responses of the finance officers in the respective local government jurisdictions with responses from chief executives from the same jurisdiction: the sample sizes are relatively small compared to the total survey because both respondents had to be present to make the comparison. As indicated in Chapter 2, response rates were somewhat lower for chief executive officers generally, and there were many cases in smaller communities where only one interview was taken. No data are shown for communities with over 300,000 population, since few chief executive interviews were obtained in those cities. Townships are also omitted, mainly because only one interview was typically conducted there.

Table 3-9 contains exactly the same types of comparisons as Table 3-8, except that the comparison involves survey responses from finance officers with data from the Use Reports. As in Table 3-8, comparisons involve positive or negative indications of program impact in each of the four program areas that seem to have been principally affected by GRS.

The cell frequencies in these tables indicate the degree to which both reports agree that there was a particular program impact of GRS (lower right-hand cell), both agree that there was no program

Table 3-8
Comparison of Program Impact Estimates of GRS for Public Safety, Environmental Control, Amenities, and Transportation
SRC Survey of Local Government Officials:
Finance Officer vs. Chief Executive Estimates*

Chief Executive Program Impact	Cities Between 100,000 and 299,000 (N=23) Finance Officer Program Impact			Cities Between 25,000 and 99,999 (N=108) Finance Officer Program Impact			Cities Between 10,000 and 24,999 (N=35) Finance Officer Program Impact			Cities Between 2,500 and 9,999 (N=35) Finance Officer Program Impact		
	No	Yes	Total	No	Yes	Total	No	Yes	Total	No	Yes	Total
No	48	14	62	234	64	298	64	20	84	64	22	86
Yes	16	14	30	56	78	134	25	31	56	24	30	54
Total	64	28	92	290	142	432	89	51	140	88	52	140

	Cities Between 100 and 2,499 (N=62) Finance Officer Program Impact			Counties Over 500,000 (N=8) Finance Officer Program Impact			Counties Between 100,000 and 499,000 (N=23) Finance Officer Program Impact			Counties Under 100,000 (N=37) Finance Officer Program Impact		
	No	Yes	Total	No	Yes	Total	No	Yes	Total	No	Yes	Total
No	121	41	162	23	4	27	58	13	71	96	16	112
Yes	33	53	86	3	2	5	12	9	21	19	17	36
Total	154	94	248	26	6	32	70	22	92	115	33	148

*Table 3-8 is arranged as a 2 x 2 contingency table, with the cells representing the number of specific programs where the finance officer responses either agreed or disagreed with the chief executive officer responses. Agreement would be indicated in the upper left-hand corner, where both responses agreed that there was no impact of revenue sharing on a particular program, and the lower right-hand corner, where both respondents agreed that there was a particular program impact. The lower left-hand corner and the upper right-hand corner represent disagreement, where one report indicated that revenue sharing had impacted on a particular program, the other did not. Thus in the first of the sub-tables in Table 3-8, 48 represents the number of responses from finance officers and chief executive officers reporting that revenue sharing, in cities between 100,000 and 299,999 population, had no impact on expenditures in the public safety, environmental controls transportation or amenities areas, 14 is the number of responses from finance officers and chief executive officers reporting that, in these same cities, there was a program impact, and 16 and 14 represent the number of cases where either the finance officer reported a program impact but the chief executive officer did not, or vice versa.

Table 3-9
Comparison of Program Impact Estimates of GRS for Public Safety, Environmental Control, Amenities, and Transportation, Official Use Reports vs. Finance Officer Response
from the SRC Survey of Local Government Officials

Finance Officer Program Impact	Cities Between 100,000 and 299,000 (N=29) Use Report Program Impact			Cities Between 25,000 and 99,999 (N=150) Use Report Program Impact			Cities Between 10,000 and 24,999 (N=53) Use Report Program Impact			Cities Between 2,500 and 9,999 (N=48) Use Report Program Impact		
	No	Yes	Total	No	Yes	Total	No	Yes	Total	No	Yes	Total
No	24	51	75	201	189	390	63	63	126	76	44	120
Yes	5	36	41	52	158	210	22	64	86	20	52	72
Total	29	87	116	253	347	600	85	127	212	96	96	192

	Cities Between 100 and 2,499 (N=73) Finance Officer Program Impact			Counties Over 500,000 (N=16) Finance Officer Program Impact			Counties Between 100,000 and 499,999 (N=33) Finance Officer Program Impact			Counties Under 100,000 (N=46) Finance Officer Program Impact		
	No	Yes	Total	No	Yes	Total	No	Yes	Total	No	Yes	Total
No	143	44	187	15	35	50	51	45	96	85	50	135
Yes	44	61	105	4	10	14	8	28	36	14	35	49
Total	187	105	292	19	45	64	59	73	132	99	85	184

impact (upper left-hand cell), or one indicates a particular program impact and the other does not (lower left-hand and upper right-hand corners). Perfect agreement, either between the two survey respondents or between the finance officer and the Use Reports, would put all cell frequencies along the upper left to lower right diagonal, while perfect disagreement would put all along the opposite diagonal. The association measure (Cramer's V) indicates the degree to which it is possible to predict one of the program impact responses from knowledge of the other; V varies between 0 and 1. Table 3-10 summarizes the association statistic.

The results of these comparisons are roughly in accordance with the aggregate analysis discussed earlier. Agreement between finance officers and chief executives on program impact is substantially stronger in smaller-sized communities than in larger ones, as is agreement between finance officer responses from the survey and the Use Reports. Although the associations are not overwhelmingly strong, they are by no means weak either. In particular, they are not weak for the smaller-sized communities, concerning that microlevel comparisons like these are affected by differences in the reporting and coding of the survey data on program impact. For example, it is entirely possible for exactly the same program, say construction of a community center, to be reported by one respondent as construction of a community center, by another as construction of a senior citizens' facility, and by a third as construction of a recreational facility. Although these might all be descriptions of exactly the same facility, they would be coded into different expenditure categories. Thus there is a sizable misclassification component, which is bound to have the effect of producing significant numbers of off-diagonal entries.

Table 3-10
Association Between Different Estimates of the Program Impact of Revenue Sharing

	Relationship Between (Cramer's V):	
	Finance Officer Response and Chief Executive Response	Finance Officer Response and Use Report Estimate
Municipalities		
100,000-299,999....	.23	.22
25,000-99,999......	.36	.26
10,000-24,999......	.32	.25
2,500-9,999........	.30	.34
100-2,499..........	.36	.35
Counties		
500,000 or more....	.13	.01
100,000-499,999....	.24	.28
Less than 100,000...	.34	.31

One might speculate as to why the Use Report and survey estimates of program impact are not more different than the data in this chapter suggest. Virtually everyone who has analyzed the Use Reports has come to the conclusion that they tend to represent allocations of GRS funds designated to meet Office of Revenue Sharing reporting requirements, and tend not to have much relation to the underlying realities of program changes as they relate to GRS.[4] But this picture of the Use Reports can be quite misleading, especially if it is derived from examination of data for large urban cities and counties. The analysis above suggests that the Use Reports are by and large thoroughly misleading for large cities or counties, but this is much less true for moderate or small cities. In retrospect, it is easy to see why that might be true.

For the most part, the notion that the Use Reports are apt to give an inaccurate picture of how GRS funds were actually used lies in the fungibility of money notion—funds officially earmarked for one purpose might simply replace local sources of revenue, with the true impact being on some quite different expenditure program or not on expenditure programs at all.[5] It is unquestionably true that for municipalities and counties in most size classes, money is in fact fungible, and it would not be difficult to produce a Use Report that varied markedly from a good estimate of how GRS funds affected the local pattern of expenditures. But what is true in principle need not be true in practice, and it may be that many local officials simply take the view that they are asked to report how GRS funds were used and do a reasonably adequate job of such reporting, without paying much attention to the fact that it would be easier to provide misleading reports if they had any strong incentive to do so. The priority categories are, after all, rather broad and cover most of the kinds of programs that local government officials would like to see come into being. Hence the simplest solution for most local officials may be to provide exactly the same kind of information on an official Use Report as they do when they answer the question "what programs would have been cut if GRS funds had not been available," and both answers may be accurate.

In addition, there must be many communities in which the use of the GRS funds is not mysterious at all but consists of a single clearly defined and fairly

[4]For example, see Lovell, et al,. "The Effects of General Revenue Sharing on Ninety-Seven Cities in Southern California," and Anton, et al., "Understanding the Fiscal Impact of General Revenue Sharing."

[5]Fungibility in this sense depends partly on the size of the GRS allocation relative to the community's budget. A small amount of money is more fungible than a large (relative) amount.

conspicous program use. If a relatively small community uses GRS funds to replace its fire equipment earlier than had been scheduled, or to construct a recreation facility, or to build a new administrative building, that may exhaust the full amount of GRS allocations for a number of years. In situations of that sort, it is hard to see what else these officials would report, on either the Use Report or on the survey, other than the fact that fire equipment had been bought with GRS funds and would not have been bought if the funds had not been available, or that a recreation facility was constructed with GRS money and would not have been constructed if the funds had not been available, etc. In short, the fungibility of money notion, which tends to suggest to most analysts that the Use Reports are apt to be misleading, may not make a great deal of difference except in places where programs are large and comprehensive, where GRS funds are a modest addition to local resources, and where deciding how GRS funds were actually used is complex and far from obvious.

The report by the General Accounting Office on revenue sharing[6] indicates that the Actual Use Reports are an unreliable source of information on the actual uses of GRS funds. The GAO report cites the usual reasons—money is fungible and local funds can be transferred into and out of areas with complete flexibility, thus providing a potentially misleading picture of how revenue-sharing funds were "really" used as compared to how they were accounted in the Use Reports. However, this was not found to be a universal pattern. To quote the GAO report, in Hardyville, South Carolina, "town officials said they did not view revenue sharing as merely a part of total local resources. They considered revenue sharing funds a special Federal subsidy separate from the town's own resources and spent the funds on what they considered very visible capital items. The mayor stated that revenue sharing permitted Hardyville to [make major capital expenditures], including a backhold for the water department and a metal utility building."

The story of Hardyville is one that shows up, by implication, in much of the SRC sample data on small communities. Thus, even though it is almost certainly true that Use Reports are greatly misleading for large municipalities and larger counties, it is far from evident that the same applies to the enormous number of small local governments receiving revenue-sharing funds.

6"Revenue Sharing: An Opportunity for Improved Public Awareness of State and Local Government Operations," Department of the Treasury, General Accounting Office, GGD-76-2, September 9, 1975.

PUBLIC SAFETY AND GRS FUNDS

Some of the earlier results from analysis of the first Use Reports suggested that public safety was the dominant use of GRS funds, and both the fiscal year 1974 Use Reports as well as the survey estimates of program impact continue to suggest that public safety is the single most important use of GRS monies. Because so many analysts have concluded, on the basis of evidence derived mainly from large cities, that the Use Reports are misleading as a measure of program impact, it is important to validate the survey estimates of large public safety expenditures from GRS funds. One way to do that is to divide public safety into two of its principal components—police services and fire services. Neither the Use Reports nor the Census of Governments data permit this distinction, but the survey estimates of program impact do. And the results can be compared against the analysis of GRS program impact from the detailed examination of budget data in Chapter 5 of this monograph.

The survey estimates for fiscal year 1974 show that program impacts clearly defined as relating to police services came to a bit more, overall, than those related to fire services (Table 3-11). But the pattern among communities is very different. In very large cities, GRS uses of funds for police services were reported to be much larger than for fire, and the same is true for counties. But for all cities except the very largest ones, expenditures on fire services tended to be much larger (with one exception) than expenditures for police. Interestingly enough, the analysis in Chapter 5, based on expenditure and revenue data for a small subset of the sample communities in the survey, shows a significant impact of GRS money on expenditures for fire services, no impact on expenditures for police services. But the sample used for the analysis consists of cities in size classes between 25,000 and 300,000—city size classes where the survey estimates of program impact indicate that expenditures for fire are twice as high or more as expenditures for police. These results thus serve as an interesting corroboration of the basic survey data, although obviously for only one area of expenditure and a small subgroup of all community types.

IMPACT ON POPULATION GROUPS

Although it proved possible in the survey to obtain information from responding officials about the program impact of GRS, an attempt to do the same with respect to the impact of GRS on population groups proved totally unsuccessful. The basic

Table 3-11
Program Impact Estimates From the Survey:
Police vs. Fire Services
(millions of dollars)

Size Class	Fiscal Year 1974		Fiscal Year 1975	
	Police	Fire	Police	Fire
Municipalities				
300,000 and over	22.9	5.0	25.8	11.3
100,000-299,999	10.8	21.2	6.5	19.3
25,000-99,999	13.2	30.6	12.2	19.0
10,000-24,999	17.0	31.8	3.9	22.1
2,500-9,999	5.7	12.7	6.9	2.0
Less than 2,500	8.3	6.1	4.6	6.3
Townships, 9,000 and over.	2.4	2.4	2.4	2.4
Townships, less than 9,000	0.6	3.0	—	—
Counties				
500,000 and over	16.5	—	18.2	—
100,000-499,999	24.5	12.2	7.1	1.5
Less than 100,000	50.8	12.6	31.9	—
All	172.0	137.7	119.5	84.0

idea was to ask officials which particular population group or groups would have been affected by the absence of the programs that GRS facilitated.

In planning the survey, we were aware from the beginning of the great interest that attached to the distributional effects of the GRS program. Thus, we conducted extensive training sessions for the interviewers and devoted particular attention to the importance of getting responses that would indicate not only program but also population impact. Our interviewers were instructed to try to get specific information where possible about programs that would have been reduced or eliminated in the absence of GRS: if GRS facilitated a recreational building, where would it have been located, who would have used it, etc. If police or fire services were facilitated, which areas of the community and which population groups would have benefitted from the additional services, and so forth.

But despite all this preparation and our considerable interest in attempting to get population impact via the survey, it proved to be virtually impossible to do so. Almost all respondents were reluctant to pinpoint GRS program impact on particular population groups. The overwhelming response we got was that "everybody would have been affected." In consequence, there are virtually no data with which one can examine the apparent impact of GRS on different population groups, insofar as impact is measured by the incidence of programs across different population groups.

In one sense, the result we got is understandable. In large communities with many programs, it is certainly conventional for public officials to take the view that everybody in the community benefits from every program conducted by the jurisdiction. True, some programs benefit older people, poor

people, etc., more than others, but it is often not so obvious when talking about broad-based programs like public safety, libraries, sewers, etc. In small communities, it may often be true that "everybody" benefits, simply because such a community may have only one recreation facility, and it makes little difference where it is located. Similarly with improved police or fire protection—it may matter hardly at all where the next fire truck acquired with GRS funds is housed, since it may provide protection to all members of the community in proportion to their property holding.

It is worth noting that any estimate of the program impact of GRS obtained by trying to measure the particular types of expenditures facilitated by GRS is only part of the story. In this chapter we make no attempt to assess the distributional impact of the tax or borrowing abatement aspect of GRS. In principle, the beneficiaries of such use of the GRS funds are clear enough: if local property taxes are abated as a consequence of GRS, local property holders are the beneficiaries in proportion to their tax payments, and renters are benefitted in proportion to the property taxes included in rent.

One criticism often leveled against the GRS program is that it has operated to the relative detriment of the poor, the elderly, and the disadvantaged. Evidence on this point seems to come in part from examination of the official Use Reports, which suggest that a very small fraction of GRS funds went to social services—predominantly an expenditure category benefiting the disadvantaged. Our program impact data tells the same tale, in that we show very little use of GRS funds for social services. But that is far from an adequate basis for judging that a distributional impact of

GRS is perverse in the sense of benefitting the haves at the expense of the have-nots. After all, the disadvantaged also use police and fire services, sewerage services, and transportation services, and these were all major program areas that appeared to have benefitted from GRS. But we have no way of knowing, from our program impact data, whether the particular aspects in which these kinds of services were improved tended to convey disproportionate benefits on one population group or another. As indicated above, attempts to do so proved to be fruitless.

APPENDIX TO CHAPTER 3

Comparison of Survey, Use Report & Census Classifications

This appendix outlines procedures for developing a unified set of expenditure categories to facilitate comparisons of program impact from the survey estimates, the Official Use Report estimates, and the Census of Governments expenditure data.

We decided to use the basic structure implied by the survey, making whatever adjustments were needed to bring that structure in line with the Use Report priority categories and the Census expenditure categories. Differences between the survey-based categories and the Use Reports are minimal, but that is not the case for differences relating to the Census data. These differences, and the allocation procedures used to put Census data into the survey categories, are described below. The category headings are those used by the Census.

General Control

This Census category includes expenditures for the city legislative body, the city executive, the offices of the city clerk and recorder, local courts, personnel, planning and zoning, and the city legal staff. Expenditures were divided between public safety (planning and zoning, courts and legal staff) and general and financial administration. It was assumed that 80 percent of expenditures in this category were in the public safety area, the remaining 20 percent in general and financial administration.

Utilities

This category includes expenditures on locally operated gas and water systems, electrical power systems, and transit and bus systems. Based on an examination of State-local data on the relative size of these categories, we assumed that 5 percent of utility expenditures represented costs of operating transit systems in municipality size classes 2-7

(cities from 100,000-299,999 down to those under 2,500 and counties), while 35 percent of utility expenditures were for transit systems in municipality size class 1 (cities over 300,000). The remainder of the expenditures under utilities were categorized as environmental protection, which in the survey categories includes sanitation and sewerage.

General Health

The Census category includes all public health activity except provision of or payment for hospital services. Expenditures must be distributed between public safety (regulation, inspection and licensing) and direct care activities such as innoculations, disease screening, etc. We assume that expenditures are divided equally between these two activities.

Housing and Urban Renewal

Expenditures must be split between public safety (code enforcement and building inspection) and land-use planning. On the basis of data published by the Douglas Commission in 1968, we assume that enforcement functions comprise 25 percent of expenditures in size class 1 cities, 35 percent in size classes 2-7.

Since tax payments for public assistance were not an eligible use of revenue sharing funds, we eliminated public assistance and Medicaid payments from the Census public welfare category and thus from the expenditure base. In addition to the prohibition on the use of revenue-sharing funds for this purpose, the level of these payments is set by the States and the overwhelming proportion of funds spent are State/Federal rather than local. Thus retaining public assistance and Medicaid expenditures for the purpose of allocating responses would, in cases where respondents reported expenditure on social services, seriously overstate the amount of revenue-sharing funds involved.

Comparison of Expenditure Categories Between the Survey, the Use Reports, and the Census of Governments

Survey Categories	Use Reports	Census of Governments
Public Safety (police, fire protection, courts)	Public Safety	% General Control, Police, Fire, % Health, % Housing,[1] Corrections[2]
Environmental Control (sanitation, sewerage)	Environmental Protection	Sewage, Sanitation, % Utilities[1], Natural Resources[2]
Land Use	Housing and Community Development, Economic Development[3]	% Housing and Urban Renewal[1]
Transportation (streets, highways)	Public Transportation	Highways, % Utilities[1]
Amenities (recreation facilities, libraries)	Recreation, Libraries	Libraries, Parks
Education	Education[3]	Education
Health	Health	% Health, Hospitals
Social Services	Social Services for Aged and Poor	% Public Welfare
Administrative and Financial	Financial Administration, General Government[3]	% General Control, Financial Adminis., Public Buildings, Debt Interest
Other	Other	Other General Expenditures

[1]Cities only
[2]Counties only
[3]Capital expenditures only

The removal of Medicaid payments presented certain problems. The Census public welfare category for the cities is subdivided into both cash assistance (AFDC, OAA, etc.) and "other expenditures," which includes Medicaid payments. It was assumed that the ratio of Medicaid to total cash expenditure payments is the same for each locality as the national average. More precisely, it is assumed that the figure for reported cash assistance represents 56 percent of total public assistance payments for all localities. The difference between the cash assistance figure and the imputed expenditure for total assistance was subtracted from the "other" expenditure category, and we hypothesize that the remaining expenditures represent programs such as day care, homemaker and other social services over which local governments have primary jurisdiction. These calculations are not necessary for counties, as medical vender payments are separately reported.

The census categories where allocations are necessary account for about 30 percent of the total city expenditures, and less than one-eighth of general expenditures. The allocations are least satisfactory in the utilities and housing categories, which unfortunately account for 80 percent of the total for which allocations are necessary. And here, it is likely to be true that the allocations are least satisfactory for size class 1 cities.

The allocation of municipal and county expenditures according to the expenditure categories developed from the survey are shown in the text above in Table 3-6. The categories themselves are listed below in Table A, with a brief explanation of the activities included in each category and an indication of how the Use Report and Census expenditure categories relate to the survey categories.

CHAPTER 4

Modeling the Fiscal Impact
of Revenue Sharing

Gail R. Wilensky*

INTRODUCTION

Understanding the fiscal impact of general revenue sharing has been a major concern of both policymakers and researchers. As noted earlier, this study is concerned with only a portion of the fiscal impact—that which occurs at the State and local Level. This chapter is limited to analysis of the fiscal impact of revenue sharing on local governments.

There are several ways to proceed in modeling the fiscal impact of revenue sharing. We could specify models which predict local government receipts and expenditures and which include general revenue sharing as one of the explanatory variables in the equation. This is essentially the procedure used in Chapter 5, where data collected on the information forms sent to local governments in the SRC sample are examined. Alternatively, we could model the responses obtained from interviews with the chief finance officers. That is the procedure used here.

It will be recalled that as part of the survey we used a detailed sequence of questions which in essence asked finance officers to describe how their budgets would have been different if there had been no general revenue sharing. More specifically, we asked if their operating expenditures would have been lower, if their capital expenditures would have been lower, if their tax rates would have been higher, and so forth. Each of these was followed by questions regarding the degree to which expenditures would have been lower, taxes higher, and so forth. By the procedures described in the appendix to Chapter 2, we were able to derive quantitative estimates of the fiscal impact of revenue sharing from these responses.

In this chapter attention is focused on the economic and other determinants of the share of a juristiction's revenue-sharing allocation "spent" on operating expenditures, capital expenditures,

tax reduction and borrowing reduction. Economic theory provides little guidance on this question. It does suggest that a program like revenue sharing is likely to result in some net increase in expenditure-as long as a community's demand for public goods is not completely insensitive to an increase in its income. Theory also suggests that a substantial portion should go into tax reduction or displacement. In a recent empirical study, Gramlich and Galper[1] estimate that a pure "lump sum" grant (where the amount received is the same irrespective of the unit's behavior) is likely to decrease local taxes by 56-75 cents for each dollar of grant received. Since revenue sharing provides a small incentive to increase expenditures rather than reduce taxes (the allocation formula rewards local tax effort), we might expect a slightly smaller decrease in taxes than reported by Gramlich and Galper. Moreover, the tax adjustment process takes some time to occur, which again leads us to expect that a smaller fraction of revenue sharing funds would be expected to go for tax reduction during fiscal year 1974 or 1975 than implied by the above analysis.

The process literature, which includes studies by Crecine, Meltsner, and others[2] does provide some specific *a priori* expectations about the allocation of additional revenue such as would result from a revenue-sharing grant. According to Crecine's model of municipal budgeting, the first use of a budget surplus is to increase salaries. The residual is then distributed among departments for use in the next highest priority account category, with the last use being to increase expenditures on equipment. The overriding tone of these models is one of incrementalism: this year's budget is like last year's budget with small changes at the margin to eliminate surpluses or deficits or accommodate some unexpected fiscal pressure point.

*Visiting Assistant Professor, Department of Economics and Associate Research Scientist, Institute for Public Policy Studies, The University of Michigan.

[1]Edward Gramlich and Harvey Galper, "State and Local Fiscal Behavior and Federal Grant Policy," *Brookings Papers on Economic Activity* I 1973, pp. 15-58.

[2]John P. Crecine, "A computer Simulation Model of Municipal Budgeting," *Management Science*, 13 (July 1967), pp. 786-815; A. Meltsner and Aaron Wildavsky, "Leave City Budgeting Alone," in J. P. Crecine (ed.) *Financing the Metropolis*, Sage Publications, 1970.

In general, revenue sharing does not appear to have been allocated in a manner consistent with the expectations of the process studies. For the period 1970-72, the ratio of current (operating) expenditures to capital expenditures for all local governments was approximately 5:1. For cities over 300,000 this was roughly the ratio of operating to capital expenditures in 1974. In 1975, however, it dropped down to 4:1. Survey findings on the allocation of GRS funds between the operating and capital expenditure categories were, however, substantially different from these recent historical averages. For cities between 100,000 and 300,000 the ratio of operating to capital was approximately 1:1 for both 1974 and 1975. For smaller cities the ratio was at most 1:3.5 operating to capital for 1974; and at most 1:2.5 operating to capital in 1975. Furthermore, one of the least important uses of the revenue-sharing money was to increase salaries. A major reason for the relatively heavy use for capital expenditures, as indicated below, appears to have been the uncertainty of revenue sharing's continuation after 1976. This also may have been one of the reasons that so little revenue-sharing funds were put into salary increases.

Overall, the share which went to tax reduction, according to the survey, was only a little lower than would have been expected given the economic literature on the effects of grants. Aside from the largest cities, other jurisdictions were typically reporting at least 20 percent of GRS going to tax abatement, with cities between 100,000 and 300,000 reporting about 40 percent.[3] In most instances, the share going to tax reduction increased in 1975 relative to what was reported for 1974. And as Chapter 2 indicates, there is good reason to suppose that the survey estimates of tax abatement are too low, by perhaps 5 to 10 percentage points on average.

For analytical purposes, we have grouped local jurisdictions into three categories: city size classes 1-3 (i.e. populations of 300,000+, 100,000-299,999 and 25,000-99,999), city size classes 4-6 (i.e. populations of 10,000-24,999, 2,500-9,999 and less than 2,500) and all counties. As will become clear from the regression analyses, the characteristics which influence behavior in the larger cities are not

the same or do not operate in the same way as the characteristics which influence behavior in the smaller areas. Furthermore, they do not appear to influence the counties in the same way they do the cities. For each of these three groups, we use multiple regression to analyze the characteristics which influence the percent of revenue sharing going to operating expenditures, capital expenditures, tax reduction and borrowing reduction for the years 1974 and 1975.[4]

CITIES IN SIZE CLASSES 1, 2 and 3

The results of the regression analyses for city size classes 1-3 are shown in Table 4-1. The independent or predictor variables are a combination of Census variables such as per capita income, percent of the population under 18, and subjective survey cata, such as agreement with the statement that the temporary nature of the revenue-sharing program has led to the use of revenue-sharing funds for capital expenditures. These predictor variables are listed in the left hand column of Table 4-1 and are shown as row variables. The dependent variables are the percent of revenue-sharing funds spent for operating expenditures in fiscal year 1974, the percent spent for operating expenditures in fiscal year 1975, and so forth; they are shown as column variables. Within each cell of the table, the regression coefficients are shown first and the t-values for each coefficient are shown below in parentheses. Coefficients whose t-values are at least 2.0 have been designated by an asterisk.

As a result of using both subjective survey responses and objective Census information, the regression coefficients for Census variables become difficult to interpret in conventional terms. The effects of the Census variables shown in these regressions are not the true effects of these variables but only the effects net of whatever differences in attitudinal responses are generated by differences in the Census variables. Thus, for example, the income effect indicated by the per capital income coefficient is affected by any impact on the revenue-sharing allocation of differences in the response to questions about the uncertain nature of revenue sharing, including any such differences that happen to be associated with differences in per capita income.

From Table 4-1 we can see that as per capita income increases, the share going to operating expenditures increases while the share going to tax

[3]Cities over 300,000 reported only 10 percent going to tax reduction in 1974. It may be that we have simply underestimated this effect for 1974 or it may be that many of the very financially pressed large cities had already included revenue sharing money in their 1973 and 1974 budgets prior to the time that the legislation was passed and it was only in 1975 that response could be given to community pressures for tax reduction. In any case, we estimate that about 34 percent of the revenue sharing money in the large cities went to tax reduction in 1975, which is within the range we would have expected.

[4]Multiple regression analysis measures show the influence of each independent variable on the dependent variable, say the influence of per capita income on the percent of revenue sharing used for operating expenditures, with the influence of all the other independent variables like city size or racial composition held constant.

Table 4-1
Regression Analyses for City Size Classes 1-3[a]

Independent Variables	Percent of Revenue Sharing Going To Operating Expend.		Percent of Revenue Sharing To Capital Expend.		Percent of Revenue Sharing to Tax Abatement		Percent of Revenue Sharing to Borrowing Reduction	
	1974	1975	1974	1975	1974	1975	1974	1975
Per Capita Income	.0001*	.0000	-.0000	-.0000	.0000*	.0000	.0000	-.0001*
	(2.93)	(.74)	(.78)	(.91)	(2.33)	(1.57)	(.59)	(4.97)
City Size 1	.205*	.145*	-.129*	-.113*	-.165*	-.074	-.084*	-.057
	(4.18)	(2.91)	(2.51)	(2.17)	(3.09)	(1.19)	(2.55)	(1.77)
City Size 2	.032	-.007	-.109	.007	.064	-.025	.051	-.035
	(.59)	(.13)	(1.90)	(.12)	(1.08)	(.36)	(1.39)	(.96)
Temporary Nature Discourages Innovative Use	.073	.117*	NA	NA	NA	NA	NA	NA
	(1.62)	(2.57)						
Percent Under 18	.605	.483	1.02*	.979*	-1.36*	-.743	-.071	-.435
	(1.43)	(1.12)	(2.31)	(2.16)	(2.93)	(1.37)	(.25)	(1.54)
Percent White	-.078	-.403*	.334*	-.172	-.080	-.014	-.047	.06
	(.51)	(2.62)	(2.09)	(1.06)	(.48)	(.07)	(.46)	(.59)
Mentions Fiscal or Economic Problems	.103*	.05	-.156*	-.182*	.113*	.108*	-.042	.015
	(2.72)	(1.22)	(4.02)	(4.60)	(2.78)	(2.30)	(1.69)	(.60)
Per Capita Grants	-.001*	-.0002	-.001*	-.0008*	.002*	.002*	.0004	.0004
	(3.11)	(.64)	(2.09)	(2.15)	(5.94)	(3.47)	(1.80)	(1.87)
Per Capita Revenue Sharing	.051*	.051*	-.011	-.031	-.019*	.009	.002	-.01*
	(8.14)	(2.35)	(1.67)	(1.99)	(2.70)	(1.04)	(.40)	(2.46)
"Uncertainty", Mentions Temporary Nature of Revenue Sharing	-.134*	.043	.074	-.061	NA	NA	NA	NA
	(2.82)	(.88)	(1.48)	(1.19)				
Temporary Nature Leads to Capital Expenditure	NA	NA	.231*	-.053	NA	NA	NA	NA
			(4.43)	(1.0)				
Best Thing is to Reduce Taxes	NA	NA	NA	NA	.184*	.068	NA	NA
					(4.02)	(1.28)		
Adjusted R².	.44	.20	.34	.26	.33	.13	.07	.10

*designates t value >2.0

[a]City size class 1 has population of 300,000 or more, size class 2 has population from 100,000-299,999, size class 3 has population from 25,000-99,999. N=270, t values in parentheses.

reduction and borrowing reduction declines. There is no significant relationship between income and the share going to capital expenditures. From the size of the coefficient it is clear that the income effect is very small. As per capita income increases by $1.00, the share going to operating expenditures increases by 1/100th of a percent or, using somewhat more relevant units, as per capita income increases by $100.00, the share going to operating expenditures increases by 1 percent. The negative sign of income tax reduction is consistent with the notion of Neenan[5] and others that the demand for public goods is positively related to income. The implied income elasticity of demand is approximately one, which is not unreasonable, but for the reasons indicated above it is not clear how much confidence we can place in this specific numerical value. The positive sign of income on operating expenditures is also expected for the same reason— we expect expenditures to be positively related to income. It is not clear whether the coefficient should be larger for capital or for operating expenditures. Since capital expenditures are more postponable and less pressing, we might therefore expect them to be more income elastic. In fact, the coefficient is not significantly different from zero.

City Size classes 1 and 2 are categorical variables. The suppressed category, from which these are shown as deviations, is City Size class 3. Being in City Size class 1 rather than in size class 3 is almost always significant; it increases the share going into operating expenditures and decreases the share going to capital expenditures, tax reduction and borrowing reduction, and the differences are rather sizeable. Being in size class 1 rather than three increases the share going into operating expenditures by 21 percent (1974), decreases the share going into capital expenditures by 13 percent (1974), and so forth. Being in size class 2 rather than 3 was not significant, although it was close to significance for capital expenditures in 1974.

Throughtout this chapter, we will see emerging evidence that the largest cities have been using their revenue sharing funds primarily to maintain

[5]William B. Neenan, *Political Economy of Urban Areas*, Markham, Chicago 1972, Chapter 4.

ongoing programs rather than to innovate, to expand capital facilities, or to reduce taxes, thus confirming an image of the largest cities as governments which are facing a significant financial crunch. A substantial amount of evidence supports the notion that large cities are using their funds to maintain existing programs. When asked how they would characterize their use of revenue sharing dollars, 94 percent of the finance officers of the largest cities indicated continuing activities rather than new activities or both. The percent saying continuing activities for city size class 2 was 68 percent and with the exception of the smallest cities (less than 2500) and the smallest township (less than 9000), all the other groups reported a smaller percent saying continuing activities. By way of contrast, cities below 300,000 are much more likely to use their revenue sharing for capital projects or for tax reduction. Those that are particularly concerned about the possibility of revenue sharing being discontinued tend to put their revenue-sharing money into capital expenditures. Those that are not so concerned put their revenue-sharing funds into tax reduction or new programs, both of which may incur future financial obligation.

We expected that agreement with the statement "concern over the continuation of general revenue sharing may discourage some governments from using revenue-sharing funds for experimental programs" would be negatively related with the share going to operating expenditures or not related at all. Instead, it was positively related. Our expectation was based on the presumption that innovative programs are more likely to involve operating expenditures, but Chapter 8 below, where innovation is discussed at length, indicates this is not often the case. A second expectation was that agreement with the statement would indicate concern over the continuation of the program, and that jurisdictions which had this concern would be less likely to go into operating expenditures because of the implication for future obligations. Another attitudinal statement which deals more directly with the uncertainty issue was also included in the regression and is discussed below. Furthermore, the respondent could agree that governments in general would behave in this manner without regard to what his/her unit actually does.

The percent of the population under 18 is a proxy for a service demand variable. The larger the population under 18, the more likely the additional funds to be used for the provision of public goods and the less likely they are to be used for tax reduction. Our results support this expectation.

The percent of the population which is white is also a service demand variable. We expect that jurisdictions having a large white population would be less likely to use their revenue-sharing funds to increase expenditures and more likely to use them to reduce taxes. The significant coefficient for operating expenditures on percent of the population white was negative, but the significant coefficient for capital expenditures was positive. While this is not what might have been expected a priori, it is consistent with an image of communities which tend to spend their revenue-sharing funds on capital expenditures as being under less financial pressure.

As part of the survey, local officials were asked to list what they thought were the most important problems faced by their jurisdictions. From these responses we constructed a dummy variable for fiscal pressure: jurisdictions whose finance officers listed fiscal or economic problems as the first or second of the most important problems facing their community were assigned 1, other jurisdictions were assigned zero. The coefficient of this fiscal pressure variable was significant in five of eight equations shown in Table 4-1, generally with the expected signs. A mention of fiscal or economic problems increased the proportion of revenue-sharing monies going to operating expenditures, decreased the share going to capital outlays, and increased the share going to tax abatement. The first two results are clearly consistent with an image of these communities as having a mismatch between fiscal capacity and fiscal requirements, while the results for tax abatement are unavoidably ambiguous. On the one hand, the existence of fiscal or economic pressure should increase the demand for tax reduction: but on the other hand, the existence of financial problems should tend to make the tax abatement option less feasible. Thus while it is not difficult to explain our finding of a positive relationship, it would be just as easy to explain a negative relationship.

Some additional supportive evidence that large cities feeling financially pressed were likely to allocate a substantial share of their revenue-sharing money to operating expenditures can also be seen from the relation between revenue-sharing funds and responses to the question, "we have been able to stay afloat financially." Communities who agree with the statement, and can therefore be assumed to be under less pressure than those who disagree with it, tend to spend less revenue-sharing money on operating outlays than communities who disagree, as indicated by Table 4-2 below.

Per capita governmental grants (other than revenue sharing) were found to be negatively related to both operating and capital expenditures and positively related to tax reduction and borrowing reduction. Some caution should be used in interpreting these coefficients, since States differ enormously in the degree to which they themselves

Table 4-2

Share of GRS Funds Going to Operating Expenditures Related to Opinions About the Statement, "Revenue Sharing has Enabled us to Stay Afloat Financially," Cities with 300,000 or More Population

Opinion Question	Percent of GRS Funds Used for Operating Outlays		
	None	Less Than Average	More Than Average
Agree	33%	40	27
Disagree................	17%	14	69

perform certain functions versus their appropriation of funds as grants to lower governments who in turn perform the same functions. Nonetheless, it seems reasonable that the higher the level of per capital grants, the less dependent is the jurisdiction on its own sources for revenue. This makes it less necessary for the jurisdiction to devote its revenue sharing to increasing expenditures and more able to cut its taxes. In other words, revenue sharing appears to be serving as slack in high grant jurisdictions.

Per capita revenue sharing is positively related to the share going to operating expenditures and negatively related to the share going to capital expenditures, to tax reduction and to borrowing reduction. It should be noted that this pattern corresponds to the pattern observed for per capita income and for city size class 1. The reason is that the revenue-sharing grant serves as a proxy for the characteristics of a jurisdiction which are associated with grants of different sizes. In particular, the per capita revenue-sharing allocation is positively correlated with being a big city (.4), negatively correlated with the percent under 18 (−.33), and negatively correlated with the percent white (−.47). In addition and of equal importance, to the extent that the community regards the revenue-sharing allocation as being similar to an increase in the community's income, which is the way economic theory regards block grants, we would expect that the signs on the income coefficient and the revenue-sharing coefficient would be the same, which turns out to be the case.

The last question of the survey asked local officials if there was "anything else they would like to tell us about the revenue-sharing program." A variable was constructed treating all jurisdictions whose finance officers mentioned concern about the temporary nature of revenue sharing as equal to 1; all other jurisdictions were coded zero. This variable is the more direct measure of the effects of uncertainty referred to earlier. The only significant coefficient for this variable was in the operating expenditure equation for 1974, where it showed the

expected negative relationship—jurisdictions who are concerned about incurring future obligations are unlikely to allocate their funds to operating projects. This result is supported by the next independent variable in Table 4-1: agreement with the statement that "concern about the temporary nature of revenue-sharing funds may have led some governments to spend most of their revenue-sharing money on capital items." We included this variable only in the capital expenditure equation, and at least for 1974 it was positively and significantly related to the share allocated to capital expenditures.

The final independent variable in Table 4-1 is agreement with the statement that "the best use of revenue-sharing funds may be to reduce taxes." This variable was only included in the tax reduction equation, and was highly significant and positively related to the dependent variable, at least for 1974. This attitudinal response was included in the equation to measure a predisposition towards tax reduction on the part of the local officials. We recognize, however, that some elements of a tautology are introduced by including this response.

Looking at Table 4-1 as a whole, it is possible to make the following generalizations. The variables which tend to be most important in explaining variations in the share of revenue sharing going to operating expenditures, capital expenditures, tax reduction and borrowing reduction are per capita income, city size, fiscal pressure, per capita grants and uncertainty about the continuation of the program. It is clear that we have difficulty explaining variation in the share going to borrowing. The most obvious explanations of this difficulty is that the share going to borrowing is very small and that there is not much variation in that share across the jurisdictional characteristics we are considering. Also clear is that, except for the borrowing reduction equations, we do a much poorer job of explaining variations in the 1975 equations than we do for the 1974 equations. It is not obvious why this is so. One possibility is that the quality of the responses may not be as good for 1975 as it was for 1974. For jurisdictions whose fiscal years coincide with calendar years, we were asking questions about budgets for years which did not even begin until three to four months after our survey.

We expected—particularly for the largest cities—that agreement with two survey questions relating inflation and strong employee unions to salary increases would be positively related to the share of revenue-sharing monies going to operating expenditures. In fact, this expectation was not borne out and was, therefore, not included in the equations. The primary reason in both cases appears to be that one or two large urban cities, who did not agree with the statement, spent most of their revenue sharing on operating expenditures. Of those who agreed with the statement, "high rates of inflation mean that much of revenue sharing goes for salary increases," 19 percent spent no GRS funds on operating expenditures, 51 percent spent less than the average amount, and 30 percent spent more than the average amount. Overall, those who disagreed with the statement showed a larger percentage spending "none," 31 percent, and only 8 percent spending less than the average, which is as expected. Surprisingly, 62 percent reported spending more than the average. Focusing only on those who disagreed somewhat, we find 79 percent who reported spending "none" and 21 percent who reported spending less than the average, with none reporting that more than the average amount was spent—about what would be expected.

The same basic pattern prevailed for the statement "Active employee organizations mean that much of the revenue-sharing money goes for salary increases." For the largest cities, those who agreed showed a smaller percent in the "none" category and larger percent in the less than average category, with the more than average category being dominated by one or two major cities. As before, there were no cases in the more than average category for those who disagree "somewhat." For cities with less than 300,000 population, there is very little difference between those agreeing and those disagreeing with the statement about employee organizations and revenue-sharing monies.

CITIES IN SIZE
CLASSES 4, 5 and 6

The results of the regression analyses for city size classes 4-6 (10,000-24,999, 2500-9,999 and less than 2500 respectively), are shown in Table 4-3. It is clear that we are not able to explain nearly as much variance for these smaller cities as we were for larger ones, in large part because there is not nearly as much variance to explain. As before, with the exception of the share going to operating expenditures, we have more difficulty explaining variance in 1975 than we do for 1974.

Once again, per capita income is important in several of the equations, but the signs in most of the equations are reversed from the ones in Table 4-1. For small cities, the share going to operating expenditures declines as income increases, as does the share going to capital expenditures; the share going to tax reduction increases. The reader will recall that the coefficients of Census variables may be difficult to interpret in conventional terms, but

this result suggests that in small cities, as income increases, the demand for private goods increase relative to the demand for public goods.

City size classes 4 and 5 are categorical variables. The suppressed category here is size class 6 and the coefficients are shown as deviations from the suppressed category. With one exception, city size is not significant.

Agreement with the statement that concern over the continuation of revenue sharing may discourage its use for experimental programs is negatively related to the share going to operating expenditures. Although this is what we expected a priori, the ambiguous nature of the question remains and the more direct measure of the effect of uncertainty seems superior.

An increase in the percent of the population under 18 increases the share going to operating expenditures and decreases the share going for capital expenditures. Since this is a proxy for a service demand variable, we would expect it in general to be positively related to expenditures and negatively related to tax reduction. The negative sign on the share going to capital expenditures is usually regarded as representing less pressing needs. The other service demand variable, the percent of the population which is white, was not significant in any of the equations.

A high priority given to fiscal or economic problems in response to the question "What are the three most important problems facing this unit?" is a significant variable in three of the equations. The signs on the coefficients are reasonable in all cases: a perception that fiscal or economic problems are high priority is positively related to the fraction of GRS funds going to operating expenditures, and negatively related to borrowing reduction.

Per capita grants is significant in only one equation but the signs on the coefficients are almost identical to those for city size classes 1-3. This provides some weak support for the notion that revenue sharing serves as slack in high grant jurisdictions. The per capita revenue-sharing allocation is also significant in only one equation but this time the signs are not the same as those for per capita income, city size, etc. This time the variable is proxying only for low per capita income and high nonwhite populations, with negative intercorrelations of .46 and .37 respectively.

Finally, an expressed concern about the temporary nature of revenue sharing is generally not significant but the signs are as we would expect—a negative relation to operating expenditures and a positive relation to capital expenditures. This pattern is strengthened when coupled with the next variable, agreement with the statement that the temporary nature of revenue sharing will lead to

Table 4-3
Regression Analyses for City Size Classes 4-6[a]

Independent Variables	Percent of Revenue Sharing Going To Operating Expend.		Percent of Revenue Sharing To Capital Expend.		Percent of Revenue Sharing to Tax Reduction		Percent of Revenue Sharing to Borrowing Reduction	
	1974	1975	1974	1975	1974	1975	1974	1975
Per Capita Income	-.0000* (2.32)	-.0000 (1.82)	-.0001* (2.57)	-.0000 (1.52)	.0001 (2.47)*	.0001* (2.33)	.0000 (.49)	.0000 (.05)
City Size 4	-.114 (1.75)	-.119 (1.55)	.163 (1.27)	.034 (.28)	-.025 (.24)	.111 (.85)	.087 (1.13)	.052 (.78)
City Size 5	-.147* (2.21)	-.128 (1.65)	.086 (.66)	-.018 (.15)	-.045 (.44)	.128 (.98)	.113 (1.46)	.078 (1.16)
Temporary Nature Discourages Innovative Use	-.051 (1.5)	-.093* (2.34)	NA	NA	NA	NA	NA	NA
Percent Under 18	.130 (.61)	.598* (2.39)	-.840 (2.03)	-.544 (1.37)	-.157 (.49)	-.170 (.41)	.022 (.09)	.046 (.22)
Percent White	.199 (1.90)	-.224 (1.82)	.393 (1.99)	.193 (1.04)	.074 (.46)	.171 (.85)	.026 (1.74)	.099 (.96)
Mentions Fiscal or Economic Problems	.025 (.71)	.093* (2.27)	.073 (1.07)	-.007 (.10)	-.055 (1.00)	-.065 (.95)	-.109* (2.68)	-.072* (2.04)
Per Capita Grants	-.0007 (1.71)	-.0008 (1.52)	-.002* (2.26)	-.001 (1.76)	.0007 (1.06)	.002 (1.74)	.0003 (.60)	-.0001 (.26)
Per Capita Revenue Sharing	-.0004 (1.90)	.0003 (.06)	.019* (2.08)	.014 (1.59)	-.006 (.88)	-.005 (.52)	.0003 (.50)	-.0009 (.20)
"Uncertainty", Mentions Temporary Nature of Revenue Sharing	-.007 (.17)	-.0320 (.70)	.151 (1.97)	.186* (2.53)	NA	NA	NA	NA
Temporary Nature Leads to Capital Expenses	NA	NA	.051 (.72)	.160* (2.33)	NA	NA	NA	NA
Best Thing is to Reduce Taxes	NA	NA	NA	NA	.248* (5.22)	.221* (3.67)	NA	NA
Adjusted R².	.05	.14	.12	.09	.17	.12	.02	.0

*designates t value >2.0
[a]City size class 4 has population of 10,000-24,999, size class 5 has population from 2500-9,999, size class 6 has population less than 2500. N=195, t values in parentheses.

capital expenditures. And to the extent that agreement with the statement that the best thing to do with revenue sharing is to reduce taxes represents a predisposition towards tax reduction, we find such a predisposition to be very strong in the smaller cities. This result is consistent with the relationship observed for per capita income, where the small city data suggest a relative preference for private goods as opposed to public goods.

COUNTY SIZE CLASSES 1, 2, and 3

The results of the regression analyses for county sizes 1, 2 and 3 (500,000 and above, 100,000-499,999 and less than 100,000, respectively) are shown in Table 4-4. It is clear that we are not very successful in explaining variations among counties, which appears to be a common problem.

Per capita income is significant in only one equation. The sign is the same as for large cities, with higher income decreasing the share going to borrowing reduction.

County size classes 1 and 2 are categorical variables, with county class 3 the suppressed category and the other two coefficients shown as deviations from it. Being in county class 1 (having a population greater than 500,000) decreases the share going to capital expenditures and increases the share going to tax reduction and borrowing reduction. This image is clearly not consistent with the image evoked by the large cities. Except for the share going to borrowing reduction, being in county size 2 rather than 3 does not result in significant differences.

The percent of the population under 18 is significant in only one equation but the signs are generally consistent with our interpretation of this as a service demand variable. The same is true of the percent of the population which is white, which serves as a negative service demand variable.

Mentioning fiscal or economic problems as being the most important problems facing the county is generally not significant nor is agreement

Table 4-4
Regression Analyses for Counties[a]

Independent Variables	Percent of Revenue Sharing Going To Operating Expend.		Percent of Revenue Sharing To Capital Expend.		Percent of Revenue Sharing to Tax reduction		Percent of Revenue Sharing to Borrowing Reduction	
	1974	1975	1974	1975	1974	1975	1974	1975
Per Capita Income	-.0000 (.57)	.0001 (1.77)	.0001 (1.31)	.0000 (1.02)	-.0000 (.95)	-.0001 (1.90)	-.0001* (2.47)	-.0001* (3.13)
County Size 1	.023 (.27)	-.038 (.54)	-.234* (2.45)	-.264* (3.02)	.103 (1.27)	.297* (2.89)	.287* (3.19)	.275* (3.44)
County Size 2	-.045 (.60)	-.068 (1.11)	-.147 (1.82)	-.119 (1.57)	.042 (.60)	.143 (1.61)	.188* (2.43)	.177* (2.57)
Temporary Nature Discourages Innovative Use	-.009 (.16)	.012 (.24)	NA	NA	NA	NA	NA	NA
Percent Under 18	.885 (1.11)	1.37* (2.11)	-1.288 (1.43)	-.556 (.69)	-.686 (.92)	-.220 (.23)	.031 (.04)	.279 (.38)
Percent White	-.327 (1.35)	-.821* (4.11)*	.242 (.92)	.227 (.93)	-.106 (.46)	.485 (1.69)	.121 (.48)	.459* (2.05)
Mentions Fiscal or Economic Problems	.025 (.44)	.028 (.82)	.062 (.99)	-.026 (.45)	-.137* (2.52)	-.006 (.08)	-.087 (1.46)	.021 (.39)
Per Capita Grants	.0002 (.28)	-.000 (.05)	-.001* (2.09)	-.0006 (1.05)	.002* (4.08)	.002* (2.35)	.0003 (.48)	.0005 (.94)
Per Capita Revenue Sharing	-.015 (1.10)	-.002 (.14)	.036* (2.43)	.012 (.87)	-.034* (2.70)	-.034* (2.13)	-.019 (1.38)	-.019 (1.52)
"Uncertainty", Mentions Temporary Nature of Revenue Sharing	NA	NA	NA	NA	NA	NA	NA	NA
Temporary Nature Leads to Capital Expenses	NA	NA	.215* (2.63)	.264* (3.45)	NA	NA	NA	NA
Best Thing is to Reduce Taxes	NA	NA	NA	NA	.182* (3.53)	.228* (3.49)	NA	NA
Adjusted R²	0	.14	.13	.13	.15	.14	.07	.10

*designates t value >2.0

[a]County size class 1 has population of 500,000 or more, and size class 2 has population of 100,000-499,999. N=138, t values in parentheses.

with the statement that the temporary nature of revenue sharing discourages experimental uses.

Per capita grants are negatively related to capital expenditures and positively related to tax reduction, again lending support to the notion that high grant county jurisdictions tend to regard the revenue sharing allocation as financial slack.

As the per capita revenue-sharing allocation increases, the county data show that the share of GRS monies going into capital increases and the share going to tax reduction declines. There is a high simple correlation between the per capita revenue-sharing allocation and other per capita grants but the effects of the revenue-sharing allocation are clearly different. With only one exception, the signs are the same as those for per capita income, a result that is consistent with our earlier finding for large cities and with our expectations about the impact of what is essentially a block grant.

Agreement with the statement that the temporary nature of revenue sharing will result in capital expenditures is significant and positively related to the share going to capital expenditures. Thus, the effect of uncertainty is the same here as in the cities: it leads jurisdictions to dispose of their funds in such a way as not to increase their future obligations. And a predisposition towards reducing taxes is significant, and is positively related to the share going for tax reduction.

The variables which seem to be important for the counties are concern about uncertainty, a predisposition towards reducing taxes and being in size class 1. The coefficients for the revenue-sharing allocation and for other grants are significant in three equations. The latter finding supports the notion that units with a good deal of other grant money are more likely to regard revenue-sharing money as slack.

REGION

From Chapter 2, it is clear that there are some striking differences in the way jurisdictions in different regions allocate their revenue-sharing funds. We have not included region as a variable in the equations shown above for two reasons. First, region is correlated with several variables already in the equation, such as percent white, per capita income, and so forth. Second and of equal importance, it is not at all clear what the region variable stands for: most researchers are therefore reluctant to include it directly in the analyses. We think that in this case region may be serving as a proxy for the age of the jurisdiction and/or a different distribution of functional responsibility for the provision of various public goods.

Tables 4-5 and 4-6 show the variation by region and city size in the proportion of general revenue-sharing funds allocated to operating expenditures, using the qualitative categories none, below average, and above average. Tables 4-7 and 4-8 provide the same information for the share allocated to capital expenditures. These tables present somewhat more detailed data than presented earlier, but provide little more in the way of explanation as to why these differences are occurring.

Looking first at the share allocated to operating expenditures, it is clear that the biggest cities in the Northeast and the Northcentral behave differently than the biggest cities in the South and West, and that big cities behave differently than other cities in their own regions. In the Northeast, 92 percent of the revenue-sharing money is in the "above average" category with the rest in the "none" category. It is interesting to note that the allocation for city size classes 1 and 2-6 are almost identical in the South and the West, while the smaller cities in the Northeast and Northcentral allocate even less to operating expenditures than do their counterparts in the South and West.

The differences among the share allocated to capital expenditures are very striking. Among the biggest cities there is a direct progression from the Northeast to the West with nothing going to capital expenditures in the Northeast and 24 percent in the "above average" category in the West. For the other cities, it is primarily the Northeast which differs from the others with more in the "none" category and less in the above average category.

In terms of the share allocated to tax reduction (Tables 4-9 and 4-10), all of the largest cities have very large "none" categories although the South has the smallest "none" and the biggest above average category. Looking at city sizes, lumping all cities under 300,000 misses the dramatic use of revenue-sharing funds for tax reduction among city size class 2 in the Northeast, but it is still clear that the Northeast is much more likely to have used revenue sharing for tax reduction than other areas. Their "none" category is approximately half the size of the other regions.

SUMMARY AND CONCLUSIONS

The above analysis makes it clear that many of the characteristics that influence behavior in the

Table 4-5

Share of GRS Allocated to Operating Expenditures, Cities with 300,000 or More Population

Region	None	Below Average	Above Average
Northeast	7.9%	0.0	92.1
Northcentral	7.4%	37.0	55.5
South	57.4%	35.5	7.1
West	39.9%	60.1	0.0

Table 4-6

Share of GRS Allocated to Operating Expenditures, Cities with Less than 300,000 Population

Region	None	Below Average	Above Average
Northeast	74.6%	24.4	1.0
Northcentral	65.2%	31.8	3.0
South	54.4%	45.4	0.3
West	58.7%	36.5	4.8

Table 4-7

Share of GRS Allocated to Capital Expenditures, Cities with 300,000 or More Population

Region	None	Below Average	Above Average
Northeast	100.0%	0.0	0.0
Northcentral	63.0%	37.0	0.0
South	44.5%	55.5	0.0
West	16.1%	60.1	23.8

Table 4-8

Share of GRS Allocated to Capital Expenditures, Cities with Less than 300,000 Population

Region	None	Below Average	Above Average
Northeast	46.2%	44.3	9.5
Northcentral	26.5%	43.5	30.0
South	19.9%	53.9	26.2
West	15.8%	44.0	40.2

Table 4-9

Share of GRS Allocated to Tax Reduction, Cities with 300,000 or More Population

Region	None	Below Average	Above Average
Northeast	92.1%	3.4	4.6
Northcentral	83.8%	8.8	7.4
South	78.9%	10.5	10.6
West	86.5%	13.5	0.0

Table 4-10

Share of GRS Allocated to Tax Reduction, Cities with Less Than 300,000 Population

Region	None	Below Average	Above Average
Northeast	39.6%	43.7	16.7
Northcentral	74.1%	23.8	2.1
South	70.2%	28.2	1.6
West	84.9%	13.8	1.3

larger cities are not the same or do not operate in the same way as the characteristics that influence behavior in smaller cities or in counties. Furthermore, it is evident that we are less successful in explaining variation in the share of revenue-sharing monies going to alternative uses in 1975 than in 1974, in smaller cities than in larger cities, and in counties than in cities.

A major conclusion of this chapter is that jurisdictions which spend significant amounts of their revenue-sharing funds on operating expenditures are using their GRS money primarily to maintain ongoing programs. These jurisdictions are more likely than others to mention fiscal or economic problems as either the first or second most important problem facing their community. They are also less likely than other communities to be concerned about the temporary nature of the revenue-sharing program. It is not clear whether this lack of concern reflects confidence that the program will be extended, or some other factor. A plausible alternative interpretation is that for these cities, concerns about getting through the next year or two override any concern about an event several years into the future.

A second major conclusion is that city size makes a big difference to the use of revenue-sharing funds. Being in city size class one rather than in three (300,000 or more compared to 25,000-99,999) increases the share going into operating expenditures by 21 percentage points. And large cities are much more likely than smaller ones facing their jurisdictions, a view which is strongly associated with the use of GRS funds on operating programs. Our results thus confirm the popular image of large cities as being financially hard pressed, and using the revenue sharing program to maintain existing programs rather than to expand programs or begin innovative new ones.

A very different set of characteristics are associated with jurisdictions which allocate major portions of their revenue-sharing funds to capital expenditures or tax reduction. In general, we can characterize cities and counties allocating substantial shares to capital expenditures as having a population less than 300,000; as not mentioning fiscal or economic problems as major problems; as

not having many other governmental grants; and as being concerned about the temporary nature of the revenue-sharing program. These responses conjure up an image of smaller jurisdictions that are not financially pressed, but that are concerned about the possibility of revenue sharing being discontinued, and therefore allocate their funds in such a way as not to incur future obligations.

Cities which allocate substantial shares to tax reduction can be characterized as also having a population less than 300,000 but in other ways as being different from the high capital expenditure jurisdictions. These cities are even more likely than those allocating large shares to operating expenditures to have mentioned fiscal and economic problems as being the major ones they face. And unlike either of the other groups, the higher their other grants, the higher the share going to tax reduction. Finally, both big and small cities showed a strong relationship between the share that went to tax reduction and agreement that the best thing to do with revenue sharing and to reduce taxes. The image evoked is thus one of smaller jurisdictions who are very concerned about fiscal or economic problems (which may include anything from inflation and unemployment to expected deficits) but who also have a substantial amount of other grant money. This may mean that such cities can afford to treat revenue sharing money as slack, or it may simply reflect the fact that these jurisdictions are indeed hard pressed and have a lower preference for public goods than other cities.

Counties allocating large shares of GRS funds to tax reduction behave somewhat differently. Big counties were much more likely to devote large shares to tax reduction than small ones, and those who did not mention fiscal or economic problems were more likely to use their revenue sharing in this way than those that did. Once again there was a strong relationship between tax abatement uses of GRS funds and agreement with the statement that the best thing to do with revenue sharing funds is reduce taxes. Although there is nothing intuitively surprising about these findings for counties, it is curious that on two important variables the signs are opposite those for cities. It should be noted, however, that the two variables with the most significant impact (other grants and the predisposition to tax abatement question) have the same signs in both city and county equations.

Two other variables were of some importance: income and region. The signs on the income variables were reasonable and of some interest, but we have not included them in the earlier part of the summary because of the difficulty of interpreting financial variables used in conjunction with survey measures. For bigger cities, our results suggest that the demand for public goods is positively related to income and that the implied income elasticity of demand is approximately one. For smaller cities, we had a very different finding. Here as income increases, the demand for private goods increases relative to the demand for public goods. Income was generally not important in the county equations.

As indicated in Chapter 2, region differentiates communities in terms of their uses of revenue sharing. There are two reasons why we have not included region in the equations. First, there is substantial correlation between region and several of the other variables in the model. Second, and more importantly, we have no theory of what region means as an explanatory variable. We think it may stand for the age of the community, but it might also reflect historical differences and/or a different distribution of functional responsibilities.

It was noted earlier that big cities tend to use most of their revenue-sharing funds for operating expenditures. The data by region qualify this finding somewhat. Operating outlay uses of GRS funds are far and away the dominant use for big cities in the Northeast and Northcentral region, but a much less important use for big cities in the South and West. There also exist striking differences among big cities in different regions in the share of GRS monies going to capital outlays. In the Northeast, no big city in our sample allocates revenue-sharing funds to capital expenditures, whereas in the West, 84 percent allocate some. Again as noted in Chapter 2, the Northeast was much more likely to have used revenue-sharing funds for tax reduction than other areas.

CHAPTER 5

Measuring the Fiscal Effects of Revenue Sharing Through Analysis of Budget Data

*Robin Barlow**

SUMMARY

As part of the revenue-sharing survey, local governments were asked to complete a form requesting expenditure and revenue data for each of the fiscal years 1972-75. The forms returned by a group of 75 cities with population between 25,000 and 300,000 were sufficiently detailed to permit a statistical analysis of the effects of revenue sharing on local expenditures and revenues.

The main conclusions of this analysis are as follows:

1. Only a small part of revenue-sharing funds seems to have been devoted to increasing local expenditures.

2. What little expansion of services did occur in fiscal years 1973 and 1974 was mostly in the current operations of the larger cities within the group studied.

3. In fiscal year 1975 the tax reductions caused by the grants were more significant on a per capita basis in the larger cities than in the smaller.

4. There was no evidence that a significant fraction of revenue-sharing funds were spent on capital projects.

5. The specific functions apparently expanded as a result of revenue sharing were fire protection, sewerage, highways, health, and general control.

Conclusions (2), (3), and (5), it might be noted, are to some extent consistent with the opinions of the officials interviewed in the main survey. Conclusions (1) and (4) contradict what the officials said.

---

*Professor, Department of Economics, The University of Michigan

INTRODUCTION

For measuring the effects of revenue sharing on State and local government expenditures and revenues, a number of different methodologies are available. The first relies on the judgments of government officials close to the problem. The Actual Use Reports submitted to the Office of Revenue Sharing and the interviews obtained by the Institute for Social Research survey reported in this volume are examples of this approach. A second approach, exemplified by the Brookings Institution's project of "Monitoring Revenue Sharing," uses the judgments of outside experts who are not employees of the governments being studied. A third approach is to collect historical budget data for a sample of communities and subject the data to statistical analysis to see what correlation exists between revenue-sharing grants on the one hand and local expenditures or revenues or other fiscal variables on the other.

This third method has both strengths and weaknesses. It avoids the subjective biases present in the individual responses on which the other two methods rely. But it is vulnerable to econometric problems like multicolinearity which make it difficult to disentangle the effects of revenue sharing from the effects of all the other influences bearing on the State and local fisc.

The annual historical data on which the third method must rely will eventually be available from the U.S. Bureau of the Census. But it will be some time before the Census releases data for all of the first three years of the revenue-sharing program. In the meantime, it is possible to carry out a preliminary analysis with some admittedly inferior but nonetheless serviceable data collected in the Institute for Social Research survey. These data consist of reports on expenditures and revenues for each of the four fiscal years 1972-75 provided for a group of 75 medium-sized cities located across the entire United States. A multiple regression analysis, described in the sections below, was performed on these data with the objective of discovering how the revenue-sharing funds had been spent.

THE SAMPLE

Each of the local governments contacted by the Institute for Social Research for the survey of officials' opinions on revenue sharing was asked also to complete a "General Information Form" requesting budget data for the previous four years. The information which was requested involved seven types of revenue (of which revenue-sharing funds were one), and current and capital expenditures on each of 16 functions.[1]

Attention was eventually focused on cities with 1970 population between 25,000 and 300,000. (Cities in this category received about 12 percent of revenue sharing allocations going to all State and local governments in 1972.) Cities with populations over 300,000 returned the information forms in too few numbers to make their inclusion worthwhile. Cities with populations under 25,000 did not have available from Census sources certain data needed for the statistical analysis (in particular, the ratio of manufacturing employment to the city's population).

Of the cities in between, 241 were successfully contacted for the survey of officials' opinions. Of this number, 123 also returned information forms which were fairly completely filled out. Eleven of these forms were rejected when inspection revealed wide discrepancies between their expenditure reports for fiscal year 1972 and what was indicated in the Census of Governments for those cities in that year. A further 37 cases had to be discarded for other reasons, usually because the manufacturing employment variable was not available.

Thus 75 cities were left for the statistical analysis of historical budget data. (This was the maximum number of cities used for any regression equation. For some of the regression analyses, further losses occurred because information was lacking on the particular dependent variable in question.) Preliminary examination indicates that certain important characteristics of the 75 cities used in the statistical analysis were not very different from those of the 166 other cities in the same population

group where interviews were obtained. The characteristics in question were mean-per-capita personal income, mean-per-capita tax effort, and mean-per-capita revenue-sharing grant. Thus *faute de mieux*, the 75 cities can be accepted as reasonably representative of all U.S. cities with populations between 25,000 and 300,000.

THE BASIC MODEL

We can define our first objective as measuring the effect of revenue sharing on city expenditues (either *in toto* or any component thereof, like capital expenditures or police expenditures). It must be recognized that expenditures are influenced by many factors besides revenue sharing, and that to isolate the effect of revenue sharing therefore involves holding constant the effects of the other important factors. Multiple regression analysis is the method employed here for holding the other effects constant.

The particular model used for this analysis is based on consumer demand theory, and takes the following general form:

$$E = f (Y, P, Z)$$

This equation says that city expenditure per capita on the public service (or group of services) in question is a function of certain independent variables, among which are the community's income (Y), the relative price of the service (P), and a set of community characteristics of an economic, social, political, demographic, or environmental nature (Z).[2] How should the revenue-sharing grant be fitted into this equation? More specifically, should the grant be treated as an addition to the community's income (a Y-variable) or as a reduction in the price of public services (a P-variable)? As Gramlich has shown, a price-reducing grant (like a matching grant) should appear in a regression equation explaining expenditures as an adjustment to price rather than as an addition to income.[3] This is because, in the case of a matching grant, the dollar amount of the grant is not independent of the amount of expenditures. Causation flows both ways between the allegedly dependent variable (expenditures) and the allegedly independent

---

[1]Police, fire, sewerage, other sanitation, education, highways, public transportation, welfare, hospitals, health, parks and recreation, housing and urban renewal, general control, libraries, utilities, and other functions.

[2]In a more complete analysis, demand and supply equations would be specified and estimated separately. It would be particularly important to do this if attention were focused on an explanatory variable which appeared simultaneously on both the demand and supply sides. In the present case, however, the variable of principal concern—the revenue sharing grant—would seem to enter the system on the demand side only. Hence the single-equation approach is fairly defensible.

[3]Edward M. Gramlich, "The Effect of Federal Grants on State-Local Expenditures: A Review of the Econometric Literature," *1969 Proceedings of the National Tax Association*, pp. 569-93.

variable (the grant), and the regression coefficient applying to the grant becomes difficult to interpret.

In fact, the dollar amount of the revenue-sharing grant is genuinely independent of the current level of municipal expenditures, and hence it would seem proper to treat the amount of the grant as an independent variable. The amount of the grant received in, say, fiscal year 1976 depends on the city's population, personal income, and taxes in prior years, but does not depend on anything that the city does in fiscal year 1976. In a regression equation relating municipal expenditures to the amount of the revenue sharing grant as well as to other Y-, P-, and Z-variables, the coefficient on the grant variable should then provide an unbiased estimate of the extent to which the grants lead to increased expenditures. (In fact other sources of bias are present, as we shall see shortly).

Of course the grants can logically produce other fiscal results besides an increase in public expenditures. There are three other possibilities: a reduction in local taxes (or in other locally raised revenues like user charges), a reduction in borrowing, or an increase in fund balances. It would be desirable therefore to conduct a more general analysis, and measure the effects of the revenue-sharing grants not only on public expenditures but also on the other three possibilities. In such an analysis, the coefficients on the revenue-sharing variables appearing in the equations for the four types of dependent variables would be so constrained that 100 percent of the revenue-sharing grants—no more and no less—would be distributed between the four possible uses.[4]

This cannot be done in the present case, because no attempt was made in the information forms to collect data on changes in indebtedness and in fund balances. Data were collected, however, on locally raised revenues, which were therefore analyzed as an additional dependent variable. With this exception, all of the dependent variables were some form of public expenditure: total current plus capital expenditures on all 16 functions, total current expenditure on all 16 functions, total capital expenditures on all 16 functions, and current plus capital expenditures on each of the 11 functions provided by enough cities to make analysis worthwhile.[5] That made a total of 15 dependent variables.

---

[4]A model of this type is contained in Edward M. Gramlich and Harvey Galper, "State and Local Fiscal Behavior and Federal Grant Policy," *Brookings Papers on Economic Activity,* 1973:1, pp. 15-58.

[5]The eleven frequently provided functions were police, fire, sewerage, other sanitation, highways, health, parks and recreation, general control, libraries, utilities, and "other functions." The five rarely provided functions were education, public transportation, welfare, hospitals, and housing and urban renewal.

EXPECTATIONS ABOUT THE EFFECTS OF REVENUE SHARING

What relationship, expressed in the form of a regression coefficient, should be expected between the revenue-sharing grant on the one hand and expenditures or taxes on the other? One body of theory, known sometimes as the "theory of grants," would suggest that revenue-sharing funds are mostly devoted to tax reduction.[6] In the framework offered by the simpler versions of this theory, a community is seen as dividing its income between the purchase of public commodities (via taxation) and the purchase of private commodities in such a way as to maximize utility. A lump-sum addition to community income, such as a revenue-sharing grant could be interpreted to be, would result in both increased private consumption (via tax reduction) and increased public consumption. The percentage increase in either category of consumption would be equal to the percentage increase in community income multiplied by the income-elasticity of the demand for that category of consumption.

For example, suppose that a city with personal income of $100 million was spending $5 million of that amount on municipal services, for which the income-elasticity of demand is assumed to be unity. A grant of $1 million is then received. The theory of grants would predict that expenditures on municipal services would rise by $50,000, and that taxes would be reduced by $950,000.

Many observers would argue that this prediction is more likely to be accurate in the long run than in the short run. In the long run, taxes might be expected to correspond fairly closely with collective preferences between public and private consumption. In the short run, taxes might be very little affected by the arrival of a grant, as bureaucrats seize the opportunity to expand their empires, or as politicians seize the opportunity to improve public services at no cost to local voters. A large and immediate tax cut would also be unlikely if politicians regarded the new program as temporary. A tax cut now would involve a politically painful tax increase later when the revenue-sharing program was terminated. On the other hand, one can well imagine circumstances in which politicians with limited time horizons see a tax cut as the way of obtaining maximum political advantage from the receipt of the grant.

At any rate, it is clear that empirical research should allow for the possibility that the short-run

---

[6]For a representative example of this theory, see James A. Wilde, "The Expenditure Effects of Grant-in-Aid Programs," *National Tax Journal,* XXI (September 1968), pp. 340-48.

response of expenditures and taxes to revenue-sharing grants may differ from the long-run response. In the present case, this means estimating the effects of revenue sharing separately in each of the first three years of the program, and noting whether any trend is apparent.

A further complication enters when it is realized that the revenue-sharing grant is somewhat different from a lump-sum grant. The formula used in allocating revenue-sharing funds among cities gives a reward for local tax effort. Compared with a lump-sum grant of equal size, a revenue-sharing grant might be expected to cause a larger increase in municipal expenditures and a smaller reduction in municipal taxes. However, the reward for tax effort (or the penalty for reducing taxes) is postponed one or more years into the future. A decision to cut taxes does not reduce this year's grant, but only next year's. If local politicians and bureaucrats are somewhat myopic (focusing their attention mostly on this year's budget), the response to a revenue-sharing grant would differ little from the response to a lump-sum grant.

SOME STATISTICAL PROBLEMS

Unfortunately there are some statistical problems which make it difficult to measure the true effects of revenue sharing from cross-sectional data, either in the short run or the long run. Because of the particular formula used in allocating revenue-sharing funds among cities, cross-sectional correlations exist between the amounts of the grants and certain municipal characteristics, and these correlations tend to bias the estimates of the effects of the grants on expenditures and taxes.

Most importantly, the allocation formula gives more money on a per capita basis to cities with lower personal incomes (in the previous year) and also more money to cities with higher local taxes (in the previous year). The cross-sectional negative correlation which the formula produces between personal income per capita and the amount of the revenue-sharing grant per capita makes it difficult to interpret the regression coefficient describing the effects of revenue sharing on expenditures. This coefficient will partly reflect the "pure" effect of the grants on expenditures, and partly the effect of personal income on expenditures (which other studies have usually found to be positive). The severity of the problem depends, of course, on the degree of correlation between per capita income and the per capita grant. In the equations estimated here, the correlation coefficient for these two variables was always in the neighborhood of 0.5—close to the borderline, perhaps, between being acceptably low and unacceptably high.

The appearance of lagged tax effort in the allocation formula causes some difficulties which must be discussed at greater length. It can be shown that the presence of this formula element will cause an overestimation of the effect of revenue sharing on both expenditures and taxes, regardless of whether the dependent variable is expressed in terms of levels or year-to-year changes. Suppose that in two cities A and B, with equal per capita personal incomes, expenditures and taxes were actually determined according to the following systems of three equations:

City A	City B

1a) $E_t = .1Y_t + .1R_t$ 1b) $E_t = .05Y_t + .1R_t$

2) $R_t = .1\,T_{t-1}$ 2) $R_t = .1\,T_{t-1}$

3) $T_{t-1} = E_{t-1} - R_{t-1}$ 3) $T_{t-1} = E_{t-1} - R_{t-1}$

where E is municipal expenditures, Y is personal income, R is the revenue-sharing grant, and T is municipal taxes (all expressed in per capita terms). Equations (1) indicate that 10¢ of each revenue-sharing dollar is devoted to raising municipal expenditures (and hence 90¢ to reducing taxes). Equation (2) is a simplification of the revenue-sharing allocation formula. Equation (3) is an accounting identity, based on the assumption of a balanced budget.

If income in each city is 1,000 in 1972 and grows by 10 percent annually, the E, R, and T variables will change as indicated in Table 5-1. (The revenue sharing program starts in 1973).

Given that the actual relationship between revenue sharing and expenditures is as indicated in Equation (1) above, what relationship would be obtained with cross-sectional regression analysis? The answer to this question is suggested in Figure 5-1, where the data from Table 5-1 are plotted, and it is clear that the answer would depend on whether the dependent variable (expenditures) is expressed in terms of levels or year-to-year changes.

If the dependent variable is defined as the annual level of expenditures, then Figure 5-1(a) indicates that $\partial E/\partial R$ estimated by least-squares regression would be approximately 12, regardless of whether the regression were performed for each of the years 1973-75 separately or for all years pooled. This is a highly exaggerated estimate of $\partial E/\partial R$, whose actual value is by assumption 0.1. Defining the dependent variable as the change in expenditures since the base year of 1972 [Figure 5-1(b)] or as the change in expenditures since the previous year [Figure 5-1(c)] likewise yields gross overestimates of $\partial E/\partial R$.

Figure 5
Relationships Between Revenue Sharing and Alternative Measures of City Expenditures

E . . . actual city expenditures per capita
E* . . . city expenditures per capita in absence of revenue sharing
R . . . revenue sharing grant per capita

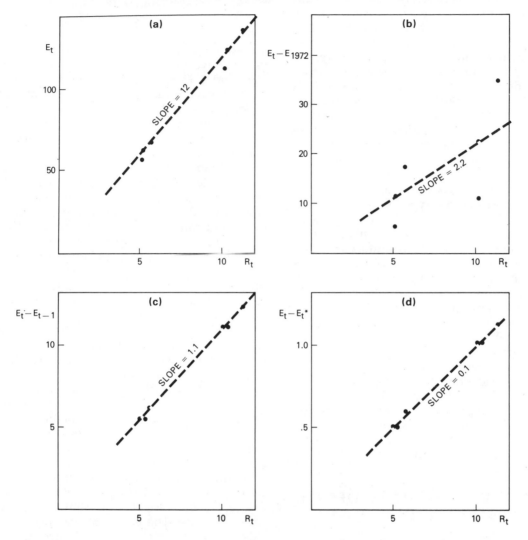

TABLE 5-1

Hypothetical Per Capita Data for Two Cities

		Personal Income (Y)	City Expenditures (E)	Revenue Sharing Grant (R)	City Taxes (T)	City Expenditures in Absence of Revenue Sharing (E*)
City A	1972.............	1,000	100.0	0.0	100.0	100.0
	1973.............	1,100	111.0	10.0	101.0	110.0
	1974.............	1,210	122.0	10.1	111.9	121.0
	1975.............	1,331	134.2	11.2	123.0	133.1
City B	1972.............	1,000	50.0	0.0	50.0	50.0
	1973.............	1,100	55.5	5.0	50.5	55.0
	1974.............	1,210	61.0	5.0	56.0	60.5
	1975.............	1,331	67.1	5.6	61.5	66.5

An unbiased estimate of $\partial E/\partial R$ could be obtained by expressing the dependent variable as the difference between the actual level of expenditures with revenue sharing (E) and what expenditures would have been in the absence of revenue sharing (E*). The relationship between the revenue-sharing grant and this version of the dependent variable is shown in Figure 5-1(d). We have attempted to estimate this particular relationship, but the results so far are inconclusive and are not reported here. It is obviously difficult to develop an equation for accurately predicting what expenditures would have been year by year without revenue sharing, because information is not available on a year-by-year basis for most of the predictors that might be useful in such an equation. We are continuing work along this line, and there may be results to report at some point in the future.

For the time being, however, we can report only those relationships of the type shown in Figures 5-1(a) and 5-1(b). This means that the regression coefficients shown below for the relationships between revenue sharing and expenditures must be regarded as overestimates of the true $\partial E/\partial R$. Where a significantly positive coefficient is obtained, its absolute value should be scaled down. Where a coefficient not significantly different from zero is obtained, some extra confidence can be placed in the conclusion that, expenditures responded little if at all to the grants.

Similarly, it can also be shown that our estimates of how taxes responded to revenue sharing are biased. In the numerical example discussed in this section, the actual $\partial T/\partial R$ is a *negative* 0.9. But regression analyses of the types shown in Figures 5-1(a), 5-1(b), and 5-1(c) will all show a *positive* relationship between taxes and revenue sharing.

ALTERNATIVE VERSIONS OF THE BASIC MODEL

Four different versions of the basic model discussed above were used for estimation purposes. In the first of these (Model I), each of the 15 dependent variables (expenditures or taxes) were expressed in terms of annual levels. Experimentation with the independent variables available—either from our own information forms or from Census sources—led to the selection of the following variables as representing the Y, P, and Z factors:

Y-variables ... personal income per capita
revenue sharing grant per capita
other intergovernmental grants per capita

P-variables ... ratio of manufacturing employment to city population[7]

Z-variables[8] ... percentage of population aged 65 or over
percentage of population aged under 18
percentage of population white

The equations containing these seven independent variables were estimated for each of the years 1973, 1974 and 1975 separately.

In Model II an eighth independent variable was added: the lagged value of the dependent variable. This was intended to represent all of the municipal characteristics which had been omitted as explanatory factors in Model I.

For Model III, three adjustments were made. First, the demographic variable describing the percentage of the population aged under 18 was excluded, on the grounds of its general nonsignificance and rather high correlation with the other age-structure variable. Second, a term reflecting interaction between city population and per capita revenue sharing was introduced. This term, the product of the two variables in question (population × per capita revenue sharing = revenue sharing), served to test whether larger cities within the group responded differently to revenue sharing than did the smaller ones. Third, the observations for the three years 1973-75 were pooled. At the same time, the independent variables which for any one city had different values in the different years (revenue sharing and other grants) were so defined as to yield a separate coefficient for each year. Revenue sharing per capita, for example, appears in each equation of Model III as three separate variables, identified by fiscal year. The variable "revenue sharing per capita in fiscal 1973" had the value of the actual 1973 per capita amount when the dependent variable was similarly dated, and zero otherwise. The effects of pooling are to provide a large sample size (and hence more stable coefficients) and to constrain to a single value the coefficients on the independent variables where

---

[7]This variable roughly measures the ability of a community to shift its local taxes to outsiders (through imposing taxes on business property), thus effectively lowering the price paid for local public services. Another possible P-variable—the ratio of retail and wholesale trade employment to city population—was found to be much weaker than the manufacturing employment variable as an explanatory factor.

[8]Other Z-variables which were tried but rejected on grounds of nonsignificance or multicolinearity include city population, percentage of housing units renter-occupied, percentage of families with female heads and children under 18, and region.

only one observation per city was available (like per capita personal income).

In Model IV, the dependent variable was expressed as the change since the base year of 1972. The independent variables were the same as those appearing in Model I, except that "other grants" were now expressed as changes since 1972 rather than as absolute levels.

THE RESULTS

The results of using Models I-IV to explain variations in each of the 15 dependent variables are shown in Tables 5-2—5-16. In general, Models I and III behaved in a fairly orderly way. Personal income and other grants per capita were frequently significant as explanatory factors (t-values greater than 2.0), and always with the expected positive sign.[9] The manufacturing variable, when significant in these models, usually possessed the expected positive sign. In the few cases where a significantly negative coefficient appeared, this variable was presumably reflecting some other influences besides the intended one of public service price.[10]

In Model II, the inclusion of the lagged dependent variable as an additional explanatory variable added greatly, not surprisingly, to the proportion of variance explained, but substantially reduced the explanatory power of other variables. Personal income and other grants per capita, in particular, were significant predictors much less often in Model II than in Models I and III, and occasionally possessed perverse (significantly negative) coefficients. Model IV in general had little explanatory power. This was to be expected, since the definition of its dependent variables (*changes* in expenditures or taxes) required that its independent variables also be defined in terms of changes, but only two of the independent variables (revenue sharing and other variables) could be so defined in view of data limitations. Some of this model's results, such as the significantly negative coefficients appearing from time to time on changes in other grants, were clearly perverse.

---

[9]Of the 60 coefficients on personal income per capita in Models I and III, 24 were significantly positive. Of the 105 coefficients on other grants per capita in these same models, 43 were significantly positive.

[10]This phenomenon was noted for three dependent variables: total capital expenditures, sewerage expenditures, and parks and recreation expenditures.

The main interest in the present context is in the coefficients of the revenue-sharing variables. The following observations can be offered:

1. In none of the first three years of revenue sharing were total city expenditures significantly correlated with the revenue-sharing grants (Table 5-1). In view of the bias noted earlier towards overstating the effect of revenue sharing on expenditures, this makes it seem very unlikely that a large fraction of the grants were devoted to raising expenditures. The result suggests that most of the grants were devoted to the other three possible dispositions: reductions in local taxes and other locally raised revenues, reductions in borrowing, and increases in fund balances.

2. The extent to which the grants led to tax reductions is difficult to measure, since the same bias which exaggerated the effect on expenditures tends to show that grants lead to higher taxes when the opposite may actually be the case. It is therefore interesting to see that despite this bias, Model I indicates a negative (though nonsignificant) relationship between taxes and the grants in 1975, Model II does the same for both 1974 and 1975, and Model III does the same for all of the three years analyzed (the coefficient on revenue sharing becoming significantly negative in 1975). These results, presented in Table 5-3, are consistent with the view that an increasingly large fraction of the revenue sharing grants were devoted to tax reduction as time proceeded. The behavior of the interaction term in Model III suggests that the per capita tax reductions were larger in the larger cities. (It should be noted that the significantly positive coefficient on 1975 revenue sharing per capita in Model III can only be understood in conjunction with the significantly negative coefficient on 1975 revenue sharing unadjusted for population. The impact of per capita revenue sharing on per capita expenditures is the net result of these two influences, and this net result becomes more negative as city size increases.)

3. In line with what was noted earlier about total expenditures, neither current nor capital expenditures were significantly increased by revenue sharing. However, in the case of current expenditures (Table 5-4) in 1973 and perhaps also in 1974, any increase that did occur was apparently concentrated in the larger

87

cities within the group studied. This conclusion can be derived from the conjunction of the negative coefficient on revenue sharing per capita with the positive coefficient on revenue sharing unadjusted for population, the interaction term. That larger cities were more likely than smaller cities to spend their revenue-sharing grants on current operations is in line with conclusions from the survey of officials' opinions.

4. It seems that the revenue-sharing grants not only failed to stimulate capital spending, they even produced a decline in such spending (Table 5-5). This at least is the conclusion which the four models suggest for 1973 and 1974. The result is anomalous, and contradicts some widely accepted views about the short-run effects of revenue sharing. A further search for data errors is clearly indicated before attempts are made to rationalize the result.

5. Of the 11 specific expenditure functions studied, 5 appear to have been significantly expanded by the revenue-sharing program: fire, health, sewerage, highways, and general control. According to Models I and III, fire expenditures per capita were significantly related to the revenue-sharing grants per capita in all of the first three years of the program (Table 5-7). In the second year, fiscal year 1974, there was some indication that the increases in fire expenditures per capita were greatest in the larger cities. The positive coefficient on the interaction term in Model III leads to this conclusion. Similarly, increases in health expenditures per capita seem to have been greatest in the larger cities (Table 5-11). As for sewerage and highways, however, the interaction terms tended to be negative, indicating that the per capita contributions of revenue sharing to these functions were greatest in the smaller cities (Tables 5-8 and 5-10). No difference between large and small cities appeared in the increases in per capita general control spending apparently stimulated by revenue sharing (Table 5-13).

6. In the regression analyses of expenditures on the other six specific functions, the coefficients on the revenue sharing variables were in general not significantly different from zero. The pattern formed by the few significant coefficients in these analyses does not point to any strong impact of revenue sharing on the expenditure areas in question, which are police (Table 5-6), other sanitation (Table 5-9), parks and recreation (Table 5-12), libraries (Table 5-14), public utilities (Table 5-15), and other functions (Table 5-16).

CONCLUDING REMARKS

The study reported here attempts to provide, on short notice and with inferior data, an econometric answer to the question of how revenue sharing has affected municipal expenditures and taxes. It is worth repeating what should be done to carry out a more satisfactory analysis:

—a large and representative sample (or even the universe) of all U.S. municipalities should be analysed, not merely a rather small and possibly unrepresentative sample of medium-sized cities

—data should be gathered not only on expenditures and receipts but on the other two elements in the budget equation—borrowing and fund withdrawals—and econometric techniques like stacking should be employed in measuring the fraction of a revenue-sharing grant which is devoted to each of the four possible budgetary dispositions (expenditure increase, tax decrease, fund accumulation, borrowing decrease).

—the positive cross-sectional correlation which the allocation formula produces between grants on the one hand and expenditures or taxes on the other should be taken into account, so that biases in estimating the causation from grants to expenditures or taxes can be avoided.

Unfortunately a study which accomplished all that would not be finished in time to enlighten the current debate about extending the revenue-sharing program, so inferior sources of information must be used instead.

Table 5-2
Multiple Regression Analysis of the Effects of Revenue Sharing on Per Capita Total Expenditures in Cities with 1970 Population Between 25,000 and 300,000

(Coefficients with t-values greater than 2.0 are marked with an asterisk)

Independent variables	Model number						
	I			II			III
	Form of dependent variable						
	1973 level	1974 level	1975 level	1973 level	1974 level	1975 level	1972-75 levels pooled
1. Personal income per capita ($)	0.018	0.050*	0.068*	0.012	0.020	0.012	0.025*
Revenue sharing grant per capita ($)							
2. Fiscal 1973	2.85			0.06			0.41
3. Fiscal 1974		0.22			0.09		−1.75
4. Fiscal 1975			1.33			1.03	3.15
Revenue sharing grant ($m.)							
5. Fiscal 1973							4.31
6. Fiscal 1974							23.33
7. Fiscal 1975							−20.45
Other grants per capita ($)							
8. Fiscal 1972							2.57*
9. Fiscal 1973	2.77*			3.42*			2.20*
10. Fiscal 1974		2.44*			0.27		2.47*
11. Fiscal 1975			1.89*			0.08	2.73*
12. Manufacturing employment as percent of population	1.73	3.12*	5.46*	−2.12*	0.10	0.66	3.67*
13. Percent of population aged 65 or older.	11.22	10.61*	6.53	−1.44	−2.21	−0.40	7.74*
14. Percentage of population aged under 18	2.85	5.08	5.89	2.49	−0.33	0.29	
15. Percent of population white	0.36	−3.25*	−3.08	0.19	−0.64	0.39	−0.96
16. Dependent variable lagged one year				0.60*	0.99*	0.98*	
Constant term	−267	−78	−119	5	27	−55	−14
Number of cases	56	62	64	43	57	57	277
Adjusted R²	.50	.45	.27	.93	.86	.79	.48

Independent variables	Model number IV		
	Form of dependent variable		
	1972-73 change	1972-74 change	1972-75 change
1. Personal income per capita ($)	0.010	0.022	0.060*
Revenue sharing grant per capita ($)			
2. Fiscal 1973	1.24		
3. Fiscal 1974		−0.10	
4. Fiscal 1975			2.01
5. Change in other grants per capita ($)	0.26	−0.07	2.49*
6. Manufacturing employment as percent of population	−2.69*	−1.09	−2.29
7. Percent of population aged 65 or over	2.78	1.52	−12.21*
8. Percent of population aged under 18	2.03	1.62	−3.10
9. Percent of population white	−0.10	−0.80	−1.53
Constant term	−94	−15	98
Number of cases	42	45	43
Adjusted R²	.00	.00	.43

Table 5-3
Multiple Regression Analysis of the Effects of Revenue Sharing on Per Capita Locally Raised Revenue in Cities with 1970 Population Between 25,000 and 300,000
(Coefficients with t-values greater than 2.0 are marked with an asterisk)

Independent variables	Model number I — Form of dependent variable			Model number II			Model number III
	1973 level	1974 level	1975 level	1973 level	1974 level	1975 level	1972-75 levels pooled
1. Personal income per capita ($)	0.047*	0.058*	0.023	0.000	−0.010	−0.015	0.032*
Revenue sharing grant per capita ($)							
2. Fiscal 1973	7.88*	....	....	−0.06	....	....	2.35
3. Fiscal 1974	....	2.04	....	....	−1.56	....	0.34
4. Fiscal 1975	....	....	−2.83	....	....	−4.13*	4.22*
Revenue sharing grant ($m.)							
5. Fiscal 1973	....	....	....	....	....	....	11.04
6. Fiscal 1974	....	....	....	....	....	....	22.80
7. Fiscal 1975	....	....	....	....	....	....	−23.79*
Other grants per capita ($)							
8. Fiscal 1972	....	....	....	....	....	....	3.07*
9. Fiscal 1973	1.58*	....	....	0.10	....	....	1.75*
10. Fiscal 1974	....	2.62*	....	....	0.47*	....	2.05*
11. Fiscal 1975	....	....	1.96*	....	....	0.16	2.04
12. Manufacturing employment as percent of population	1.41	3.61*	2.55	−0.26	−0.09	−1.17	1.91*
13. Percent of population aged 65 or older	16.98*	11.43*	14.82*	−1.97*	−1.15	4.84	9.67*
14. Percentage of population aged under 18	6.86	6.24	−3.61	0.98	−0.18	−8.52*	....
15. Percent of population white	0.94	−3.75*	−2.49	0.15	−0.20	0.39	−1.07
16. Dependent variable lagged one year	....	....	....	1.07*	1.13*	0.89*	....
Constant term	−649	−181	245	34	70	357	−77
Number of cases	69	73	68	74	74	68	277
Adjusted R²	.45	.38	.27	.98	.92	.72	.39

Independent variables	Model number IV — Form of dependent variable		
	1972-73 change	1972-74 change	1972-75 change
1. Personal income per capita ($)	0.004	−0.008	−0.026
Revenue sharing grant per capita ($)			
2. Fiscal 1973	0.67	....	....
3. Fiscal 1974	....	−1.70	....
4. Fiscal 1975	....	....	−4.33
5. Change in other grants per capita ($)	0.54	0.54	0.59
6. Manufacturing employment as percent of population	0.11	1.14	−0.14
7. Percent of population aged 65 or over	−0.06	3.44	4.44
8. Percent of population aged under 18	0.05	1.82	−9.90*
9. Percent of population white	0.16	−0.73	1.33
Constant term	−33	50	347
Number of cases	54	54	53
Adjusted R²	.00	.00	.13

Table 5-4
Multiple Regression Analysis of the Effects of Revenue Sharing on Per Capita
Current Expenditures in Cities with 1970 population between 25,000 and 300,000

(Coefficients with t-values greater than 2.0 are marked with an asterisk)

Independent variables	Model number						
	I			II			III
	Form of dependent variable						1972-75 levels pooled
	1973 level	1974 level	1975 level	1973 level	1974 level	1975 level	
1. Personal income per capita ($)	0.016	0.057*	0.033	0.035	0.016	−0.008	0.013
Revenue sharing grant per capita ($)							
2. Fiscal 1973	0.36	....	....	12.48*	....	....	−5.96*
3. Fiscal 1974	....	2.26	....	....	−2.00	....	−1.82
4. Fiscal 1975	....	....	−2.29	....	....	−1.92	1.10
Revenue sharing grant ($m.)							
5. Fiscal 1973	....	....	....	....	....	....	66.49*
6. Fiscal 1974	....	....	....	....	....	....	35.09*
7. Fiscal 1975	....	....	....	....	....	....	−8.71
Other grants per capita ($)							
8. Fiscal 1972	....	....	....	....	....	....	1.95*
9. Fiscal 1973	2.17*	....	....	5.36*	....	....	3.49*
10. Fiscal 1974	....	1.12	....	....	0.67	....	1.62*
11. Fiscal 1975	....	....	0.68	....	....	0.39	2.26*
12. Manufacturing employment as percent of population	−1.10	4.46*	1.22	1.26	−0.58	0.23	4.62
13. Percent of population aged 65 or older.	3.79	12.38*	−4.25	−3.02	3.30	3.70	8.14
14. Percentage of population aged under 18	−1.01	7.08	−4.86	5.01	−0.43	−4.41	....
15. Percent of population white	0.28	−3.72*	−1.37	1.59	−0.72	0.70	−2.37*
16. Dependent variable lagged one year	....	....	....	1.86*	0.36*	0.78*	....
Constant term	−10	−172	339	−841	106	218	113
Number of cases	33	42	42	24	36	38	242
Adjusted R²	.40	.47	.15	.96	.87	.77	.46

Independent variables	Model number IV		
	Form of dependent variable		
	1972-73 change	1972-74 change	1972-75 change
1. Personal income per capita ($)	−0.060	0.018	0.001
Revenue sharing grant per capita ($)			
2. Fiscal 1973	3.22	....	....
3. Fiscal 1974	....	0.43	....
4. Fiscal 1975	....	....	−1.86
5. Change in other grants per capita ($)	−10.05*	0.26	0.40
6. Manufacturing employment as percent of population	17.77*	0.70	0.58
7. Percent of population aged 65 or over	28.99*	2.46	−3.73
8. Percent of population aged under 18	12.46	1.80	−1.83
9. Percent of population white	−3.52	−0.63	0.17
Constant term	−260	−70	202
Number of cases	24	27	26
Adjusted R²	.77	.22	.00

Table 5-5
Multiple Regression Analysis of the Effects of Revenue Sharing on Per Capita Capital Expenditures in Cities with 1970 Population Between 25,000 and 300,000
(Coefficients with t-values greater than 2.0 are marked with an asterisk)

Independent variables	Model number I			Model number II			Model number III
	Form of dependent variable						
	1973 level	1974 level	1975 level	1973 level	1974 level	1975 level	1972-75 levels pooled
1. Personal income per capita ($)	0.002	−0.003	0.016	−0.018	−0.014	0.024	−0.003
Revenue sharing grant per capita ($)							
2. Fiscal 1973	−0.46	....	....	−1.57	....	....	−1.51*
3. Fiscal 1974	....	−2.15*	....	....	−1.84*	....	−0.48
4. Fiscal 1975	....	....	1.71	....	....	3.66*	−0.51
Revenue sharing grant ($m.)							
5. Fiscal 1973	....	....	....	....	....	....	6.72
6. Fiscal 1974	....	....	....	....	....	....	−8.96
7. Fiscal 1975	....	....	....	....	....	....	−5.66
Other grants per capita ($)							
8. Fiscal 1972	....	....	....	....	....	....	0.41
9. Fiscal 1973	0.44	....	....	0.05	....	....	0.66*
10. Fiscal 1974	....	0.74*	....	....	0.48*	....	0.80*
11. Fiscal 1975	....	....	1.09*	....	....	0.55	1.07*
12. Manufacturing employment as percent of population	−0.40	−1.15*	−0.64	0.74	−1.21*	−0.33	−0.99*
13. Percent of population aged 65 or older	0.65	1.78	1.94	0.71	1.99	0.49	0.78
14. Percentage of population aged under 18	0.61	−0.08	3.86	−0.06	−0.93	3.11	....
15. Percent of population white	0.52	−0.02	−0.72	0.09	0.85	−0.20	−0.03
16. Dependent variable lagged one year	....	....	....	1.42*	0.32	0.53*	....
Constant term	−54	50	-141	73	35	−209	38
Number of cases	31	40	43	23	33	36	241
Adjusted R²	.03	.44	.38	.47	.55	.36	.17

Independent variables	Model number IV		
	Form of dependent variable		
	1972-73 change	1972-74 change	1972-75 change
1. Personal income per capita ($)	−0.005	−0.011	0.018
Revenue sharing grant per capita ($)			
2. Fiscal 1973	−0.62	....	....
3. Fiscal 1974	....	−0.67	....
4. Fiscal 1975	....	....	3.28
5. Change in other grants per capita ($)	1.09	0.94*	1.74*
6. Manufacturing employment as percent of population	0.31	0.15	0.13
7. Percent of population aged 65 or over	−0.92	1.24	−2.42
8. Percent of population aged under 18	0.43	−0.60	1.71
9. Percent of population white	0.53	0.78	0.87
Constant term	−23	−5	−208
Number of cases	23	28	27
Adjusted R²	.00	.60	.57

Table 5-6
Multiple Regression Analysis of the Effects of Revenue Sharing on Per Capita Police Expenditures in Cities with 1970 Population Between 25,000 and 300,000
(Coefficients with t-values greater than 2.0 are marked with an asterisk)

Independent variables	Model I 1973 level	1974 level	1975 level	Model II 1973 level	1974 level	1975 level	Model III 1972-75 levels pooled
1. Personal income per capita ($)	0.000	0.008*	0.008	0.008*	0.008*		0.006*
Revenue sharing grant per capita ($)						NOT AVAILABLE	
2. Fiscal 1973	0.50	....	....	0.34	....		0.07
3. Fiscal 1974	....	−0.05	....	....	−0.04		−0.29
4. Fiscal 1975	....	....	0.01	....	....		−0.02
Revenue sharing grant ($m.)							
5. Fiscal 1973	....	....	....	....	....		−0.90
6. Fiscal 1974	....	....	....	....	....		4.12
7. Fiscal 1975	....	....	....	....	....		4.93
Other grants per capita ($)							
8. Fiscal 1972	....	....	....	....	....		0.09
9. Fiscal 1973	0.05	....	....	0.17*	....		0.13
10. Fiscal 1974	....	0.13	....	....	0.47		0.12
11. Fiscal 1975	....	....	0.17*	....	....		0.14*
12. Manufacturing employment as percent of population	0.45	−0.02	0.03	−0.16	−0.08		0.14
13. Percent of population aged 65 or older.	2.01	0.89	0.67	1.04	0.70		1.19*
14. Percentage of population aged under 18	−0.37	−0.10	−0.26	0.25	0.12		....
15. Percent of population white	−0.07	−0.68*	−0.72*	−0.43*	−0.61*		−0.53*
16. Dependent variable lagged one year	....	....	....	0.11*	0.27*		....
Constant term	17	54	62	7	41		40
Number of cases	69	74	70	55	75		276
Adjusted R²	.11	.24	.19	.46	.34		.23

Independent variables	Model IV 1972-73 change	1972-74 change	1972-75 change
1. Personal income per capita ($)	0.002	0.000	0.001
Revenue sharing grant per capita ($)			
2. Fiscal 1973	0.32	....	....
3. Fiscal 1974	....	−0.11	....
4. Fiscal 1975	....	....	−0.56
5. Change in other grants per capita ($)	0.01	−0.49	0.35
6. Manufacturing employment as percent of population	−1.43*	−1.54*	−1.85*
7. Percent of population aged 65 or over	1.43	1.96	−0.32
8. Percent of population aged under 18	1.38	1.20	0.29
9. Percent of population white	−0.40	−0.40	−0.80
Constant term	−20	7	78
Number of cases	54	54	53
Adjusted R²	.06	.15	.14

Table 5-7

Multiple Regression Analysis of the Effects of Revenue Sharing on Per Capita Fire Expenditures in Cities with 1970 Population between 25,000 and 300,000

(Coefficients with t-values greater than 2.0 are marked with an asterisk)

Independent variables	Model I 1973 level	Model I 1974 level	Model I 1975 level	Model II 1973 level	Model II 1974 level	Model II 1975 level	Model III 1972-75 levels pooled
1. Personal income per capita ($)	0.003*	0.007*	0.004	0.002	0.003	−0.001	0.004*
Revenue sharing grant per capita ($)							
2. Fiscal 1973	0.44*	....	....	0.34	....	....	0.34*
3. Fiscal 1974	....	0.74*	....	....	0.36*	....	0.33*
4. Fiscal 1975	....	....	0.89*	....	....	0.12	1.02*
Revenue sharing grant ($m.)							
5. Fiscal 1973							0.20
6. Fiscal 1974							2.72*
7. Fiscal 1975							2.03
Other grants per capita ($)							
8. Fiscal 1972							0.22*
9. Fiscal 1973	0.17*	....	....	0.06	....	....	0.12*
10. Fiscal 1974	....	0.10*	....	....	0.05	....	0.08*
11. Fiscal 1975	....	....	−0.02	....	....	−0.05	0.00
12. Manufacturing employment as percent of population	0.14	0.19	0.19	0.00	0.07	0.11	0.24*
13. Percent of population aged 65 or older.	0.87*	0.51	0.65	0.49	0.00	0.65*	0.79*
14. Percentage of population aged under 18	−0.08	−0.10	−0.27	0.02	−0.23	0.19	....
15. Percent of population white	−0.12	−0.22	−0.33*	−0.01	−0.01	−0.23*	−0.24*
16. Dependent variable lagged one year	....	....	....	0.62*	0.58*	0.87*	....
Constant term	−1	−1	31	−10	0	17	8
Number of cases	65	72	67	51	73	67	264
Adjusted R²	.49	.50	.41	.64	.66	.78	.53

Independent variables	Model IV 1972-73 change	Model IV 1972-74 change	Model IV 1972-75 change
1. Personal income per capita ($)	0.001	0.002	0.001
Revenue sharing grant per capita ($)			
2. Fiscal 1973	0.17	....	....
3. Fiscal 1974	....	0.24*	....
4. Fiscal 1975	....	....	−0.49
5. Change in other grants per capita ($)	−0.12	0.01	0.13*
6. Manufacturing employment as percent of population.	−0.13	−0.21*	−0.24
7. Percent of population aged 65 or over	0.09	−0.04	−0.23
8. Percent of population aged under 18.	−0.08	−0.08	−0.06
9. Percent of population white	0.05	−0.02	−0.01
Constant term	−3	1	9
Number of cases	50	52	51
Adjusted R²	.00	.17	.17

Table 5-8

Multiple Regression Analysis of the Effects of Revenue Sharing on Per Capita Sewerage Expenditures in Cities with 1970 Population Between 25,000 and 300,000

(Coefficients with t-values greater than 2.0 are marked with an asterisk)

Independent variables	Model number I			Model number II			Model number III
	Form of dependent variable						1972-75 levels pooled
	1973 level	1974 level	1975 level	1973 level	1974 level	1975 level	
1. Personal income per capita ($)	0.000	0.001	0.004	0.000	0.002	0.003	0.002
Revenue sharing grant per capita ($)							
2. Fiscal 1973	0.41*			0.00			0.47
3. Fiscal 1974		−0.06			0.04		0.32
4. Fiscal 1975			1.54*			1.52*	2.67*
Revenue sharing grant ($m.)							
5. Fiscal 1973							−1.23
6. Fiscal 1974							−1.82
7. Fiscal 1975							−10.57*
Other grants per capita ($)							
8. Fiscal 1972							0.16
9. Fiscal 1973	0.02			−0.05			0.09
10. Fiscal 1974		0.17*			0.15*		0.19*
11. Fiscal 1975			0.09			0.05	−0.04
12. Manufacturing employment as percent of population	−0.17	−0.46*	−1.22*	0.07	−0.31	−1.07*	−0.58*
13. Percent of population aged 65 or older	1.34	0.93	−3.13	1.36*	0.19	−3.90*	0.23
14. Percentage of population aged under 18	0.82	0.33	−2.46	1.07*	−0.10	−2.81*	
15. Percent of population white	−0.01	−0.11	−0.34	−0.10	0.05	0.42	−0.10
16. Dependent variable lagged one year				0.86*	0.70*	0.58*	
Constant term	−31	−1	79	−36	−9	85	9
Number of cases	55	60	58	43	61	58	223
Adjusted R^2	.14	.06	.24	.74	.19	.32	.27

Independent variables	Model number IV		
	Form of dependent variable		
	1972-73 change	1972-74 change	1972-75 change
1. Personal income per capita ($)	0.001	0.004	0.012
Revenue sharing grant per capita ($)			
2. Fiscal 1973	−0.12		
3. Fiscal 1974		0.25	
4. Fiscal 1975			1.89
5. Change in other grants per capita ($)	−0.19	0.59*	0.34
6. Manufacturing employment as percent of population	0.10	−0.18	−1.85*
7. Percent of population aged 65 or over	1.21*	0.70	−5.14*
8. Percent of population aged under 18	1.08*	0.51	−3.21
9. Percent of population white	−0.11	−0.50	0.58
Constant term	−39	4	46
Number of cases	41	41	40
Adjusted R^2	.26	.30	.26

Table 5-9
Multiple Regression Analysis of the Effects of Revenue Sharing on Per Capita Other Sanitation Expenditures in Cities with 1970 Population Between 25,000 and 300,000
(Coefficients with t-values greater than 2.0 are marked with an asterisk)

Independent variables	Model number I 1973 level	I 1974 level	I 1975 level	II 1973 level	II 1974 level	II 1975 level	III 1972-75 levels pooled
1. Personal income per capita ($)	0.003*	0.002	0.003	0.000	0.000	0.000	0.004*
Revenue sharing grant per capita ($)							
2. Fiscal 1973	0.16	....	....	0.08	....	....	0.03
3. Fiscal 1974	....	−0.26	....	....	−0.15*	....	−0.07
4. Fiscal 1975	....	....	−0.07	....	....	0.02	0.08
Revenue sharing grant ($m.)							
5. Fiscal 1973							0.12
6. Fiscal 1974							0.24
7. Fiscal 1975							−0.13
Other grants per capita ($)							
8. Fiscal 1972							0.03
9. Fiscal 1973	0.07	....	....	−0.01	....	....	0.03
10. Fiscal 1974	....	0.05	....	....	0.01	....	0.06*
11. Fiscal 1975	....	....	0.05	....	....	0.01	0.03
12. Manufacturing employment as percent of population	−0.12	−0.03	0.08	−0.04	0.00	0.05	0.01
13. Percent of population aged 65 or older	0.73	0.25	−0.22	0.28	0.03	−0.12	0.48*
14. Percentage of population aged under 18	0.12	−0.42	−0.32	0.23	−0.20	−0.03	....
15. Percent of population white	−0.48*	−0.52*	−0.60*	0.05	−0.19*	−0.02	−0.54*
16. Dependent variable lagged one year	....	....	....	1.16*	0.82*	1.06*	....
Constant term	25	63	60	−6	28	4	38
Number of cases	62	65	62	49	66	62	243
Adjusted R²	.42	.45	.39	.88	.93	.95	.41

Independent variables	Model number IV 1972-73 change	1972-74 change	1972-75 change
1. Personal income per capita ($)	0.001	0.000	0.000
Revenue sharing grant per capita ($)			
2. Fiscal 1973	0.09	....	....
3. Fiscal 1974	....	−0.08	....
4. Fiscal 1975	....	....	0.01
5. Change in other grants per capita ($)	0.09	0.01	0.00
6. Manufacturing employment as percent of population	−0.05	−0.04	0.04
7. Percent of population aged 65 or over	0.34	−0.09	0.25
8. Percent of population aged under 18	0.26	−0.11	−0.03
9. Percent of population white	−0.11	−0.18*	−0.25*
Constant term	−4	23	22
Number of cases	48	48	47
Adjusted R²	.08	.50	.44

Table 5-10
Multiple Regression Analysis of the Effects of Revenue Sharing on Per Capita Highway Expenditures in Cities with 1970 Population Between 25,000 and 300,000
(Coefficients with t-values greater than 2.0 are marked with an asterisk)

Independent variables	Model I — 1973 level	Model I — 1974 level	Model I — 1975 level	Model II — 1973 level	Model II — 1974 level	Model II — 1975 level	Model III — 1972-75 levels pooled
1. Personal income per capita ($)	0.001	0.002	0.002	−0.003	0.002	0.002	0.003
Revenue sharing grant per capita ($)							
2. Fiscal 1973	−0.30	....	....	−0.86	....	....	0.09
3. Fiscal 1974	....	0.42	....	....	0.50	....	0.70*
4. Fiscal 1975	....	....	0.25	....	....	0.15	0.93*
Revenue sharing grant ($m.)							
5. Fiscal 1973	....	....	....	....	....	....	−2.84
6. Fiscal 1974	....	....	....	....	....	....	−4.92*
7. Fiscal 1975	....	....	....	....	....	....	−5.94*
Other grants per capita ($)							
8. Fiscal 1972	....	....	....	....	....	....	−0.07
9. Fiscal 1973	0.14	....	....	0.23	....	....	0.05
10. Fiscal 1974	....	−0.07	....	....	−0.08	....	0.00
11. Fiscal 1975	....	....	0.05	....	....	0.10	0.05
12. Manufacturing employment as percent of population	−0.12	0.01	0.26	−0.49	0.04	0.00	−0.06
13. Percent of population aged 65 or over	−0.35	1.33	0.64	−1.51	1.38*	1.05	0.08
14. Percentage of population aged under 18	−0.59	1.48*	0.96	−1.96	1.62*	−0.59	....
15. Percent of population white	0.31	0.37	−0.05	0.18	0.25	0.20	0.32*
16. Dependent variable lagged one year	....	....	....	0.94*	0.24*	0.92*	....
Constant term	15	−77	−18	85	−79	38	−16
Number of cases	67	68	68	53	69	67	261
Adjusted R²	.00	.19	.00	.09	.30	.35	.12

Independent variables	Model IV — 1972-73 change	Model IV — 1972-74 change	Model IV — 1972-75 change
1. Personal income per capita ($)	−0.003	−0.001	0.000
Revenue sharing grant per capita ($)			
2. Fiscal 1973	−0.62	....	....
3. Fiscal 1974	....	0.25	....
4. Fiscal 1975	....	....	−0.11
5. Change in other grants per capita ($)	−0.04	0.11	0.21*
6. Manufacturing employment as percent of population	−0.37	−0.22	−0.52
7. Percent of population aged 65 or over	−0.77	1.19*	−0.92
8. Percent of population aged under 18	−1.73	0.45	−0.91
9. Percent of population white	0.32	0.17	−0.20
Constant term	64	−33	65
Number of cases	51	50	50
Adjusted R²	.00	.11	.09

TABLE 5-11
Multiple Regression Analysis of the Effects of Revenue Sharing on Per Capita Health Expenditures in Cities with 1970 Population between 25,000 and 300,000
(Coefficients with t-values greater than 2.0 are marked with an asterisk)

Independent variables	Model number I Form of dependent variable 1973 level	1974 level	1975 level	Model number II Form of dependent variable 1973 level	1974 level	1975 level	Model number III 1972-75 levels pooled
1. Personal income per capita ($)	0.002	0.001	0.001*	0.000	0.000	0.001*	−0.001
Revenue sharing grant per capita ($)							
2. Fiscal 1973	−0.04	....	....	−0.04*	....	....	0.01
3. Fiscal 1974	....	0.11*	....	....	0.04	....	−0.16*
4. Fiscal 1975	....	....	0.23*	....	....	0.27*	−0.11
Revenue sharing grant ($m.)							
5. Fiscal 1973							0.13
6. Fiscal 1974							1.94*
7. Fiscal 1975							1.67*
Other grants per capita ($)							
8. Fiscal 1972							0.03*
9. Fiscal 1973	0.01	....	....	0.00	....	....	0.02
10. Fiscal 1974	....	0.02	....	....	0.02*	....	0.02*
11. Fiscal 1975	....	....	0.00	....	....	−0.02*	0.01
12. Manufacturing employment as percent of population	0.09*	0.11*	0.08	0.01	−0.01	0.02	0.06*
13. Percent of population aged 65 or over	0.47*	0.50*	0.53*	0.02	−0.14	0.23	0.11*
14. Percentage of population aged under 18	0.40*	0.47*	0.43*	0.04	−0.05	0.18	....
15. Percent of population white	−0.06	−0.17*	−0.09	0.01	−0.06	−0.01	−0.02
16. Dependent variable lagged one year				0.88*	1.02*	0.96*	....
Constant term	−12	−10	−18	−1	6	−14	3
Number of cases	34	40	37	21	40	37	137
Adjusted R²	.41	.48	.32	.98	.75	.56	.49

Independent variables	Model number IV Form of dependent variable 1972-73 change	1972-74 change	1972-75 change
1. Personal income per capita ($)	0.000	0.000	0.002*
Revenue sharing grant per capita ($)			
2. Fiscal 1973	−0.04*	....	....
3. Fiscal 1974	....	0.01	....
4. Fiscal 1975	....	....	0.34*
5. Change in other grants per capita ($)	0.03	−0.02	−0.03*
6. Manufacturing employment as percent of population	−0.01	−0.04	0.04
7. Percent of population aged 65 or over	−0.04	−0.07	0.25
8. Percent of population aged under 18	0.00	−0.01	0.23
9. Percent of population white	−0.02	−0.02	0.03
Constant term	0	1	−22
Number of cases	21	23	22
Adjusted R²	.70	.04	.65

Table 5-12
Multiple Regression Analysis of the Effects of Revenue Sharing on Per Capita Parks and Recreation Expenditures in Cities with 1970 Population between 25,000 and 300,000
(Coefficients with t-values greater than 2.0 are marked with an asterisk)

Independent variables	Model I 1973 level	Model I 1974 level	Model I 1975 level	Model II 1973 level	Model II 1974 level	Model II 1975 level	Model III 1972-75 levels pooled
1. Personal income per capita ($)	0.005*	0.008*	0.009*	−0.001	0.004*	0.000	0.007*
Revenue sharing grant per capita ($)							
2. Fiscal 1973	0.45*	....	....	0.21	....	....	0.07
3. Fiscal 1974	....	0.16	....	....	0.10	....	0.05
4. Fiscal 1975	....	....	0.27	....	....	0.04	0.22
Revenue sharing grant ($m.)							
5. Fiscal 1973							0.92
6. Fiscal 1974							1.31
7. Fiscal 1975							−0.07
Other grants per capita ($)							
8. Fiscal 1972							0.07
9. Fiscal 1973	0.04	....	....	0.04	....	....	0.06
10. Fiscal 1974	....	0.11*	....	....	0.05	....	0.09*
11. Fiscal 1975	....	....	0.18*	....	....	0.07	0.15*
12. Manufacturing employment as percent of population	−0.05	−0.30*	−0.30	−0.15	−0.12	−0.21	−0.21*
13. Percent of population aged 65 or over	1.35*	−0.06	−0.77	0.38	−0.45	−0.80	0.23
14. Percentage of population aged under 18	0.51	−0.25	−0.59	0.27	−0.30	−0.44	....
15. Percent of population white	−0.25	−0.21	−0.11	−0.08	0.02	0.18	−0.20*
16. Dependent variable lagged one year	....	....	....	1.25*	0.81*	1.14*	....
Constant term	−17	12	17	−8	3	5	4
Number of cases	62	66	63	50	66	63	247
Adjusted R²	.19	.18	.16	.64	.74	.72	.21

Independent variables	Model IV 1972-73 change	Model IV 1972-74 change	Model IV 1972-75 change
1. Personal income per capita ($)	0.001	0.005	0.007
Revenue sharing grant per capita ($)			
2. Fiscal 1973	0.24	....	....
3. Fiscal 1974	....	0.14	....
4. Fiscal 1975	....	....	0.27
5. Change in other grants per capita ($)	0.00	0.04	0.19*
6. Manufacturing employment as percent of population	−0.11	−0.20	−0.50*
7. Percent of population aged 65 or over	0.70	−0.08	−1.40
8. Percent of population aged under 18	0.41	−0.14	−0.57
9. Percent of population white	0.12	−0.15	0.00
Constant term	−12	−2	7
Number of cases	49	49	48
Adjusted R²	.03	.01	.11

Table 5-13
Multiple Regression Analysis of the Effects of Revenue Sharing on Per Capita General Control Expenditures in Cities with 1970 population between 25,000 and 300,000

(Coefficients with t-values greater than 2.0 are marked with an asterisk)

	Model number						
	I			II			III
Independent variables	Form of dependent variable						
	1973 level	1974 level	1975 level	1973 level	1974 level	1975 level	1972-75 levels pooled
1. Personal income per capita ($)	−0.001	0.000	0.003	0.001	0.000	0.001	0.000
Revenue sharing grant per capita ($)							
2. Fiscal 1973	−0.01	....	....	0.13*	....	....	0.17
3. Fiscal 1974	....	−0.03	....	....	−0.13	....	0.12
4. Fiscal 1975	....	....	0.60*	....	....	0.30*	0.16
Revenue sharing grant ($m.)							
5. Fiscal 1973							−2.70
6. Fiscal 1974							0.31
7. Fiscal 1975							1.26
Other grants per capita ($)							
8. Fiscal 1972							0.00
9. Fiscal 1973	−0.05	....	....	−0.01	....	....	0.09
10. Fiscal 1974	....	0.02	....	....	0.07	....	0.00
11. Fiscal 1975	....	....	0.03	....	....	0.00	0.01
12. Manufacturing employment as percent of population	0.54*	0.01	0.18	−0.07	0.14	0.12	0.18*
13. Percent of population aged 65 or over	1.33	−0.07	0.14	0.07	−0.39	0.20	0.54*
14. Percentage of population aged under 18	0.39	−0.48	−0.06	−0.05	−0.66	0.11	....
15. Percent of population white	0.20	−0.11	0.12	0.03	0.00	0.05	0.12
16. Dependent variable lagged one year	....	....	....	1.09*	0.34*	0.75*	....
Constant term	−27	21	−18	−5	36	−16	−7
Number of cases	69	74	71	55	75	71	278
Adjusted R²	.11	.00	.09	.92	.07	.70	.08

	Model number IV		
Independent variables	Form of dependent variable		
	1972-73 change	1972-74 change	1972-75 change
1. Personal income per capita ($)	0.001	0.000	0.003
Revenue sharing grant per capita ($)			
2. Fiscal 1973	0.11*	....	....
3. Fiscal 1974	....	0.06	....
4. Fiscal 1975	....	....	0.44*
5. Change in other grants per capita ($)	−0.08	−0.04	−0.01
6. Manufacturing employment as percent of population	−0.05	−0.07	−0.03
7. Percent of population aged 65 or over	−0.05	0.00	−0.21
8. Percent of population aged under 18	−0.13	−0.27	−0.05
9. Percent of population white	−0.04	−0.06	0.13
Constant term	−1	7	−19
Number of cases	54	54	53
Adjusted R²	.09	.00	.11

Table 5-14
Multiple Regression Analysis of the Effects of Revenue Sharing on Per Capita
Library Expenditures in Cities with 1970 Population between 25,000 and 300,000

(Coefficients with t-values greater than 2.0 are marked with an asterisk)

Independent variables	Model number						
	I			II			III
	Form of dependent variable						
							1972-75 levels pooled
	1973 level	1974 level	1975 level	1973 level	1974 level	1975 level	
1. Personal income per capita ($)	0.000	0.003*	0.003*	−0.003*	0.002*	0.000	0.002*
Revenue sharing grant per capita ($)							
2. Fiscal 1973	−0.06	....	....	−0.13	....	....	0.02
3. Fiscal 1974	....	0.16*	....	....	0.08	....	0.09
4. Fiscal 1975	....	....	0.03	....	....	−0.17*	−0.06
Revenue sharing grant ($m.)							
5. Fiscal 1973	....	....	....	....	....	....	−0.42
6. Fiscal 1974	....	....	....	....	....	....	−0.81
7. Fiscal 1975	....	....	....	....	....	....	0.25
Other grants per capita ($)							
8. Fiscal 1972	....	....	....	....	....	....	0.02
9. Fiscal 1973	0.00	....	....	−0.02	....	....	0.03
10. Fiscal 1974	....	0.02	....	....	0.01	....	−0.01
11. Fiscal 1975	....	....	0.06*	....	....	0.05*	0.04
12. Manufacturing employment as percent of population	0.02	−0.06	−0.02	−0.01	0.04	0.03	−0.03
13. Percent of population aged 65 or over	0.64	0.09	−0.03	4.98*	−0.14	−0.15	0.26*
14. Percent of population aged under 18	0.22	−0.03	−0.03	1.03	−0.14	−0.02	....
15. Percent of population white	0.09	0.03	−0.01	....	....	....	0.08*
16. Dependent variable lagged one year	....	....	....	0.59*	0.42*	0.99*	....
Constant term	−16	−8	−4	6	4	6	−9
Number of cases	44	52	48	40	53	48	192
Adjusted R²	.02	.32	.23	.71	.64	.73	.11

Independent variables	Model number IV		
	Form of dependent variable		
	1972-73 change	1972-74 change	1972-75 change
1. Personal income per capita ($)	−0.003*	−0.001	−0.002
Revenue sharing grant per capita ($)			
2. Fiscal 1973	−0.09	....	....
3. Fiscal 1974	....	−0.03	....
4. Fiscal 1975	....	....	−0.30
5. Change in other grants per capita ($)	0.17	−0.03	0.08
6. Manufacturing employment as percent of population	−0.09	−0.09	−0.12
7. Percent of population aged 65 or over	0.21	−0.08	−0.47
8. Percent of population aged under 18	−0.04	−0.09	−0.36
9. Percent of population white	0.00	−0.07	−0.12
Constant term	10	17	37
Number of cases	38	41	39
Adjusted R²	.20	.00	.00

Table 5-15
Multiple Regression Analysis of the Effects of Revenue Sharing on Per Capita Public Utility Expenditures in Cities with 1970 Population between 25,000 and 300,000

(Coefficients with t-values greater than 2.0 are marked with an asterisk)

Independent variables	Model number I			Model number II			Model number III
	Form of dependent variable						
	1973 level	1974 level	1975 level	1973 level	1974 level	1975 level	1972-75 levels pooled
1. Personal income per capita ($)	−0.006	−0.006	−0.010	0.009	0.003	0.001	0.000
Revenue sharing grant per capita ($)							
2. Fiscal 1973	1.81	....	....	2.04	....	....	1.51
3. Fiscal 1974	....	−1.30	....	....	0.37	....	−1.90
4. Fiscal 1975	....	....	−2.10	....	....	−0.28	3.00
Revenue sharing grant ($m.)							
5. Fiscal 1973							−4.35
6. Fiscal 1974							−3.00
7. Fiscal 1975							−19.88*
Other grants per capita ($)							
8. Fiscal 1972							0.32
9. Fiscal 1973	0.26	....	....	0.12	....	....	−0.20
10. Fiscal 1974	....	0.83*	....	....	−0.05	....	0.74*
11. Fiscal 1975	....	....	0.14	....	....	−0.45*	0.11
12. Manufacturing employment as percent of population	0.40	0.73	1.84	−0.87	0.08	0.79	1.24*
13. Percent of population aged 65 or over	−5.18	−3.48	1.87	−4.94*	−0.18	4.30	1.26
14. Percent of population aged under 18	−5.33	−3.94	−1.49	−3.62	−0.76	3.49	....
15. Percent of population white	0.87	0.03	1.63	0.56	−0.29	0.83	0.16
16. Dependent variable lagged one year	....	....	....	0.91*	1.13*	1.21*	....
Constant term	176	198	−30	66	−13	−215	−8
Number of cases	46	49	47	35	50	47	182
Adjusted R²	.01	.08	.00	.79	.95	.76	.06

Independent variables	Model number IV		
	Form of dependent variable		
	1972-73 change	1972-74 change	1972-75 change
1. Personal income per capita ($)	0.009	0.002	0.013
Revenue sharing grant per capita ($)			
2. Fiscal 1973	2.47*	....	....
3. Fiscal 1974	....	−1.21	....
4. Fiscal 1975	....	....	0.11
5. Change in other grants per capita ($)	1.16	0.13	0.44
6. Manufacturing employment as percent of population	−1.62*	−0.07	−0.08
7. Percent of population aged 65 or over	−6.67*	−3.39	−8.19
8. Percent of population aged under 18	−5.00*	−3.56	−5.54
9. Percent of population white	0.91	−0.06	−0.15
Constant term	96	164	219
Number of cases	33	33	33
Adjusted R²	.29	.12	.05

Table 5-16
Multiple Regression Analysis of the Effects of Revenue Sharing on Per Capita
Expenditures on Other Functions in Cities with 1970 Population between 25,000 and 300,000

(Coefficients with t values greater than 2.0 are marked with an asterisk)

Independent variables	Model number I			II			III
	Form of dependent variable						
	1973 level	1974 level	1975 level	1973 level	1974 level	1975 level	1972-75 levels pooled
1. Personal income per capita ($)	0.009*	0.013	0.011	0.002	0.002	−0.001	0.007*
Revenue sharing grant per capita ($)							
2. Fiscal 1973	0.02	....	....	0.38	....	....	−0.86
3. Fiscal 1974	....	−0.47	....	....	−0.02	....	−1.26*
4. Fiscal 1975	....	....	−0.26	....	....	−0.05	−0.17
Revenue sharing grant ($m.)							
5. Fiscal 1973							4.46
6. Fiscal 1974							6.30
7. Fiscal 1975							0.70
Other grants per capita ($)							
8. Fiscal 1972							0.05
9. Fiscal 1973	0.02	....	....	−0.19	....	....	0.14
10. Fiscal 1974	....	0.28	....	....	0.11	....	0.32*
11. Fiscal 1975	....	....	0.07	....	....	−0.06	0.20
12. Manufacturing employment as percent of population	0.91*	1.15*	1.69*	0.73*	0.04	0.41*	0.91*
13. Percent of population aged 65 or over	3.30*	3.06	3.45*	2.15*	−1.32	0.55	0.44
14. Percentage of population aged under 18	2.95*	3.26*	3.25*	1.91*	−0.78	0.33	....
15. Percent of population white	−1.41*	−1.87*	−2.16*	−0.34	0.23	−0.51*	−1.12*
16. Dependent variable lagged one year	....	....	....	0.70*	1.27*	0.91*	....
Constant term	−10	5	43	−54	1	42	94
Number of cases	67	69	67	55	70	65	265
Adjusted R²	.20	.28	.25	.69	.87	.88	.23

Independent variables	Model number IV		
	Form of dependent variable		
	1972-73 change	1972-74 change	1972-75 change
1. Personal income per capita ($)	0.000	0.006	0.000
Revenue sharing grant per capita ($)			
2. Fiscal 1973	0.31	....	....
3. Fiscal 1974	....	0.27	....
4. Fiscal 1975	....	....	−0.07
5. Change in other grants per capita ($)	−0.25	0.09	−0.05
6. Manufacturing employment as percent of population	0.06	0.53	1.01*
7. Percent of population aged 65 or over	−0.01	−0.38	−0.20
8. Percent of population aged under 18	0.06	0.50	0.20
9. Percent of population white	0.36*	0.02	−0.27
Constant term	−36	−40	27
Number of cases	53	53	52
Adjusted R²	.02	.00	.02

CHAPTER 6

The States and General Revenue Sharing

Harvey E. Brazer *

The data that provide the basis for the findings presented in this chapter are drawn from comprehensive personal interviews obtained during the Fall of 1974 with all 50 of the principal finance officers (typically Director of the Budget Office) of the states, 45 chairmen of Upper House appropriations committees, and 48 of the chairmen of Lower House appropriations committees. Shorter, less comprehensive, interviews of 36 governors were obtained as well.

The first part of this chapter presents our findings with respect to the opinions of our respondents on various aspects of General Revenue Sharing, including its impact on innovative activity, on the fiscal freedom or independence of the states vis-a-vis the Federal Government, and on various elements of the allocation of revenue-sharing funds under the Fiscal Assistance Act of 1972. The second part presents our estimates of the impact of General Revenue Sharing in fiscal years 1974 and 1975 on operating expenditures and capital outlays, tax levels, indebtedness, and surplus or deficit. The third and last part of the chapter offers the results of our effort to explain variance among the States in their responses to GRS using multiple regression analysis.

While reading the analysis that follows one should keep in mind the overall dimensions of GRS as it affects the States. The State and Local Fiscal Assistance Act of 1972 provided for the distribution to the States and local subdivisions of approximately $6 billion per year for the five calendar years beginning with 1972 and ending with 1976. One-third of each year's funds allocated to each of the State areas is apportioned to State government. Thus the States receive about $2 billion per year. For the last fiscal year prior to the receipt of GRS

allocations, fiscal year 1971-72, total State revenue from all sources exceeded $112 billion, "general revenue" from own sources amounted to $70.7 billion, and State tax receipts to $59.9 billion.[1] In that same year the States received Federal grants-in-aid amounting to $28 billion.[2] The States' annual share of GRS funds amounts to about one-quarter of the roughly $8 billion per year increase in State tax collections realized between 1971 and 1973, or almost exactly the annual increase for that period in State general sales tax receipts alone.[3] In this context, therefore, GRS does not loom large as a source of revenue for the States.

Nonetheless, GRS receipts constitute a new kind of revenue source for the States. They became available during fiscal year 1972-73 without imposing the political and other scars typically associated with the imposition of new State taxes or raising the rates on old ones. Unlike almost all other Federal aid to the States, GRS requires no State matching, and, with respect to the States' share, is essentially entirely unconditional. Given these unique and innovative aspects of revenue sharing as a part of Federal-State fiscal relations, it is both specially interesting and particularly important to observe reactions and opinions to it of those who play a leading role in State fiscal policy—top fiscal officers in the executive branch and the heads of legislative appropriations committees.

Another aspect of the overall fiscal picture that should be kept in mind is the trend in recent years in the amount of total Federal assistance to State and local governments. It is often alleged that GRS has supplanted a substantial part of Federal conditional grants-in-aid rather than supplemented

---

*Professor, Department of Economics, The University of Michigan

[1] U. S. Bureau of the Census, *Governmental Finances in 1971-72* (U. S. Government Printing Office, Washington, DC, 1973), p. 1.
[2] *Ibid.*
[3] U. S. Bureau of the Census, *State Tax Collections in 1973* (U. S. Government Printing Office, Washington, DC, 1973), p. 5.

them. Looking at the aggregate data for the years 1970 through fiscal year 1975, while the allegation may have some validity for local units of government, the figures do not support it for the States. Federal aid in fiscal years 1969-70 amounted to $24.0 billion. It increased at the rate of about $6 billion per year for the next two years, reaching $35.9 billion in fiscal year 1972. The increase to fiscal year 1973, the first year in which GRS was in effect, amounted to more than $8 billion. Fiscal year 1974 saw Federal aid increase by a little more than $2 billion, partly because one-and one-half rather than one year's revenue sharing disbursements were made in fiscal year 1973. By 1975, however, the estimated increase in Federal aid once again exceeded $6 billion, bringing total Federal aid, including GRS, to $52.6 billion for that fiscal year.[4]

VIEWS ON REVENUE SHARING IN THE STATES

In this section we present primarily the responses of chief State fiscal officers and the heads of legislative appropriations committees to closed-ended questions, asked either in the form of statements with which the respondents were asked to agree or disagree or as questions answerable in yes-no terms. These statements and questions are reproduced in Tables 6-1—6-4. In these tables the States are divided into upper and lower income groups according to whether they rank above or below the median in terms of 1973 per capita personal income. This grouping reflects our hypothesis that income level plays a major role in accounting for differences among the States in their response to revenue sharing.

An abbreviated questionnaire was administered to the governors of 36 States. Where it seems apt we shall note their responses to questions relating to various aspects of revenue sharing. In addition, in cases where open-ended questions asked of fiscal officers and appropriations committee chairmen elicited useful information we shall bring it into our analysis.

General Revenue Sharing and Innovation in State Government

Ongoing programs of State governments seem always to be underfinanced in the sense that levels of service performance are never "adequate."

Litigants and people accused of criminal activity wait months or even years to be heard in the courts, prisons are overcrowded and little or nothing by way of rehabilitation is accomplished, "needs" in higher education are unmet, too many patients in mental hospitals are simply "warehoused" and uncared for, and so it goes down the list of State functional responsibilities. Tax increases are always unpopular and politically difficult and few, if any, States appear able to avoid moving agonizingly from one real or apparent fiscal crisis to another. Under these circumstances the prospects for innovations in the form of new and even experimental programs are normally dim in the absence of such irresistible prods as Federal conditional grants-in-aid. But general revenue-sharing receipts may be seen as a more or less unfettered windfall and may therefore offer a challenge to innovation or experimentation by the recipient States.

The timing of the first payments under the State and Local Assistance Act of 1972 may have been particularly conducive to the breaking of some traditional budgetary barriers. The Act was passed in October 1972 and called for payments to begin almost immediately for the two 6-month "entitlement periods" of calendar year 1972. Thus before the end of fiscal year 1973 (typically June 30, 1973) the states had received one-and-one-half years' revenue-sharing payments, some $3 billion, which most of them had not taken into account in their 1973 budgets.

In our interview schedule administered to chief State fiscal officers and the heads of legislative appropriations committees, several questions were asked designed to elicit information about the extent, if any, to which revenue sharing did inspire innovations. Responses to the ten statements or questions are presented in Table 6-1. In each segment of the table we distinguish between respondents from States with per capita personal income above and below the median for all 50 States, and between the responses of chief State fiscal officers and chairmen of the appropriations committees of the Upper Houses and of the Lower Houses of the State legislatures. The responses of those interviewed are presented as percentages weighted by the population size of the State in which the interview was conducted. The data relate only to those respondents (and States) who clearly answered the question. The number who do so is indicated in each case. Thus, for example, the number 53 that appears in Table 6-1 is to be interpreted as follows: respondents from States in which 53 percent of the people resident in all 47 states in which the chief fiscal officer replied to the question "agree somewhat" with the first statement.

---

[4]U. S. Office of Management and Budget, *Special Analyses, Budget of the United States Government, Fiscal Year 1976* (U. S. Government Printing Office, Washington, DC, 1975), p. 242.

Table 6-1
General Revenue Sharing and Innovation
in State Government

(Percentages)

	Upper Half of Personal Income Per Capita[a]			Lower Half of Personal Income Per Capita[b]			Grand Mean		
	FO[c]	UH[d]	LH[e]	FO	UH	LH	FO	UH	LH
1. "Concern over the continuation of general revenue sharing may discourage some governments from using revenue sharing funds for experimental programs."									
Agree strongly	5	18	47	45	33	37	23	25	44
Agree somewhat	53	59	33	35	53	42	45	56	36
Disagree somewhat	27	23	19	10	15	9	20	19	15
Disagree strongly	15	0	0	10	0	12	13	0	4
Total	100	100	100	100	100	100	100	100	100

N = FO UH LH
     47   42   41

	FO	UH	LH	FO	UH	LH	FO	UH	LH
2. "Overall, would you say that your state government has used revenue sharing dollars to finance ongoing activities or to start new ones?"									
New activities	5	0	6	16	14	6	9	6	6
Ongoing activities	80	68	74	55	73	63	71	70	70
Both	15	32	20	29	13	30	20	24	24
Total	100	100	100	100	100	100	100	100	100

N = FO UH LH
     43   45   47

	FO	UH	LH	FO	UH	LH	FO	UH	LH
3. "Because of revenue sharing we have been able to develop some new programs at the state level."									
Agree strongly	10	24	8	54	21	20	26	23	13
Agree somewhat	49	23	65	20	47	47	38	33	58
Disagree somewhat	4	36	8	14	23	7	7	30	8
Disagree strongly	37	16	18	13	9	26	28	13	21
Total	100	100	100	100	100	100	100	100	100

N = FO UH LH
     48   42   47

	FO	UH	LH	FO	UH	LH	FO	UH	LH
4. "Inflation has cut down the use of revenue sharing funds for innovative programs."									
Agree strongly	30	46	14	1	15	31	19	30	21
Agree somewhat	37	36	73	43	60	30	39	48	57
Disagree somewhat	22	9	12	44	16	17	30	13	14
Disagree strongly	11	10	0	12	8	22	12	9	9
Total	100	100	100	100	100	100	100	100	100

N = FO UH LH
     43   40   45

	FO	UH	LH	FO	UH	LH	FO	UH	LH
5. "High rates of inflation mean that much of revenue sharing goes for salary increases."									
Agree strongly	13	16	1	1	11	20	9	14	8
Agree somewhat	38	46	37	35	13	17	37	29	30
Disagree somewhat	40	33	25	29	59	28	36	47	26
Disagree strongly	9	4	36	35	16	35	18	10	36
Total	100	100	100	100	100	100	100	100	100

N = FO UH LH
     48   40   43

	Upper Half of Personal Income Per Capita[a]			Lower Half of Personal Income Per Capita[b]			Grand Mean		
	FO[c]	UH[d]	LH[e]	FO	UH	LH	FO	UH	LH
6. "Active employee organizations mean that much of the revenue sharing money goes for salary increases."									
Agree strongly	20	16	1	1	15	16	13	16	6
Agree somewhat	32	22	48	8	20	17	23	21	36
Disagree somewhat	39	53	23	45	30	40	41	42	30
Disagree strongly	10	9	28	46	35	28	23	22	28
Total	100	100	100	100	100	100	100	100	100

N = FO UH LH
     47 39 42

	FO[c]	UH[d]	LH[e]	FO	UH	LH	FO	UH	LH
7. "Do you find yourself paying attention to different kinds of issues or problems in this state because of revenue sharing?"									
Yes	5	29	43	17	32	23	9	30	34
No	95	71	57	83	68	77	91	70	66
Total	100	100	100	100	100	100	100	100	100

N = FO UH LH
     50 45 46

	FO[c]	UH[d]	LH[e]	FO	UH	LH	FO	UH	LH
8. "Local governments have been able to develop some new programs."									
Agree strongly	17	42	36	15	34	30	16	39	34
Agree somewhat	83	47	56	80	55	49	82	51	53
Disagree somewhat	0	4	0	0	7	7	0	5	3
Disagree strongly	0	6	8	6	3	14	2	5	10
Total	100	100	100	100	100	100	100	100	100

N = FO UH LH
     39 41 42

	FO[c]	UH[d]	LH[e]	FO	UH	LH	FO	UH	LH
9. "As a result of revenue sharing has your state undergone any changes in its taxing structure?"									
Yes	17	8	31	24	15	10	19	11	23
No	83	92	68	76	85	90	81	89	77
Total	100	100	100	100	100	100	100	100	100

N = FO UH LH
     49 44 47

	FO[c]	UH[d]	LH[e]	FO	UH	LH	FO	UH	LH
10. "Are there plans for such changes?"									
Yes	5	13	16	13	15	11	8	14	13
No	95	87	84	87	85	89	92	86	86
Total	100	100	100	100	100	100	100	100	100

N = FO UH LH
     37 37 39

[a]Upper half of states ranked by per capita income: Alaska, California, Colorado, Connecticut, Delaware, Florida, Hawaii, Illinois, Indiana, Iowa, Kansas, Maryland, Massachusetts, Michigan, Minnesota, Missouri, Nebraska, Nevada, New Jersey, New York, North Dakota, Ohio, Pennsylvania, Virginia, Washington.

[b]Lower half of states ranked by per capita income: Alabama, Arizona, Arkansas, Georgia, Idaho, Kentucky, Louisiana, Maine, Mississippi, Montana, New Hampshire, New Mexico, North Carolina, Oklahoma, Oregon, Rhode Island, South Carolina, South Dakota, Tennessee, Texas, Utah, Vermont, West Virginia, Wisconsin, Wyoming.

[c]Chief State Fiscal Officer

[d]Chairman, Appropriations Committee, Upper House

[e]Chairman, Appropriations Committee, Lower House

One of the first statements in the interview schedule to which the respondents were asked to react was, "Because of revenue sharing we have been able to develop some new programs at the State level." They were given the options of agreeing "strongly" or "somewhat" or disagreeing "somewhat" or "strongly." We find that approximately two-thirds of our respondents agree with the statement, the proportion being somewhat higher than that for chairmen of Lower House appropriations committees and appreciably lower for heads of the Upper House committees. Respondents from the poorer States appear to be more widely in agreement with the statement than those from the richer States, but this is not consistently the case.

Later on in the interview, however, when asked whether GRS dollars had been used "to finance ongoing activities or to start new ones," respondents indicate that GRS has been responsible for some new program activity in only about a quarter to a third of the States. The proportion reporting new activities was somewhat higher among the poorer States than it was among those with higher incomes. The areas of expenditure most frequently mentioned as being involved in new activities started with revenue-sharing funds were education and health. Annual costs of such new activities were estimated at as little as $100,000 and as much as $100 million.

Another indication of the possible relationship between GRS and innovation in State government may be seen in responses to the question, "Do you find yourself paying attention to different kinds of issues or problems in this state because of revenue sharing?" The extraordinary nature of revenue-sharing receipts, in terms of the source and the timing of the first payments, would, as we have noted, lead one to expect a positive response to this question. It must be borne in mind, however, that despite these features of revenue-sharing receipts, they nevertheless constituted less than 2 percent of total State spending for fiscal year 1973, and may have readily mingled with all other revenues in an atmosphere in which demand for budgetary allocations to ongoing programs is strong and competes with politically attractive prospects for tax reduction. For these reasons, perhaps, fiscal officers in States with only 5 and 17 percent, respectively, of the populations of the richer and poorer States responded affirmatively to this question. It is interesting to note, however, that legislative leaders represented by our respondents are far more inclined than fiscal officers to respond to GRS by attending to "different kinds of issues or problems" in their States.

Apart from the factors already noted, at least three other circumstances may have inhibited the use of revenue sharing for innovative purposes in State government. One of these is the fact that the State and Local Assistance Act of 1972 provides for the distribution of GRS funds only for the calendar years 1972 through 1976. By the time budget officers and legislative leaders were in a position to deliberate about the uses to which they might put their receipts they were already into the second year of a program limited by Congress initially to a five-year duration. They might well, in this circumstance, have been reluctant to enter into new programs involving obligations that would carry over into years beyond the scheduled expiration of the Act. Close to half of the budget officers from the lower income States agreed strongly with the suggestion that concern about the continuation of GRS after 1976 may discourage some governments from financing experimental programs out of revenue-sharing funds. On the whole respondents representing some 80 percent of the population of the poorer States held to this position in some degree. This was true as well of close to three-quarters of higher income state respondents. Only a very small minority of the people are represented by respondents who disagreed strongly with this statement. The opinions on this issue of the governors who were interviewed were divided in about the same way as those of our other respondents.

Another inhibiting factor may have been the upsurge in the rate of inflation that more or less coincided with the enactment of GRS in late 1972. We asked those interviewed to indicate agreement or disagreement with the statement, "Inflation has cut down the use of revenue sharing funds for innovative programs." In all, about three-quarters of the respondents agreed with this statement, as did all but five of the thirty-three Governors who expressed an opinion on it. Agreement tends to be found rather more frequently among the poorer than the richer States and very much more frequently among fiscal officers than legislators. If a high rate of inflation led to GRS funds being used largely for salary increases for State employees, it might well be argued that in this indirect fashion inflation cut down on the use of revenue sharing for experimental or innovative programs. Between about 40 and 50 percent of those interviewed, including the governors, indicated agreement with the statement that, "High rates of inflation mean that much of revenue sharing goes for salary increases," thus lending some credence to this view.

A third possible inhibiting factor may be that employer organizations succeeded in using the fact that a substantial increment in revenues had been realized from outside State sources as the basis for successful negotiation of substantial increases in wages and salaries. About 40 percent of State respondents agreed with the statement that the existence of active employee organizations meant that a substantial part of revenue-sharing money went into salary increases. There is no discernible pattern suggested either by differences among type of respondents or income level of the states.

We find, therefore, that there is evidence to the effect that, at least in limited ways and among some States, revenue sharing has resulted in the introduction of new programs, attention to new kinds of problems, and even some experimentation. It would seem clear that such activities might have been substantially more important and more widespread in the absence of inflation and uncertainty with respect to the continuation beyond 1976 of GRS.

It is of some interest to observe a sharp contrast in the views of State fiscal officers and legislators with respect to the extent to which local governments, as compared with the States, have been seen as able to develop new programs as a consequence of the receipt of revenue-sharing funds. Almost all of our respondents at the State level agreed that "Local governments have been able to develop some new programs." This response may, of course, simply suggest that the grass always looks greener outside of one's own backyard.

Apart from budget programs and expenditures, another kind of innovation that might be inspired by revenue sharing involves changes in the States' tax structures or plans for such changes. But only a small proportion of our respondents indicate that their States had either undertaken or were planning changes in tax structures. This seems surprising in light of the fact that legislative sessions at the State level in 1973 and 1974 produced a large number and volume of tax reductions as well as some structural changes. The basic question, however, may, in retrospect, have been somewhat ambiguous. We asked "As a result of revenue sharing has your state undergone any changes in its taxing structure?" Respondents may have interpreted the question in such a way as to rule out a positive answer where existing taxes were changed either with respect to their base or rate. Such changes may not have been viewed as "structural."

Perceptions of the Influence of General Revenue Sharing on Local Governments

We turn now to the broad question as to whether and, if so, to what extent, GRS has influenced some aspects of the activities of local government jurisdictions. Table 6-2 offers a brief summary statement relating to this question. We asked, first, whether or not in the last two or three

Table 6-2
Perceptions of the Influence of General Revenue Sharing
on Local Governments

(Percentages)

	Upper Half of Personal Income Per Capita			Lower Half of Personal Income Per Capita			Grand Mean		
	FO	UH	LH	FO	UH	LH	FO	UH	LH
1. "In the last two or three years has your state government felt any pressure to expand local government functions?"									
Yes	41	60	70	40	55	77	41	57	73
No	59	40	29	60	45	23	59	42	27
Total	100	100	100	100	100	100	100	100	100
N = FO UH LH / 48 43 46									
2. "To what extent is this pressure due to general revenue sharing—entirely, to some extent, or not at all?"									
Entirely	23	0	0	0	5	0	14	2	0
To some extent	0	29	1	24	11	14	10	20	7
Not at all	77	70	99	76	84	85	76	77	93
Total	100	100	100	100	100	100	100	100	100
N = FO UH LH / 23 25 29									

	Upper Half of Personal Income Per Capita[a]			Lower Half of Personal Income Per Capita[b]			Grand Mean		
	FO[c]	UH[d]	LH[e]	FO	UH	LH	FO	UH	LH
3. "Some people have argued that revenue sharing will encourage certain changes among local government jurisdictions. Do you think revenue sharing will encourage cities and towns to annex outlying areas?"									
Yes	15	24	9	24	30	52	18	27	26
No	85	76	90	76	70	48	82	73	74
Total.........	100	100	100	100	100	100	100	100	100

N = FO UH LH
    40 41 42

	FO	UH	LH	FO	UH	LH	FO	UH	LH
4. "Do you think that revenue sharing will encourage municipalities and counties to take over some functions now being performed by special districts?"									
Yes	47	47	20	10	36	66	34	42	39
No	53	53	80	90	64	34	66	58	61
Total.........	100	100	100	100	100	100	100	100	100

N = FO UH LH
    43 38 39

	FO	UH	LH	FO	UH	LH	FO	UH	LH
5. "Do you think that revenue sharing will encourage some small governments to increase the range of their activities?"									
Yes	96	69	90	72	81	79	87	75	86
No	4	31	10	27	19	21	13	25	14
Total.........	100	100	100	100	100	100	100	100	100

N = FO UH LH
    47 43 44

	FO	UH	LH	FO	UH	LH	FO	UH	LH
6. "Do you think that revenue sharing will encourage less reliance on user charges by local governments?"									
Yes	32	63	53	35	38	40	33	52	49
No	68	37	47	65	61	60	67	48	51
Total.........	100	100	100	100	100	100	100	100	100

N = FO UH LH
    44 42 39

years the State government had been under any pressure to expand local government functions. A majority of respondents replied affirmatively to the question, but only chairmen of Lower House appropriations committees were overwhelmingly positive in their response. When asked the extent to which this pressure was attributable to GRS, however, there was very little inclination to believe that this had been the case, irrespective of whether the respondent was from a rich or poor State or whether he was a member of the executive or legislative branch of the government. Significantly, perhaps, only a little over half of all of our inter-

viewees were able or willing to answer this question, a far smaller proportion than applied to any of the others.

One way in which municipalities might seek to increase their allotment of GRS funds is through annexation of adjacent unincorporated areas. We asked those interviewed, not whether they thought that municipalities had annexed such areas in response to revenue sharing, but rather, whether they believed that revenue sharing would encourage annexations. In the higher income states only a small minority are of the view that revenue sharing will encourage annexation, while in the poorer States the proportion ranges from about one-quarter to one-half. The difference between the two sets of responses may be due to two factors. The first is that a large proportion of the lower income States are located in the South and Southwestern regions where cities are generally newer and annexations are easier to achieve. In other parts of the country, particularly in the Northeast and Midwest, cities tend to be older, more commonly surrounded by well-established incorporated suburban cities or villages, and the procedures involved in annexation are beset with an array of difficult obstacles. The second factor is that revenue sharing represents a larger part of budget receipts in poorer than in richer parts of the country and the incentive to annexation seen in adjacent areas' revenue-sharing allocations may be more tempting targets than they would be in richer communities.

The State and Local Fiscal Assistance Act of 1972 specifically excludes special districts from participation in GRS. Nevertheless, many of these special districts do levy property and other taxes. One may imagine, therefore, that some municipalities or counties might seek to take over the functions now being performed by special districts in order to gain credit for their tax receipts. We asked legislative appropriation committee chairmen, chief fiscal officers, and governors whether, in their opinion, revenue sharing will in fact encourage this kind of activity. We find that views on this matter vary widely among groups of respondents. Only 10 percent of the fiscal officers in the poorer States responded affirmatively to the question, in contrast to 66 percent of the chairmen of lower house appropriations committees in the same group of States and more than half of the governors. On the whole something over a third of our respondents do believe that revenue sharing will encourage municipalities and counties to move into areas of activity that are now the responsibilities of special districts.

The State and Local Fiscal Assistance Act permits revenue-sharing funds to comprise as much as one-third of the sum of local tax revenue and intergovernmental transfers (including GRS) of the immediately preceding fiscal year. In the case of a substantial number of very small jurisdictions, therefore, revenue sharing may add up to 50 percent to the amounts of funds otherwise available each year. This could lead to a variety of outcomes, clearly one of which is that small local governmental units might seek to expand their range of activities. This, in fact, is the predominant view of State chief fiscal officers, legislative appropriations committee chairmen, and governors. Few questions asked in the course of interviewing State officials elicited as much agreement among groups of respondents as did this one.

User charges of various kinds, including fees, prices charged for services, certain licenses, and special assessments are not included in the tax receipts or measure of tax effort that determine a local government's portion of general revenue-sharing funds. We should expect, therefore, that some jurisdictions would be encouraged to reduce their reliance on such user charges in favor of the levying of "taxes." Rather surprisingly, we believe, only about a third of chief State fiscal officers and governors responded affirmatively when asked whether or not they thought that GRS would encourage less reliance on user charges by local governments. Legislative leaders interviewed, on the other hand, were about equally divided on the question.

In summary, neither fiscal officers nor legislative leaders interviewed appear to believe that the advent of GRS will stimulate major changes in those aspects of local governmental activities examined in this chapter. The exception appears to relate to opinions regarding expansion of the range of activities of small local jurisdictions. And, as we saw in the preceding section, there is a widespread belief among State administrative and legislative leaders that revenue sharing has enabled local governments to develop new programs.

Opinions Relating to the Allocation Formula

Responses to the set of questions relating either to the allocation formula or to the consequences of its application are summarized in Table 6-3. The first set of questions with which we are concerned has to do with opinions regarding the income tax factor in the allocation formula. State individual income tax collections are afforded one-sixth of the total of weights assigned to the five factors used in the allocation formula devised by the House of Representatives. The House formula provides a larger allocation than the Senate formula to 20 of the States, but in 6 of these the difference is less than 5 percent. Thus there are only 14 states for which the level of income tax receipts affects appreciably the amount of revenue sharing funds received.[5] It is not surprising, therefore, that virtually all of the chairmen of appropriations committees of the State Lower Houses and all but a small handful of State fiscal officers and chairmen of appropriations committees in the Upper Houses responded negatively to the question, "Has the income tax factor in the revenue sharing allocation

[5]Staff of the Joint Committee on Internal Revenue Taxation, *General Explanation of the State and Local Assistance Act and the Federal-State Tax Collection Act of 1972* (U.S. Government Printing Office, Washington, DC, 1973), pp. 26-7.

Table 6-3
Opinions Relating to the Allocation Formula

(Percentages)

	Upper Half of Personal Income Per Capita			Lower Half of Personal Income Per Capita			Grand Mean		
	FO	UH	LH	FO	UH	LH	FO	UH	LH
1. "Has the income tax factor in the revenue sharing allocation formula had any influence on tax policy in this state?"									
Yes	15	0	1	1	20	1	9	10	1
No	85	100	99	99	80	99	90	90	99
Total	100	100	100	100	100	100	100	100	100

N =
  FO UH LH
  47 42 43

	FO	UH	LH	FO	UH	LH	FO	UH	LH
2. "Do you favor keeping the present income tax provisions in the revenue sharing allocation formula, or do you think they should be changed?"									
Keep	74	60	76	55	74	51	66	66	66
Changed	26	39	24	45	26	49	34	34	34
Total	100	100	100	100	100	100	100	100	100

N =
  FO UH LH
  40 00 04

	FO	UH	LH	FO	UH	LH	FO	UH	LH
3. "With respect to the *state* government, how do you feel about changing the allocation formula to increase the reward going to the states which have their own income taxes?"									
Strongly favor	46	69	69	34	31	23	41	53	51
Somewhat favor	20	8	6	22	23	29	21	15	15
Somewhat oppose	0	4	16	7	15	0	2	8	10
Strongly oppose	34	19	9	37	31	48	35	24	24
Total	100	100	100	100	100	100	100	100	100

N =
  FO UH LH
  48 45 45

	FO	UH	LH	FO	UH	LH	FO	UH	LH
4. "With respect to the *state* government, how do you feel about changing the allocation formula to give a larger share of the funds to states and a smaller share to local units?"									
Strongly favor	15	19	1	26	13	23	19	16	9
Somewhat favor	55	52	49	36	28	18	48	41	38
Somewhat oppose	30	28	44	23	49	51	27	37	47
Strongly oppose	0	0	6	15	10	7	6	5	6
Total	100	100	100	100	100	100	100	100	100

N =
  FO UH LH
  48 44 45

	FO	UH	LH	FO	UH	LH	FO	UH	LH
5. "With respect to the *state* government, how do you feel about changing the allocation formula to give a smaller share of the funds to states and a larger share to local units?"									
Strongly favor	0	0	5	4	10	5	2	4	5
Somewhat favor	8	22	15	4	13	10	6	18	13
Somewhat oppose	63	39	44	29	57	34	50	46	41
Strongly oppose	29	39	32	62	19	51	42	31	38
Total	100	100	100	100	100	100	100	100	100

N =
  FO UH LH
  48 45 45

	Upper Half of Personal Income Per Capita			Lower Half of Personal Income Per Capita			Grand Mean		
	FO	UH	LH	FO	UH	LH	FO	UH	LH
6. "With respect to the *state* government, how do you feel about changing the allocation formula to give the states and local governments shares proportional to their respective tax efforts?"									
Strongly favor	33	66	27	26	13	20	31	43	24
Somewhat favor	27	20	30	36	67	30	31	41	30
Somewhat oppose	31	5	11	17	19	17	25	11	14
Strongly oppose	9	9	32	20	1	33	13	5	32
Total	100	100	100	100	100	100	100	100	100

N = FO UH LH
    44 48 46

	FO	UH	LH	FO	UH	LH	FO	UH	LH
7. "With respect to local governments in this state, how do you feel about changing the allocation formula to give more money to poorer communities?"									
Strongly favor	19	52	45	37	21	22	26	38	33
Somewhat favor	54	35	23	31	55	37	46	44	30
Somewhat oppose	23	12	11	15	18	20	20	15	16
Strongly oppose	3	1	20	17	5	21	8	3	21
Total	100	100	100	100	100	100	100	100	100

N = FO UH LH
    47 44 43

	FO	UH	LH	FO	UH	LH	FO	UH	LH
8. "With respect to local governments in this state, how do you feel about changing the allocation formula to omit very small government units?"									
Strongly favor	26	15	22	22	10	21	25	13	22
Somewhat favor	27	33	14	20	15	27	25	25	18
Somewhat oppose	39	13	26	20	22	16	32	17	22
Strongly oppose	8	46	38	37	53	36	19	45	37
Total	100	100	100	100	100	100	100	100	100

N = FO UH LH
    48 44 45

	FO	UH	LH	FO	UH	LH	FO	UH	LH
9. "With respect to local governments in this state, how do you feel about changing the allocation formula to give more to big city areas?"									
Strongly favor	36	16	30	11	9	11	27	13	23
Somewhat favor	40	15	9	21	23	41	33	19	21
Somewhat oppose	17	39	31	29	21	21	21	30	27
Strongly oppose	8	30	30	39	47	28	19	38	29
Total	100	100	100	100	100	100	100	100	100

N = FO UH LH
    48 42 44

	FO	UH	LH	FO	UH	LH	FO	UH	LH
10. "With respect to local governments in this state, how do you feel about changing the allocation formula to discourage reduction in local tax rates?"									
Strongly favor	9	1	0	13	20	32	10	9	13
Somewhat favor	10	9	40	19	7	31	13	8	37
Somewhat oppose	39	46	52	42	44	9	40	45	35
Strongly oppose	42	44	7	26	29	27	36	38	15
Total	100	100	100	100	100	100	100	100	100

N = FO UH LH
    46 44 45

	Upper Half of Personal Income Per Capita			Lower Half of Personal Income Per Capita			Grand Mean		
	FO	UH	LH	FO	UH	LH	FO	UH	LH
11. "With respect to local governments in this state, how do you feel about changing the allocation formula to encourage the consolidation of small government units?"									
Strongly favor	36	21	24	41	33	43	38	27	31
Somewhat favor	26	61	22	13	28	35	21	47	27
Somewhat oppose	27	11	39	7	20	5	19	15	26
Strongly oppose	11	7	15	39	18	17	21	12	16
Total	100	100	100	100	100	100	100	100	100

N =
FO	UH	LH
48	44	46

	Upper Half			Lower Half			Grand Mean		
12. "With respect to local governments in this state, how do you feel about changing the allocation formula to remove the penalty against getting revenue from user charges by including them in the definition of tax effort?"									
Strongly favor	47	33	24	40	22	43	45	29	31
Somewhat favor	29	43	22	20	42	35	26	43	27
Somewhat oppose	17	13	39	32	30	5	23	20	26
Strongly oppose	6	10	15	8	6	17	7	8	16
Total	100	100	100	100	100	100	100	100	100

N =
FO	UH	LH
43	44	37

formula had any influence on tax laws in this state?" Nevertheless, a substantial majority of all three groups of respondents favored keeping the present income tax provisions in the allocation formula. Perhaps the clue to this otherwise somewhat paradoxical juxtaposition of responses may be found in the fact that just under two-thirds of the fiscal officers interviewed and a somewhat larger proportion of the legislative respondents favor changing the allocation formula so as to increase the reward going to the States that impose their own income taxes. This view was expressed with appreciably more frequency among respondents in the richer States than it was by those in the poorer States.

What all of this seems to mean is that the existing weight attached to the income tax factor in the allocation formula is relatively small and therefore is seen as not having a major impact on tax policy, and at the same time State fiscal officers and legislative appropriations committee chairmen would apparently like to see the influence of the income tax in determining the distribution of GRS funds among the States increased. The proportion of re-

spondents who strongly oppose such a change is quite close to the proportion of States that now do *not* levy a personal income tax. Of 35 governors who responded to the question on increasing the importance in the allocation formula of the income tax factor, 25 took a position in favor of the change. On the whole, we conclude that State chief fiscal officers and legislative appropriations committee chairmen in general are not much exercised about the role of the individual income tax in the GRS allocation formula. We suspect that this follows from the fact that the five-factor House formula applies to only 20 States and for 3 of them (Connecticut, Nevada and New Jersey) the income tax factor is currently irrelevant because they do not levy the tax.

We turn next to the distribution of total revenue-sharing funds between the States and their local subdivisions. Our respondents, including 36 of the 50 governors, were asked whether they would prefer changing this distribution in favor of the States, in favor of the local jurisdictions, or changing it so as to make it proportional to tax effort. A majority of the governors appear to be opposed to changing the distribution in favor of either the States or the local units, with the majority being substantially greater in opposition to providing a larger share to local units. But the governors did, to the extent of 25 in favor as against 7 opposed, approve providing the States and their local subdivisions with shares proportional to their respective tax efforts. With respect, however, to the chief State fiscal officers and the chairmen of the appropriations committees, there is wide variance in response among them and also a substantial difference in the responses obtained from those representative of poorer States as compared with respondents from the richer States. A large majority of the fiscal officers favor giving a larger share of available funds to the States and, as might be expected, oppose giving a larger share to local units. A rather smaller majority of them approve of changing the allocation formula so as to distribute funds within each State in accordance with the relative tax efforts of the States and their eligible local jurisdictions. Legislative officers, particularly those from the poorer States, appear to favor the status quo, for they oppose both giving a larger share to the States and giving a larger share to local units. But, on the matter of whether or not shares should be distributed within each State between the State and its local subdivisions in accordance with tax effort, we find that legislative officers join the governors and chief State fiscal officers in being among the substantial majority of respondents who favor distribution between the states and their local subdivisions on the basis of respective tax effort.

One of the major issues that continues to hold the front of the stage in the debate on the merits of GRS has to do with the impact of this program on big cities versus smaller communities, rich versus poor communities, and very small governmental jurisdictions versus the rest of the country. Our survey results suggest that there is rather strong sentiment among the leadership in both the executive and legislative branches of State government in favor of changing the allocation formula so as to direct more money toward the poorer communities. Almost two-thirds of the governors and the chairmen of Lower House appropriations committees and about three-quarters of the State chief fiscal officers and chairmen of Upper House appropriations committees took this position when interviewed.

On the matter of changing the allocation formula so as to exclude from the distribution of funds "very small government units," only the chief State fiscal officers from the richer States supplied a majority in favor of such action. The proportion of governors who oppose it is about equal to that found among the legislative committee chairmen.

We asked all four groups of respondents the following question, "With respect to local governments in this State, how do you feel about changing the allocation formula to give more to big city areas?" The conclusion we draw from the responses received is that, with the modest exception of Lower House appropriations committee chairmen from the poorer States, all groups of elected respondents, including 25 of 32 governors who replied to the question, would oppose such action. On the other hand, more than three-quarters of the chief State fiscal officers from the richer States favor it, probably because the richer States are, in general, also those in which the larger, older cities experiencing severe fiscal difficulties are located. In light especially of the fact that the State and Local Assistance Act of 1972 places a ceiling of 145 percent of the average State-wide per capita amount distributed to local jurisdictions on the allocation of revenue-sharing funds to cities, it would appear that the governors and State legislative leaders tend not to believe that the fiscal salvation of the big city should come in any measure at the expense of other jurisdictions in the State.

Section 103 of the Act lists nine "priority categories" for which funds distributed to local governments may be spent. They include "ordinary and necessary maintenance and operating expenses" for eight functional categories of expenditure and "ordinary and necessary capital expenditures authorized by law."[6] But clearly, with local government expenditures rising at an average rate of 8-12 percent per year it is impossible to insure that GRS funds are in fact used as intended by the Congress; one of the purposes to which GRS funds may be put is reduction in local tax rates. This use is, of course, discouraged by the major role played by tax effort in determining the allocation of revenue-sharing funds within the States. Nevertheless, the question continues to arise as to whether or not further means of discouraging such use of revenue-sharing receipts is appropriate. We find relatively little support for this position among our respondents. Only 14 of 35 governors who expressed an opinion on this matter favor changing the within-State allocation formula so as to discourage reduction of local tax rates. And, as may be seen in Section 10 of Table 6-3, only one of our six groups of respondents—chairmen of Lower House appropriations committees in the poorer States—presents a majority in its favor.

Some people have seen GRS as an opportunity for bringing about consolidation of "inefficiently

[6]See General Explanation, op. cit., pp. 20-1, for a detailed discussion of the priority expenditure categories.

small" local governmental units. Should the allocation formula be changed so as to encourage such consolidation? Chief State fiscal officers from the poorer States constitute the only group of respondents among whom a substantial minority, close to 40 percent, indicated that they are strongly opposed to such action. And only the chairmen of Lower House appropriations committees in the richer States offer a majority (54 percent) in opposition to it, most of which opposition is expressed as "somewhat" rather than "strongly." It is interesting to note that within these same richer States the chairmen of Upper House appropriations committees differ sharply from their Lower House confreres. Less than one-fifth of that group opposes changing the allocation formula so as to encourage consolidation of small jurisdictions. This contrast may be due to the fact that members of Upper chambers typically represent larger constituencies than their Lower House counterparts, and frequently hold longer terms. The strength of this position is substantially weakened, however, when one observes that among the poorer States it is the chairmen of Upper House appropriations committees who are more frequently in opposition to the indicated change than are chairmen of the Lower House committees. Moreover, the elected State officials with the largest constituencies, namely the governors, split right down the middle on this issue. In general, however, apart from the governors, we find that all but one of our six groups of respondents offer a majority in favor of the indicated change.

Various user charges, essentially public prices charged for services rendered or goods delivered, such as water supply, sewage disposal, parking fees, patient charges in public hospitals, and so forth, are frequently major sources of revenue for both the States and their local jurisdictions. Such charges, however, are not included in tax revenues for purposes of allocating GRS funds either among the States or, within the States, among local jurisdictions. And yet it is difficult to draw a clear line of distinction between taxes and user charges, either in principle or even in terms of impact and distributional consequences among tax payers. Thus it may be argued that the Act discriminates unfairly against those jurisdictions that rely relatively heavily on user charges as opposed to those revenue sources that meet the definition of "taxation." In an effort to ascertain the views of State government officials on this issue we asked, "With respect to local governments in this state, how do you feel about changing the allocation formula to remove the penalty against getting revenue from user charges by including them in the definition of tax effort?" Close to three-quarters of the chief State fiscal officers indicated that they were either strongly or "somewhat" in favor of such a change. Approximately the same proportion of Upper House appropriations committee chairmen favored the change, but with less enthusiasm. In the case of Lower House appropriations committee chairmen, there is a substantial difference in the responses obtained from representatives from the richer States as compared with those from the poorer states. The latter are overwhelmingly in favor of the change, whereas the former group split more or less evenly. Obviously an explanation for this difference is not readily seen because similar differences do not appear with respect to chief State fiscal officers and Upper House committee chairmen. On the whole, it seems clear that amending the Act so as to include at least some user charges, perhaps those most closely resembling excise or selective sales taxes, would be welcomed by State officials, including the governors, more than two-thirds of whom favor the change.

General Attitudes Toward Revenue Sharing

Especially in some of the larger cities of the Nation debate continues on whether or not a fair share of GRS money is being used to help poor people. Some observers believe that the poor have been shortchanged under GRS, in part because they believe that GRS has either supplanted some Federal grant-in-aid programs or stifled their growth, and in part for a variety of other reasons. Thus we asked all of our respondents, including the governors, whether they agreed or disagreed with the statement, "A fair share of revenue sharing money goes to government services to poor people." On this issue we find a rather wide divergence of opinion among groups of respondents. The governors and chief State fiscal officers indicate agreement with this statement in proportions ranging from about 2:1 to as high as 3:1. Far more of those agreeing with the statement do so "somewhat," as compared with the proportion agreeing "strongly." A majority of chairmen of Lower House appropriations committees, however, disagree with the statement, albeit about two-thirds of them only "somewhat." With respect to Upper House appropriations committees chairmen, there is a substantial difference in the responses obtained depending on whether the person interviewed was from a rich or a poor State. Among chairmen from the richer States close to two-thirds agree that poor people are getting a fair share of GRS funds, whereas in the case of those from the poorer States less than half believe this to be the case.

Table 6-4

General Attitudes Toward Revenue Sharing

(Percentages)

	Upper Half of Personal Income Per Capita			Lower Half of Personal Income Per Capita			Grand Mean		
	FO	UH	LH	FO	UH	LH	FO	UH	LH
1. "A fair share of revenue sharing money goes to government services for poor people."									
Agree strongly	22	21	17	12	10	0	18	15	10
Agree somewhat	44	42	32	61	34	41	50	38	36
Disagree somewhat	22	37	36	17	40	40	20	39	38
Disagree strongly	12	0	15	11	16	18	12	8	16
Total	100	100	100	100	100	100	100	100	100

N = FO UH LH
      42 37 41

	FO	UH	LH	FO	UH	LH	FO	UH	LH
2. "Because the local jurisdictions are not permitted to spend their revenue sharing funds on operating expenses for education, there is increased pressure on state government to assist local units in financing education."									
Agree strongly	13	35	65	33	34	47	20	34	58
Agree somewhat	53	27	14	38	30	29	48	29	20
Disagree somewhat	31	31	10	12	32	19	24	31	19
Disagree strongly	-3	7	11	16	4	4	8	5	4
Total	100	100	100	100	100	100	100	100	100

N = FO UH LH
      47 40 42

	FO	UH	LH	FO	UH	LH	FO	UH	LH
3. "How do you feel about developing more complete budget reporting categories?"									
Strongly favor	11	48	23	5	24	20	9	36	22
Somewhat favor	15	5	27	18	14	20	17	9	24
Somewhat oppose	45	27	46	50	44	32	47	35	41
Strongly oppose	28	20	4	27	18	28	28	19	13
Total	100	100	100	100	100	100	100	100	100

N = FO UH LH
      45 43 40

	FO	UH	LH	FO	UH	LH	FO	UH	LH
4. "Do you view revenue sharing as a supplement or as a substitute to other forms of federal support to state and local governments?"									
Supplement	84	67	85	90	46	80	86	56	83
Substitute	16	32	15	10	54	20	14	44	17
Total	100	100	100	100	100	100	100	100	100

N = FO UH LH
      43 39 40

	FO	UH	LH	FO	UH	LH	FO	UH	LH
5. "Revenue sharing has undermined categorical grant-in-aid programs."									
Agree strongly	14	49	12	33	22	26	20	36	17
Agree somewhat	23	13	13	38	44	14	48	28	14
Disagree somewhat	41	20	56	12	14	49	24	17	54
Disagree strongly	22	17	18	16	20	10	8	19	15
Total	100	100	100	100	100	100	100	100	100

N = FO UH LH
      48 41 44

	FO	UH	LH	FO	UH	LH	FO	UH	LH
6. "How do you feel about adjusting payments to keep up with inflation?"									
Strongly favor	66	40	55	44	16	24	58	30	43
Somewhat favor	16	21	38	30	43	22	21	31	32
Somewhat oppose	2	38	2	8	35	9	4	37	5
Strongly oppose	16	0	4	19	5	44	17	3	19
Total	100	100	100	100	100	100	100	100	100

N = FO UH LH
      47 43 47

	Upper Half of Personal Income Per Capita			Lower Half of Personal Income Per Capita			Grand Mean		
	FO	UH	LH	FO	UH	LH	FO	UH	LH
7. "With respect to state government how do you feel about adjusting payments to keep up with inflation?"									
Strongly favor	68	41	67	51	44	29	61	42	52
Somewhat favor	14	40	29	20	8	26	17	27	28
Somewhat oppose	2	8	3	11	34	18	5	18	9
Strongly oppose	16	11	1	18	14	27	17	17	11
Total	100	100	100	100	100	100	100	100	100

N = FO UH LH
48 43 46

	FO	UH	LH	FO	UH	LH	FO	UH	LH
8. "Concern about the temporary nature of revenue sharing funds may have led some governments to spend most of their revenue sharing money on capital items."									
Agree strongly	50	56	67	65	64	60	55	60	70
Agree somewhat	00	42	21	28	28	26	29	35	23
Disagree somewhat	6	2	5	7	7	6	6	4	5
Disagree strongly	14	0	7	0	1	8	9	1	7
Total	100	100	100	100	100	100	100	100	100

N = FO UH LH
47 41 42

	FO	UH	LH	FO	UH	LH	FO	UH	LH
9. "With respect to *local governments* in this state, how do you feel about eliminating priority expenditure requirements?"									
Strongly favor	30	39	32	34	35	36	31	38	34
Somewhat favor	47	15	33	55	21	22	50	17	28
Somewhat oppose	20	14	26	10	19	20	16	16	23
Strongly oppose	3	32	9	1	25	22	2	29	14
Total	100	100	100	100	100	100	100	100	100

N = FO UH LH
46 45 43

	FO	UH	LH	FO	UH	LH	FO	UH	LH
10. "Is revenue sharing likely to make any difference in your ability to deal with the three most important problems facing your state?"									
Yes	84	84	81	84	64	78	84	76	80
No	16	16	19	16	36	22	16	24	20
Total	100	100	100	100	100	100	100	100	100

N = FO UH LH
50 43 46

	FO	UH	LH	FO	UH	LH	FO	UH	LH
11. "If you were free to allocate your state revenue sharing funds all over again, would you do it the same way or do it differently?"									
Do it the same way	85	61	79	96	82	71	89	70	76
Do it differently	15	39	21	4	17	29	11	29	24
Total	100	100	100	100	100	100	100	100	100

N = FO UH LH
48 42 47

It is rather difficult to know what conclusions to draw from the responses to this question as presented in the first block of numbers in Table 6-4. It is, perhaps, significant to note that very few of our respondents either agree or disagree *strongly* with the statement. Most, rather; seem to be hedging their positions, perhaps because they are unsure of the "true facts," or perhaps because avoiding a strong stand on the issue may appear to be the "safest" posture to assume.

In the immediately following question it was suggested that increased pressure on the States to provide additional fiscal assistance for education results from the prohibition against the use of local receipts under GRS for education. More than two-thirds of the governors and their chief state fiscal officers who responded to this question express agreement with the statement. Among Upper House appropriations committee chairmen the proportion in agreement is even higher, with fully two-thirds of those representing the richer States agreeing strongly. Since in most States education is the responsibility of independent school districts rather than districts that are dependent upon the general municipal budget, it is by no means clear why the indicated opinion should be so widely held by both executive and legislative branch State government officials. That they do agree with the statement in such large proportions may reflect simply the continuation of perennial pressures that long antedate GRS. But there may be more to it than that. In at least some States, awareness of the fact that the state is now receiving an infusion of untied funds may inspire school districts to intensify efforts to obtain more State aid. Unfortunately the question is so phrased that one cannot be sure whether those interviewed are agreeing with the causal implications contained in the statement with which they were confronted or whether they are merely agreeing with the latter part of it which suggests that there is "increased pressure on state government to assist local units in financing education."

As we have noted above, the State and Local Assistance Act of 1972 sets out in Section 103 certain "priority categories" of expenditures for the use of funds received by local jurisdictions. Budget reporting categories employed in the Use Reports required under the Act of local governments employ these same priority categories of expenditure. We asked our respondents whether they favor or oppose the development of more complete budget reporting categories. Two-thirds of the governors who replied to this question express opposition to the suggestion that "more complete" budget reporting categories be required and between just over half and three-quarters of the other three groups of respondents oppose it as well, with

the strongest opposition coming from chief State fiscal officers.

At the same time we find that an overwhelmingly large majority, over 80 percent, of the chief State fiscal officers favor eliminating entirely the provisions regarding priority expenditures as they apply to local governmental jurisdictions. The governors are somewhat less solidly in favor of this position, with 22 of the 36 governors interviewed being equally divided between those strongly favoring it and those only "somewhat" in favor of it. A majority of each of the four groups of appropriations committee chairmen favor eliminating the restrictive priority expenditure requirements, but these majorities are substantially smaller than those found among the governors and their chief fiscal officers.

Two questions were asked at different points in the interview schedule which were designed to elicit opinions on the relationship between GRS and other Federal aid programs. In the first of these questions our respondents were asked whether they regard revenue sharing as a supplement or as a substitute for other forms of Federal support to State and local governments. Some 85 percent of State fiscal officers and a similar proportion of Lower House appropriations committee chairmen regard GRS as a supplement· to rather than a substitute for other forms of Federal aid. Upper House committee chairmen, however, particularly those representing the poorer States, seem much more evenly divided on this issue.

The other closely related question asked the respondent whether he agrees or disagrees, "strongly" or "somewhat", with the statement "Revenue sharing has undermined categorical grant-in-aid programs." One might reasonably presume that consistency would require those who believe that GRS is a substitute for other forms of Federal support to express agreement with this statement, and vice versa. In fact some degree of consistency does emerge. That is, the group of respondents that most frequently expresses the view that GRS is a substitute for other forms of Federal support also most frequently agrees with the suggestion that revenue sharing has "undermined" the categorical grant-in-aid programs. Thus a substantial majority, approximately two-thirds of Upper House appropriations committee chairmen agree with the statement, while only some one-third of Lower House committee chairmen do so. Inconsistency seems to appear most strongly among chief State fiscal officers in the poorer States, where we find that 90 percent of them express the view that GRS is a supplement rather than a substitute for other Federal support programs and, at the same time, 71 percent of them managed to agree as well with the view that revenue sharing has undermined categorical grant-in-aid programs.[7] Thus one may find the responses to these closely related questions interesting, but it is, indeed, difficult to know how to interpret them in terms of relevant policy implications.

Should payments under GRS to local governments and the States be adjusted so as to keep up with inflation? Two questions were asked on this subject, one with respect to local jurisdictions and the other with respect to the States. In the case of the question relating to local jurisdictions (number 6, Table 6-4), we find considerable opposition expressed to the idea that payments to local governments should "keep up with inflation." That opposition is especially strong among Lower House appropriations committee chairmen in the poorer States, where 44 percent registered strong opposition. This contrasts sharply with the figure of 4 percent for their counterparts representing the richer States. The reasons for this disparity are by no means obvious. One may speculate, perhaps, that appropriations committee chairmen in the poorer States may envisage the State having to contribute toward the budgetary costs of adjusting payments to local governments in general if GRS payments are adjusted for inflation. Be that as it may, among all respondents we find that a substantial majority favors adjusting payments under GRS for price increases.

Somewhat more surprising, perhaps, is the fact that when the question is rephrased so that it relates to *State* government, while 30 of 35 governors and more than three-quarters of the chief State fiscal officers favor adjusting payments under GRS for inflation, again substantial opposition to doing so appears among legislative appropriations committee chairmen in the poorer States. Approximately half of the chairmen of both houses among the States oppose adjustments for inflation. This finding simply defies rational explanation.

A widely held hypothesis argues that the fact that the State and Local Assistance Act of 1972 carries an expiration date of December 31, 1976, introduces uncertainty regarding the future of GRS, and that this uncertainty has led some governments to spend most of their allotments on capital assets rather than expansion of operations. Thus we asked all respondents to express agreement or disagreement with the following statement: "Concern about the temporary nature of revenue sharing funds may have led some governments to spend most of their revenue sharing money on

capital items." A majority of each of the seven groups of respondents who answered this question, including 19 of 32 governors, agree *strongly* with the statement. The proportion disagreeing either strongly or "somewhat" ranges from only 2 percent for Upper House appropriations committee chairmen in the richer states to a high of 20 percent for chief State fiscal officers in these same States. In fact, no other question asked of respondents representing State governments elicited as strong or as uniform agreement as did this one. Nevertheless, this widespread agreement certainly cannot be said to "prove" the truth of the hypothesis. It may stem as much from the wording of the question, wording that includes such terms as "may" and "some," as from belief on the part of our respondents that the hypothesis is in fact true. Some evidence on this matter is presented in Chapter 2, dealing with estimates of the actual uses to which local jurisdictions have put their GRS receipts and in a later section of this chapter which offers similar estimates for State governments.

Those interviewed were asked to name the three most important problems facing their State. A further question asked whether revenue sharing would be likely to make any difference in the States' ability to deal with these problems. The vast majority of each of our categories of respondents, between three-quarters and five-sixths of them, do believe that GRS funds make a difference in the State's ability to deal with its most important problems. This is, of course, hardly surprising, particularly in light of the answers obtained to the question, "What would you say are the three most important problems facing your State?" The problems mentioned by more than a third of our respondents are education, planning, general fiscal problems and inflation. Other frequently mentioned problems are environmental improvement, transportation, health, the need for more jobs, and the general ability of government to function effectively. And, for the most part, these are problems the solution of which clearly requires substantial sums of money.[8]

Interviewers probed respondents for explanations as to why revenue sharing did or did not make a difference in the State's ability to deal with its most important problems. For the most part, those who believe that revenue sharing does make a difference do so because in their States they see GRS funds being used to finance programs specifically designed to cope with the main problems. Others indicate that GRS does make a difference because of its contribution to the State's

---

[7]It should be noted that, prior to the State and Local Assistance Act of 1972 and subsequent legislative action introducing the so-called special revenue sharing programs, virtually all federal support to state and local governments came in the form of categorical grants-in-aid.

[8]It is interesting to note that crime, race relations, and housing were rarely mentioned as being among the three most important problems facing the state.

total revenues. On the other hand those who claim that revenue sharing is not likely to make any difference most often cited one or more of the following reasons: revenue-sharing funds are not used to solve the specific problem mentioned; the problem cannot be solved or is not being solved; the problem is too big relative to GRS for the latter to have a significant effect; or the problem is not amenable to solution by the use of more money.

Finally, we have a question as to whether the chief State fiscal officers and chairmen of legislative appropriations committees, if they were free to allocate State GRS funds all over again, would do it the same way or would they do it differently. We find that chief State fiscal officers are apparently quite well satisfied with the way in which their States have allocated GRS funds. Nine out of ten of them would do it the same way if they had the opportunity to change the allocation. For the chairmen of Upper and Lower House appropriations committees there appears to be less satisfaction with the way in which GRS funds were allocated as of the time of the interviews. In total roughly a quarter of these chairmen would "do it differently," the highest proportion expressing this view being the 39 percent of Upper House appropriations committee chairmen in the richer States.

THE FISCAL IMPACT OF REVENUE SHARING ON STATE GOVERNMENTS

One way in which some early indications may be uncovered with respect to what State governments did in fiscal year 1974 with the funds received under GRS is to ask those playing a major role in fiscal decisions what they believe would have happened if GRS funds had not been forthcoming. We find, as indicated in Table 6-5, that most of the chief State fiscal officers and chairmen of Upper and Lower House appropriations committees believe that their States would have reduced expenditures. There is considerable variance in the extent to which this view is held as between those representing the richer States and those representing the poorer States. By and large the view that expenditures would have been reduced in the absence of GRS is substantially more widespread among respondents from the richer States.

In general it appears that less than 40 percent of the States would have cut expenditures by the full amount of their revenue-sharing allocation and that some States would have cut operating expenditures, some capital expenditures, and, especially in the view of chief State fiscal officers, a large proportion of the States would have reduced both categories of expenditure.

There is a good deal of disagreement among respondents as to the extent to which the States would have reduced expenditures in the form of transfers to local jurisdictions. About 70 percent of the chief State fiscal officers from the richer States believe that this would happen, but less than 40 percent of those from the poorer States believe it. The contrast between the two groups of chairmen of Upper House appropriations committees is even sharper, while the proportions with respect to Lower House appropriations committee chairmen, as shown in the last column of Table 6-5, are virtually identical.

Since most States, according to our respondents, would have reduced expenditures in fiscal year 1974 by less than the full amount of their revenue-sharing allocation, it follows that for a large proportion of the States reduced expenditures would have been accompanied by higher taxes and/or increased borrowing, while for some the response might simply have been higher taxes. Table 6-6, when read in conjunction with Table 6-5, casts some light on the opinions of our respondents in this matter. The wide variance on whether or not taxes would have been higher in 1974 without GRS

Table 6-5
Percent of All States That Would Have Reduced Expenditures in 1974
Without General Revenue Sharing

	Percent of States That Would Have Reduced Expenditures			Percent of (All) States That Would Have Reduced Expenditures by the Amount of the Revenue Sharing Allocation			Percent of States That Would Have Reduced Operating Expenditures			Percent of States That Would Have Reduced Capital Expenditures			Percent of States That Would Have Reduced Transfers To Localities		
	FO	UH	LH	FO	UH	LH	FO	UH	LH	FO	UH	LH	FO	UH	LH
Richer States	83.3	83.3	70.2	35.0	40.0	55.9	58.8	40.0	46.9	20.2	57.6	48.6	69.4	72.9	51.6
Poorer States	63.8	51.3	62.4	39.5	40.0	29.2	34.9	9.7	40.6	50.4	35.4	61.3	38.7	23.3	51.8
Grand Mean	76.1	69.8	67.2	36.7	39.6	45.5	49.9	21.2	44.4	31.4	48.2	53.5	58.1	51.9	51.6

N =   FO   UH   LH
        50   45   47

	Higher Taxes			Increased Borrowing		
	FO	UH	LH	FO	UH	LH
Richer States	48	29	12	2	0	1
Poorer States	19	29	16	5	16	20
Grand Mean	37	29	14	3	7	8

$$N = \frac{FO \quad UH \quad LH}{50 \quad 45 \quad 47}$$

suggests that the opinions of our respondents are just that and can hardly be construed as "the truth." For example, among the richer States we find that almost half of the chief fiscal officers express the view that taxes would have been higher in the absence of GRS, but only 12 percent of chairmen of Lower House appropriations committees express this opinion. The range of opinion is widest among the poorer States, not between the executive and legislative branch respondents, but between the Upper and Lower House committee chairmen. In this instance, almost twice as large a proportion of the Upper House as compared with the Lower House committee chairmen believe that taxes would have gone up had revenue sharing not been forthcoming. Only among respondents from the poorer States do we find any appreciable expectation that borrowing would have increased had there been no revenue sharing for 1974.

On the whole, the impressions gained from results presented in Tables 6-5 and 6-6 indicate considerable difference of opinion among those who "should know" as to the fiscal consequences for their States of the availability of GRS for fiscal year 1974. Nevertheless, applying to the States the methodology detailed in Chapter 2 with respect to the fiscal impact of GRS on local units of government, we have estimated the percentage distribution as well as the absolute dollar distribution of the fiscal impact of GRS on the States for fiscal years 1974 and 1975, using fiscal officer responses as well as the responses of Upper and Lower House appropriations committee chairmen. These estimates are presented in Tables 6-7—6-12. The fiscal impact categories used are: "maintained or increased operating expenditures," "maintained or increased capital expenditures," "maintained or increased transfers to local governments," "stabilized or reduced taxes," "stabilized or reduced borrowing," and "additions to surplus." The States are grouped both by major region and by income level.

Looking first at the estimates based on the responses of State fiscal officers, we find that for 1974 GRS funds are estimated to have been used to maintain or increase the three categories of expenditures to the extent of about 60 percent of the total

received, while lower levels of taxes or borrowing and additions to surpluses accounted for the remainder of the funds. For fiscal year 1975 the proportion purported to be going toward maintenance or expansion of expenditures increases to about two-thirds, while the other categories of use of funds account for less than one-third. For both years there appear to be substantial differences in the way in which GRS funds were used as between Upper and Lower income States. Lower income States appear to have used GRS funds much less extensively than the richer States for maintenance or increases in operating expenditures and more extensively for adding to surpluses. On the other hand, the richer States used GRS much more to stabilize or reduce taxes than did the poorer States. Differences among regions are substantial, particularly as between the South and the rest of the country. This regional difference seems largely to support the observed difference with respect to level of income.

Overall, on the basis of State fiscal officers replies to the relevant questions in our interview schedule, it would appear that of the $2 billion in State receipts under GRS, in actual dollar terms the major beneficiaries were the local jurisdictions whose transfers from the State governments were maintained or increased. The next most important single category for 1974 was "stabilized or reduced taxes." The picture differs somewhat for 1975, when we find that maintenance or increases in transfers to local jurisdictions is still, at $559 million, most important, but maintenance or increase in operating expenditures at approximately $500 million is substantially higher than the amount accounted for by stabilization or reduction in taxes.

Comparison of the estimates presented in Table 6-7 with those found in Tables 6-9 and 6-11 permits us to gain some impressions as to the extent to which there is agreement among the three main groups of respondents for the effects in fiscal year 1974. Because we were able to interview all 50 chief State fiscal officers but only 45 chairmen of Upper House appropriations committees and 48 chairmen of Lower House appropriations committees, the numbers in the nonresponse columns of Tables 6-9—6-11 are very much larger than those found in the same column of Table 6-7. This factor reduces but does not destroy the comparability we seek. Nevertheless, it is difficult to generalize about the direction and structure of differences based on the three sets of interviews. For example, the State fiscal officers and chairmen of Upper House appropriations committees are reasonably close, with respect to totals, under the column headed "stabilized or reduced taxes." But when one compares estimates by region large differences appear and the ostensible similarity in the totals emerges as a consequence of offsetting differences among the regions. Most disturbing, perhaps, are such differences as may be seen in the column relating to maintenance or increase in operating expenditures for Table 6-9 and Table 6-11. For the North-central States, for example, we find that Lower House committee chairmen appear to allocate more than three times as much of the States' GRS funds to maintenance or increases in operating expenditures as do their Upper House counterparts. Similar differences may be found in various other segments

of the tables and between the estimates based on responses of fiscal officers and each of the two groups of committee chairmen.

Turning to Tables 6-8, 6-10 and 6-12, which relate to fiscal year 1975, there does not appear to be an appreciable improvement in consistency of results. Conceivably one of the three groups of respondents provides a basis for reasonably accurate estimates. Our basic data and methodology at best lend themselves to rough estimates. Nevertheless, estimates such as those presented in Tables 6-7–6-12, despite their obvious shortcomings, may still be superior to any other estimates currently available. From them we believe that one can safely conclude that for 1975, for example, it is likely that about one-half to three-quarters of a billion dollars of State proceeds under GRS went into stabilizing or reducing taxes, stabilizing or reducing borrowing, and additions to surplus, while something between $1.2 and 1.5 billion was devoted to maintaining or increasing expenditures in the form of operating and capital expenditures and transfers to

Table 6-7
Estimated Fiscal Impact of GRS on the States, Fiscal Year 1974,
Finance Officer Responses, by Region and Income Level

	Number of Cases	Fiscal Impact Categories							Total Revenue Sharing Allocation
		Maintained or Increased Operating Expenditures	Maintained or Increased Capital Expenditures	Maintained or Increased Transfers to Local Governments	Stabilized or Reduced Taxes	Stabilized or Reduced Borrowing	Additions to Surplus	Non-Response	
		(millions of dollars)							
Region[a]									
Northeast	9	127.4	11.5	206.3	176.9	10.0	−14.2	. . . .	518.0
North Central	12	98.8	96.9	137.0	74.0	52.0	20.6	43.2	522.5
South	16	83.6	137.4	67.2	55.4	7.2	279.6	. . . .	630.5
West	13	68.2	35.0	121.9	149.4	. . . .	−2.6	. . . .	371.9
Total	50	378.0	280.7	532.5	455.7	69.2	283.5	43.2	2,042.9
Income[b]									
Upper Half	25	304.8	86.3	400.6	397.4	52.0	2.0	43.2	1,286.4
Lower Half	25	73.2	194.4	131.8	58.3	17.2	281.5	. . . .	756.5
		(percent of total)							
Region									
Northeast	9	24.6	2.2	39.8	34.2	1.9	−2.7	. . . .	100.0
North Central	12	18.9	18.5	26.2	14.2	10.0	3.9	8.3	100.0
South	16	13.3	21.8	10.7	8.8	1.1	44.3	. . . .	100.0
West	13	18.3	9.4	32.8	40.2	. . . .	−0.7	. . . .	100.0
Total	50	18.5	13.7	26.1	22.3	3.4	13.9	2.1	100.0
Income									
Upper Half	25	23.7	6.7	31.1	30.9	4.0	0.2	3.4	100.0
Lower Half	25	9.7	25.7	17.4	7.7	2.3	37.2	. . . .	100.0

[a]Northeast: Connecticut, Maine, Massachusetts, New Hampshire, New Jersey, New York, Pennsylvania, Rhode Island, Vermont.
North Central: Illinois, Indiana, Iowa, Kansas, Michigan, Minnesota, Missouri, Nebraska, North Dakota, Ohio, South Dakota, Wisconsin.
South: Alabama, Arkansas, Delaware, Florida, Georgia, Kentucky, Louisiana, Maryland, Mississippi, North Carolina, Oklahoma, South Carolina, Tennessee, Texas, Virginia, West Virginia.
West: Alaska, Arizona, California, Colorado, Hawaii, Idaho, Montana, Nevada, New Mexico, Oregon, Utah, Washington, Wyoming.
[b]See Table 1 for listing of states by per capita income.

Table 6-8

Estimated Fiscal Impact of GRS on the States, Fiscal Year 1975,
Finance Officer Responses, by Region and Income Level

		Fiscal Impact Categories							
	Number of Cases	Maintained or Increased Operating Expenditures	Maintained or Increased Capital Expenditures	Maintained or Increased Transfers to Local Governments	Stabilized or Reduced Taxes	Stabilized or Reduced Borrowing	Additions to Surplus	Non-Response	Total Revenue Sharing Allocation
		(millions of dollars)							
Region[a]									
Northeast	9	121.4	54.6	134.4	197.9	6.2	−49.7	66.0	530.8
North Central	12	148.7	64.4	133.4	60.0	52.0	76.9	. . . .	535.4
South	16	166.7	195.0	165.5	62.7	21.6	34.5	. . . .	646.0
West	13	62.1	28.4	125.7	112.2	. . . .	32.3	20.4	381.1
Total	50	498.9	342.5	558.9	432.8	79.8	94.1	86.4	2,093.2
Income[b]									
Upper Half	25	340.7	92.2	336.7	363.8	52.0	46.4	86.4	1,318.1
Lower Half	25	158.2	250.3	222.2	68.9	27.8	47.7	. . . .	775.1
		(percent of total)							
Region									
Northeast	9	22.9	10.3	25.3	37.3	1.2	−9.4	12.4	100.0
North Central	12	27.8	12.0	24.9	11.2	9.7	14.4	. . . .	100.0
South	16	25.8	30.2	25.6	9.7	3.3	5.3	. . . .	100.0
West	13	16.3	7.5	33.0	29.4	. . . .	8.5	5.4	100.0
Total	50	23.8	16.4	26.7	20.7	3.8	4.5	4.1	100.0
Income									
Upper Half	25	25.8	7.0	25.5	27.6	3.9	3.5	6.6	100.0
Lower Half	25	20.4	32.3	28.7	8.9	3.8	6.2	. . . .	100.0

[a]See Table 6-7 for listing of states by region.
[b]See Table 6-1 for listing of states by per capita income.

Table 6-9

Estimated Fiscal Impact of GRS on the States, Fiscal Year 1974, Responses of Chairmen,
Appropriations Committees, Upper Houses, by Region and Income Level

		Fiscal Impact Categories							
	Number of Cases	Maintained or Increased Operating Expenditures	Maintained or Increased Capital Expenditures	Maintained or Increased Transfers to Local Governments	Stabilized or Reduced Taxes	Stabilized or Reduced Borrowing	Additions to Surplus	Non-Response	Total Revenue Sharing Allocation
		(millions of dollars)							
Region[a]									
Northeast	9	93.8	120.5	170.0	32.4	. . . .	29.9	71.4	518.0
North Central	11	18.7	109.9	80.6	210.3	. . . .	−0.1	103.1	522.5
South	14	21.6	79.5	68.8	119.2	141.7	29.8	169.9	630.5
West	11	42.6	15.4	45.6	28.9	. . . .	12.5	226.9	371.9
Total	45	176.8	325.2	365.0	390.8	141.7	72.1	571.3	2,042.9
Income[b]									
Upper Half	22	150.8	159.6	259.7	216.2	. . . .	72.1	428.0	1,286.4
Lower Half	23	26.0	165.6	105.3	174.6	141.7	−0.0	143.3	756.5
		(percent of total)							
Region									
Northeast	9	18.1	23.2	32.8	6.2	. . . .	5.8	13.8	100.0
North Central	11	3.6	21.0	15.4	40.2	. . . .	−0.0	19.7	100.0
South	14	3.4	12.6	10.9	18.9	22.5	4.7	26.9	100.0
West	11	11.4	4.1	12.3	7.8	. . . .	3.3	61.0	100.0
Total	45	8.6	15.9	17.9	19.1	6.9	3.5	28.0	100.0
Income									
Upper Half	22	11.7	12.4	20.2	16.8	. . . .	5.6	33.3	100.0
Lower Half	23	3.4	21.9	13.9	23.1	18.7	−0.0	18.9	100.0

[a]See Table 6-7 for listing of states by region.
[b]See Table 6-1 for listing of states by per capita income.

Table 6-10

Estimated Fiscal Impact of GRS on the States, Fiscal Year 1975, Responses of Chairmen, Appropriations Committees, Upper Houses, by Region and Income Level

	Number of Cases	Fiscal Impact Categories							Total Revenue Sharing Allocation
		Maintained or Increased Operating Expenditures	Maintained or Increased Capital Expenditures	Maintained or Increased Transfers to Local Governments	Stabilized or Reduced Taxes	Stabilized or Reduced Borrowing	Additions to Surplus	Non-Response	
		(millions of dollars)							
Region[a]									
Northeast	9	153.5	112.5	130.5	178.5	2.9	−120.4	73.3	530.8
North Central	11	26.7	74.0	81.3	228.1	. . . .	20.5	104.8	535.4
South.	14	58.2	210.1	79.7	47.9	39.2	76.7	134.2	646.0
West	11	9.3	14.2	29.2	23.4	2.3	40.1	262.6	381.1
Total	45	247.6	410.7	320.8	477.9	44.5	16.9	574.8	2,093.2
Income[b]									
Upper Half	22	203.7	115.2	225.4	384.9	2.3	−72.6	459.2	1,318.1
Lower Half	23	43.9	295.5	95.4	93.0	42.2	89.5	115.6	775.1
		(percent of total)							
Region									
Northeast	9	28.9	21.2	24.6	33.6	0.5	−22.7	13.8	100.0
North Central	11	5.0	13.8	15.2	42.6	. . . .	3.8	19.5	100.0
South.	14	9.0	32.5	12.3	7.4	6.1	11.9	20.8	100.0
West	11	2.4	3.7	7.7	6.1	0.0	10.5	60.0	100.0
Total	45	11.8	19.6	15.3	22.8	2.1	0.8	27.5	100.0
Income									
Upper Half	22	15.4	8.7	17.1	29.2	0.2	−5.5	34.9	100.0
Lower Half	23	5.7	38.1	12.3	12.0	5.4	11.5	14.9	100.0

[a]See Table 6-7 for listing of states by region.
[b]See Table 6-1 for listing of states by per capita income.

Table 6-11

Estimated Fiscal Impact of GRS on the States, Fiscal Year 1974, Responses of Chairmen, Appropriations Committees, Lower Houses, by Region and Income Level

	Number of Cases	Fiscal Impact Categories							Total Revenue Sharing Allocation
		Maintained or Increased Operating Expenditures	Maintained or Increased Capital Expenditures	Maintained or Increased Transfers to Local Governments	Stabilized or Reduced Taxes	Stabilized or Reduced Borrowing	Additions to Surplus	Non-Response	
		(millions of dollars)							
Region[a]									
Northeast	9	130.3	92.7	130.3	112.2	12.8	39.7	. . . .	518.0
North Central	10	66.9	193.5	85.9	50.9	. . . .	24.2	101.1	522.5
South.	16	53.8	92.9	105.6	63.3	107.6	167.4	39.9	630.5
West	13	49.6	29.6	29.1	14.1	. . . .	4.6	244.8	371.9
Total	48	300.6	408.8	350.9	240.6	120.4	235.9	385.8	2,042.9
Income[b]									
Upper Half	23	231.6	275.4	233.7	120.0	5.0	74.8	345.9	1,286.4
Lower Half	25	69.0	133.4	117.2	120.5	115.4	161.1	39.9	756.5
		(percent of total)							
Region									
Northeast	9	25.2	17.9	25.1	21.7	2.5	7.7	. . . .	100.0
North Central	10	12.8	37.0	16.4	9.7	. . . .	4.6	19.3	100.0
South.	16	8.5	14.7	16.7	10.0	17.1	26.5	6.3	100.0
West	13	13.3	8.0	7.8	3.8	. . . .	1.2	65.8	100.0
Total	48	14.7	20.0	17.2	11.8	5.9	11.5	18.8	100.0
Income									
Upper Half	23	18.0	21.4	18.2	9.3	0.4	5.8	26.8	100.0
Lower Half	25	9.1	17.6	15.5	15.9	15.2	21.3	5.3	100.0

[a]See Table 6-7 for listing of states by region.
[b]See Table 6-1 for listing of states by per capita income.

Table 6-12
Estimated Fiscal Impact of GRS on the States, Fiscal Year 1975, Responses of Chairmen,
Appropriations Committees, Lower Houses, by Region and Income Level

	Number of Cases	Maintained or Increased Operating Expenditures	Maintained or Increased Capital Expenditures	Maintained or Increased Transfers to Local Governments	Stabilized or Reduced Taxes	Stabilized or Reduced Borrowing	Additions to Surplus	Non-Response	Total Revenue Sharing Allocation
				(millions of dollars)					
Region[a]									
Northeast.......	9	91.0	71.4	84.4	124.4	3.2	156.2	....	530.8
North Central....	10	55.3	174.2	98.6	92.1	....	3.0	112.2	535.4
South...........	16	93.6	122.2	199.6	19.5	98.1	113.0	....	646.0
West	13	49.8	13.6	29.5	21.0	....	12.1	254.9	381.1
Total	48	289.7	381.4	412.0	257.1	101.3	284.5	367.1	2,093.2
Income[b]									
Upper Half	23	168.3	233.8	205.3	184.8	3.5	180.6	341.7	1,318.1
Lower Half	25	121.4	147.6	206.7	72.4	97.8	103.9	25.4	775.1
				(percent of total)					
Region									
Northeast.......	9	17.1	13.4	15.9	23.4	0.6	29.4	....	100.0
North Central....	10	10.3	32.5	18.4	17.2	....	0.6	20.9	100.0
South...........	16	14.5	18.9	30.9	3.0	15.2	17.5	....	100.0
West	13	13.1	3.6	7.7	5.5	....	3.2	66.9	100.0
Total	48	13.8	18.2	19.7	12.3	4.8	13.6	17.5	100.0
Income									
Upper Half	23	12.8	17.7	15.6	14.0	0.3	13.7	25.9	100.0
Lower Half	25	15.7	19.0	26.5	9.3	12.6	13.4	3.3	100.0

[a]See Table 6-7 for listing of states by region.
[b]See Table 6-1 for listing of states by per capita income.

local jurisdictions. It may, however, be pressing the data too far to attempt to draw from them any major inferences about differences in the fiscal impact of GRS among States grouped either by region or by income level.

REGRESSION ANALYSIS

We have little or nothing in the form of rigorously developed theoretical explanations, either for the variance among respondents in their opinions regarding the many aspects of GRS on which responses are reported in this chapter, or for the variance among the States in the uses to which GRS funds have been put. We believe it of interest, nevertheless, to test several intuitively plausible hypotheses. To this end we have estimated a number of regression equations, using ordinary least squares techniques, equations that assume a linear relationship between the variable whose behavior we wish to explain and selected independent or "predictor" variables.

Respondents' Views on Selected Aspects of GRS

Responses to four questions asked of State fiscal officers and chairmen of Upper and Lower House appropriations committees were selected for analysis. They relate to whether or not more funds should be channeled to the big cities; whether the State-local allocation should be changed from one-third and two-thirds to proportionality to tax effort; whether the State share should be increased at the expense of local units of government; and whether GRS has led to the introduction of new State programs. In each case the dependent variable has been expressed as a dichotomous "dummy," taking on a value of 1 for a "yes" or "agree" response and 0 otherwise. The responses thus coded of all of the State officials interviewed (except the governors) constitute the set of observations for each of the dependent variables.

Our hypotheses reflect the intuitive expectation that preferences with respect to the distribution formula are governed by the level of per capita income in the State (PCY); the location, by major region, of the State (LOC);[9] its population density (DEN) or an alternative measure in the form of the proportion of the population that lives in cities with a population of more than 50,000 (URB); the degree of State centralization of State-local fiscal responsibility, as measured by the ratio of State to total State-local revenue (GR); GRS funds per capita (GPC); the level of State expenditures per capita (EXP); and whether or not the respondent is a chief State fiscal officer (FO). In the estimating

---

[9]LOC 1 is location in the South; LOC 2 is location in the West; LOC 3 is location in the North Central region; and the Northeastern States are the "control" group.

equations reported here some of these variables were dropped after preliminary analysis.

The equation for whether or not respondents favor increasing the share of big cities in GRS funds (GBC) is (with 't' values in parentheses):

$$GBC = -.0670 + .0001\ PCY - .1225\ LOC\ 1 - .2039\ LOC2$$
$$(1.25) \qquad (0.98) \qquad (1.68)$$
$$- .0530\ LOC\ 3 + .1485\ URB + .2798\ FO$$
$$(0.41) \qquad (0.52) \qquad (3.35)$$

$$R^2 = .08;\ \text{'F' ratio} = 3.22$$

In combination the location of the State, its per-capita income, "urbanness," and whether or not the respondent is a fiscal officer account for only about 8 percent of total variance in the dependent variable. The signs of the coefficients presented in the estimation equation are all as expected, but only the coefficient for FO is clearly statistically significant.

The corresponding equation for whether or not respondents favor the distribution of GRS funds between the States and their local subdivisions in accordance with relative tax effort (DPT) is:

$$DPT = .7689 - .0001\ PCY + .2200\ LOC\ 1 + .1139\ LOC\ 2$$
$$(1.77) \qquad (1.74) \qquad (0.89)$$
$$+ .3581\ LOC\ 3 + .0006\ EXP - .0606\ FO$$
$$(2.73) \qquad (2.70) \qquad (0.71)$$

$$R^2 = .06;\ \text{'F' ratio} = 252$$

Again, R^2, at .06, is unimpressive. As expected, being located outside of the Northeast region, where traditions of strong local autonomy and major local fiscal responsibility make for decentralization of State-local finances, is associated with a greater likelihood that the respondent favors distribution of GRS funds according to the ratio of state to total state-local tax receipts. High per capita state expenditures are positively associated as well with favoring this approach.

The equation for whether or not respondents favor giving more GRS funds to the States at the expense of local governments does not yield a statistically significant 'F' ratio and is not of sufficient interest to warrant its reproduction here. Perhaps, with respect to this variable as well as the two for which the estimating equations are presented above, the most interesting finding is that such factors as level of income, population density or concentration of the population in large cities, and our measure of State centralization of State-local finances do not consistently explain an appreciable proportion of total variance.

A fourth variable, whether or not GRS has led to the introduction of new programs, was believed to be one that might reasonably be expected to be influenced by a set of predictor variables such as that employed in the regression equations relating to views expressed on possible changes in the allocation of GRS funds. Here again, however, the regression coefficients estimated turned out to be anything but "robust," and the equation yielded an R^2 of .01.

Obviously respondents differ sharply, as we have seen, on their views with regard to most aspects of GRS covered in our survey of State officials. But, just as obviously, we are unable to explain these differences in terms of those characteristics of the States suggested by our intuitive expectations for inclusion in our analysis.

Fiscal Impact of GRS

Assuming that the chief fiscal officers in the States are likely to be the most knowledgable of our three principal groups of respondents, we have selected for purposes of analysis of the fiscal impact of GRS the estimates based on their interviews (see Tables 6-7 and 6-8). Our objective is to account for the variance in the proportions of GRS funds said to be applied in 1974 and 1975 to maintaining or increasing operating expenditures (OP74 and OP75), to maintaining or increasing capital outlays (CAP74 and CAP75), to maintaining or increasing transfers to local units (TR74 and TR75), and to stabilizing or reducing taxes (TAX 74 and TAX 75).

With respect to OP74 and OP75 we expect that there is a positive association with DEN, CEN, location outside of the Northeast region, and EXP, and a negative association with GPC and GR. The estimated equations are as follows:

$$OP74 = -.2061 + .0000\ PCY + .0976\ LOC\ 1 + .2959\ LOC\ 2$$
$$(.302) \qquad (.843) \qquad (2.87)$$
$$+ .0485\ LOC\ 3 - .0010\ DEN + .1224\ CEN$$
$$(.419) \qquad (3.00) \qquad (.165)$$
$$+ 192.5\ GR - 3.945\ GPC + .0009\ EXP$$
$$(1.16) \qquad (1.67) \qquad (1.89)$$

$$R^2 = .29;\ \text{'F' ratio} = 3.2$$

$$OP75 = -.7662 + .0002\ PCY + .1418\ LOC\ 1 + .2098\ LOC\ 2$$
$$(1.78) \qquad (.986) \qquad (1.57)$$
$$- .0647\ LOC\ 3 + .0000\ DEN + .5995\ CEN$$
$$(.453) \qquad (.097) \qquad (.636)$$
$$+ 253.9\ GR - 1.634\ GPC - .0005\ EXP$$
$$(1.25) \qquad (.562) \qquad (.892)$$

$$R^2 = .03;\ \text{'F' ratio} = 1.17$$

We find little consistency from 1974 to 1975 in the equations. Population density appears to have a negative effect on the allocation of GRS funds to operating expenditures in 1974 and no effect at all in 1975. Whereas in 1974 location in the West

(LOC 2) adds substantially to the proportion of GRS funds used to maintain or increase operating expenditures, in 1975 its coefficient is not statistically significant. The explanatory power of the equation drops from .29 to .03 as measured by R^2 corrected for the number of degrees of freedom.

For CAP74 and CAP75 the regression equations yield not a single coefficient that is significant at the .95 confidence level. The adjusted R^2 for CAP74 is .13, but it falls to 0 for CAP75.

In the case of TR74 only the variable GRS funds per capita (GPC) exhibits a statistically significant positive association with the dependent variable. The R^2 is .18. Again, as in the equation for CAP75, R^2 falls to 0 for TR75.

Finally, our regression equation for predicting the proportion of GRS funds allocated in fiscal year 1974 to reducing or stabilizing taxes, according to our estimates based on responses of chief State fiscal officers, explains none of the variance among the States in this dimension. But this same equation is of considerable interest for TAX75. It is:

$$\begin{aligned}
\text{TAX75} = 1.161 &- .0001 \text{ PCY} - .2392 \text{ LOC 1} - .3112 \text{ LOC 2} \\
&\quad (.913) \qquad (2.09) \qquad\quad (2.93) \\
&- .2554 \text{ LOC 3} - .0005 \text{ DEN} - 1.075 \text{ CEN} \\
&\quad (2.24) \qquad\quad (1.64) \qquad\quad (1.43) \\
&- 102.6 \text{ GR} - 1.642 \text{ GPC} + .0008 \text{ EXP} \\
&\quad (.643) \qquad\quad (.710) \qquad\quad (1.607)
\end{aligned}$$

$$R^2 = .18; \text{ 'F' ratio} = 2.14$$

Thus the proportion of GRS used to reduce or stabilize taxes in 1975 appears to be most significantly a matter of the regional location of the State, with location outside of the Northeast region resulting in a reduction in TAX75 of between .24 and .31, relative to the expected outcome associated with the State being in that region. This is consistent with the further finding that the more centralized State-local finances (CEN) the less likely are GRS funds to go to tax reduction.

The failure of our estimating equations to yield more impressive results may be due to a number of factors. First, as we noted earlier in this chapter, we have only limited confidence in our estimates of the uses to which GRS funds were in fact allocated in 1974 and 1975; second, we may have failed to specify the estimating equations correctly; and, third, we have undoubtedly omitted some important predictor variables, either because of lack of data or because we simply do not know what they are.

CHAPTER 7

General Revenue Sharing and State-Local Governmental Structure

Thomas J. Anton

SUMMARY

The evidence summarized here suggests that revenue sharing has had little or no impact on the existing structure of State-local relations. Very few respondents report changes in tax systems or governmental responsibilities as a result of revenue sharing. Some changes in informal patterns of interaction seem to have occurred, particularly in the largest urban centers, but the evidence linking such changes to GRS is amgibuous, and quite difficult to interpret. No one should be surprised at the lack of apparent impact, of course; revenue sharing is far too recent an innovation to have yet caused major structural change.

On the other hand, it is important to realize that revenue sharing has appeared at a time when intergovernmental relationships are changing for reasons quite unrelated to the program itself. State officials among these respondents report increasing pressure from local governments to expand State assistance during the past several years. These data also suggest that urban-area officials have begun to dominate State governments all across the country. State and urban-area officials now generally agree that revenue sharing should be used, in part, to encourage or even force the consolidation of smaller local units. Significantly enough, that opinion is held most firmly in regions—the Mid-West and the South—that are most noted for the existence of large numbers of small governments. In this context, urban control of the State house promises to breed considerable interest in rural governmental reform. Revenue sharing has had nothing to do with the rise of urban power, but it provides a likely vehicle for exploitation should interest in reform become linked to effective political leadership. Under such conditions, revenue sharing might well contribute to, if not cause, significant intergovernmental change.

INTRODUCTION

General Revenue Sharing was not designed to change governmental systems in the American States; it was merely a device to transfer a portion of Federal tax revenues back to *existing* State and local units of government. It is nevertheless clear that GRS cannot be regarded as neutral with regard to governmental structure. School districts and special districts are not eligible to receive funds, while many thousands of "general" local governments with few people and fewer governmental functions qualify as recipients. Moreover, the GRS formula appears to encourage a variety of changes: States are rewarded for adopting income taxes, communities are given incentives to shift from user charges to taxes, and relatively inactive units are apparently encouraged to expand their service provision activities as a means of qualifying for more Federal support. Apart from the recognized bias in favor of "general" rather than "special purpose" governmental structures, the consequences flowing from the formula were dimly perceived, if at all, and remain a matter of considerable interest. Has GRS caused, or is it likely to cause, major adjustments in the structure of American federalism? Should GRS be used to encourage changes in local and/or State governments? If so, what kinds of changes are desirable?

In this chapter we analyze responses to a series of questions that bear on these problems. To simplify the analysis we present local responses according to a three-fold classification: cities of 100,000 and above, medium-sized communities of 25,000-99,999 and communities of under 25,000. Readers who may want to compare this classification to the more detailed breakdown provided in our appendix tables can easily do so. Large units here are those contained in size classes 1 and 2 in the appendices; medium units here are those reported in size class 3 in the appendix tables; and small units here are units contained in size classes 4, 5 and 6 in the appendices. Except for some references where appropriate, we do not deal with township responses here. Interpretation of the results reported for large, medium and small communities may be helped by recalling the nature of these units: with only a few exceptions, "large" units are cities; roughly 80 percent of the "medium" communities are suburbs, and the remainder are cities; "small" units are divided almost evenly between smaller suburbs (55 percent) and non-SMSA cities (45 percent).

ESTIMATES OF IMPACT

From one point of view, of course, the very existence of GRS is itself a major structural adjustment. Of the 37,000 townships, municipalities and counties eligible to receive GRS funds, more than 33,000 (90 percent) are units of 10,000 or fewer people. Most of these small units have had no direct fiscal relationship to the Federal Government in the past, but each of them now receives an annual revenue-sharing allotment from Washington. For the first time in American political history, a direct and continuing national-local link, unconstrained by program requirements, has been established. Although it is far too early to assess the long-term consequences of that link, it is clear that officials in the smaller municipal units are wary of what those consequences might be: large majorities reject the idea that they are subject to "less control" by the Federal Government because of revenue sharing, and a substantial majority of fiscal officers believe they are now subject to more Federal control. (Table 7-1). These views are notably different from the perspectives held by officials in larger

TABLE 7-1
Impact of Revenue Sharing on Attitudes Toward Federal Government Control
by Size Class for City and County Executives and Finance Officers
(Percentages)

Size Class	Now Subject to Less Federal Government Control				Now Subject to More Federal Government Control			
	Strongly Agree	Somewhat Agree	Somewhat Disagree	Strongly Disagree	Strongly Agree	Somewhat Agree	Somewhat Disagree	Strongly Disagree
City Executives								
Over 100,000 inhabitants	53.2	29.3	14.7	2.8	9.8	12.4	31.5	46.3
25,000-100,000 inhabitants	23.2	44.0	20.6	12.2	2.3	16.6	39.3	41.9
Under 25,000 inhabitants	11.1	17.6	47.6	23.7	12.6	34.8	36.4	16.1
Total	11.8	18.7	46.4	23.2	12.2	34.0	36.5	17.3
City Finance Officers								
Over 100,000 inhabitants	37.0	33.4	19.1	10.5	2.9	18.7	37.4	41.0
25,000-100,000 inhabitants	8.1	42.4	30.0	19.6	8.1	34.6	33.7	23.6
Under 25,000 inhabitants	7.1	22.0	48.2	22.7	11.3	43.6	31.9	13.3
Total	7.3	22.9	47.3	22.5	11.1	43.0	32.0	13.9
County Executives								
Over 100,000 inhabitants	15.0	45.2	32.6	7.1	8.0	22.0	35.0	35.1
25,000-100,000 inhabitants	21.2	36.7	31.2	10.8	12.3	25.2	45.6	16.9
Under 25,000 inhabitants	19.3	21.2	18.8	40.7	11.4	12.8	43.2	32.6
Total	19.3	27.2	23.1	30.4	11.3	16.2	43.0	29.6
County Finance Officers								
Over 100,000 inhabitants	24.7	24.5	28.4	22.4	12.1	27.4	22.4	38.1
25,000-100,000 inhabitants	7.2	33.5	39.2	20.2	3.5	43.5	22.1	30.9
Under 25,000 inhabitants	15.1	13.9	33.6	37.3	24.2	31.1	25.9	18.7
Total	14.0	20.0	34.6	31.5	18.0	33.8	24.6	23.5

municipalities, who overwhelmingly see themselves as subject to less Federal interference. On the fundamental issue of whether Federal money implies federal control, then, local officials in large and small communities are in sharp disagreement.

Disagreement over an issue as new and important as the control implied by Federal revenue sharing is hardly surprising; it will be some time before clear patterns emerge. In the meantime, the more immediate impact of revenue sharing is easier to judge. Local and county officials were asked whether revenue sharing had caused them to make changes in their tax structures or whether, as a result of revenue sharing, their units had taken over activities formerly performed by special districts (Table 7-2). Responses from both executives and financial officers were uniformly negative. These responses were confirmed by the State officials to whom we talked: neither chief fiscal officers nor upper and lower house Appropriate Committee chairpersons at the State level perceive any significant pressure from local units for changing tax structures or assumption of special district responsibilities. On these issues, State and local officials are in complete agreement.

State officials also agree among themselves that revenue sharing has had virtually no impact on State-level tax systems. The income tax factor in the revenue-sharing formula has not influenced tax policy, and only a handful of State officials (25 percent of fiscal officials and 15 percent of legislators) report that revenue sharing has caused changes in tax structure. At the same time, State officials report considerable pressure to expand local government functions: nearly 44 percent of State fiscal officers and 62 percent of legislative appropriation chairpersons indicate that they have experienced such pressure "in the last two or three years." Note, however, that they do not attribute that pressure to GRS. When asked the extent to which requests to expand local governmental authority was due to GRS, nearly 80 percent of State respondents indicated "not at all." One-fifth of the fiscal officers and just over a quarter of the legislators we talked to believe that GRS has increased the pressure to provide additional State services or State funding to local units, but this does not appear to have had a major impact on State budgets. Of the State respondents who report some change in State budget pressure after GRS, most

Table 7-2
Impact of Revenue Sharing on Tax Structures and on Special District Functions
by Size Class for City and County Executives and Finance Officers and State Officials
(Percentages)

Size Class	Tax Structure Has Changed		Unit Has Taken on Special District Functions	
	Yes	No	Yes	No
City Executives				
Over 100,000 inhabitants	9.1	90.9	7.9	92.1
25,000-100,000 inhabitants	7.6	92.4	3.8	96.2
Under 25,000 inhabitants	7.4	92.6	3.4	96.6
Total	7.4	92.6	3.4	96.6
City Finance Officers				
Over 100,000 inhabitants	15.1	84.9	0.0	100.0
25,000-100,000 inhabitants	10.7	89.3	2.1	97.9
Under 25,000 inhabitants	7.3	92.7	0.8	99.2
Total	7.4	92.6	0.8	99.2
County Executives				
Over 100,000 inhabitants	17.6	82.4	5.5	94.5
25,000-100,000 inhabitants	10.4	89.6	7.2	92.8
Under 25,000 inhabitants	5.5	94.5	0.0	100.0
Total	7.7	92.3	2.0	98.0
County Finance Officers				
Over 100,000 inhabitants	7.4	92.6	0.6	99.4
25,000-100,000 inhabitants	10.3	89.1	0.3	99.7
Under 25,000 inhabitants	0.0	100.0	3.6	96.4
Total	3.3	96.7	2.5	97.5
State Officials				
Finance officers	8.5	91.5	4.2	95.8
Appropriation Committee Chairman	15.9	84.1	4.9	95.1

believe that GRS has decreased, rather than increased, that pressure. Perhaps this explains why so very few State officials report any interest in changing State tax systems as a result of revenue sharing. (Table 7-3).

The immediate impact of GRS thus appears to have been slight. Very few State or local officials report changes in tax structures or functional responsibilities as a result of revenue sharing. Local government pressure on the States for expanded financial assistance or enlarged authority seems apparent, but few State-level officials attribute these pressures to GRS. On the contrary, GRS seems to be viewed as simply a revenue increment that, if anything, helps to reduce the intensity of those pressures without changing their causes or their direction. For the moment, at least, the structural impact of GRS seems to have been generally insignificant.

Judging "significance" by formal changes in taxation or functional authority, of course, is a very difficult test. A revenue increment such as GRS is likely to produce a variety of informal changes

prior to more lasting adjustments—for example, the number of contacts between officials might be expected to increase in order to determine the disposition of the additional revenue. At the State level, there is only moderate support for this supposition. Although 30 percent of fiscal officers and 37 percent of legislators report more contact with their State colleagues, more than four of five indicate that contacts with either congressmen or Federal officials (apart from ORS officials) are about the same as they were before revenue sharing. Revenue sharing appears to have encouraged state officials to interact more among themselves but it has had little effect on cross-level contacts.

Local and county officials, on the other hand, do report more cross-level interaction. Data Appendix Tables 89 to 97, available on request from the Survey Research Center, display responses of local and county executives and finance officers regarding changes in their contacts with officials from other units and levels of government. On the whole, reports of increased contact tend to decrease as size of unit decreases, and finance officers are less likely to report increases in contact than are local and county executives. But there are some interesting exceptions to these familiar themes. The most obvious is the set of responses from the smallest counties. Although these counties do not represent a large fraction of either the population or total GRS allotments, officials in these units report significant changes in their contacts with other units: congressmen, Federal officials (non-GRS), State legislators and officials, and municipalities. Moreover, finance officers in these counties are generally more likely to report "more" contact than are executives. It seems reasonable to suppose that GRS represents a new relationship for such units and that more contact with other units arises from both uncertainty and the perceived benefits of coordinating action with the other GRS recipients (i.e., municipalities) within small-county boundaries. The smallest *municipal* units, on the other hand, are generally *least* likely to report "more contact" with any other units.

For municipalities as a whole, it is clear that revenue sharing is perceived to have had the greatest impact by officials from the larger cities, particularly the big-city executives. Nearly half of big-city mayors report more contact with congressmen, roughly a third report more contact with Federal non-ORS officials and with State officials, and just under a third report more contact with county officials. Big-city finance officers also report (36 percent) more contact with county officials. Since county officials from the largest units give very similar responses—just over a third of big-county executives and nearly 42 percent of county finance officers report more contact with

Table 7-3

Impact of Revenue Sharing on State Tax Structure and Pressure to Expand Local Government Functions (Percentages)

		State Finance Officer	State Appropriations Committee Chairmen
Income Tax Factor in Revenue Sharing Formula Affected Tax Policy	YES	10.6	5.9
	NO	89.4	94.1
Revenue Sharing Affected Tax Structure	YES	24.5	15.4
	NO	75.5	84.6
State Government Pressured to Expand Local Functions	YES	43.8	61.8
	NO	56.3	38.2
Extent Pressure is Due to Revenue Sharing	ENTIRELY	4.3	1.8
	SOME EXTENT	13.0	18.2
	NOT AT ALL	78.3	80.0
Revenue Sharing Changed Pressure to Provide Services to Local Governments	INCREASED	20.5	27.5
	NO CHANGE	65.9	55.0
	DECREASED	13.6	17.5
Revenue Sharing Changed Pressure From Local Governments on State Budget	INCREASED	2.0	20.2
	NO CHANGE	61.2	27.0
	DECREASED	36.7	52.8

municipalities—there is reason to conclude that city-county relationships have been significantly affected in the largest urban areas. Without a clear metric it is impossible to be precise about these reports: "much more" contact may mean a telephone call for one official and ten meetings for another. There is some reason to believe, however, that increased city-county interaction in urban areas was largely concerned with new program initiatives. All respondents were asked whether GRS monies were used to support "new" activities, and whether these "new" activities were undertaken alone or "in cooperation with other government units or private agencies?" Table 7-4 displays local and county responses to the first-mentioned new activity. Local respondents mention "county" as the other cooperating unit more frequently than any other unit, and county respondents mention "municipalities" as the cooperating unit more frequently than any other unit. Again, there is unavoidable ambiguity in these responses, since the adjective "new" is subject to varying interpretations. Taken at face value, they suggest that increases in municipal-county contact were indeed stimulated by the opportunity to use incremental funds for activities not currently supported.

Increased contact need not, of course, lead to more cooperation; greater conflict may also be created, particularly when fund disposition is the issue. Table 7-5 reveals that nearly 40 percent of

Table 7-5
Change in Conflict for State Government Because of Revenue Sharing
(Percentages)

Conflict Between		State Finance Officer	Appropriations Committee Chairmen
Executive and	LESS	6.1	3.4
Legislative	MORE	16.3	39.3
Branches of State Government	SAME	77.6	57.3
	LESS	6.0	9.0
State Government	MORE	8.0	28.1
and Local Units	SAME	86.0	62.9
State Government	LESS	2.0	4.6
and Local	MORE	8.0	27.6
Citizens' Groups	SAME	90.0	67.8
State Government	LESS	2.3	1.2
and the Media	MORE	9.3	23.5
	SAME	88.3	75.3

State appropriation committee chairpersons believe that conflict between executive and legislative branches of State governments has increased after revenue sharing. More than a quarter of legislative respondents also perceive an increase in conflict between the State government and local government units, and between the State government and

Table 7-4
Other Government Units or Agencies Cooperating on New Activities Undertaken with GRS Funds by Size Class for City and County Executives and Finance Officers
(Percentages)

Size Class	State	County	Munic.	Special District	Regional Assoc.	Private Agency	Other
City Executives							
Over 100,000 inhabitants	20.5	39.3	0.0	0.0	0.0	0.0	40.2
25,000-100,000 inhabitants	12.4	9.6	15.4	11.3	1.6	25.1	24.6
Under 25,000 inhabitants	14.7	29.0	16.2	2.6	0.0	23.3	14.2
Total	14.6	28.1	16.0	3.1	0.1	23.2	15.0
City Finance Officers							
Over 100,000 inhabitants	4.5	36.7	25.4	0.0	0.0	33.4	0.0
25,000-100,000 inhabitants	5.5	11.8	28.7	1.6	0.0	16.8	35.7
Under 25,000 inhabitants	13.4	30.9	7.8	9.6	1.3	22.1	14.9
Total	12.9	29.9	9.2	9.0	1.2	22.0	15.9
County Executives							
Over 100,000 inhabitants	16.3	5.3	55.3	0.0	0.0	16.5	6.5
25,000-100,000 inhabitants	8.4	0.0	36.1	0.0	2.2	0.0	53.4
Under 25,000 inhabitants	0.0	0.0	27.3	19.1	11.7	26.2	15.7
Total	1.7	0.2	29.4	15.8	10.0	22.2	20.9
County Finance Officers							
Over 100,000 inhabitants	0.0	30.0	41.5	0.0	0.0	6.2	22.3
25,000-100,000 inhabitants	2.0	9.4	50.9	0.0	0.0	0.0	37.7
Under 25,000 inhabitants	0.0	0.0	24.6	0.0	0.0	75.4	0.0
Total	0.4	4.5	31.6	0.0	0.0	53.7	9.9

local citizens' groups. Only a handful of State fiscal officers accepts any of these judgments—suggesting again that position has a powerful impact on perception.

At the local level, there seems to be agreement that GRS has either had little impact on, or has reduced, conflict within and across agencies (Table 7-6). Some big-city mayors and big-county executives disagree, and the same groups perceive some increase in conflict between administrators and local governing councils. The most noticeable reports of conflict increase come from the largest cities, where substantial proportions of both mayors and finance officer report increases in conflict between the governing bodies and the general public or between the governing bodies and local citizens' groups. An increment of citizen group-governing body conflict is also reported by a fraction of officials from the larger counties. Conflict *between* governments, however, seems not to have been affected very much: only big-city mayors report much perceived impact, toward reducing intergovernmental conflict. Reports of conflict change at the local level are therefore as ambiguous as State-level reports. Big-city officials report increases in conflict between governing bodies and local citizens, but at the same time most officials fail to detect much change in other categories of conflict or perceive an amelioration of conflict due to revenue sharing.

For the moment, then, GRS can hardly be said to have had much of an impact on government structure. Formal changes in systems of taxation or in the scope of governmental authority are reported very rarely. Reports of changes in informal patterns of contact or conflict are more numerous but ambiguous, in part because officials often disagree, in part because the measures we have are far too gross to permit very precise conclusions. Perhaps the strongest evidence of significant informal change emerges from the larger urban areas, where local and county officials both report more interaction with one another, and where reports of new program initiatives tend to confirm these reports of increased contact. In our largest urban areas, at least, GRS appears to have stimulated changes in contact patterns that are noticeable and of some potential significance.

EXPECTATIONS

However significant or insignificant the actual impact of GRS to date, the formula remains, and with it the incentives for changing the behavior of local and state officials. Those officials appear sensitive to the possibility of change, as Table 7-7 reveals, whatever they may think of the current record of GRS impacts. Recall, for example, that

Table 7-6
Change in Amount of Conflict Over Local Budget Due to Revenue Sharing
by Size Class for City and County Executives and Finance Officers
(Percentages)

Size Class	Conflict Within Agencies			Conflict Across Agencies			Conflict Between Administrators and Local Gov't Bodies			Conflict Between Gov't and Public		
	Less	More	Same	Less	More	Same	Less	More	Same	Less	More	Same
City Executives												
Over 100,000 inhabitants	11.0	20.4	68.6	15.0	20.2	64.8	9.9	23.0	67.1	9.0	33.2	57.8
25,000-100,000 inhabitants	12.4	4.2	83.4	7.2	7.9	84.9	13.8	15.4	70.8	12.6	14.0	73.3
Under 25,000 inhabitants	7.3	2.3	90.4	4.1	1.0	94.9	3.4	1.9	94.6	4.0	0.9	95.1
Total	7.5	2.5	90.0	4.2	1.4	94.3	3.9	2.6	93.5	4.4	1.6	94.1
City Finance Officers												
Over 100,000 inhabitants	11.9	7.1	81.1	7.3	12.4	80.4	3.7	9.5	86.9	5.8	23.7	70.5
25,000-100,000 inhabitants	7.3	15.4	77.2	6.7	10.2	83.0	6.5	22.1	71.4	5.9	6.1	88.0
Under 25,000 inhabitants	7.3	4.2	88.5	6.3	2.4	91.3	6.2	3.0	90.9	5.2	1.4	93.3
Total	7.3	4.6	88.0	6.3	2.8	90.9	6.2	3.8	90.0	5.3	1.8	93.0
County Executives												
Over 100,000 inhabitants	12.8	11.7	75.5	12.5	15.1	72.3	11.0	10.4	78.6	9.4	9.2	81.4
25,000-100,000 inhabitants	4.9	0.0	95.1	4.2	5.6	90.2	4.2	2.8	93.0	4.2	14.3	81.5
Under 25,000 inhabitants	14.0	0.0	86.0	14.0	0.0	86.0	14.0	0.0	86.0	14.0	0.4	85.6
Total	11.8	1.0	87.2	11.7	2.6	85.8	11.5	1.5	87.0	11.4	4.3	84.3
County Finance Officers												
Over 100,000 inhabitants	8.3	3.4	88.3	6.3	2.5	91.2	4.2	10.3	85.5	5.6	14.7	79.7
25,000-100,000 inhabitants	2.2	5.0	92.7	1.1	5.8	93.1	0.4	6.7	92.9	0.0	10.7	89.3
Under 25,000 inhabitants	14.5	9.5	76.0	14.5	4.5	81.0	14.6	0.0	85.4	14.5	0.0	85.5
Total	10.9	7.8	81.3	10.4	4.7	84.9	10.1	2.6	87.3	10.1	3.9	85.9

Table 7-6 (continued)

Size Class	Conflict Between Citizens' Groups			Conflict Between Government and the Media			Conflict Between This and Other Governments		
	Less	More	Same	Less	More	Same	Less	More	Same
City Executives									
Over 100,000 inhabitants........	9.4	47.4	43.2	5.9	4.8	89.3	18.8	8.4	72.9
25,000-100,000 inhabitants......	10.8	21.6	67.5	2.8	3.6	93.6	8.5	6.8	84.7
Under 25,000 inhabitants........	4.0	2.1	93.9	3.1	2.7	94.2	1.7	2.1	96.2
Total.........................	4.3	3.1	92.6	3.1	2.7	94.2	2.0	2.3	95.6
City Finance Officers									
Over 100,000 inhabitants........	5.1	23.6	71.3	3.7	5.9	90.4	1.4	5.4	93.3
25,000-100,000 inhabitants......	3.8	21.8	74.4	1.0	4.7	94.3	2.8	5.3	91.9
Under 25,000 inhabitants........	6.1	2.0	91.8	4.0	1.7	94.3	4.0	1.7	94.3
Total.........................	6.0	3.0	91.0	3.8	1.9	94.3	3.9	1.9	94.2
County Executives									
Over 100,000 inhabitants........	12.7	15.8	71.5	8.9	9.3	81.8	9.7	5.6	84.7
25,000-100,000 inhabitants......	4.3	10.7	85.0	0.4	13.9	85.7	4.1	4.6	91.3
Under 25,000 inhabitants........	14.0	0.0	86.0	0.0	0.0	100.0	14.0	5.5	80.5
Total.........................	11.7	3.7	84.6	0.8	3.9	95.2	11.4	5.3	83.3
County Finance Officers									
Over 100,000 inhabitants........	5.3	17.6	77.1	3.6	5.5	91.0	2.2	9.2	88.5
25,000-100,000 inhabitants......	0.0	10.9	89.1	0.0	5.7	94.3	0.0	0.7	99.3
Under 25,000 inhabitants........	14.6	0.0	85.4	0.0	0.0	100.0	14.5	0.0	85.5
Total.........................	10.1	4.3	85.6	0.3	1.9	97.8	9.8	1.0	89.2

very few officials reported any changes in functional activities due to GRS. Now consider Table 7-7, which reveals that overwhelming proportions of State, local and county officials believe that revenue sharing will "encourage some small governments to increase the range of their activities." In only one group—fiscal officers of medium-sized counties—does the proportion agreeing to this proposition fall below 70 percent, while as many as 95 percent of executives agree. Given this level of agreement, slight differences between officials of different size-class communities seem insignificant. Quite clearly, the vast majority of local and State officials believe that incentives to do more and tax more will work.

State and local officials are nearly as agreed that GRS will *not* encourage "the consolidation of existing governmental units such as cities and counties." Here, a size-related difference seems apparent: only in municipalities and counties of the smallest size class is there much support for the idea that GRS will encourage consolidation. Smaller communities, of course, are natural targets of consolidation efforts. The opinions reported here may thus be expressions of concern as much as expressions of belief. Larger units, with less reason for concern, are far less persuaded of the power of GRS to induce consolidation.

A similar size-related difference colors responses to the question of whether GRS will encourage

cities and towns to annex outlying areas. Very few officials believe that revenue sharing will encourage annexation, except in the smaller municipalities, where nearly half of the mayors and more than 40 percent of the finance officers express that belief. A substantial proportion of county officials, particularly finance officers in the medium and smaller counties, also expect GRS to encourage annexation. On this issue, as with the issue of consolidation, officials from units likely to be targets of change are far more sensitive to the potential effect of GRS than are their colleagues in larger jurisdictions.

Size-related responses are far more difficult to detect on the issue of whether GRS will encourage municipalities and counties to take over some functions now being performed by special districts. More than half of the mayors in the largest municipalities believe that revenue sharing will have that effect—but so do nearly half of the mayors in the smallest communities, and almost two-thirds of the finance officers in the smallest units. County officials on the whole are less inclined to anticipate take-over of special district functions, but more than 40 percent of executives in the largest counties and almost 57 percent of finance officers from the smallest counties do believe that GRS will encourage such action. Although there are obvious differences of opinion here, size

Table 7-7

**Attitudes Toward Change in Local Government Structure
by Size Class for City and County Executives and Finance Officers and State Officials
(Percentages)**

Size Class	Encourages Increase in Small Government Activities		Encourages Consolidation		Encourages Annexation		Encourages Take-Over of Special Districts		Encourages Less User Charges	
	Yes	No	Yes	No	Yes	No	Yes	No	Yes	No
City Executives										
Over 100,000 inhabitants	96.4	3.6	19.9	80.1	27.5	72.5	54.6	45.6	49.8	50.2
25,000-100,000 inhabitants	79.5	20.5	15.3	84.7	31.9	68.1	36.0	64.0	24.8	75.2
Under 25,000 inhabitants	82.8	17.2	34.6	65.4	49.8	50.2	48.9	51.1	45.9	54.1
Total	82.7	17.3	33.7	66.3	48.8	51.2	48.4	51.6	44.9	55.1
City Finance Officers										
Over 100,000 inhabitants	74.7	25.3	16.1	83.9	28.1	71.9	31.5	68.5	32.7	67.3
25,000-100,000 inhabitants	84.0	16.0	18.7	81.3	19.3	80.7	35.5	64.5	31.5	68.5
Under 25,000 inhabitants	81.7	18.3	31.7	68.3	40.2	59.8	64.5	53.5	39.5	60.5
Total	81.7	18.3	31.0	60.0	30.2	60.8	45.9	54.1	39.1	60.9
County Executives										
Over 100,000 inhabitants	83.5	16.5	22.8	77.2	25.3	76.7	40.4	59.6	36.8	63.2
25,000-100,000 inhabitants	95.3	4.7	17.9	82.1	48.3	51.7	29.9	79.1	43.8	56.2
Under 25,000 inhabitants	70.3	29.7	37.8	62.2	32.4	67.6	26.7	73.3	53.8	46.2
Total	77.2	22.8	32.0	68.0	35.0	65.0	28.4	71.6	50.6	49.4
County Finance Officers										
Over 100,000 inhabitants	74.2	25.8	15.8	84.2	25.5	76.5	29.6	70.4	30.1	69.9
25,000-100,000 inhabitants	69.1	30.9	23.0	77.0	52.0	48.0	34.3	65.7	32.7	67.3
Under 25,000 inhabitants	77.2	22.8	53.4	46.6	60.3	39.7	56.9	43.1	50.2	49.8
Total	75.0	25.0	40.9	59.1	54.4	45.6	48.3	51.7	43.4	56.6
State Officials										
Finance officers	78.7	21.3	13.3	86.7	25.0	75.0	27.9	72.1	29.5	70.5
Appropriation Committee Chairmen	85.0	15.0	31.0	69.0	31.0	69.0	41.0	59.0	46.3	53.7
Governors*	85.0	15.0	27.0	65.0	12.0	71.0	45.5	39.4	25.7	57.1

*Not all Governors were interviewed and some of those who were chose not to respond to these questions. These responses should be treated with caution.

is probably less important than position in interpreting them. In large municipalities and counties, executives are more likely to anticipate takeover of special district functions than finance officers; in the smallest communities, finance officers, rather than executives are more likely to anticipate such changes. A plausible interpretation of these differences is that the positions held by these two groups of officials give them more involvement with GRS and thus a greater willingness to anticipate change.

In addition to administrative change, we were interested in official views of the impact GRS is likely to have on tax structure. Many observers have speculated that GRS would lead local units to abandon user charges for public services in favor of taxes, on grounds that user charges are excluded

from the "tax effort" base in calculating unit allotments. A rather substantial fraction of State and local officials agree with that speculation. Nearly half of the mayors in the largest and smallest size classes agree, and more than 50 percent of executives and finance officers in the smallest counties agree. Only among mayors in medium-sized communities—heavily dominated by suburban units—is the proportion who agree under 30 percent. Curiously, the finance officers of medium-sized municipalities, normally more skeptical, express more agreement regarding a possible move away from user charges than their mayoral colleagues. Among county officials, there seems to be a clear thrust toward greater agreement as county size decreases. For a considerable proportion of local and State officials, then, GRS represents a potential for adjustments in types of resources utilized, as well as in total funding.

It would not be unfair to summarize these responses as cautious. Very few respondents expect GRS to encourage consolidation or annexation; those who do are concentrated in the smaller communities and counties. Substantial fractions expect GRS to encourage municipal take-over of some special district functions and a movement away from user charges to taxes to support local public services. For the most part, however, these fractions do not reach a majority of officials in any size class. On the other hand, very large majorities do expect that *existing* units of local government will expand or seek to expand their activities as a means of demonstrating their "general" purpose significance. The central expectation of these respondents, therefore, is not major structural change but rather a variety of efforts to expand and/or enlarge the capacities of existing systems.

This may appear to be a cautious estimate of future impact, but it stands in sharp contrast to the earlier estimate of current impact. Nor is it at all clear that this cautious estimate of future impact is considered to be desirable by all of these respondents. When asked whether they thought GRS might encourage "the continued existence of inefficient units of local government," for example, some 60.5 percent of State fiscal officers and 54 percent of legislative appropriation committee chairmen said "yes." The belief that GRS will "prop up" inefficient units is stronger among lower house (60.5 percent) than upper house (45.9 percent) chairmen, and is strongest in the North Central (70 percent) and Southern (66.7 percent) states. Officials traditionally thought of as being closest to their constituencies, in short, are most likely to accept the "prop up" hypothesis in areas where there are large numbers of townships and rural units to prop up. This suggests both that "expected" consequences are not the same as "desired" consequences and that the differences between anticipations and preferences may be a source of some tension between state and local officials.

PREFERENCES

We can begin to appreciate the nature of this possible tension by referring to Table 7-8, which displays State and local officials' preferences on changing the revenue-sharing formula "to omit very small government units." From the point of view of local officials, this is a very harsh proposal and predictably enough, very few local officials endorse it. Some support is expressed by officials in the largest cities and counties, but only among big-city mayors does the proportion in favor exceed

one-third. State officials, on the other hand, express considerable support: some 54 percent of fiscal officers and 39 percent of legislators favor this very harsh proposal. Among officials from the North Central states two-thirds of the fiscal officers, 60 percent of lower and 55 percent of upper house appropriation chairmen support omission of very small units. Township officials' responses are not displayed in Table 7-8, but another tabulation reveals the sharp contrast in opinion: 90 percent of executives and 100 percent of fiscal officers in townships of under 9,000 population *oppose* the omission of very small units from the revenue sharing program. On this issue, the preferences of local and State officials seem very different indeed.

When the same question is posed in a less harsh fashion—"Do you think there should be a minimum size for eligibility?"—the distribution of responses changes, but not much. Officials from the largest and smallest municipalities increase their support somewhat, and state fiscal officers are slightly less favorable, but over-all, the distribution of support and opposition closely resembles responses to the more extreme formulation. Posing the issue as one of "encouraging the consolidation of small government units" rather than minimum eligibility requirements or omission, however, does alter responses. Framed this way, the issue is far less threatening and the result is considerably more agreement. At the State level 69 percent of fiscal officers and 67 percent of appropriations chairmen are in favor of using revenue sharing to encourage small-unit consolidation. Although a majority of all local and county officials oppose the idea, officials from the larger cities and counties are as supportive as State officials.

Local and State perspectives on the issue of using GRS as a lever for local government reform are as significant as they are interesting. Most State officials, particularly those in the North Central and Southern States, do *not* think that GRS will encourage local consolidation, annexation or other structural changes; yet most State officials, particularly those in the North Central and Southern States, would *prefer* to use revenue sharing to "encourage" local consolidation and very substantial proportions would go as far as introducing minimum population requirements or even omitting very small units from the GRS program. Among local officials, those who least anticipate structural change—officials in the larger cities and counties—are those who would most prefer to use GRS as an agent for such change. Similarly, those who are most likely to anticipate GRS-induced structural change—officials in the smallest cities and counties—are least likely to prefer such change. Nation-wide, a wide discrepancy between

Table 7-8
Attitudes Toward Possible Changes in Revenue Sharing Program by Size Class for City and County Executives and Finance Officers and State Officials
(Percentages)

Size Class	Change Allocation Formula to Omit Small Governments				Establish Minimum Population for Revenue Sharing Eligibility		Encourage Consolidation of Small Government Units			
	Yes!	Yes	No	No!	Yes	No	Yes!	Yes	No	No!
City Executives										
Over 100,000 inhabitants	17.6%	18.5	39.0	24.9	40.3	59.7	47.7	20.8	11.0	20.6
25,000-100,000 inhabitants ...	6.5	9.3	30.7	53.5	12.0	88.0	20.4	31.7	23.5	24.5
Under 25,000 inhabitants	3.4	10.2	15.8	70.7	9.3	90.7	15.4	29.1	13.9	41.6
Total	3.6	10.2	16.5	69.8	9.5	90.5	15.8	29.2	14.2	40.8
City Finance Officers										
Over 100,000 inhabitants	10.3	21.7	35.1	32.9	47.8	52.2	25.8	35.2	24.4	14.5
25,000-100,000 inhabitants ...	6.2	17.6	25.1	51.1	21.4	78.6	26.5	25.3	20.7	27.5
Under 25,000 inhabitants	2.9	5.4	22.2	69.5	3.4	96.6	12.5	22.4	23.9	41.2
Total	3.1	6.0	22.4	68.6	4.4	95.6	13.2	22.6	23.8	40.5
County Executives										
Over 100,000 inhabitants	16.1	16.4	28.6	38.9	24.6	75.4	30.9	38.0	14.7	16.4
25,000-100,000 inhabitants ...	5.9	8.8	30.2	54.9	9.7	90.3	7.0	40.0	24.3	28.8
Under 25,000 inhabitants	0.0	7.0	23.2	69.7	20.2	79.8	21.0	22.1	35.0	21.8
Total	2.7	8.3	25.1	63.9	18.3	81.7	18.7	27.6	30.8	22.9
County Finance Officers										
Over 100,000 inhabitants	10.3	21.7	35.1	32.9	40.5	59.5	28.6	28.3	30.3	12.7
25,000-100,000 inhabitants ...	6.2	17.6	25.1	51.1	26.7	73.3	24.4	23.0	26.1	26.4
Under 25,000 inhabitants	2.9	5.4	22.2	69.5	14.5	85.5	30.5	7.0	22.8	39.7
Total	3.1	6.0	22.4	68.6	19.9	80.1	28.8	12.9	24.3	34.0
State Officals										
Finance officers	29.2	25.0	22.9	22.9	46.8	53.2	43.8	25.0	8.3	22.9
Appropriation Committee Chairmen	20.0	18.9	22.2	38.9	38.5	61.5	33.0	34.1	13.2	19.8

the preference of State officials and officials in smaller communities seems apparent. Attitudinal similarities between State officials and officials in the largest cities and counties are equally apparent. A potential alliance between State and urban-area officials on the issue of local reform is quite evident. Should that potential be realized in the North Central and Southern States, where there is most concern over the inefficiences of tiny governmental units, significant structural reform might well take place. The fact that legislators in our sample express opinions similar to urban-area officials, rather than small-town officials, is especially significant, because local government reform will have to be initiated by legislative bodies, if it is to come at all.

Two other issues on which we can compare State and local responses suggest a similar cleavage between State and urban-area officials on one side, and small-town officials on the other. Majorities of State fiscal officers, appropriations chairmen and officials from the larger cities and counties support the inclusion of special district assessments as part of the local tax base. A majority of officials who represent cities and counties of less than 25,000, however, are opposed. To be sure, the majorities in opposition are not unusually large, but even slight majorities in opposition offer a sharp contrast to the very considerable majorities that support the idea among officials of the largest size classes. Precisely the same pattern emerges in responses to the question of including user charges in the definition of local tax effort.

The majorities in favor of this proposal are somewhat larger in the largest size classes, and only among finance officials in the smallest counties is there an actual majority opposed. But again, the least favorable officials are those in the smallest communities and again, responses of State and urban-area officials appear very similar. Substantively, it appears, small-town officials are most interested in encouraging movement toward "general purpose" government, funded by taxes rather than charges, while officials in larger communities are more strongly inclined to maintain the present structure but improve it financially by expanding the base on which revenue sharing allotments are calculated.

Superficially, these responses seem contradictory. Small-town mayors and finance officers are most opposed to structural changes but most in favor of proposals that would weaken special districts and shift service support away from user charges and toward taxes. Big-unit officials would most prefer to see structural changes yet do not support proposals that might adjust the present mixture of special districts and local units or the present mixture of taxes and user charges. If we assume that these patterns of response are determined primarily by institutional self-interest, however, and if we take account of recent changes in American State governments, a resolution of these apparently contradictory sentiments is possible.

We have already pointed out that support for reforming small units is strongest in the States of the South and the Mid-West, where a large number of tiny townships and other rural units exist. Consolidating or otherwise reforming small units of local governments receives the support of urban-area officials, in part because such reforms would not affect *their* constituencies, in part because this kind of reform fits comfortably into the "rationality" and "efficiency" goals that better-educated urban politicians are likely to support. Policies that might put pressure on special districts or subvert user charges are opposed for similar reasons: such policies *do* affect urban governmental structure and thus threaten the viability of urban and suburban political bases. Both special districts and user charges can also be supported on "efficiency" grounds, giving the urban politician a plausible justification for this political stance. At the same time, institutional reforms of the past decade, particularly changes in State legislative apportionment, have begun to give urban-based politicians control over the legislative processes that would have to be used to bring about local structural change. The preferences of State and urban-area politicians appear similar, therefore, because they are increasingly the same kinds of people. Preferences are a long way from action, of course, but these data suggest that the urban politicians who may now dominate the state house agree on the desirability of reforming nonurban governments. Should these preferences be translated into action, major structural changes could become a widespread reality.

CIVIL RIGHTS AND GRS

Section 122a of the State and Local Fiscal Assistance Act contains an explicit prohibition against discrimination: "No person in the United States shall, on the ground of race, color, national origin, or sex, be excluded from participating in, be denied the benefits of, or be subject to discrimination under any program or activity funded in whole or in part with (revenue sharing) funds." Because it precludes discrimination based on sex as well as race, color or national origin, this provision is actually more comprehensive than Title VI of the Civil Rights Act of 1964. And because revenue-sharing checks are now being distributed to many thousands of governments that otherwise have little interaction with the Federal Government, section 122a carries with it the potential of restructuring the behavior of many governments that do not now accept or comply with national standards against discrimination. Whereas the current or anticipated impact of formula provisions may be regarded as indirect and to a large extent unintentional, Section 122a is a very direct and intentional effort to structure the behavior of recipient jurisdictions.

As Table 7-9 reveals, however, neither State nor local officials interviewed in our survey perceived the expanded scope of the civil rights provision. When asked "Have the prohibitions against discrimination in revenue sharing been more restrictive, less restrictive, or about the same as those in other Federal grants?", nearly all respondents indicated that the revenue sharing provision was the same as restrictions in other Federal grants. Among the few who perceived any difference in restrictiveness, virtually all believed that the revenue sharing was less, rather than more, restrictive. Quite obviously, State and local officials do not interpret revenue sharing to imply any change in their civil rights responsibilities, whatever the language of Section 122a.

Table 7-9
Compared to Other Federal Grants, Revenue Sharing Is
(Percentages)

	Less Restrictive	Same	More Restrictive
State Finance Officers	12.8	87.2	0.0
County Executives ...	1.5	97.8	0.7
Local Executives.....	11.7	85.7	2.6

One probable reason for this widespread interpretation is a general lack of interaction among officials on the civil rights provision. All State and local respondents were asked whether Federal (for local officials, Federal *or* State) officials had "communicated with you about civil rights enforcement in the revenue-sharing program?" Table 9-10 displays the responses of State fiscal officers, county and municipal executives to this question. Overall, fewer than 30 percent of these respondents report any contact with higher level governments over civil rights. Although not shown on this table, it is clear that such contacts were reported more frequently by officials from the larger cities and counties. Fewer than 20 percent of officials from the smallest municipalities report such contact, for example, as compared to 41 percent of big-city executives. At the State level, only 3 of 15 (20 percent) of fiscal officers in the South report such contact, and only 2 of 11 (15.4 percent) western-State fiscal officers report communication with Federal officials on this issue. Both the generally low level of intergovernmental contact and the absence of State-national contact in some regions, nearly two years after enactment of the program, suggest that national officials have regarded section 122a as something less than a high priority.

Table 7-10
Have Federal (or State) Officials Communicated with you About Civil Rights Enforcement in the Revenue Sharing Program?
(Percentages)

	YES	NO
State Finance Officers.............	30.6%	69.4%
County Executives	27.6	72.4
Local Executives..................	29.8	70.2

RECAPITULATION

I. Revenue sharing has had little or no impact on the existing structure of State-local relations.

   A. There were few reported changes in tax systems or governmental responsibilities as a result of GRS.

   B. Some changes in informal patterns of interaction seem to have occurred, particularly in large urban centers, but may have been unrelated to revenue sharing.

II. Revenue sharing has appeared at a time when intergovernmental relationships are changing for reasons quite unrelated to the program itself.

   A. State government respondents report increasing pressure from local governments to expand State assistance during the recent past.

   B. State officials and urban-area legislators—now beginning to dominate State governments across the country—agree that revenue sharing funds should be used to encourage consolidation of smaller local units.

   C. Urban control of State legislatures promises to breed considerable interest in other kinds of rural governmental reform.

   D. While GRS has had nothing to do with the rise of urban power, it provides a likely vehicle for exploitation should interest in reform become linked to effective political leadership.

CHAPTER 8

GRS and Decisionmaking in Local Government

*James Fossett**

SUMMARY OF MAJOR FINDINGS

1. GRS does not appear to have had a substantial impact on the budget process in American cities. Most local officials do not report that revenue sharing has had any impact on their ability to set priorities, control expenditures, or make changes in the local tax structure. While they do indicate that planning has been made easier, it appears that this improvement refers only to the current budget and not to long-term assessments of needs and resources.

2. Officials in large cities report an extremely favorable impact, while officials in smaller cities are less enthusiastic. Again, both groups define the impact of GRS in terms of the current budget, rather than in terms of long-run improvements.

3. Cities appear to have been only modestly successful in spending GRS funds on programs which address their problems. The correlation between spending and local priorities is extremely low in big cities, and only moderate in smaller ones.

4. Both the priority categories and the requirement that GRS not be used to match other grants have had an impact on direct allocations of funds. The no-match prohibition seems to have had a larger impact.

5. There is relatively little evidence that GRS has been used to finance many new innovative programs. Many of the programs defined as new by our respondents appear to be capital projects whose construction was accelerated by the use of GRS funds or programs which were previously being financed by other grants.

6. The relationship between the program area of new programs which GRS was used to fund and local priorities is relatively small.

INTRODUCTION

Most attempts to review the impact of revenue sharing on local decision making have focused on the structural arrangements used to make, review and implement plans, and on the feasibility of using revenue sharing as a device to encourage governmental modernization. Considerable attention has been devoted to criticizing the managerial adequacy of current procedures for defining local problems and planning programs to meet them.

These studies, while useful, are somewhat incomplete. They take the formal administrative structure for developing and processing plans as the primary indicator of the health of the local decision process. They generally fail to take account of changes in the informal patterns of relationship which surround the formal decisionmaking apparatus and, to a major extent, determine its results. Finally, they fail to consider the possibility that different communities may have differing standards of success and may have altogether different goals and priorities.

Our data allow us to capture some of this variation in standards by focusing on whether or not local officials see their capacity to make decisions to have been enhanced by GRS. While the concept of local "capacity" is a difficult one to operationalize, we suggest that the following three factors provide a useful approximation:

1. Improvements in process. A local government can be said to be better off if, in the view of its officials, it is easier to plan for and control expenditures, make modifications in the tax structure, and assimilate community desires

---

*Graduate student in the Department of Political Science, The University of Michigan.

into the budget process in a more effective fashion.

2. Definition of local problems. City government which can define and address the problems it considers to be important in a more effective manner as a result of revenue sharing is obviously better off than it was before the program. While this factor obviously has a number of different dimensions, we shall confine ourselves here to evaluating whether local officials can spend GRS funds reasonably efficiently on programs which address local problems.

3. Spending on new programs. Local government can be said to be better off as a result of revenue sharing if it has the ability to develop programs which represent new and innovative approaches to local problems, rather than being forced to merely maintain existing programs. Revenue sharing can be said to have improved this dimension of local "capacity" if it has created the financial or political slack required for the development of new programs.

In this chapter, we wish to examine the views of local officials on whether or not they see themselves as being better off in any of the above ways as a result of revenue sharing. We will be particularly interested in identifying the types of circumstances associated by local officials with favorable changes. If improvements in local decisionmaking are associated with conditions that cannot be expected to persist over time, then the effects of the program are merely the result of its being novel and probably represent no long-term changes in local capacity to define and address local problems.

LOCAL GOVERNMENT PROCESSES

Perhaps one of the most striking effects of revenue sharing on the budget process is its reported impact on local governments' reported ability to plan for future expenditures. A considerable amount of criticism was directed towards revenue sharing during its adoption and early implementation because of its impermanence. It was argued that the need to renew appropriations for the program, even at intervals of several years, would create considerable misgivings among local governments about the program's future and would neutralize any advantages in local financial planning which would accrue if the funding were "guaranteed." Table 8-1 suggests that these misgivings were by and large unfounded. A majority of both executives and finance officers in cities of all sizes report that revenue sharing has had favorable impact on their ability to plan for future expenditures.

The major reasons given for the impact of GRS are presented in Table 8-2. Contrary to many expectations, the uncertainty of continued funding is mentioned only by officials in large cities. The long-term nature of the program is mentioned more frequently than the uncertainty of continued funding by officials at all levels.

The large number of respondents who indicate that GRS has enabled desirable expenditures or simply that it has provided more money suggests that the "planning" to which most officials referred was for the current budget, rather than for a long-term assessment of needs and resources. Relatively few officials indicated that GRS had provided for increased citizen input or had provided resources to otherwise improve the planning process itself. This focus on the current budget suggests that the major "planning" effect of GRS has

Table 8-1

Relation Between GRS and Difficulty in Planning New Expenditures

Percent of Local Officials Indicating that GRS Has Made
Planning More or Less Difficult

Community Size	Executives			Finance Officers		
	More Difficult	Less Difficult	No Change	More Difficult	Less Difficult	No Change
300,000 +	33.8	62.5	3.7	20.6	44.1	35.3
100,000-299,999	12.1	73.3	10.5	3.5	51.0	39.6
25,000-99,999	10.5	62.6	26.5	9.8	63.0	27.2
10,000-24,999	12.3	57.0	30.7	7.3	56.5	36.2
2,500-9,999	3.6	60.9	35.5	1.9	63.3	34.8
Less Than 2,500	4.4	67.2	28.4	3.4	58.8	37.1
All	11.3	62.9	25.4	9.7	55.7	33.9
	(N=45)	(N=342)	(N=150)	(N=42)	(N=333)	(N=191)

Table 8-2

Table 8-2
Impact of GRS on Ability to Plan

Percent of Local Officials Giving Indicated Reason Why GRS Has/Has Not
Had Impact on Ability to Plan for Future Expenditures*

Population	Un-Certainty	Certainty	Reduced Conflict	Better Planning	More Money, n.e.c.	Enables Needed Expenditures	Increase Community Awareness/ Participation
				A. Executives			
100,000 + ...	23.5	28.0	2.5	0.0	32.0	4.3	0.0
25,000-99,999	8.7	28.1	1.0	0.6	34.3	18.0	0.0
Less Than 25,000 ..	8.1	38.6	2.1	0.3	24.1	20.1	0.0
				B. Finance Officers			
100,000 + ...	16.5	16.0	0.5	0.0	32.2	20.4	0.0
25,000-99,999	6.6	32.9	1.2	0.0	17.0	18.6	0.0
Less Than 25,000 ..	3.6	25.4	2.1	0.3	36.8	18.4	0.0

been to remove some short-term uncertainty about how particular programs would have been financed.

There is some evidence which indicates that this reduction of uncertainty has operated in different ways in cities of varying size. In larger cities, the major effect of revenue sharing appears to have been the provision of funds to support programs that otherwise would have been cut, or to remove the necessity of convincing local electorates to increase taxes. Big city officials who indicate that planning has been made easier report that their cities devoted larger percentages of GRS funds to operating expenses than cities which indicated that planning had become more difficult and, in the case of executives, than cities which reported no change in the ability to plan. The data also indicate the connection between tax avoidance and improvements in planning (Table 8-3, top). Over three-quarters of the executives and half of the finance officers who indicated a tax increase would have been required without GRS report that planning had been made easier. It would appear, therefore, that GRS is seen by big city officials as having aided current planning by providing funds for programs that otherwise would have been cut

Table 8-3
Impact of GRS on Planning for Future Expenditures, Classified by Whether
Tax Increase Would Have Been Needed Without GRS
Percent of Local Officials Indicating that GRS Has Made
Planning More or Less Difficult

		Executives			Finance Officers		
		More Difficult	Less Difficult	No Change	More Difficult	Less Difficult	No Change
			A. Cities Greater Than 100,000 Population				
Percent of GRS going to Operating Expenses, FY74		11.5	35.5	17.4	24.4	50.8	59.2
Tax Increase Needed Without GRS	Yes	19.5	76.4	1.1	18.6	51.8	29.6
	No	29.5	44.7	25.8	4.9	26.7	60.6
			B. Cities Less Than 100,000 Population				
Percent of GRS going to Operating Expenses, FY74		19.7	16.5	12.1	17.1	13.1	11.8
Tax Increase Needed Without GRS	Yes	8.3	54.3	37.4	6.9	56.3	36.3
	No	8.6	63.9	27.4	6.5	62.3	31.2

or have been financed by a tax increase. In smaller cities, the situation is somewhat different. Officials who indicated that planning had become easier report spending a smaller percentage of GRS funds on operating expenses than those who indicated that planning had become more difficult, although more than those who indicated there had been no change. Further, those officials who report that a tax increase would have been required without GRS are less likely to indicate that planning had become easier than those who indicate that no tax increase would have been necessary (Table 8-3, bottom). These results suggest that officials were more likely to evaluate the "planning" utility of the program favorably if it supplemented, rather than replaced, local resources. It should be noted, again, however, that both groups of officials appear to have evaluated the "planning" effects of GRS in terms of the current budget, rather than in terms of their long-term financial situation.

Table 8-4 summarizes the reported effects of revenue sharing on controlling expenditures, which appear to be negligible. The overwhelming majority of respondents at all levels report that revenue sharing has had no impact on their ability to control expenditures, and that small minority which reports any effect at all indicates that control was made easier.

Respondents were also asked to indicate if they felt that revenue sharing had an impact on their ability to change or reform the local tax structure. These responses are presented in Table 8-5. Again, most respondents do not report any change. A sizeable minority of officials in smaller cities, however, feel that they are better off, and an equally sizeable minority of big city mayors feel

Table 8-4
Impact of GRS on Ability to Control Expenditures

Percent of Local Officials Indicating that GRS Has Made
Control of Expenditures More or Less Difficult

Community Size	Executives			Finance Officers		
	More Difficult	Less Difficult	No Change	More Difficult	Less Difficult	No Change
300,000 +	0.0	7.1	92.9	6.1	0.0	93.9
100,00-299,999	23.4	18.9	57.7	6.0	7.2	86.8
25,000-99,999	5.5	17.0	77.5	7.0	13.1	79.9
10,000-24,999	11.6	9.2	79.2	5.1	21.0	73.9
2,500-9,999	7.5	17.3	75.2	5.6	14.9	79.3
Less Than 2,500	0.7	20.1	78.2	3.9	22.2	74.0
Total	7.9	15.2	76.8	5.9	11.5	82.6
	(N=32)	(N=98)	(N=407)	(N=38)	(N=75)	(N=457)

Table 8-5
Impact of GRS on Ability to Change Tax Structure

Percent of Local Officials Reporting GRS Has Made
Change in Tax Structure More or Less Difficult

Community Size	Executives			Finance Officers		
	More Difficult	Less Difficult	No Change	More Difficult	Less Difficult	No Change
300,000 +	37.8	6.3	55.8	11.1	15.0	73.9
100,000-299,999	32.6	13.7	53.7	7.5	33.8	58.8
25,000-99,999	5.0	21.1	73.9	3.1	15.2	81.7
10,000-24,999	1.7	12.8	85.5	1.8	25.6	72.6
2,500-9,999	0.0	24.5	75.5	0.0	23.5	76.5
Less Than 2,500	0.7	25.8	73.5	0.8	24.6	74.6
All	9.0	18.5	72.5	4.7	20.8	74.5
	(N=20)	(N=115)	(N=404)	(N=17)	(N=120)	(N=429)

Table 8-6
Impact of GRS on Tax Change

Percent of Officials Giving Indicated Reason for
Revenue Sharing Impact on Tax Change

Community Size	Uncertainty	Other Problems	Certainty	Prevents Tax/Borrowing Increase
	A. EXECUTIVES			
100,000 +	29.0	27.2	0.0	40.0
25,000-99,999	1.2	1.7	15.4	70.7
Less Than 25,000	0.0	0.0	0.8	82.1
	B. FINANCE OFFICERS			
100,000 +	0.0	0.0	0.0	93.5
25,000-99,999	7.4	1.3	5.7	67.2
Less Than 25,000	1.4	0.0	1.5	77.4

Table 8-7
Impact of GRS on Ability to Set Priorities

Percent of Local Officials Indicating that GRS Has Made
Priority Setting More or Less Difficult

Community Size	Executives			Finance Officers		
	More Difficult	Less Difficult	No Change	More Difficult	Less Difficult	No Change
300,000 +	22.9	17.5	59.7	9.5	26.4	64.1
100,000-299,999	18.1	39.7	41.3	8.6	32.6	58.7
25,000-99,999	5.4	41.2	53.3	10.8	37.9	51.3
10,000-24,999	7.7	35.1	57.2	5.4	41.4	53.2
2,500-9,999	0.0	44.1	55.9	2.7	35.5	61.9
Less Than 2,500	4.7	28.3	67.0	2.9	26.0	71.1
All	7.8	36.9	55.2	7.5	33.5	59.0
	(N=30)	(N=217)	(N=290)	(N=30)	(N=199)	(N=339)

themselves to be worse off. The reasons for these responses, presented in Table 8-6, suggest that the question was generally interpreted as, "Has revenue sharing helped you keep taxes down?" The bulk of small city respondents who indicate that changes in the tax structure were easier report that revenue sharing allowed them to undertake desireable spending without the necessity of increasing taxes or borrowing. Big city mayors, on the other hand, expressed considerable misgivings about the uncertainty and reported other difficulties in modifying the tax structure.

While the small cell sizes make generalization hazardous, we can offer some speculations about the mayor's intentions. The apparent conflict between certainty on planning and uncertainty on taxes reflects a different time persepective on revenues and expenditures. For the purpose of a budget process that operates on a year-to-year basis, the program's stability between years is more or less irrelevant. Since revenue sharing is stable for the annual budget cycle, it allows better "planning" by removing a small percentage of a city's short-term financial uncertainty. Its use to replace revenue which officials feel might be lost as a result of tax relief or reform is more problematic: since, if. the program is discontinued, they may be faced with the necessity of trying to convince the electorate to agree to tax increases to recover the lost revenue.

A second explanation, mentioned by several of the mayors, is more interesting. The increased funds provided by revenue sharing, which may have been used to prevent tax increases, may also have reduced political pressure to make changes in the local tax structure. Since revenue sharing was

Table 8-8

Reported Reasons for Impact of GRS on Ability to Set Priorities

Percent of Local Officials Giving Indicated Reason Why GRS Has/Has Not Had
Impact on Ability to Set Priorities

Population	Conflict Over Spending	Citizen Involvement	Certainty	Reduced Conflict	Better Planning	More Money, n.e.c.	Enables Needed Expenditures	Increase Community Awareness/ Participation
			A. Executives					
100,000 + ...	29.5	1.2	3.0	1.4	1.2	22.4	35.7	0.0
25,000-99,999 ...	2.7	0.0	8.8	3.4	3.0	21.0	39.3	5.2
Less Than 25,000	6.2	0.0	12.5	8.6	2.5	35.0	26.8	0.0
			B. Finance Officers					
100,000 + ...	16.5	0.6	9.2	9.5	0.6	37.6	19.0	0.0
25,000-99,999 ...	3.2	0.0	11.8	5.8	0.0	21.5	37.3	0.0
Less Than 25,000	6.1	0.0	14.4	13.7	5.0	29.7	20.3	0.0

used to replace tax increases that otherwise would have taken place, tax relief or restructuring may have lost some of its salience for the general public and groups interested in tax reform may find it harder to develop sufficient support to make tax change a realistic possibility.[1]

Data on the impact of revenue sharing on local government's ability to set priorities, reported in Table 8-7, follow the same general pattern as the data on planning—most respondents at all levels report no changes, but a substantial number report themselves better off. As demonstrated in Table 8-8, the primary reason for this perceived improvement is much the same as that for improved planning—the increased ability to scratch a larger number of itches.

Table 8-9 indicates both groups of cities follow the same general pattern noted earlier: smaller cities receive a larger share of revenue sharing relative to their total budget and are generally more favorable than big cities. Likewise, big cities which report themselves better off are more likely to report having spent larger percentages of their budget on operating expenses—again, reflecting a temporary relaxation of financial pressures.

A substantial minority of big city mayors report that setting priorities has been more difficult by increased conflict both within the city government and outside of it over how funds should be used. This suggests that some attention should be

---

[1]This finding is taken from an unpublished paper prepared by Jean Guptill on the responses of big city mayors.

Table 8-9

Financial Correlates of Views of Impact of GRS on Setting Priorities

Percent of Local Officials Indicating That GRS Has Made Setting Priorities More or Less Difficult

	More Difficult	Less Difficult	No Change
	A. Cities Greater Than 100,000		
Revenue Sharing as Average Percent of Budget			
Executives...............	7.2	8.2	7.4
Finance Officers..........	8.0	7.3	8.3
Average Percent Revenue Sharing to Operating Expenses FY74			
Executives...............	29.8	33.6	23.5
Finance Officers..........	30.7	58.9	49.2
	B. Cities Less Than 100,000		
Revenue Sharing as Average Percent of Budget			
Executives...............	10.3	12.6	11.8
Finance Officers..........	13.3	12.2	11.4
Average Percent Revenue Sharing to Operating Expenses FY74			
Executives...............	16.4	16.4	14.8
Finance Officers..........	14.0	13.7	12.5

given to the political environment surrounding the process by which revenue sharing was allocated and its influence on officials' perception of improvements in the budget process.

Table 8-10 reports the relationships between a number of measures of increased public participation on mayors' perceptions of their ability to set priorities. We have chosen to rely here solely on the mayors and exclude the finance officers, since the executives are presumably more sensitive to the emergence of new groups and are in a better position to judge the relative level of activity before and after revenue sharing.

Table 8-10 suggests some differences between large and small cities that are of some interest. In smaller cities, executives who reported increases in public participation were more likely to indicate a favorable impact on their ability to set priorities than those who reported no such increases. This pattern holds for three of the five participation measures. There is no major difference between groups on the other two measures. In larger cities, by contrast, the only increases in participation associated with improvements in the ability to set priorities were the presence of groups that had not been active prior to revenue sharing and hearings having been held on the initial GRS allocation. Large city officials appear to perceive the articulation of presumably new problems by new groups as useful in making expenditure decisions, but do not appear to perceive the institutionalization of public attention, either through continued hearings or through the presence of advisory committees, as being particularly useful in this regard.

Table 8-11 presents the views of local officials on the final process question: that of whether or not they feel that they are better able to tell what the community wants as a result of revenue sharing. Large city officials report more success than do officers of smaller units, who tend to report that there was no change. The explanation for this increase in perceived access to public views is provided by findings elsewhere in this report, which indicate that citizen participation in the revenue sharing allocation process is considerably higher in big cities than elsewhere.

Summary

General revenue sharing appears to have had relatively little impact on the decisionmaking process in American cities, as perceived by those who are involved in this process on a day-to-day basis. It is argued elsewhere in this volume that GRS has produced relatively few changes of consequence in the structure of American local government. If the data reported here reflect reality, the impact of GRS on the process by which American cities accumulate and allocate resources has been equally slight.

It may be argued that the program is simply too small or too new to have any noticeable effect yet. While the long-term impact of GRS may be somewhat different from the initial results reported here, there is some evidence to suggest that the trend will be towards less impact rather than more. The fiscal analyses reported here indicate that GRS is being substituted into local budgets at a relatively rapid rate, suggesting that the program is losing its identity as a separate, visible source of funds in most cities. The sharp decline in special hearings noted over the program's first two years suggests that the same type of effect may be occurring in local decision processes. Whatever effect GRS may have had on the budget process in American cities appears to be largely a function of its being "new," visible, and being allocated in a different fashion from other funds.

Much the same argument may be made against the contention that the program's lack of effect is primarily a function of its size and that increased appropriations will increase its effect on local decisionmaking. The data reported here suggest that most local officials do not look upon increases in revenue that are more or less stable across time as providing opportunities to devise more efficient mechanisms for setting goals, defining priorities, and planning spending. The additional funds are viewed rather simply as an extra source of revenue to be allocated to programs that might otherwise have received less support. It would seem reasonable to assume that the provision of additional funds through GRS would produce more or less the same result on a larger scale.

GRS AND LOCAL PROBLEMS

One of the major questions in an evaluation of GRS should be the extent to which it has enhanced local ability to address community problems. A major argument advanced in favor of the program has been its flexibility relative to other forms of grants in allowing adaptation to differences in local problems. It is clearly of some interest, therefore, to examine the extent to which local offices report that their ability to address community problems has been affected by GRS.

In order to examine this question, it is first necessary to define local officials' perceptions of their communities' major problems. Our respondents were asked to name three such problems. Their responses, consolidated and arranged by

Table 8-10

**Percent of Executives Indicating Setting Priorities
Easier Because of GRS, by Changes in Participation**

Process Change	Cities Greater Than 100,000	Cities Less Than 100,000
Were any groups interested in GRS?		
Yes	*	42.4
No	*	34.0
Were the interested groups new?		
Yes	38.6	48.9
No	26.1	39.0
Were groups critical of GRS disposition?		
Yes	14.5	39.7
No	51.4	39.0
Is a citizen's advisory committee present?		
Yes	27.3	39.6
No	27.9	38.6
Were hearings held on the initial allocation?		
Yes	25.8	44.6
No	22.2	39.8
Were hearings held on 1974 allocations?		
Yes	13.4	52.2
No	37.0	36.9

*Only one case in "no" category

Table 8-11

Impact of GRS on Ability to Discover Community Preferences

Community Size	Percent of Local Officials Indicating that GRS Has Made Discovering Community Preferences:					
	Executives			Finance Officers		
	More Difficult	Less Difficult	No Change	More Difficult	Less Difficult	No Change
300,000 +	0.0	50.9	49.1	5.2	25.4	69.4
100,000-299,999	13.9	36.4	49.7	10.0	25.0	65.0
25,000-99,999	2.6	21.4	76.0	9.5	14.8	75.7
10,000-24,999	1.7	9.9	88.4	0.9	11.9	87.3
2,500-9,999	2.7	21.0	76.2	1.8	10.6	87.6
Less Than 2,500	4.1	13.7	82.2	4.3	15.8	79.9
All	3.6 (N=23)	22.6 (N=100)	73.7 (N=416)	5.6 (N=28)	17.3 (N=90)	77.1 (N=446)

issue area, are presented in Table 8-12.[2] As might be expected, these data indicate that officials in cities of different sizes are concerned with different types of problems. The basic dichotomy appears to be between "survival" in big cities and "housekeeping" in smaller ones.

Officials in big cities are concerned with three major problems—inadequate financial resources; general physical deterioration, both of housing and commercial areas; and such social problems as crime and unemployment. Rather than developing innovative programs in response to emerging social problems, officials in big cities appear to view their major concern as preventing further deterioration of a dilapidated building stock and financing existing services from an increasingly constrained revenue base. Labeling these problems as "survival" does not appear to overstate their magnitude.

Smaller cities do not appear to confront problems of such a critical nature. Their officials do not report financial problems at the same level as their big city counterparts, and do not report comparable deterioration of the building stock. Rather, they report their major problems to be the provision of basic services such as sewage, the regulation

of land use, and the maintenance of roads. While these problems are important, they do not reflect the same concern over physical and financial survival found in the larger cities. Hence the "housekeeping" label seems appropriate.

Our respondents were asked to indicate if GRS had an impact on their ability to deal with these problems. Their responses, again consolidated, are presented in Table 8-13. Contrary to the general pattern displayed in the process questions, GRS is reported to have had a more positive impact in larger cities. Since smaller cities received a larger percentage of their budgets from revenue sharing and were generally more likely to indicate that the program had a favorable impact on their budget processes, it is somewhat surprising they should indicate in such large numbers that GRS has had no impact on their ability to deal with local problems.

The reasons given for GRS' impact, or lack of impact, are presented in Table 8-14. These responses follow a pattern noted earlier—evaluation of the effects of GRS in terms of the current budget, rather than in terms of changes in capacity over a longer period of time. Our respondents tend to see their ability to addresss a particular program to have been enhanced by GRS if they have been able to spend it on programs in the current budget which address the problem.

The more favorable perceptions of big-city officials appear to be a consequence of the type of

---

[2]Tables 8-12, 8-13 and 8-14 are consolidated from questions relating to three community problems. The reader wishing a separate display of each question may obtain them from the Survey Research Center.

Table 8-12
Summary of Problem Areas Mentioned by Local Officials

(percentages)

Problem Area Mentioned	Cities Over 100,000		Cities Under 100,000	
	Executives	Finance Officers	Executives	Finance Officers
Public safety, crime	14.9	9.7	10.5	9.3
Environmental control	5.2	5.4	26.3	26.3
Housing planning and land use	23.1	25.0	17.0	19.2
Transportation	9.9	11.8	13.4	12.3
Amenities	0.4	2.3	6.2	5.8
Education	2.6	2.1	2.0	2.6
Health	0.0	0.1	0.4	0.8
Social services, problems	11.2	8.5	6.0	3.3
General government	7.5	5.6	4.9	4.5
Taxes/Debt too high	5.9	7.8	2.1	2.8
Inadequate revenue	7.3	5.7	4.9	5.1
Inflation & other financial	9.8	15.0	5.5	6.7
Other responses	2.1	1.0	1.9	0.9
Total	100.0	100.0	100.0	100.0
	(N= 152)*	(N= 198)	(N=1351)	(N=1360)

*This table was produced by consolidating responses to questions asking for three major community problems. Hence the number of respondents is larger than for other questions.

Table 8-13
**Percentage of Officials Indicating GRS Has/Has Not
Had Impact on Ability to Deal With
Local Problems, by Size Class**

	Yes	No	TOTAL
	A. Cities Over 100,000		
Finance Officers	78.5	21.5	100
Executives	63.3	36.7	100
	B. Cities Under 100,000		
Finance Officers	49.3	50.7	100
Executives	53.3	46.7	100

problems they report. Since they indicate considerable concern with financial problems which affect all program areas, it is to be expected that they would receive any increase in resources more favorably than smaller city officials, who are concerned with increasing expenditures in a particular program area. One would also expect big city officials to place a higher marginal value on resources which do not have to be raised locally than officials from smaller places, who do not report comparable difficulty with raising revenue

Since our respondents appear to define impact on community problems in terms of spending in the current budget, it is of some interest to examine the relationship between their expressions of local priorities and the way in which they report revenue sharing funds to have been spent. This relationship is presented in Table 8-15, which displays rank order correlations between the first problem mentioned and expenditures in both 1974 and 1975. These figures suggest that smaller cities have been more successful in spending GRS funds in a manner consistent with their priorities. The relationship between priorities and spending in these cities is roughly comparable to the degree of "success" reported by their officials. By contrast, big city officials, who were more likely to report that GRS had a favorable impact on their ability to deal with community problems, report spending program funds in a pattern that is only weakly related to their ranking of these problems.

There are two alternate explanations of this inconsistency in big cities. The first is that, since GRS represents a relatively small percentage of the big cities' budgets, their officials may have been less concerned with how it was spent than officials in

Table 8-14
**Percent of Local Officials Citing Given Reason
Why GRS Has/Has Not Had Impact on
Ability to Deal With Local Problems**

Response	Cities Over 100,000		Cities Under 100,000	
	Executives	Finance Officers	Executives	Finance Officers
Revenue sharing used, NA how	18.5	30.4	22.1	19.7
Start program	5.4	4.1	7.9	8.1
Continue/expand program	31.3	29.3	17.9	15.7
Release funds	1.7	1.5	2.9	2.0
Relieve taxes, borrowing	14.2	5.0	4.1	5.7
Other help	2.1	8.9	2.5	1.0
Restrictions on GRS	2.1	1.5	4.9	4.8
Problem being studied	0.2	2.2	3.5	2.7
Revenue sharing too small	3.3	1.5	7.2	10.4
Other governments involved	1.4	4.4	2.4	2.0
Problem can't be solved	3.4	3.5	5.4	7.7
GRS being spent on something else	14.3	4.0	16.0	16.8
Other funds being used	1.3	2.4	2.5	2.4
Other no help	0.9	0.7	0.8	0.7
Total	100.0	100.0	100.0	100.0
N	123*	182	1311	1253

*This table was produced by consolidating responses to questions asking for three major community problems. Hence the number of respondents is larger than for other questions.

Cities Greater Than 100,000	FY74	FY75
Executives	.34	.33
Finance Officers	.12	.13
Cities Less Than 100,000		
Executives	.48	.56
Finance Officers	.57	.59

smaller cities, making their reports of its usage less precise than those of officials from smaller places. Since many of the problems cited by big city officials relate to a general lack of resources rather than to deficiencies in particular programs, they may have accurately reported that GRS had a favorable impact, but may have been somewhat less precise in reporting how it was spent.

An alternate, and more persuasive explanation, is that the expenditure figures for big cities should be taken seriously and that the inconsistency is the result of the higher marginal value that big city officials seem to place on additional resources. There is no reason, either internal or external to the survey, that would lead one to suspect that big city officials' expenditure reports are any less accurate than those of officials elsewhere, and the general tenor of the big city responses suggests that their officials would be more likely than their small city counterparts to report *any* increase in spending on a particular program as representing a favorable impact. If one has to take either perceptions or spending reports as representing the "true" impact of GRS on community problems, it would appear more reasonable to accept the latter.

We now wish to examine the impact of the restrictions placed on GRS on officials' perceptions of their ability to address local problems. One set of restrictions which was frequently mentioned, but emerged too late in the processing of the survey schedules to be coded separately, was the requirement that capital projects funded with GRS be subject to the prevailing wage provisions of the Davis-Bacon Act. While we are unable to make any formal analysis, examination of a number of the interview schedules indicates that this provision may have been one of the major motivations for "fungibility" by local governments. Local governments perceive their potential capital costs to have been increased considerably by this regulation and may have used released funds to finance capital projects or used GRS to finance less than 25 percent of projects costs required for Davis-Bacon to apply. While again, we are unable to give any formal in-

dication of how many governments were thus affected by Davis-Bacon, it was cited as a major complicating factor on the use of GRS by a number of respondents.

Our respondents were asked to evaluate the impact of the priority categories and the prohibition against using revenue-sharing funds as the local share of a Federal grant. The proportions of local officials reporting that the direct allocation of funds would have been different in the absence of the priority categories is presented in Table 8-16. While a small percentage of our respondents indicated that allocations would have been different, it is somewhat surprising that larger cities are as likely, if not more so, than smaller cities to indicate that their spending patterns would have been different.

The types of programs that finance officers indicated would have been affected by the removal of the priority categories are represented in Tables 8-17 and 8-18. Table 8-17 indicates the program areas that would have received more direct funds. General government and education are mentioned by large numbers of officials in cities of all sizes. Since GRS may be used to fund capital expenditures in both these areas, it would appear reasonable to conclude that the main impact of the priorities was to reduce operating expenditures in both these areas. Taken on balance with the figures in Table 8-18, which indicate the program areas that would have received fewer funds in the absence of the priorities, these data suggest that the main impact of the priority categories was to divert some GRS funds away from education and general government and into amenities, transportation, and public safety.

Some caution should be exercised in the interpretation of these results, both in the extent to which they show that the priorities had an effect, and in the programs which they show to be impacted. It is not entirely clear that the results

Table 8-16
**Percent of Local Officials Indicating that
Direct Expenditures of GRS Funds Would Have
Been Different Without Priority
Categories**

Community Size	Executives (N=524)	Finance Officers (N=555)
300,000 +	39.8	13.4
100,000-299,999	51.2	35.6
25,000-99,999	19.8	17.0
10,000-24,999	19.6	20.3
2,500-9,999	22.7	25.8
Less Than 2,500	17.7	11.3
All	25.4	19.3

Table 8-17
**Program Areas on Which More GRS Funds Would Have Been Spent
in Absence of Priority Categories**

(Percent of Finance Officers)

	Public Safety	Environ-mental Control	Land Use	Private Transpor-tation	Public Transpor-tation	Amenities	Education	Health	Social Services	General Govern-ment
Cities Greater Than 100,000 (N=10)	23.1	0.0	0.0	6.0	0.0	15.8	30.0	13.1	0.0	18.0
Cities Less Than 100,000 (N=59)	4.1	14.0	7.4	17.1	1.8	3.7	16.9	0.0	10.7	23.7

Table 8-18
**Program Areas on Which Fewer GRS Funds Would Have Been Spent
in Absence of Priority Categories**

(Percent of Finance Officers)

	Public Safety	Environ-mental Control	Land Use	Private Transpor-tation	Public Transpor-tation	Amenities	Education	Health	Social Services	General Govern-ment
Cities Greater Than 100,000 (N=8)	25.7	0.0	0.0	18.7	0.0	32.9	0.0	3.7	2.8	16.2
Cities Less Than 100,000 (N=46)	21.9	3.7	0.0	30.5	4.1	26.0	0.0	4.2	2.8	7.4

reported here represent real losses, rather than accounting losses, by any particular program. Given the fact that the question included a reference to the Actual Use Reports, it seems prudent to treat responses as answers to the question "would the official Use Reports have been different without the priority categories?"

As the program impact analysis reported here and a number of other studies of what "happened" to GRS funds indicate, these responses represent different levels of "real" dollar impacts for different types of cities. In smaller cities, our program impact analysis suggests that the impacts may be regarded as real, as the correlation between Actual Use Reports and how local governments actually spent the money is quite high. In large cities, the correspondence between the Actual Use Reports and where the funds were "spent" is smaller. Thus, some portion of the results reported for large cities in Tables 8-17 and 8-18 represent accounting losses, rather than real ones, and do not entirely reflect the impact of the priority categories. Even so, these results are somewhat surprising, given the widespread conception that large cities can hide funds more easily than small ones and the findings of a number of studies, including this one,

that "fungibility" has been a larger problem in big cities than elsewhere.

One explanation is relatively simple. Many large city officials apparently would have preferred to see GRS used as a means of general financial relief by replacing funds that otherwise would have been raised locally. Given the requirement that all GRS funds must be completely "spent," however, they were faced with the necessity of clearing the funds through priority categories before they can be applied to reduce debts or to replace local revenue. Given the uncertain legal state of such pass-throughs and the apparently high levels of public involvement and conflict which appear to have accompanied the initial process of allocating GRS funds, it is not surprising that they were only partially successful in doing so, and hence report themselves dissatisfied with the priorities.

Small cities see themselves as having been less constrained by the priority categories, and what discontent they express is of a different sort. Their expression of their problems is not grossly out of line with the priority categories, and they are more likely to object to the priorities as unwarranted. Federal intrusions on how they should spend their money. Small city officials were more likely to indicate that the categories had been restrictive because "local units know their own needs best" and were more likely to express anti-Federal sentiments at other points in the questionnaire.

In spite of the fact that local officials see themselves as being restricted to some degree by the priority categories, they do not favor the abolition of the categories and are not particularly interested in seeing them expanded. As Tables 8-19 and 8-20 suggest, there is relatively little support for either abolition or expansion of the categories.

The impact of the no-match requirement on local government seems to have been less ambiguous. As indicated in Table 8-21, a relatively large number of officials indicate that the direct allocation of GRS funds would have been different without the no-match prohibition. Tables 8-22 and 8-23 indicate the programs that finance officers reported would have been impacted. As might be expected, those areas which are perceived as being most affected are those in which the majority of Federal grants to cities are concentrated—health and social services in large cities and amenities, land use and environmental control in smaller places. With relatively few deviations, these categories also parallel closely the major expressed substantive concerns of officials in these cities.

We are still confronted with the difficulty of separating changes in formal accounting from changes in diversion of resources. There is evidence to suggest that these figures are somewhat "harder" than those reported for the priority categories. The program regulations prohibit the use of released funds, as well as direct allocations, as local match. By contrast, no prohibitions or limitations are specified on the use of funds released by allocations to priority categories. In addition, Federal enforcement and surveillance seems

Table 8-19
Percent of Officials Favoring
Abolition of Priority Categories

Community Size	Executives (N=533)	Finance Officers (N=568)
300,000 +	11.4	34.9
100,000-299,999	24.9	23.4
25,000-99,999	36.8	40.1
10,000-24,999	26.3	34.5
2,500-9,999	23.9	30.5
Less Than 2,500	25.0	26.9
All	27.7	33.6

to have been somewhat stronger for this provision than for the priority categories.[3] It would seem likely, therefore, that these responses are more likely to reflect real resources lost to the indicated programs than the priority figures.

The real, as opposed to the accounting, impact that we have imputed to the responses to the questions on the restrictiveness of the no-match prohibition is given some further support by the strength of sentiment among our respondents for abolishing it. As indicated in Table 8-24, a majority of officials in cities of all sizes favor allowing revenue sharing to be used as the local share of matching grants.

Some further indication of the relative impact of the priority categories and the no-match requirement is provided by Table 8-25, which compares rank order correlations between priorities and spending in cities that reported being affected by either requirement and those that did not report being affected. While both requirements appear to

[3] P. R. Dommel, *The Politics of Revenue Sharing*, 1975.

Table 8-20
Percent of Officials Favoring Indicated Additions to GRS
Priority Categories

	Operating Expenses	Education	Other Programs	Match Allowed	No Change Mentioned	Other Change	Total	N
Cities Greater Than 100,000								
Executives	0.0	4.4	17.5	3.7	74.4	0.0	100	14
Finance Officers	3.0	2.9	8.5	1.5	56.9	8.0	100	65
Cities Less Than 100,000								
Executives	1.8	2.9	14.6	6.0	76.8	0.8	100	442
Finance Officers	4.7	3.4	9.1	2.1	79.3	1.4	100	460

Table 8-21
**Percent of Local Officials Indicating that Direct Allocations
of GRS Would Have Been Different Without
No-Match Restrictions**

Community Size	Executives (N= 514)	Finance Officers (N= 546)
300,000 + ...	85.0	39.8
100,000-299,999......	52.8	35.1
25,000-99,999........	47.5	41.9
10,000-24,999........	29.5	29.0
2,500-9,999	33.2	31.0
Less Than 2,500	19.9	16.3
All	42.3	35.0

lower the correlation between priorities and spending in both large and small cities, the reduction is considerably larger for those cities who report being·affected by the no-match requirement.

One further factor which should be considered in connection with the impact of the restrictions is the extent to which reductions in other Federal grants affected the way in which GRS was spent. Shortly after GRS was adopted, funds for a number of Federal programs, largely social services and sewage plant construction, were either cut sharply or impounded, and the Administration announced plans to dismantle several others (see Dommel, pp. 168-175). GRS was subsequently advanced by the Administration as an appropriate substitute funding source for those programs for cities that wished to continue them.

Our respondents were asked to indicate if the reduction in Federal grants, or the possibility of a reduction, had any impact on the way GRS funds were spent. A sizeable minority of local officials, particularly in large cities, agreed that their use of GRS funds had been affected by changes in other grants. It is of some interest to ascertain what the affected areas were and what factors are associated with reduced spending. While we have no direct evidence on what these programs were, there is some indirect evidence to suggest that the areas in which net spending was reduced correspond to those in which Federal grants were cut. As Table 8-26 suggests, cities which reported that GRS was used to replace Federal funds were also more likely to report that GRS allocations were affected by the no-match provisions. Since the program areas listed as being most affected by the no-match prohibition are social services in the large cities and environmental protection in the smaller ones, it appears to be a reasonable, if circumstantial, inference that a large number of cities were prevented from replacing "lost" Federal funds in two priority categories by the prohibition against using GRS to

Table 8-22
**Program Areas Which Would Have Been Increased First
in Absence of No-Match Provision**

(Percent of Finance Officers)

	Public Safety	Environmental Control	Land Use	Private Transportation	Public Transportation	Amenities	Education	Health	Social Services	General Government
Cities Greater Than 100,000 (N 23)	11.9	5.4	0.0	0.0	17.2	11.4	0.0	23.5	30.6	0.0
Cities Less Than 100,000 (N 116)	9.0	26.8	17.4	11.7	1.3	26.1	2.1	1.5	1.2	2.9

Table 8-23
**Program Areas Which Would Have Been Cut First
in Absence of No-Match Provision**

(Percent of Finance Officers)

	Public Safety	Environmental Control	Land Use	Private Transportation	Public Transportation	Amenities	Education	Health	Social Services	General Government
Cities Greater Than 100,000 (N 18)	48.4	0.0	0.0	8.1	0.0	11.0	0.0	8.9	1.1	22.5
Cities Less Than 100,000 (N 72)	23.1	7.9	2.0	18.6	0.7	30.0	0.0	7.7	0.0	10.0

Table 8-24

**Percent of Local Officials in Favor
of Allowing GRS Funds to be Used as
Local Match for Federal Grants**

Community Size	Executives (N=286)	Finance Officers (N=291)
300,000 + ...	71.3	64.3
100,000-299,999	58.5	65.2
25,000-99,999	57.8	47.2
10,000-24,999	59.5	49.1
2,500-9,999	56.5	39.1
Less Than 2,500	51.0	55.0
All	56.9	53.5

match Federal grants. There is, then, at least some indication that the restrictions imposed on the use of revenue sharing funds may have worked at cross-purposes with each other in some cities, and that, other things being the same, these cities are spending less, at least in the perception of their officials, on some categories than they were before revenue sharing was adopted. Local officials ap-

pear to have been somewhat reluctant to risk violation of the no-match provision by investing either revenue sharing funds or released funds in the replacement of lost Federal funds.

The more general argument that many cities may be no better off as a result of GRS because of the reductions in other grants is given some support by our respondents. As Table 8-27 indicates, a sizeable minority of officials in all but the smallest cities report that they are receiving fewer net Federal funds than before GRS was adopted because it has failed to replace losses in other programs.

Summary

General revenue sharing was initially posited as a counterweight to what was felt to be an over-centralized system of deciding and implementing domestic policy. It was designed, at least in part, to strengthen local executives and other "generalist" officials and to expand local capacity to define and

Table 8-25

**Rank Order Correlations Between First Local Problem
and Spending for Cities Affected by GRS
Restrictions, as Reported by Finance Officers**

	Priorities Have Impact	Priorities Have No Impact	No-Match Has Impact	No-Match Has No Impact
Cities Greater Than 100,000	.33	.49	.04	.28
Cities Less Than 100,000	.50	.66	.37	.66

Table 8-26

**Relationship Between Reports that Reductions in Other Grants Had Effect
on GRS Spending and Impact of No-Match Requirement**
(Percent of Finance Officers)

		No-Match Provision Had Impact		
		Yes	No	
		A. Cities Greater Than 100,000		
Reduction in other Grants had impact on GRS spending	Yes	66.0	34.0	100
	No	27.5	72.5	100
	All	39.0	61.0	(N=64)
		B. Cities Less Than 100,000		
Reduction in other grants had impact on GRS spending	Yes	54.9	45.1	100
	No	28.5	71.5	100
	All	32.3	67.7	(N=472)

Community Size	Executives (N= 497)	Finance Officers (N= 516)
300,000 + ...	49.7	50.3
100,000-299,999	48.7	44.3
25,000-99,999	26.2	25.6
10,000-24,999	25.4	20.3
2,500-9,999	28.7	21.5
Less Than 2,500	29.5	8.2

deal with problems independently of Federal guidelines and control.

The results reported here, we believe, present little evidence that local governments can better address local problems as a result of GRS. While a majority of local officials reported that GRS had a positive impact on their ability to deal with what they perceive to be their units' major problems, it seems clear that these responses can only be interpreted in the narrowest possible sense. According to local officials, they are better off almost exclusively because they now possess an increment of funds which does not have to be raised from local sources and can be spent with a relative degree of freedom. There is little evidence here to suggest that GRS has stimulated any mechanisms for improving the way in which local governments identify new problems, or modify programs to more efficiently address old ones.

It is not clear, even in this limited sense, that GRS has had an unambiguously positive impact on local government. A substantial number of our respondents indicated that they would have spent GRS funds differently had there been no restrictions on the way the money could be used, and there is some evidence that the restrictions hampered local ability to spend the funds on major community problems. Further, there is some circumstantial evidence that indicates the requirements may have worked at cross purposes with each other. Perhaps more significantly, it would appear that local governments have been only modestly successful in spending GRS in a manner consistent with their priorities.

The results reported here are relatively crude and should not be taken as an argument that GRS has had no impact on any local problems or that local officials are not satisfied with the program on the whole. They do indicate strongly however, that increasing the capacity of local governments to address community problems requires a somewhat more complex process than merely providing unrestricted funds.

GRS AND NEW PROGRAMS

One more tangible way in which GRS may have improved the capacity of local governments is by stimulating them to adopt programs that embody new and innovative ways of dealing with social problems. Many proponents of GRS argued that the program's adoption would revive the concept of State and local government as a social laboratory where new ideas could be tried on a small scale. The provision of extra funds, it was argued, would allow local officials to experiment with novel approaches to programs without risking their own funds and hence, would make them more amenable to new ideas.

We wish to examine the validity of this argument and define the extent to which GRS has stimulated spending on new or innovative programs by local governments. Because of the problems inherent in deciding what is "new" or "innovative" a few comments about our data and its limitations are in order. Respondents were asked to name up to three new programs that GRS was used to fund and the approximate annual cost of each. They were also asked to indicate it they considered the program to be an innovative addition to their activities and if the program would have been undertaken in the absence of revenue sharing.

It should be obvious that "innovation" and "new programs" are not the same. Examining innovative programs carries the connotation that the programs represent a more or less significant change in local goals or procedures. Adopting this type of program is more significant than building a new branch library, but trying to separate what is "significantly" different from what is new is inordinately difficult. This problem is compounded in our case because our respondents may have different standards for what they consider to be innovative. Relying on these standards without any further knowledge of the city's program mix or the respondent's ideology and program preferences creates the potential for considerable ambiguity in our results. Since the question of whether one is doing anything that was not being done before is less likely to produce different answers for the same situation than that of whether one is innovating or not, it seems safer to rely on new programs as dependent variables and avoid the question of innovation altogether.

A further problem of definition involves deciding whether or not several types of programs can reasonably be defined as new, or being stimulated by revenue sharing. Several case studies of the process of allocating GRS funds in individual cities have indicated two problems of this type. A number of cities used GRS as a means of accelerating spending; that is, building the branch library this year rather than next. While this type of program is new, in the sense that it was not being done before and would not have been done without revenue sharing, the fact that it would have been done eventually suggests that GRS had relatively little to do with its adoption besides providing the funds. A second problem arises from the programs that many local governments were forced to assume as a result of the reductions in Federal grants discussed in the last section. While these programs are technically new to the city budget, it is clear that their presence cannot be attributed to GRS, as they had been applied for and implemented earlier. It is obvious that including both these types of programs overestimates the importance of GRS in stimulating local expenditures on new programs. Nontheless, since they cannot be identified without an examination of each interview, they will be included.

Description of Results

Tables 8-28—8-31 present the reports of city finance officers on the number, cost, program, and account classification of the new programs which GRS was used to fund.

One problem encountered with some of the cost data should be mentioned. While our interviewers asked respondents for the total annual cost of new programs, the amounts we received in many cases were clearly spread over a period of several years. In order to adjust the data for this problem, the total cost of each new program was constrained so that it could not amount to more than twice the revenue-sharing allocation the city received. Since each city could cite a maximum of three programs, this means that total new expenditures were limited to six times the amount of the revenue-sharing allocation. While this procedure does eliminate some of the larger programs on which GRS was spent, it makes a reasonable correction for the problem of multi-year expenditures and provides more realistic figures.

The first finding of interest from these tables is the difference between the distributions of the number of new programs and the amount spent as a fraction of GRS allocation. As Tables 8-28 and 8-29 reveal, large cities used GRS funds to start a larger number of new programs than did smaller places, but spent smaller fractions of GRS funds on the programs they began. Table 8-30 suggests that

Table 8-28
Percent of Finance Officers Reporting Given Number of
New Programs on Which Revenue Sharing Was Spent

Community Size	Number of New Programs				Total	N
	0	1	2	3		
300,000 +	38.0	42.1	1.3	18.6	100	27
100,000-299,999	37.4	21.4	10.5	30.6	100	40
25,000-99,999	34.1	29.2	8.6	28.1	100	215
10,000-24,999	41.7	21.3	20.9	16.1	100	91
2,500-9,999	38.8	31.6	12.1	17.5	100	85
Under 2,500	65.2	19.5	8.9	6.4	100	120
All	40.0	29.9	9.3	20.0	100	578
N =	277	144	69	88	578	

Table 8-29
Average Spending on New Programs and Average
Program Cost,
as Reported by Finance Officers

Community Size	Average Total Spending*	Average Number of New Programs	Average Program Cost*	Average Expenditures/RS
300,000 +	$4,999,391	1.6	$3,995,205	26.7
100,000-299,999	1,240,439	2.1	844,897	42.2
25,000-99,999	303,010	2.0	203,669	50.7
24,999 or Less	24,252	1.8	13,483	58.0
All	51,340	1.9	33,210	46.5

*Compiled using sample weight—differential probability of selection only.

Table 8-30
Budget Account of New Programs GRS Used to Fund,
as Reported by Finance Officer
(percentages)

Community Size	Capital	Operating	Both and Not Ascertained	Total	N
300,000 + ...	42.8	10.0	47.2	100	26
100,000-299,999	41.5	2.1	56.4	100	35
25,000-99,999	49.2	4.1	46.7	100	277
24,999 or Less	56.8	10.2	32.4	100	240
All	49.3	7.3	43.3	100	528

Table 8-31
Program Area of New Programs GRS Used to Fund,
as Reported by Finance Officer
(percentages)

	Population		
Program Area	100,000 or more	Less Than 100,000	Total
Public Safety	27.4	14.7	19.3
Environmental control	7.9	16.1	13.2
Land use	9.2	4.4	6.1
Transportation	12.7	23.2	19.4
Amenities	15.0	25.5	21.7
Education	0.0	2.8	1.8
Health	18.1	3.3	8.7
Social services	11.8	8.2	9.5
Financial and general administrative	0.4	5.6	3.7
Other	0.0	0.2	0.1
Total	100.0	100.0	100.0
N = ...	60	449	509

this difference is largely a function of the budget object of the programs that were started. Smaller places were more likely to invest GRS funds in capital projects than were larger cities, which were more likely to start operating programs or projects which included both operating and capital elements.

Table 8-31 indicates the program areas in which new projects were begun. In larger cities, the bulk of new programs were begun in public safety, health, and environmental control, while amenities and private transportation received more funds in smaller places.

Tables 8-32—8-35 present descriptive information on the subset of these responses that finance officers indicate would have been begun without revenue sharing. They suggest that the impact of GRS on spending for new programs was largest at both extremes of the size distribution. Medium-sized cities (those with population of 25,000-300,000) appear to have been more likely to have started new programs without GRS than either very large or very small places, and report

Table 8-32
Percent of Finance Officers Indicating Number of New Programs
That Would Have Been Begun Without GRS

Community Size	Number of New Programs				N
	0	1	2	3	
300,000 + ...	84.9	10.7	4.4	0.0	27
100,000-299,999	68.6	17.0	6.4	8.0	40
25,000-99,999	60.6	34.7	3.7	1.0	215
10,000-24,999	65.5	23.8	9.0	1.7	91
2,500-9,999	75.6	18.5	3.6	2.3	85
Under 2,500	87.5	10.2	2.3	0.0	120
All	72.8	20.6	4.8	1.7	
N = ...	439	102	29	8	578

Table 8-33
Spending on New Programs That Would Have Begun Without GRS, as Reported by Finance Officers

Community Size	Average Total Spending	Total Spending/RS	N
300,000 + ...	$981,354	4.8	27
100,000-299,999 ...	629,685	23.4	40
25,000-99,999	151,139	26.0	215
24,999 or Less	6,653	21.5	296
All	$ 17,277	18.7	578

that they would have spent amounts equivalent to larger percentages of their allocations on new programs had the program not been in existence.

While the cells in the first two size classes are small, making generalization hazardous, these figures differ from the first set of tables in some interesting ways. As Table 8-34 suggests, cities are more likely to have spent funds on operating programs than on capital projects, suggesting that the main impact of GRS may have been on capital spending rather than on the on-going programs of local government. Table 8-35 indicates further that the impact of GRS was not neutral between program areas. While the relative ranking of program areas remains relatively constant in cities with populations of less than 25,000, the ranking of programs changes considerably in larger places.

We can define the impact of GRS more precisely by examining Tables 8-36—8-39 which describe the characteristics of those programs that city finance officers indicate would not have been done without GRS. These data represent the new programs that GRS can be said to have stimulated, and as such are worthy of some extended attention.

The most striking finding from this set of tables is from Table 8-38, which indicates the budget account of programs that were "stimulated" by GRS. As we suggested earlier, the major impact of GRS with respect to new programs appears to have been on capital expenditures. Even in large cities, the bulk of the new programs that GRS can be said

to be responsible for were capital projects rather than operating programs. Given the long lead time involved in the preparation of capital projects, this presents a strong circumstantial argument that the bulk of new programs stimulated by GRS were of the accelerated spending variety.

Tables 8-37 and 8-38 provide further evidence in support of two findings noted earlier. Large cities appear to have been stimulated to adopt more new programs, and smaller cities appear to have spent a relatively larger amount as a percentage of their allocation than other cities. The explanation for this finding is relatively simple. Smaller cities received less money in absolute terms than did bigger cities, and, given their predisposition to invest in capital projects, may have received enough funds to finance only one project. Large cities, on the other hand, received sufficient funds to distribute over several programs. It would also appear reasonable that smaller cities were more likely to finance projects completely out of GRS, while larger places, which were under considerable political pressure from a variety of groups, were more likely to spread funds available for new programs among several departments to be used in combination with funds from other sources.

The data contained in Table 8-39 also appear to confirm our earlier argument that GRS has not been neutral as concerns new programs between various departmental areas. If GRS had functioned as a general purpose grant, the program distributions for those programs which would have been done in any case and those that were stimulated would look more or less the same, as the program would have generated only income effects. The program distribution tables suggest that while the program has functioned in roughly this fashion in smaller cities, there are substantial differences in large cities between what was stimulated and what would have been done in any case.

It should be noted that the program distribution of spending on new programs is only moderately related to officials' ranking of local problems. As Table 8-40, which presents rank order correlations between local priorities and each

Table 8-34
Budget Account of New Programs that Would Have Been Begun Without GRS, as Reported by Finance Officer
(percentages)

Community Size	Capital	Operating	Both and Not Ascertained	Total	N
300,000 + ...	0.0	18.5	81.5	100	6
100,000-299,999	17.4	0.0	82.6	100	9
25,000-99,999	39.6	4.2	56.2	100	85
Less Than 25,000	51.7	16.3	32.0	100	76
All	34.6	9.9	55.5	100	176

Table 8-35
Program Area of New Programs That Would Have Been Begun Without GRS, as Reported by Finance Officers
(percentages)

Program Area	Population 100,000 or more	Less Than 100,000	Total
Public safety	26.2	10.8	15.6
Environmental control ...	7.2	19.5	15.7
Land use	27.9	4.8	12.0
Transportation	7.6	15.2	12.9
Amenities	12.1	24.7	20.8
Education	0.0	3.6	2.4
Health	12.1	5.6	7.6
Social services	7.0	8.7	8.2
Finanacial and general administrative	0.0	6.7	4.6
Other	0.0	0.0	0.0
Total	100.0	100.0	100.0
N = ...	15	152	167

Table 8-36
Percentage of Finance Officers Reporting Number of New Programs that Would Not Otherwise Have Been Begun

Community Size	Number of New Programs 0	1	2	3	N
300,000 + ...	43.0	41.4	6.9	8.6	27
100,000-299,999	57.7	15.6	20.9	5.8	40
24,000-99,999	55.2	18.9	22.5	3.3	215
10,000-24,999	55.1	25.3	18.8	0.9	91
2,500-9,999	60.7	21.3	11.5	6.5	85
Under 2,500	72.9	17.7	5.0	4.3	120
All	54.7	25.5	14.8	5.1	
N = ...	366	116	68	28	578

Table 8-37
Spending on New Programs That Would Not Have Begun Without GRS, As Reported by Finance Officers

Community Size	Average Spending	Average Spending/RS	N
300,000 + ...	$4,018,036	21.9	27
100,000-299,999 ...	610,754	18.8	40
25,000-99,999	151,871	26.6	215
24,999 or Less	17,599	41.7	296
All	$ 34,063	30.3	578

Table 8-38
Budget Account of New Programs Stimulated by GRS,
As Reported by Finance Officers

(percentages)

Community Size	Capital	Operating	Both and Not Ascertained	Total	N
300,000 + ...	53.2	7.9	38.8	100	20
100,000-299,999	53.2	3.8	43.0	100	25
25,000-99,999	58.0	4.0	38.1	100	125
24,999 or Less	60.8	7.5	31.7	100	151
All	5.7	6.2	36.8	100	321

Table 8-39
Program Area of New Programs Stimulated By
GRS, as Reported by Finance Officers

(percentages)

Program Area	Population		Total
	100,000 or more	Less Than 100,000	
Public safety	28.5	16.5	21.4
Environmental control	8.4	15.6	12.7
Land use	2.6	4.1	3.5
Transportation	11.4	19.7	16.3
Amenities	14.1	27.3	21.9
Education	0.0	2.5	1.5
Health	20.7	2.3	8.5
Social services	13.8	7.1	9.8
Financial and general adminsitrative	0.5	4.7	3.0
Other	0.0	0.0	0.0
Total	100.0	100.0	100.0
N = ...	44	233	277

of the three types of new programs we have discussed here, indicates, this correlation is particularly low in big cities. Smaller cities again appear to have experienced less difficulty in spending GRS in areas which they identify as problems. The concentration of new programs in capital areas suggests, as argued earlier, that local officials do not look upon revenue sharing as an opportunity to start new, innovative programs, but rather as an additional source of revenue that does not have to be extracted from local sources.

Table 8-40
Rank Order Correlations Between Local Problems and
Program Areas of New Programs,
as Reported by Finance Officers

	All New Programs	Programs That Would Have Been Done Without GRS	Programs Stimulated by GRS
Cities with populations of 100,000 or more	.07	.28	.02
Cities with populations Less Than 100,000	.57	.48	.53

CHAPTER 9

Citizen Participation in General Revenue Sharing

Edie Goldenberg*

SUMMARY

Outside the largest cities, revenue sharing appears to have had little impact on local political processes. In large cities (over 100,000 population), special hearings on revenue sharing were commonly held, a number of citizen advisory groups were established, and citizens were frequently active with regard to revenue sharing. Outside the big cities, citizens' groups expressed interest in revenue sharing but did little else, and special hearings and advisory committees were relatively rare.

In places with hearings and advisory committees, officials tend to find it easier to learn about community preferences. They also tend to broaden their concerns to new issues and problems.

[Over time, whatever special treatment was initially given to revenue-sharing funds declined as they were incorporated into the regular budgetary process.] Fewer cities of all sizes held special hearings on revenue sharing the second year than the first. Furthermore, local officials overwhelmingly expressed their opposition to requiring the formation of citizen advisory committees as a condition of the revenue-sharing program. As the process becomes increasingly normalized over time, we can expect a return to former levels of citizen participation in local fiscal processes.

Finally, what one learns about revenue-sharing-related citizen activity depends somewhat on whom one asks. Finance officers typically perceive less citizen activity than do local executives.

*Assistant Professor, Department of Political Science and Assistant Research Scientist, Institute for Public Policy Studies, The University of Michigan.

INTRODUCTION

A considerable amount of controversy has surrounded the question of General Revenue Sharing's effects on citizen involvement in the policy process. When GRS was first instituted, some proponents suggested that it would result in a transfer of power from Washington to State and local governments, and that this increment of power and money would generate public interest and activity. On the other hand, critics argued that the levels of citizen participation achieved under Great Society programs such as Model Cities and OEO Community Action Programs would wither away since GRS had no requirements for citizen input. Recently, some observers have claimed that no such withering away has occurred; others have noted no participation increase either.

What proponents seem to be emphasizing are increased incentives to participate as a result of GRS allocations. In contrast, critics are stressing that opportunities for citizen input are likely to decrease because local governments are no longer required to implement citizen input mechanisms. Both appear to assume that citizen participation is desirable and effectual.

Accordingly, the following discussion is presented in three parts. First, we summarize responses of city and county officials to a series of questions about governmental initiatives in seeking citizen input and their perspectives on the desirability of requiring citizen activity. Second, we examine official opinions regarding GRS effects on citizen involvement, and how they vary with varying opportunities and incentives. And third, we try to assess whether perceived citizen involvement has made any noticeable difference to the fiscal process or to policy outcomes.

For simplicity, in general only the views of executives are presented for discussion. Executives were chosen because they are probably in a better position to assess questions of interest group activity than are finance officers. However, neither set of opinions should be viewed as a "correct" description of reality. Rather, the survey responses should be understood to reflect the varying standards and viewpoints associated with differences of position and function. In fact, executives and their fiscal officers do not always agree in their perceptions of citizen activities and process effects. These differences are in and of themselves interesting and are reported when they occur.[1]

A brief word about the weights and samples used in this discussion may prove helpful since they are different from those used in discussing fiscal impacts. The weight used here is simply the inverse of the probability of selection of the government unit. Since, in general, there is only one executive and one functional finance officer per unit, this allows us to make statements about percentages of executives or finance officers. In those cases in which we compare executives and finance officers, a special matched sample of respondents is used. This second sample is somewhat smaller than either the sample of executives or the sample of finance officers since it excludes all cases missing either an executive or a fiscal officer. It also excludes those cases in which the executive *is* the functional finance officer for that government unit. Table 9-1 shows the unweighted N's for executives, functional finance officers, and the matched sample for municipalities and counties, respectively.

GOVERNMENT INITIATIVES IN SEEKING CITIZEN INPUT

There are a number of ways in which officials might take initiatives to become aware of community preferences. One of these is through a public hearing mechanism. Apart from municipalities of under 2,500 people, executives in virtually all (75-100 percent) other local governments reported that they held budgetary hearings at least once per year prior to revenue sharing. When finance officers rather than executives were asked, they tended to report hearings slightly more often. Therefore, the figures cited may even be con-

Table 9-1

Unweighted Sample Size of Municipal and County Executives, Functional Finance Officers and Matched Sample

	All Executives	All Functional Finance Officers	Matched Sample
Municipalities....	559	578	520
Counties	133	142	121

servative. In any case, one may conclude from Table 9-2 that budgetary hearings are now a common practice in American municipalities and counties.

Table 9-3 shows executive responses to a question about whether they held public hearings on the disposition of revenue-sharing funds. Initially, most large cities apparently did hold such hearings, but most small cities (under 10,000) did not. Roughly one-half of the county executives reported holding initial hearings. Those who have argued that GRS would produce changes in the budgetary process initially, but after a while would be treated like any other funds subject to the same fiscal process find some support in Table 9-3. The number of officials reporting that public hearings were held during fiscal year 1974 specifically on revenue-sharing funds was smaller in all size classes of cities and counties than those reporting initial GRS hearings. Within a fairly short time, some cities and counties which initially looked upon GRS as special money which required special hearings began to treat it like any other funding source. Contrary to other findings which suggest an *increase* in the number of large cities (over 50,000 population) which held hearings from roughly 50 percent in 1973 to "almost 60 percent" in 1974,[2] these data indicate a substantial fall off for large and small cities alike.

Table 9-4 further illuminates these trends. Most executives saw their revenue sharing money as separate from other local funds when it was received initially. Executives in larger cities and counties were more likely than others to view funds as merged, but even there around 70 percent reported viewing funds as separate. Some analysts have suggested that GRS funds were looked upon as separate money initially as an inevitable result of the bunching of revenue-sharing cash in the first entitlement periods.[3] They further suggest that with time, since the bunching effect would no longer present local jurisdictions with large sums of money after budgets had already been decided, that GRS funds would tend to be seen as merged

---

[1]This observation was first made in Thomas J. Anton and Richard Hofferbert, "Assessing the Political Impact of General Revenue Sharing: Local Perspectives," Preliminary Report No. 2, February 1975. This chapter draws heavily from the conclusions presented in that preliminary report.

[2]See Richard L. Cole, "Revenue Sharing: Citizen Participation and Social Service Aspects," *The Annals of the American Academy of Political and Social Science* 419 (May 1975): 67.

[3]Richard P. Nathan, Allen D. Manvel, Susannah E. Calkins and Associates, *Monitoring Revenue Sharing* (The Brookings Institution: Washington, DC 1975): 267,268.

Table 9-2
Number of Public Budgetary Hearings Held Before Revenue Sharing
(Question E6) by Size Class Reported by Municipal and County Executives

	Number of Hearings Per Budget Period Held Before Revenue Sharing			
	None	One	2-4	5 and More
Municipalities				
Size Class				
Over 300,000 inhabitants	7.3%	32.2%	12.9%	47.5%
100,000-300,000 inhabitants	7.9	51.5	27.2	13.3
25,000-100,000 inhabitants	5.1	56.8	24.1	14.0
10,000-25,000 inhabitants	6.5	64.9	18.2	10.4
2,500-10,000 inhabitants	25.0	46.4	18.8	9.8
100-2,500 inhabitants	45.8	44.3	5.6	4.3
Total Municipalities	34.3	47.5	11.4	6.9
Counties				
Size Class				
Within SMSA-over 500,000 inhabitants	0.0%	51.6%	26.3%	22.1%
Within SMSA-150,000-500,000 inhab.	20.1	47.3	21.4	11.2
Within SMSA-under 150,000 inhab.	20.8	63.8	9.7	5.7
Outside SMSA	18.6	72.9	4.4	4.1
Total Counties	18.6	70.9	5.8	4.8

Table entries are the weighted percent within the size class with the indicated response.

Table 9-3
Whether Public Hearings Were Held for Revenue Sharing Funds (Questions E7, E8)
by Size Class Reported by Municipal and County Executives

	Were Initial Hearings Held?		Were 1974 Hearings Held?	
	Yes	No	Yes	No
Municipalities				
Size Class				
Over 300,000 inhabitants	64.5%	35.5%	56.2%	43.8%
100,000-300,000 inhabitants	62.5	37.5	19.6	80.4
25,000-100,000 inhabitants	50.5	49.5	27.3	72.7
10,000-25,000 inhabitants	53.2	46.8	18.7	81.3
2,500-10,000 inhabitants	40.1	59.9	16.6	83.4
100-2,500 inhabitants	32.1	67.9	10.8	89.2
All Municipalities	38.6	61.4	14.6	85.4
Counties				
Size Class				
Within SMSA-over 500,000 inhabitants	44.1%	55.9%	34.2%	65.8%
Within SMSA-150,000-500,000 inhabitants	44.6	55.4	26.3	73.7
Within SMSA-under 150,000 inhabitants	45.6	54.4	27.2	72.8
Outside SMSA	56.4	43.6	30.1	69.9
All Counties	54.8	45.2	29.8	70.2

Table entries are the weighted percent of a size class with the indicated response.

with other local money. However, when asked in a follow-up question whether they still looked upon GRS money in the same way, an overwhelming majority of respondents replied "yes."

When executives and finance officers are compared, in Table 9-5 we see that finance officers were even more likely than executives to view revenue-sharing funds initially as separate from other local funds. When asked if they still viewed GRS money in the same way, finance officers, like executives, overwhelmingly responded "yes." Therefore, according to official reports, there was no marked

tendency for funds initially perceived as separate due to bunching to be subsequently viewed as merged. Those that did report changes in the way they viewed funds moved about equally from merged to separate as from separate to merged.

The findings on hearings and those on official attitudes about whether GRS funds are viewed as separate appear contradictory. The number of special hearings held declined, suggesting that over time GRS funds became merged. Official reports suggest the opposite. A more detailed study of fewer jurisdictions offers an explanation: official

Table 9-4

Whether Revenue Sharing Funds Were Viewed As Separate From or Merged with Local Funds (Questions A4, A5) by Size Reported by Municipal and County Executives

	How Were Funds Viewed Initially?		How Were Funds Viewed in 1974?	
	Separate	Merged	Same	Differently
Municipalities				
Size Class				
Over 300,000 inhabitants...................	68.2%	31.8%	66.4%	33.6%
100,000-300,000 inhabitants...............	76.7	23.3	89.5	10.5
25,000-100,000 inhabitants................	72.8	27.2	90.4	9.6
10,000-25,000 inhabitants.................	90.3	9.7	94.7	5.3
2,500-10,000 inhabitants..................	80.7	19.3	92.7	7.3
100-2,500 inhabitants.....................	86.5	13.5	95.9	4.1
All Municipalities.........................	84.7	15.3	94.6	5.4
Counties				
Size Class				
Within SMSA-over 500,000 inhabitants	70.2%	29.8%	93.4%	6.6%
Within SMSA-150,000-500,000 inhabitants...	86.0	15.0	98.0	2.0
Within SMSA-under 150,000 inhabitants	93.1	6.9	96.7	3.3
Outside SMSA.............................	88.8	11.2	89.1	10.9
All Counties	88.7	11.3	90.0	10.0

Table entries are the weighted percent of a size class with the indicated response.

Table 9-5

Whether Revenue Sharing Funds Were Viewed As Separate From Local Funds (Questions A4, A5) by Size Class Reported by Municipal and County Matched Executives and Functional Finance Officers

	Percent Initially Viewing GRS Funds as Separate		Percent Viewing Funds the Same Way in 1974	
	Executives	Finance Officers	Executives	Finance Officers
Municipalities				
Size Class				
Over 100,000 inhabitants..................	75.9%	84.2%	84.3%	91.8%
Under 100,000 inhabitants.................	85.0	86.3	94.3	91.6
All Municipalities.........................	84.9	86.2	94.3	91.6
Counties				
Size Class				
Within SMSA-Over 500,000 inhabitants	66.0%	84.9%	92.5%	93.7%
Within SMSA-150,000-500,000 inhabitants...	83.3	92.0	97.8	94.2
Within SMSA-Under 150,000 inhabitants	92.9	81.4	96.6	100.0
Outside SMSA.............................	99.6	99.6	100.0	94.2
All Counties	97.9	97.7	99.5	94.6

Table entries are the weighted percent of a size class with the indicated response.

reports that GRS money is kept separate appear to reflect the fact that GRS funds were placed in a separate account rather than that they were handled by any substantially different allocation process.[4] Since finance officers are probably more aware of this requirement, it explains differences between their reports and those of executives. Therefore, the decline in hearings probably gives a more accurate picture of what actually occurred in terms of the budgetary process.

To sum up, officials in cities and counties in- itially tended to see GRS funds as separate from other local funds. Only large-city and large-county executives showed any inclination to report that they viewed GRS as merged. They also reported holding hearings initially and in 1974 more than did officials in smaller cities and counties. Therefore, in one way or the other, almost all local units tended to treat GRS funds as different from regular sources of revenue initially. However, by 1974 there was a substantial shift toward nor- malization with respect to public hearings.

---

[4]Catherine H. Lovell, *The Effects of General Revenue Sharing on Ninety-Seven Cities in Southern California* (Riverside, California: Dry-Lands Research Institute, June 30, 1975), p. 117.

Budgetary hearings, of course, represent only one among a variety of activities likely to be associated with local fiscal decisions. In Table 9-6 we summarize responses to the question, "Has this unit set up any citizens' groups or committees which advise you on budget, financial or program matters?" Most do not have such committees, but substantial numbers do. The larger the unit, the more likely were executives to report that they have advisory committees.

While interested in the citizen input mechanisms available in local communities, we were additionally interested in whether these were begun as a result of revenue sharing or whether they had been there all along. When asked whether any of the advisory committees had been formed "because of revenue sharing," an overwhelming proportion of respondents (over 80 percent) in cities and counties responded "no." When further asked how they felt about changing revenue sharing "to require the formation of citizen advisory committees to decide how to use revenue sharing money," local officials overwhelmingly indicated their opposition. Table 9-7 shows that not only did around 80 percent of

Table 9-6
Whether Citizens' Groups Were Set Up to Advise on Budget, Financial or Program Matters (Questions E10, E11) by Size Class Reported by Municipal and County Executives

	Were Citizens' Groups Set Up?		If So, Because of Revenue Sharing	
	Yes	No	Yes	No
Municipalities				
Size Class				
Over 300,000 inhabitants	58.5%	41.5%	24.2%	75.8%
100,000-300,000 inhabitants.	76.2	23.8	12.1	87.9
25,000-100,000 inhabitants.	40.2	59.8	16.1	83.9
10,000-25,000 inhabitants.	37.7	62.3	15.7	84.3
2,500-10,000 inhabitants	22.4	77.6	9.5	90.5
100-2,500 inhabitants	8.8	91.2	9.1	90.9
All Municipalities.	17.2	82.8	11.4	88.6
Counties				
Size Class				
Within SMSA-Over 500,000 inhabitants	36.7%	63.3%	28.1%	71.9%
Within SMSA-150,000-500,000 inhabitants. . .	29.5	70.5	33.7	66.3
Within SMSA-Under 150,000 inhabitants	19.8	80.2	32.9	67.1
Outside SMSA	25.9	74.1	16.6	83.4
All Counties	25.8	74.2	18.4	81.6

Table entries are the weighted percent of a size class with the indicated response.

Table 9-7
Attitudes Toward Requiring Formation of Citizens' Advisory Committees (Question A10d) by Size Class Reported by Municipal and County Executives

	Citizen Advisory Committees Should be Required			
	Strongly Favor	Somewhat Favor	Somewhat Oppose	Strongly Oppose
Municipalities				
Size Class				
Over 300,000 inhabitants	5.7%	6.2%	37.2%	50.9%
100,000-300,000 inhabitants.	3.5	25.0	25.1	46.4
25,000-100,000 inhabitants.	5.4	19.9	28.8	45.9
10,000-25,000 inhabitants.	4.4	26.4	18.3	50.9
2,500-10,000 inhabitants	4.9	8.1	23.1	63.8
100-2,500 inhabitants	7.7	10.8	21.3	60.3
All Municipalities.	6.4	11.9	21.8	59.9
Counties				
Size Class				
Within SMSA-Over 500,000 inhabitants	9.4%	13.6%	14.6%	62.4%
Within SMSA-150,000-500,000 inhabitants. . .	2.2	14.9	25.8	57.1
Within SMSA-Under 150,000 inhabitants	12.2	5.5	17.2	65.1
Outside SMSA	5.4	7.3	28.2	59.1
All Counties	5.7	7.6	27.2	59.4

Table entries are the weighted percent of a size class with the indicated response.

Table 9-8

**Whether Citizens' Groups Were Set Up to Advise on Budget, Financial, or Program Matters
(Questions E10) by Size Class Reported by Municipal and County
Matched Executives and Functional Finance Officers**

	Executives		Finance Officers	
	Yes	No	Yes	No
Municipalities				
Size Class				
Over 100,000 inhabitants	71.8%	28.2%	37.1%	62.9%
Under 100,000 inhabitants	18.1	81.9	15.6	84.4
All Municipalities.	18.3	81.7	15.7	84.3
Counties				
Size Class				
Within SMSA-Over 500,000 inhabitants	36.9%	63.1%	27.6%	72.4%
Within SMSA-150,000-500,000 inhabitants. . .	29.7	70.3	20.4	79.6
Within SMSA-Under 150,000 inhabitants	20.4	79.6	10.9	89.1
Outside SMSA	17.2	82.8	2.4	97.6
All Counties	18.3	81.7	4.2	95.8

Table entries are the weighted percent within a size class with the indicated response.

city and county executives oppose the idea, but over 50 percent were strongly opposed. Somewhat surprisingly, whether or not a locality had an advisory committee was only slightly related to the executive's response to this question. They were likely to strongly oppose requiring citizen advisory committees whether or not they already had one.

There are some surprising differences between executives and finance officers in their responses to this question. In Table 9-8, we see that large-city (over 100,000) executives and county executives in general reported having advisory committees more than did finance officers. It is possible that the executives were reporting advisory committees which were ad hoc or which provided advice only to the executive office and not directly to the bureaucracy. It is also possible that many of these advisory committees were so ineffectual that their presence was not salient to the chief fiscal officer of the government unit. In any case, perspectives from different role positions are noticeably different, particularly in large municipalities.

Advisory committees and public hearings may be seen by some to be interchangeable aspects of the same process—seeking citizen input. It is possible that some units hold hearings, others rely on committees, but most seek citizen input in some form. Or conversely, perhaps the same government units hold hearings as have citizen committees, and therefore, some seek citizen input in a variety of ways while others do not seek input in either way. Table 9-9 shows that the pattern is not so simple as either alternative.

Quite a few government units report having no formal mechanism for citizen input. Nearly half of the cities with less than 100,000 population had neither an initial hearing nor an advisory commit-

Table 9-9

**Coincidence of Citizen Advisory Committees (Question E10)
and Initial Public Hearings (Question E7) Reported
by Municipal and County Executives**

	Were Citizen Advisory Committees Formed?	
Were Public Hearings Held?	Yes	No
Municipalities over 100,000		
Yes	52.0%	10.9%
No	17.2	19.9
Municipalities under 100,000		
Yes	9.6	28.8
No	14.2	47.4
Counties over 250,000		
Yes	17.7	31.0
No	16.6	34.6
Counties under 250,000		
Yes	27.9	27.1
No	5.7	39.3

Table entries are weighted percents.

tee. Similarly, roughly one-third of the counties had neither hearings nor committees. Only in the big cities did most places report having both hearings and committees. There, 80 percent had at least one mechanism or the other.

CITIZEN INVOLVEMENT

A General Summary by Size of Community

Above we discussed general initiatives taken by government which might encourage citizen interest and input. Describing the occurrence of public hearings and the existence of citizen advisory committees begins to describe only the opportunities available for citizen participation. It says nothing about whether participation in fact occurs or if participation that does occur is effective. Below we describe official perceptions of actual expressions of citizen interest in revenue sharing. In Part III we address the question of participation effects.

General Revenue Sharing had built into it requirements for publicizing planned and actual use reports. It also appears to have generated some number of public hearings and a few citizens' advisory committees. GRS was viewed by many as a program which should involve and interest the public. Therefore, respondents were asked for their perceptions of whether or not revenue sharing had any impact on the level of public interest in the budget. Table 9-10 shows that while most local officials saw no such impact, nearly 50 percent of the mayors in large cities (over 100,000 population) reported some impact as did about 30 percent of the county executives.

Table 9-10

Whether Revenue Sharing Had an Impact on the Level of Public Interest in the Budget (Question E9C) by Size Class Reported by Municipal and County Executives

	Revenue Sharing Has Had:	
	No Impact	Some Impact
Municipalities		
Size Class		
Over 300,000 inhabitants	52.5%	47.5%
100,000-300,000 inhabitants	52.0	48.0
25,000-100,000 inhabitants	68.4	31.6
10,000-25,000 inhabitants	91.1	8.9
2,500-10,000 inhabitants	81.5	18.5
100-2,500 inhabitants	87.8	12.2
All Municipalities	85.3	14.7
Counties		
Size Class		
Within SMSA-Over 500,000 inhabitants	79.0	21.0
Within SMSA-150,000-500,000 inhabitants	66.4	33.6
Within SMSA-Under 150,000 inhabitants	70.5	29.5
Outside SMSA	68.4	31.6
All Counties	68.6	31.4

Table entries are the weighted percent of a size class with the indicated response.

Citizen interest might have been expressed in any number of ways. There are three questions in the survey which attempt to gauge revenue sharing's impact on citizen participation in the form of attendance at hearings, expressed interest, and group criticism of the way GRS was handled locally. The opinions of executives regarding these three questions are shown in Table 9-11. Most executives did not perceive increased attendance at budget hearings or significant group criticism at either the municipal or county level. Most mayors did not even perceive group interest in revenue sharing, but 63.9 percent of the county executives did. In general, then, citizen activity was not widely perceived by officials at the local level.

Responses to the three questions varied considerably depending on the size of the unit. Over half of the mayors in cities over 300,000 population reported that attendance at budget hearings increased; 82.1 percent said that groups criticized the way GRS was handled; and almost all of the mayors in cities over 100,000 said that there has been some group interest in revenue sharing. The same trend holds at the county level, but fewer executives in large counties (over 500,000 population) reported citizen involvement than did large-city executives.

In Table 9-12 executives and finance officers are compared on these same three variables. Differences in response can be seen, particularly in large cities. For the most part, large-city mayors were more likely than finance officers to respond that attendance at budget hearings has increased since GRS, that groups have been critical of the way GRS has been handled, and that some groups have expressed interest in GRS. The differences between executives and finance officers are smaller in small municipalities than in large ones. These positional differences probably result from the requirements associated with the roles of executive and fiscal officer. In large municipalities, mayors and finance officers occupy very different role positions. Finance officers are professionals, often from other parts of the country, who are quite specialized in their concern with fiscal matters and who may be rather insulated from community politics. On the other hand, mayors tend to be generalists who have lived in the locality for years and who are relatively more aware of community politics. In smaller communities, executives and finance officers are more similar in their perspectives. If the mayor is unpaid or part time, as many small-town mayors are, the chief fiscal officer may have greater responsibilities and opportunities in the political sphere. As in smaller cities, there are few interesting differences between executives and finance officers at the county level.

In addition to three close-ended questions about community participation, local officials were also asked several open-ended questions about the types of groups which had expressed interest and been critical. Tables 9-13 and 9-14 show the results. According to the respondents, large cities had different types of groups expressing interest and being critical than did smaller cities. Mayors in

Table 9-11

Reports of Citizen Participation
(Checkpoint E, Question E16, and E13) by Size Class
Reported by Municipal and County Executives

	Attendance Increase at Budget Hearings	Group Criticism	Group Interest
Municipalities			
Size Class			
Over 300,000 inhabitants..................	54.7%	82.1%	90.4%
100,000-300,000 inhabitants...............	24.0	48.1	97.4
25,000-100,000 inhabitants................	16.7	25.4	77.0
10,000-25,000 inhabitants.................	4.4	11.6	62.4
2,500-10,000 inhabitants	6.3	5.9	49.1
100-2,500 inhabitants	3.1	0.6	31.4
All Municipalities.........................	5.0	4.4	41.6
Counties			
Size Class			
Within SMSA-over 500,000 inhabitants	17.9%	29.6%	82.9%
Within SMSA-150,000-500,000 inhabitants...	14.5	20.1	86.5
Within SMSA-under 150,000 inhabitants	21.0	13.6	71.3
Outside SMSA.............................	0.4	3.8	62.0
All Counties	2.6	5.4	63.9

Table entries are the weighted percent of a size class with the indicated response.

Table 9-12

Reports of Citizen Participation
(Checkpoint E, Question E16, and E13) by Size Class Reported by
Municipal and County Matched Executives and Functional Finance Officers

	Executives			Finance Officers		
	Increased Attendance	Group Criticism	Group Interest	Increased Attendance	Group Criticism	Group Interest
Municipalities						
Size Class						
Over 100,000 inhabitants	29.0%	55.1%	97.9%	18.7%	24.4%	79.4%
Under 100,000 inhabitants	4.9	4.7	42.4	6.7	3.5	33.3
All Municipalities..............	5.1	4.9	42.7	6.8	3.6	33.5
Counties						
Size Class						
Over 250,000 inhabitants	18.0	24.0	77.7	19.2	27.6	88.6
Under 250,000 inhabitants	1.8	5.7	55.5	2.1	3.4	47.7
All Counties	2.4	6.4	56.2	2.8	4.3	49.1

Table entries are the weighted percent of a size class with the indicated response.

large cities most frequently reported expressions of interest by social service organizations. They reported criticism most often by OEO and social service organizations. In contrast, mayors of cities under 100,000 population tended to report interest in GRS by civic organizations (e.g. Kiwanis, Little League, YMCA) and not much criticism. What criticism was reported came from a variety of types of organizations, but noticeably *not* from civic organizations which expressed interest. Instead it tended to come from community groups (e.g. Fair Housing Councils, neighborhood area associations, ethnic groups), government agencies, and social service organizations. Differences between large and small counties in the types of groups express-

ing interest were not as substantial. Respondents mentioned many different types of groups as interested in GRS and very little group criticism at all.

Thus, once again the picture in large cities is different from that in other local places. In large cities, not only was GRS-related participation more likely to be reported, but it was seen as conflictual (critical) and fairly concentrated in certain types of groups, namely social service groups. In smaller cities and in counties, participation was reported less and seen as less conflictual and more evenly spread among different types of groups.

Recent literature on political participation suggests that there are many different forms and that different forms might be more common in different

Table 9-13

Kinds of Groups Which Expressed Interest in Revenue Sharing
(Question E13) by Size Class Reported by Municipal and County Executives

	Gov't	OEO	Comm.	Bus.	Soc. Serv.	Civic	Educ.	Senior	Tax Payers	Every-body	League Women Voters	Pol. Parties
Municipalities												
Size Class												
Over 100,000 inhabitants............	3.4%	11.7%	12.9%	10.6%	28.2%	11.3%	5.4%	0.0%	3.1%	8.9%	3.4%	0.0%
Under 100,000 inhabitants............	10.9	0.5	5.6	12.6	10.5	32.6	7.2	10.3	4.2	2.5	2.9	0.0
All Municipalities............	10.9	0.6	5.7	12.6	10.7	32.4	7.2	10.3	4.2	2.6	2.9	0.0
Counties												
Size Class												
Over 250,000 inhabitants............	9.6	11.9	7.8	15.8	8.1	7.3	3.9	1.2	11.3	12.5	10.6	0.0
Under 250,000 inhabitants............	17.2	5.0	17.7	8.1	10.5	18.2	15.3	2.0	4.2	0.0	0.6	1.0
All Counties............	16.9	5.3	17.3	8.4	10.4	17.8	14.9	1.9	4.5	0.5	1.0	1.0

Table entries are the weighted percent of a size class with the indicated response.

Table 9-14

Kinds of Groups Which Were Critical of the Way Revenue Sharing Funds Were Handled
(Question E16a) by Size Class Reported by Municipal Executives

	Gov't	OEO	Comm.	Bus.	Soc. Serv.	Civic	Educ.	Senior	Other	Every-body	League Women Voters	Pol. Parties
Municipalities												
Size Class												
Over 100,000 inhabitants............	6.4%	29.7%	13.4%	0.0%	21.0%	5.9%	10.1%	3.7%	0.0%	5.3%	0.0%	4.5%
Under 100,000 inhabitants............	15.8	3.4	32.4	1.0	15.6	1.7	6.6	11.4	0.4	6.3	0.5	4.9
All Municipalities............	15.3	4.6	31.5	1.0	15.8	1.9	6.8	11.1	0.4	6.2	0.5	4.8

Table entries are the weighted percent of a size class with the indicated response.

types of communities.[5] It is difficult to ascertain how citizens participated by asking questions of officials. The most we can hope to discern is what types of activity these officials recall from interested groups. This is nontrivial information, however, since it gives us a rough picture of what types of activity those in positions of influence notice. Accordingly, local officials were asked what kinds of things groups interested in GRS had done. In Table 9-15 we see that a number of different forms of activity were mentioned. Most commonly in cities and large counties, groups reportedly attended budgetary or agency meetings. Large-city mayors also frequently mentioned (27.5 percent) group initiatives such as calling meetings, conducting surveys, and circulating petitions. In smaller cities, executives tended to remark frequently on lobbying activities and funding requests. Thus, these data add to the picture of large-city group activity as more active and more visible generally than group activity in smaller cities. In counties, groups interested in GRS engaged in a variety of activities. They attended meetings, lobbied and requested funds, and contracted local officials by letter or telephone.

Finally, Table 9-16 suggests that, on the whole, the groups that were interested in GRS were well-established local organizations rather than new groups formed specifically in response to revenue sharing. Most city officials believe that local groups expressing interest in GRS were "as active before revenue sharing as afterward." However, it appears that smaller places—those reporting less

group activity overall—were somewhat more likely to perceive what activity that did occur as new and attributable to revenue sharing.

To summarize, in most local units citizen involvement was not perceived to have increased as a result of revenue sharing. However, substantial proportions of large-city executives did report increases in attendance at budget hearings as well as citizen interest in and criticism of GRS. In general, group involvement in large cities was perceived as

Table 9-16
Whether Groups Were As Active Before Revenue Sharing As Afterward (Questions E15) by Size Class Reported by Municipal and County Executives

	Were Groups As Active Before As Afterward?	
	Yes	No
Municipalities		
Size Class		
Over 300,000 inhabitants ..	77.5%	22.5%
100,000-300,000 inhabitants	63.2	36.8
25,000-100,000 inhabitants	71.0	29.0
10,000-25,000 inhabitants .	65.4	34.6
2,500-10,000 inhabitants...	56.4	43.6
100-2,500 inhabitants......	63.2	36.8
All Municipalities	61.6	38.4
Counties		
Size Class		
Within SMSA-over 500,000 inhabitants	62.5	37.5
Within SMSA-150,000-500,000 inhabitants......	60.9	39.1
Within SMSA-under 150,000 inhabitants	54.8	45.2
Outside SMSA	32.2	67.8
All Counties...............	35.8	64.2

Table entries are the weighted percent of a size class with the indicated response.

---

[5]Sidney Verba and Norman Nie, *Participation in America* (New York: Harper and Row, 1972).

Table 9-15
Ways in Which Groups Have Expressed Interest (Question E14) by Size Class Reported by Municipal and County Executives

	Ways of Expressing Interest					
	Write Phone	Seek Info	Attend Meetings	Lobby Request $	Initiate	Other
Municipalities						
Size Class						
Over 100,000 inhabitants	13.7%	6.9%	44.0%	5.9%	27.5%	1.9%
Under 100,000 inhabitants.................	6.1	5.6	38.0	25.3	17.4	7.5
All Municipalities	6.3	5.7	38.1	24.9	17.7	7.4
Counties						
Size Class						
Over 250,000 inhabitants	29.0	7.3	31.9	21.3	10.5	0.0
Under 250,000 inhabitants.................	19.1	0.7	22.1	28.9	22.6	6.7
All Counties.............................	19.5	0.9	22.5	28.6	22.1	6.4

Table entries are the weighted percent of a size class with the indicated response.

more active, conflictual and concentrated in social service groups than it was in smaller cities. Executives and finance officers in large cities differed in their perspectives on citizen involvement resulting from revenue sharing, with mayors regularly reporting involvement in higher proportions than finance officers. In counties, the only type of citizen involvement which was reported by substantial proportions of respondents was expressions of interest by local groups. As in cities, large-county executives tended to report the various types of involvement more than executives in smaller places. Few differences between executives and finance officers at the county level were large enough to warrant reporting. Finally, in most local units the groups which participated were well-established rather than new organizations.

Formal Participation Mechanisms and Official Perceptions of Citizen Activity

Citizen participation in the revenue-sharing process was expected to be greater in situations of greater opportunity. In this section we examine this proposition. A variable for opportunity was devised as a combination of two others—whether an advisory committee was set up due to revenue sharing, and whether there were hearings held on the initial revenue-sharing allocation. Richard P. Nathan and associates referred to whether revenue-sharing funds are treated differently or merged into the regular budgetary process as "the most important distinction for the budgetary process."[6] They claimed that changes in the process and in political relations were more likely to occur and more pronounced when funds were treated as separate money, although some change also occurred in places which merged revenue-sharing funds. Their finding fits nicely with widely ac-

---

[6]Richard P. Nathan, *et al.*, p. 266.

cepted theories about the politics of the budgetary process. According to these theories, standard operating procedures dominate the usual budgetary process, and these procedures allow for very little meaningful citizen input. Exceptions come in situations of special revenue opportunities. When GRS is perceived as such an opportunity with hearings held and advisory committees established, program visibility is relatively high and citizen participation, according to this argument, should also be common. When GRS is handled just like other local funds with no special hearings or committees, opportunities for citizen involvement are relatively scarce and citizen participation should be less common.

Of course, one might question the direction of causality suggested by the preceding discussion of opportunity. Perhaps citizen and group involvement preceded and encouraged the formation of advisory committees and the scheduling of special hearings rather than the other way around. This problem cannot be resolved with the data available, but it is somewhat mitigated by building the opportunity measure from a question about *initial* hearings on the disposition of the first revenue-sharing money. It is assumed that in most cases these initial hearings preceded substantial individual and group activity *vis a vis* GRS.

Table 17 exhibits the relationship between opportunity and the three measures of citizen participation discussed above for cities. The N's for counties were too small to allow analysis. As expected, there were more reports of increases in attendance at budgetary meetings in cities which provided formal participatory mechanisms than in places which did not. There were also more reports of group interest in cities with special opportunities than elsewhere. These differences in small cities were substantial and significant since, of the three forms of citizen involvement, group interest was the one most commonly reported in small communities. The results for group criticism, however,

---

Table 9-17
Reports of Citizen Participation (Checkpoint E, Question E16 and E13)
by Opportunity and Size Class Reported by Municipal Executives

	Opportunity	Increased Attendance	Group Criticism	Group Interest
Municipal Executives				
Size Class				
Over 100,000 inhabitants	High/Med*	39.6%	46.5%	100.0%
	Low	14.2	52.5	85.8
Under 100,000 inhabitants	High	80.0	14.3	100.0
	Med	1.5	4.7	76.1
	Low	0.5	10.7	53.5

Table entries are weighted percents.
*High and Medium were combined to increase the cell size for analysis.

do not follow this pattern. In general, in small places, executives reported no group criticism of GRS decisions whether or not there were special opportunities. Roughly one-half of the large-city executives reported group criticism whether or not special opportunities existed. Of course, it is impossible with the data available to sort out just what was the content of group criticism. It is entirely possible that criticism of the way GRS was handled could have been generated *because* no hearings were held and no advisory committees were established. Without being able to sort out the different reasons for criticism, it is difficult to understand the relationship between opportunity and group criticism.

In sum, opportunity does show a positive relationship to reports of increased attendance and to mentions of group interest in the places where group interest was the most commonly reported form of citizen activity. However, the relationship between formal participation mechanisms and reports of group criticism is difficult to assess with the data at hand. If hearings and advisory committees have generated group and individual interest in revenue sharing, they will generate less in the future as fewer special hearings are held.

Incentives to Participate: Allocation Amount and Loss of Other Funds

Proponents of revenue sharing have stressed the incentives provided for citizen involvement in the fiscal process. With additional money shifted to the local level, citizens could be expected to be more interested and involved in the budgetary process. According to this logic, one might expect that those communities receiving large allocations might witness a great deal more citizen activity than those receiving relatively small allocations. In order to examine this proposition, municipalities and counties were each divided into two categories according to size—large and small—and then within each size, units were divided into high and low allocation amounts. The amounts were used rather than some other figure such as the allocation as a percent of the total budget, because we judged that groups and individuals in the community would be more aware of and concerned about the total amount of cash available than the increment to the budget. Of course, whether a unit falls into the high or low allocation category within its size class is somewhat (but not totally) a function of population. It is also a function of a number of other factors, such as tax effort, which are discussed in other sections of this report. Therefore, any relationship between allocation amount and citizen activity is at least partly the result of the relationship already described between unit size and citizen activity. This is somewhat mitigated by roughly controlling for size of community in the following tables. However, size itself is not a very satisfying variable theoretically in any case. Perhaps part of what accounts for relatively high citizen activity in large places is the added incentive provided by large allocation amounts.

Table 9-18 summarizes the relationship between allocation amount and citizen activity. Increases in attendance at budgetary meetings are weakly related to allocation amount for cities and counties. Similarly, reports of group criticism of GRS allocations are weakly related to allocation amount for counties and smaller cities. The relationship is more substantial in large cities where 74.3 percent of the high-allocation places reported group criticism as compared with only 42.5 percent of the low-allocation places. The relationship becomes more interesting for group interest. Nearly all large city and county executives reported some group interest regardless of the allocation amount received.

Table 9-18

Reports of Citizen Participation (Checkpoint E, Questions E16 and E13)
by Size of Allocation and Size Class Reported by Municipal and County Executives

	Size of Allocation	Increased Attendance	Group Criticism	Group Interest
Municipal Executives				
Size Class				
Over 100,000 inhabitants	High	33.7%	74.3%	94.7%
	Low	28.2	42.5	96.5
Under 100,000 inhabitants	High	7.3	8.2	56.4
	Low	1.7	0.0	26.0
County Executives				
Size Class				
Over 250,000 inhabitants	High	19.8	26.5	80.2
	Low	14.4	24.8	79.3
Under 250,000 inhabitants	High	4.4	8.8	94.3
	Low	0.5	0.5	33.5

Table entries are weighted percents.

However, in the smaller units, substantial differences appear. More than twice as many high-allocation cities under 100,000 population reported group interest (56.4 percent) as low-allocation cities (26.0 percent). Almost three times as many high-allocation counties under 250,000 population reported group interest (94.3 percent) as their low-allocation counterparts (33.5 percent). These are stronger relationships than we found between size and group interest. It appears that the larger units of local government all received enough money to generate citizen interest. There, allocation amount was not crucial. In the smaller units, however, allocation amount became more important as an incentive for groups to express interest.

The size of the allocation, however, does not tell the whole story. As critics of GRS have been quick to point out, a number of cities have lost categorical grants since revenue sharing was implemented. Therefore, there are really at least two forces at work providing incentives for participation: new money to allocate and the threat of the loss of other funds. Local officials were asked whether "reductions, or the possibility of reductions, in federal categorical programs for local governments affected decisions regarding the uses of revenue sharing." Their responses are shown in Table 9-19. Substantial proportions of respondents in large cities and all counties said "yes." Those that responded "yes" presumably had experienced reductions or anticipated them in the future. Those that responded "no" may have included both those who had not experienced reductions and did not anticipate them, as well as those who had experienced them (or anticipated them) but did not see them as affecting revenue-sharing decisions locally.

Below we examine the relationship between perceived reductions in Federal categorical programs and perceptions of citizen activity. Table 9-20 indicates a positive relationship between concern over the loss of other Federal funds and perceptions of citizen activity and interest in revenue sharing. Increases in attendance at budgetary meetings and critical group activity were reported by twice as many large-city and large-county executives who expressed concern over the loss of other Federal money as by those who did not. While most large-city and large-county executives mentioned group interest in GRS whether or not they also were concerned over the loss of Federal Funds, executives in small places were noticeably more likely to report group interest if they were concerned over other Federal funds than if not.

In summary, it appears that official perceptions of citizen participation were more common where allocations were large and where there was concern over the loss of other Federal funds. To the extent that citizen activity was a consequence of reactions to discontinued categorical grants, one might

Table 9-19
Whether Reductions in Federal Categorical Programs Affected Decisions on the Use of GRS Funds (Question D15) by Size Class Reported by Municipal and County Executives

	Yes	No
Municipal Executives		
Size Class		
Over 100,000 inhabitants	44.6%	55.4%
Under 100,000 inhabitants	10.6	89.4
All Executives	10.7	89.3
County Executives		
Size Class		
Over 250,000 inhabitants	42.1	57.9
Under 250,000 inhabitants	36.5	63.5
All Executives	36.7	63.3

Table entries are weighted percents.

Table 9-20
Reports of Citizen Participation (Checkpoint E, Questions E16 and E13) by Loss of Other Grants and Size Class Reported by Municipal and County Executives

	Loss of Other Grants	Increased Attendance	Group Criticism	Group Interest
Municipal Executives				
Size Class				
Over 100,000 inhabitants	Yes	43.5%	73.8%	94.5%
	No	17.5	38.7	95.9
Under 100,000 inhabitants	Yes	8.5	9.4	56.8
	No	4.3	3.3	38.8
County Executives				
Size Class				
Over 250,000 inhabitants	Yes	29.2	39.2	84.2
	No	10.1	17.8	79.2
Under 250,000 inhabitants	Yes	0.8	9.5	72.6
	No	3.0	2.0	57.7

Table entries are weighted percents.

expect participation to increase initially and then to decline over time as groups succeed in establishing a claim to new money to replace the old or as they cease to be viable organizations because of a lack of funds.

FISCAL PROCESSES AND OUTCOMES

Most advocates of citizen participation in the budgetary process are not merely concerned that citizens have an opportunity to express interest and opinions. They also want evidence that the input is heard, seriously considered, and, at least part of the time, that it makes some difference to the allocation decisions reached. Therefore, having described government initiatives in seeking citizen input on revenue sharing as well as official perspectives regarding amounts and types of citizen involvement, we turn to the question of what difference it all makes to fiscal processes and outcomes. This important question is frequently overlooked and extremely difficult to answer.[7] Given the nature of the data available here, all we can do below is to offer some highly tentative suggestions about the relationships between participation variables and several process and outcomes variables. The process variables considered are the following: (1) whether officials find it easier, harder or the same difficulty to learn community preferences; (2) whether officials say that as a result of revenue sharing they pay attention to new issues and problems, and if so (3) which problems. The outcome variable examined is expenditures on social services as a percent of total expenditures of revenue sharing dollars.

Processes

The first process variable considered is shown in Tables 9-21 and 9-22. Respondents were asked whether revenue sharing had made it harder or easier or changed at all their ability to learn about community preferences. Not surprisingly, holding hearings and establishing advisory committees is positively associated in most cases with finding it easier to learn what the community wants (Table 9-21). The only exceptions are in small cities and small counties which show no substantial relationship at all between holding hearings initially and

perceiving an easier time. Perhaps some of those executives who held hearings initially found them poorly attended or otherwise lacking in usefulness and did not hold them subsequently. In any case, the relationship between holding hearings in 1974 and finding it easier to learn community preferences for small-town and small-county executives is fairly substantial. Furthermore, those executives who noted increases in attendance at regular budgetary meetings were more likely to find it easier to learn community preferences as a result of revenue sharing than were those who did not report attendance increases.

Both of the other two participation variables are also positively associated with reports that it is easier to learn what the community wants. The presence of critical groups is substantially associated with an easier time only in cities over 100,000 population. Elsewhere it makes little difference whether groups were critical or not. It is interesting to note that the presence of critical groups is also positively related to responses that it is harder to learn community preferences (Table 9-22). Not surprisingly, group criticism is a mixed blessing from the official's perspective.

Local officials were also asked if, because of revenue sharing, they were paying attention to different issues and problems than before. As expected, those officials from places which held hearings and appointed advisory committees generally responded "yes" more often than others (Table 9-23). Increases in attendance at budgetary meetings and mentions of interested groups were also related to paying attention to different issues. However, the presence of critical groups once again did not follow the usual pattern. Critical groups cannot be credited with turning the attention of city officials from old to new problems.

There were some interesting patterns to the answers given when officials were asked what these new problems were that received their attention as a result of revenue sharing (Table 9-24). In cities with hearings, executives tended to report paying attention to amenities and social services; in cities without hearings, they paid attention to issues such as utilities, sanitation and transportation. In contrast, county executives reported just the opposite. Hearings apparently did not lead to greater attention to social services at the county level, but were associated with fewer mentions of social services as a new concern. Fiscal problems, planning and development, on the other hand, showed the strongest positive relationship to hearings in counties.

Similar results can also be seen for counties with and without advisory committees. Having a county advisory committee appears to be associated with fewer mentions of health and social services as a

---

[7]For one effort to assess the relationship between participation and outcomes for ten large cities, see Steven A. Waldhorn, et. al., *Planning and Participation: General Revenue Sharing in Ten Large Cities* (Stanford, California: Stanford Research Institute, August 1975).

Table 9-21
Percent Who Say They Have an Easier Time Finding Out What the Community Wants Because of Revenue Sharing (Question E5) by Hearings, Committees and Citizen Activity and by Size Class Reported by Municipal and County Executives

Size Class	Initial Hearings		1974 Hearings		RS Advisory Committee**		Attendance Increase		Critical Groups		Interested Groups	
	Yes	No	Yes	No	Yes	No	Yes	No	Yes	No	Yes	No
Municipal Executives												
Over 100,000 inhabitants......	54.7%	17.0%	58.7%	33.5%	52.1%	22.9%	56.4%	31.9	44.4%	28.1%	*	*
Under 100,000 inhabitants......	20.3	17.5	36.0	14.9			67.7	15.2	13.3	14.5	19.0	11.2
County Executives												
Over 250,000 inhabitants......	46.7	25.6	44.6	27.7	84.1	3.3	58.7	26.3	31.9	28.1	31.0	21.2
Under 250,000 inhabitants......	23.6	30.5	37.1	18.8			54.1	21.5	*	*	35.8	3.0

*Too few cases for analysis.
**Size classes were combined to keep N's large enough for analysis.

Table entries are weighted percents.

Table 9-22
Percent Who Say They Have a Harder Time Finding Out What the Community Wants Because of Revenue Sharing (Question E5) by Hearings, Committees, and Citizen Activity and by Size Class Reported by Municipal and County Executives

Size Class	Initial Hearings		1974 Hearings		RS Advisory Committee**		Attendance Increase		Critical Groups		Interested Groups	
	Yes	No	Yes	No	Yes	No	Yes	No	Yes	No	Yes	No
Municipal Executives												
Over 100,000 inhabitants......	4.9%	39.2%	5.2%	19.8%	6.8%	3.8%	13.2%	16.1%	18.2%	9.4%	*	*
Under 100,000 inhabitants......	3.1	2.9	0.3	3.3			4.0	3.0	9.1	2.6	3.1	2.6
County Executives												
Over 250,000 inhabitants......	8.5	13.3	3.5	9.0	7.6	0.6	5.9	10.6	20.6	9.8	15.6	0.0
Under 250,000 inhabitants......	3.7	0.0	6.2	0.0			17.4	1.4	*	*	2.1	0.0

*Too few cases for analysis.
**Size classes were combined to keep N's large enough for analysis.

Table entries are weighted percents.

Table 9-23

Percent Who Pay Attention to Different Issues or Problems Because of Revenue Sharing (Question E17) by Participation Variables and Size Class Reported by Municipal and County Executives

Size Class	Initial Hearings		1974 Hearings		RS Advisory Committee**		Attendance Increase		Critical Groups		Interested Groups	
	Yes	No	Yes	No	Yes	No	Yes	No	Yes	No	Yes	No
Municipal Executives												
Over 100,000 inhabitants	71.6%	44.1%	71.4%	55.5%	75.1%	40.1%	69.7%	57.0%	48.6%	66.0%	*	*
Under 100,000 inhabitants......	41.9	29.6	32.6	36.0			66.7	32.8	32.2	33.7	68.5	63.4
County Executives												
Over 250,000 inhabitants	47.8	50.6	43.3	48.4	91.2		*	*	53.8	44.3	85.0	46.8
Under 250,000 inhabitants......	71.3	28.9	59.5	42.3		81.6	*	*	33.1	44.5	81.9	41.7

*Too few cases for analysis.
**Size classes were combined to keep N's large enough for analysis.

Table entries are weighted percents.

Table 9-24

New Issues and Problems Attended to Because of Revenue Sharing (Question E17a) Reported by Municipal and County Executives

Issues	Initial Hearings		1974 Hearings		Advisory Committee		Increased Attendance		Group Criticism		Group Interest	
	Yes	No	Yes	No	Yes	No	Yes	No	Yes	No	Yes	No
Municipal Executives												
Utilities..................	15.7%	54.1%	25.0%	33.5%	39.5%	30.4%	29.9%	33.7%	11.7%	33.1%	19.8%	42.3%
Amenities.................	20.1	8.8	31.2	9.5	17.3	17.0	0.0	14.1	14.9	17.2	32.6	4.7
Health/Social Sciences	16.3	4.4	31.6	5.7	6.4	5.7	23.7	7.0	33.8	4.7	12.3	0.6
Government................	18.7	6.7	4.3	25.0	9.3	25.3	19.1	22.9	4.4	22.6	10.2	31.2
Other....................	29.2	26.0	7.8	26.4	27.5	21.7	36.3	22.4	35.2	22.4	25.2	21.2
County Executives												
Utilities..................	25.6	3.5	12.8	25.5	25.2	15.4	*	*	*	*	*	*
Amenities.................	0.0	0.0	0.0	0.0	0.0	28.2	*	*	*	*	*	*
Health/Social Services.......	28.0	65.0	9.5	59.2	3.9	47.3	*	*	*	*	*	*
Government................	45.7	2.6	76.4	1.0	70.2	0.2	*	*	*	*	*	*
Other....................	0.7	28.9	1.2	11.3	0.6	9.0	*	*	*	*	*	*

*Too few cases to permit analysis.

Table entries are weighted percents.

new problem attended to as a result of revenue sharing. However, there is no substantial relationship at all for cities. There are very few mentions of health and social services as new concerns whether or not the city had an advisory committee.

Roughly the same pattern holds for communities with and without reported citizen participation in the revenue-sharing process. In general, more city executives mention social services in places with participation than in places without. Fewer mention utilities, sanitation, environment, transportation, planning and development or fiscal problems. The data for counties are too skewed to permit analysis.

To sum up, officials in places which hold hearings, which have advisory committees formed because of revenue sharing, and which report citizen activity find it easier to learn community preferences as a result of revenue sharing than do officials in other places. They also report paying attention to new problems. However, the new problems they pay attention to are quite different for city than for county executives. City officials in places with hearings and citizen activity reported attention to social services more than other city officials while county executives reported just the opposite. These differences reflect the different responsibilities of city and county governments. In general, city governments have traditionally provided such services as utilities, sanitation and transportation; county governments have traditionally been heavily involved in social services. What these data suggest is that with hearings, advisory committees, and citizen involvement, local governments may be encouraged to attend to new types of problems—that is, to problems which have not been of primary concern in the past. That leads city executives to worry more about social services, but it leads county executives to worry less. Citizen involvement may speed city and county governments into new areas which make them more alike in their functional activities than they have been in the past.

Outcomes

With so many officials in places with hearings, advisory committees, and citizen activity reporting that they were paying attention to new issues and problems as a result of revenue sharing, we might expect that these same places would spend more of their revenue-sharing allocation on these new programs. In particular, some observers have suggested that in cities with citizen participation (i.e. public hearings), more revenue-sharing money is actually allocated to social services.[8] Given the results reported above, we would expect citizen participation in counties to be associated with less revenue-sharing money allocated to social services. Below in Table 9-25 we examine these propositions for 1974 revenue-sharing dollars.[9]

Cities with initial hearings did spend a greater percent of their revenue sharing allocation on social services than did other cities. As expected, the reverse is true for counties. There, less was spent on social services in places that held hearings than in places that did not. Similar findings are apparent for cities and counties with and without citizen advisory committees. In fact, for cities, the data in Table 9-25 consistently fall as expected, with formal mechanisms and reported citizen activity associated with greater social service expenditures. However, there are two exceptions for counties. Reports of increased attendance at budgetary meetings and group interest in revenue sharing are each associated with higher rather than lower social service expenditures. This is somewhat surprising in light of county officials claims for their concern with new problems, particularly in places with reported citizen activity. Unfortunately, the numbers of counties in the sample with reported citizen activity were too small to permit more detailed analysis.

---

[8]Richard L. Cole, *Loc. cit.*

[9]Initial hearings are relevant to 1974 revenue sharing dollars, but the 1974 hearings are not since they occurred after the fact.

Table 9-25
Mean Percent of Revenue Sharing Expenditures for Health and Social Services
by Participation Variables for Cities and Counties
(Estimates for FY 1974 Using Survey Data with Equal Dollar Weights)*

	Hearings		Advisory Committee		Attendance Increase		Critical Groups		Interested Groups	
	Yes	No	Yes	No	Yes	No	Yes	No	Yes	No
Municipal Executives	1.4%	0.5%	1.1%	0.5%	2.8%	0.8%	4.2%	0.4%	1.0%	0.2%
County Executives..........	9.5	26.9	4.6	19.8	18.5	15.2	7.5	15.5	16.9	12.4

*Estimates of program impacts using census weights instead of equal dollar weights yield mean percents which are very close to those cited above. See Chapter 3 of this report for a more detailed discussion of both weighting schemes.
Table entries are weighted mean percents.

In sum, the data are consistent with the idea that formal participatory mechanisms allow citizen involvement which pushes local governments (particularly cities) into new problem areas. They are also consistent with another interpretation: that officials interested in moving into new problem areas consult citizens before doing so.

CONCLUSION

A lot has been said about citizen participation in revenue-sharing decisions, most of it based on observations of large cities. From the data presented here, a number of conclusions are justified. First, large cities are quite different from other localities in terms of the types and frequency of citizen participation. It is in large cities that formal mechanisms such as hearings and citizens' committees were most common, and it is there that citizens were frequently active with regard to revenue sharing. Second, outside the big cities, citizens' groups expressed interest in revenue sharing but did little else. Third, these groups which did express interest were not newly generated but were well established prior to revenue sharing. Fourth, where hearings were held and advisory committees were established as a result of revenue sharing, officials found it easier to find out what the preferences in the community were and to broaden their concerns

to new issues and problems to which they had not formerly attended. However, fifth, far fewer cities and counties held hearings on GRS funds the second year than the first, and very few appointed citizens advisory committees as a result of revenue sharing. And when asked, local officials overwhelmingly opposed the idea of changing revenue sharing to require the formation of citizen advisory committees. With a decline in the use of formal mechanisms to encourage participation, we should expect future levels of citizen activity in revenue-sharing decisions to drop. Sixth, part of the increases in citizen activity that did occur as a result of GRS may be traced to the concerns of groups formerly funded by Federal categorical grants which had been or were about to be cut, particularly in large cities and counties. Accordingly, levels of participation in fiscal processes may also decrease in the future as these groups either cease to exist from lack of funds or establish some claim to a portion of the city budget. Finally, what one learns about revenue-sharing-related citizen activity depends somewhat on whom one asks. Differences in the respondents' positions and functions affect their perceptions of what happens in their community. Therefore, setting policy in an effort to effect certain ends with regard to citizen input is extremely complicated and requires attention to different types and sizes of local governments.

APPENDIX A

Availability and Contents
of Data Appendix

*Richard E. Barfield**

INTRODUCTION AND EXPLANATION

A tabular appendix displaying selected data gathered from State and local government officials for the General Revenue Sharing study is available to interested researchers and policymakers. Much of the available data are discussed in the body of the report, and some are displayed there; but they have been brought together in order to provide the reader with a single easily accessible source of basic responses from the interviewed officials.

To assist the reader in deciding on the usefulness of the data appendix for his/her needs, lists of questions included in Part 1 (local government officials) and Part 2 (State government officials) are provided below. Either or both parts may be requested.

FORMAT AND CLASSIFICATION SCHEME

Tables in the appendix are copied directly from computer output produced by a computer program which allows some labeling and other annotation, generally sufficient for headings and table titles but sometimes inadequate for variable category specification. Hence the reader may be faced from time to time with rather cryptic column headings which do not reflect code content as well as one would prefer. Generally, though, the headings indicate fairly well the categories constructed for the various questions, and the user who needs additional information may obtain it from the Survey Research Center. Throughout the tables the conventional reference "DK, NA" has been used to

categorize those cases in which the official responded "I don't know" or in which, for other reasons, a codable response was not obtained. Two numbers are displayed in the table cells, an unweighted ("raw") count of responses and a percent *based on weighted totals*. Since the raw and weighted totals can vary substantially, cells containing similar unweighted counts can properly have quite dissimilar percentages.

The appendix contains answers to most closed-end questions and selected open-end questions from all sections of the local and State government questionnaires except those dealing with fiscal impact (presented separately in this report). The only closed-end questions eliminated were those dependent on prior screening questions and answered by few respondents.[1] Similarly, open-end questions screened by other questions and answered by relatively few respondents (the rule of thumb was 40 percent) were omitted, as were a handful of others whose codes were unsuccessful in capturing response patterns. In all cases only the first response to a question was tabulated, even though two or three responses were coded for several open-end questions.[2] In each table, beneath the labeling information repeated from table to table, the question asked is printed (along with its number from the questionnaire), either exactly as asked or (where necessary) augmented for clarity. Each table consists of two pages: the first displays responses from the head of the local government unit or the chairs of State legislative committees; the second displays responses from the (local unit's or State's) chief financial officer.

*Research Associate, Survey Research Center, The University of Michigan.

[1]Additionally, a few personal information responses are not displayed.

[2]Inclusion of multiple responses in one table is technically awkward, and it weights disproportionately the more vocal respondents.

The classification scheme for local government units incorporates type of unit and population size. The eleven categories are defined below:

1. Cities (in all cases including townships not in New York State or the North Central region) with 300,000 or more population.

2. Cities with 100,000-299,999 population.

3. Cities with 25,000-99,999 population.

4. Cities with 10,000-24,999 population.

5. Cities with 2,500-9,999 population.

6. Cities with 100-2,499 population (municipalities with fewer than 100 inhabitants were not sampled).

7. New York State towns and North Central region townships with 9,000 or more population.

8. Towns/townships with less than 9,000 population.

9. Weighted summation of all 8 classes above.

10. Counties with 100,000 or more population.

11. Counties with less than 100,000 population.

State governments are classified by per capita personal income (upper half of income distribution vs. lower half) and by region (the Census divisions Northeast, North Central, South and West).

LIST OF INCLUDED QUESTIONS

Included in Part 1 (local government units) are the following questions:

SECTION 1. GENERAL EVALUATION OF REVENUE SHARING

A1. Particular features of GRS about which respondent feels very favorable.

A2. Particular features of GRS about which respondent feels very unfavorable.

A3A. Whether agrees/disagrees that local governments have been able to develop some new programs because of GRS.

A3B. Whether agrees/disagrees that GRS has been more trouble for local governments than it is worth.

A3C. Whether agrees/disagrees that local governments are now subject to less control by the Federal government because of GRS.

A3D. Whether agrees/disagrees that local governments are finally getting some of their tax money back because of GRS.

A3E. Whether agrees/disagrees that local governments have been able to avoid tax increases because of GRS.

A3F. Whether agrees/disagrees that local governments have been able to stay afloat, financially, because of GRS.

A3G. Whether agrees/disagrees that local governments are now subject to more control by the Federal Government because of GRS.

A3H. Whether agrees/disagrees that revenue sharing has not made up for cutbacks in Federal grants so local governments are getting less Federal money than before.

A3J. Whether agrees/disagrees that revenue sharing does not amount to enough to make a real financial difference.

A4. Whether looked upon GRS money as being kept separate from local funds or as being merged with them when revenue sharing funds were received initially.

A5. Whether looks upon revenue sharing money in the same way now.

A6. Most satisfactory and productive use to which local government has put its GRS funds.

A8-8A. Whether/how strongly respondent thinks that GRS should continue after current expiration date.

A8B. Why feels that revenue sharing should continue.

A9. Whether thinks the amounts should be increased or decreased if revenue sharing is extended.

A10A. Whether favors/opposes eliminating priority expenditure requirements.

A10B. Whether favors/opposes allowing revenue sharing money to be used as the matching share of Federal grants.

A10C. Whether favors/opposes developing more complete budget reporting categories.

A10D. Whether favors/opposes requiring the formation of citizen advisory committees to decide how to use revenue sharing money.

A10E. Whether favors/opposes adjusting payments to keep up with inflation.

A10F1. Whether favors/opposes changing the allocation formula to give more money to poorer communities.

A10F2. Whether favors/opposes changing the allocation formula to omit very small government units.

A10F3. Whether favors/opposes changing the allocation formula to give more to big city areas.

A10F4. Whether favors/opposes changing the allocation formula to discourage reduction in local tax rates.

A10F5. Whether favors/opposes changing the allocation formula to encourage the consolidation of small government units.

A10F6. Whether favors/opposes changing the allocation formula to remove the penalty against special districts by including local assessments as part of the tax base.

A10F7. Whether favors/opposes changing the allocation formula to make it easier to know one's payments over the next few years.

A10F8. Whether favors/opposes changing the allocation formula to remove the penalty against getting revenue from user charges by including them in the definition of tax effort.

A11. Other changes in GRS program respondent favors.

G1. Whether agrees/disagrees that concern about the temporary nature of revenue sharing funds may have led some governments to spend most of their revenue sharing money on capital items.

G2. Whether agrees/disagrees that concern over the continuation of general revenue sharing may discourage some governments from using revenue sharing funds for experimental programs.

G3. Whether agrees/disagrees that increased public participation may make the allocation of revenue sharing funds different from other funds.

G4. Whether agrees/disagrees that revenue sharing may not be worth its cost because of the expense involved in meeting the administrative requirements.

G5. Whether agrees/disagrees that the best use of revenue sharing funds may be to reduce taxes.

G6. Whether agrees/disagrees that the revenue sharing formula gives too much weight to tax effort and not enough to needs.

G7. Whether agrees/disagrees that a fair share of revenue sharing money goes to government services for poor people.

G8. Whether agrees/disagrees that active employee organizations mean that much of the revenue sharing money goes for salary increases.

G9. Whether agrees/disagrees that very small government units should get more revenue sharing funds because they are closer to the people than bigger units.

G10. Whether agrees/disagrees that the best system of revenue sharing is one in which local governments are allowed to use the money for whatever they think best.

G11. Whether agrees/disagrees that the administrative cost of the GRS program is much less than the cost associated with other Federal assistance programs.

G12. Whether agrees/disagrees that high rates of inflation mean that much of revenue sharing goes for salary increases.

G13. Whether agrees/disagrees that revenue sharing funds will be used differently in the future than they have been in the past.

G14. Whether agrees/disagrees that inflation has cut down the use of revenue sharing funds for innovative programs.

G15. Whether thinks that revenue sharing has/has not strengthened local government.

G15A. Why thinks that GRS has/has not strengthened local government.

G16. Other general comments about the GRS program.

SECTION 2. IMPACT OF REVENUE SHARING ON GOVERNMENT PROGRAMS

D1(1). Most important problem facing this unit.
D1(2). Second most important problem facing this unit.
D1(3). Third most important problem facing this unit.
D2/D2A. Whether/how revenue sharing has made difference in dealing with the first problem.
D3/D3A. Whether/how revenue sharing has made difference in dealing with the second problem.
D4/D4A. Whether/how revenue sharing has made difference in dealing with the third problem.
D5. Whether revenue sharing is likely to make any difference in ability to deal with major problems in the future.
D6. Whether feels that Federal categories of priority expenditures have been very restrictive, moderately restrictive, or not restrictive at all.
D7. Whether would favor greater Federal restrictions on uses of GRS funds.
D8. Whether would favor total elimination of Federal priority categories.
D8A. Why feels that priority categories should be eliminated.
D10. Whether would allocate GRS funds same way or differently if could do so again.

D12. Whether GRS funds have been used primarily to finance continuing activities or to start new ones.
D12-1. Whether any revenue sharing funds have been used to start new activities.
D13. Whether direct allocation of revenue sharing funds would have been different if the law did not restrict expenditures to priority categories.
D14. Whether direct uses of revenue sharing would have been different if there were no prohibitions on use of revenue sharing to match other federal grants.
D15. Whether reductions, or possibility of reductions, in Federal categorical programs for local governments have affected decisions regarding uses of revenue sharing.

SECTION 3. IMPACT OF REVENUE SHARING ON THE BUDGET PROCESS

E1. Whether revenue sharing has made planning for future expenditures more difficult or less difficult.
E1A. Why revenue sharing has/has not affected planning for future expenditures.
E2. Whether GRS has made controlling expenditures more or less difficult.
E3. Whether GRS has made deciding on changes or reforms in the local tax structure more or less difficult.
E4. Whether GRS has made setting priorities for local expenditures more or less difficult.
E4A. Why revenue sharing has/has not affected setting priorities for future expenditures.
E5. Whether GRS has made finding out what the community wants more or less difficult.
E7-7A. Whether/how many hearings were held on the disposition of first revenue sharing entitlement.
E8-8A. Whether/how many public hearings were held during FY 74 specifically on revenue sharing funds.
E9. Number of people who usually attended budget hearings before revenue sharing.
E9A. Number of people who attended budget hearings after revenue sharing.
CHECKPOINT E. Comparison of number of people attending public budget hearings before vs. after revenue sharing.
E9C. Whether revenue sharing has had no impact on the level of public interest in the budget.
E10. Whether local unit has set up any citizens' groups or committees which advise it on budget, financial, or program matters.
E13. Kinds of community groups or organizations which have expressed interest in revenue sharing.
E14. Kinds of things community groups/organizations have done to show their interest.
E17. Whether local unit pays attention to different kinds of issues or problems because of revenue sharing.
E19A. Whether revenue sharing has/has not made any difference in reaction of other government officials in this unit to public criticism or support.
E19B. Whether revenue sharing has/has not made any difference in public officials' desire for better information.
E19C. Whether revenue sharing has/has not made any difference in public officials' concern over fiscal problems.
E19D. Whether revenue sharing has/has not made any difference in public officials' awareness of fiscal pressures.
E20. Whether Federal or state officials have communicated with unit about civil rights enforcement in revenue sharing program.

E21. Whether prohibitions against discrimination in revenue sharing have been more restrictive, less restrictive, or about same as those in other Federal grants.

SECTION 4. IMPACT OF REVENUE SHARING ON INTERGOVERNMENTAL RELATIONSHIPS

F1A. Amount of contact with Federal administrators, other than those in the Office of Revenue Sharing, as result of GRS.

F1B. Amount of contact with congressmen and senators as a result of revenue sharing.

F1C. Amount of contact with State officials as a result of revenue sharing.

F1D. Amount of contact with State legislators as a result of revenue sharing.

F1E. Amount of contact with school district officials as a result of revenue sharing.

F1F. Amount of contact with officials in non-school special districts as a result of revenue sharing.

F1G. Amount of contact with county officials as a result of revenue sharing.

F1H. Amount of contact with municipal officials as a result of revenue sharing.

F1I. Amount of contact with township officials as a result of revenue sharing.

F2A. Amount of conflict over budget within particular departments or agencies of unit after vs. before GRS.

F2B. Amount of conflict over budget across unit departments or agencies after vs. before GRS.

F2C. Amount of conflict over budget between administrators and the unit governmental body after vs. before GRS.

F2D. Amount of conflict over budget between the unit governmental body and the general public after vs. before GRS.

F2E. Amount of conflict over budget between the unit governmental body and local citizens' groups after vs. before GRS.

F2F. Amount of conflict over budget between the unit governmental body and the media after vs. before GRS.

F2G. Amount of conflict over budget between this unit and other governments after vs. before GRS.

F3. Impact of revenue sharing on respondent's willingness to work with officials from other local governments in the future.

F4-4A. Whether revenue sharing will/will not encourage cities and towns to annex outlying areas.

F4B. Whether revenue sharing will/will not encourage municipalities and counties to take over some functions now being performed by special districts.

F4C. Whether revenue sharing will/will not encourage less reliance on user charges by local governments.

F4D. Whether revenue sharing will/will not encourage the consolidation of existing governmental units such as cities and counties.

F4E. Whether revenue sharing will/will not encourage some small governments to increase the range of their activities.

F4F. Whether revenue sharing will/will not encourage less cooperation among various units of local government.

F5. Whether unit has undergone any changes in its taxing structure as a result of revenue sharing.

F5C. Whether there are any plans for changes in taxing structure resulting from revenue sharing.

F6. Whether, as a result of revenue sharing, unit has taken on any of the functions ordinarily performed by special districts.

F6B. Whether it is likely that unit will take on some special district functions.

F7. Whether there should be minimum population size in order to be eligible for revenue sharing money.

SECTION 5. BACKGROUND INFORMATION ON RESPONDENTS

H1. Age of respondent.

H3. Length of residence in community where respondent now lives.

H4/4A. Urbanicity of place in which respondent grew up.

H5. Length of tenure in present governmental office.

H8. Education of respondent.

(A) Political characteristics of present administration in the jurisdiction (interviewer observation).

(B) Sex of respondent (interviewer observation).

(C) Apparent ethnic origin of respondent (interviewer observation).

Included in Part 2 (States) are the following questions:

SECTION 1. GENERAL EVALUATION OF REVENUE SHARING

A1. Particular features of GRS about which respondent feels very favorable.

A2. Particular features of GRS about which respondent feels very unfavorable.

A3A. Whether agrees/disagrees that states have been able to develop new programs because of GRS.

A3B. Whether agrees/disagrees that States are finally getting back some Federal tax money because of GRS.

A3C. Whether agrees/disagrees that State governments have been able to avoid tax increases because of GRS.

A3D. Whether agrees/disagrees that local governments have been able to develop new programs because of GRS.

A3E. Whether agrees/disagrees that local governments are now subject to less control by the Federal Government because of GRS.

A3F. Whether agrees/disagrees that local governments are now subject to less control by the State government because of GRS.

A3G. Whether agrees/disagrees that local governments have been able to avoid tax increases because of GRS.

A4. Most satisfactory and productive use to which State has put its share of GRS.

A4A. Most satisfactory and productive use to which local governments in State have put their share of GRS.

A5. Least satisfactory and productive use to which State has put its share of GRS.

A6-A6A. Whether/how strongly respondent thinks that GRS should continue after current expiration date.

A6B. Why respondent thinks GRS should/should not be continued.

A7A1(s).[3] Whether favors/opposes changing allocation formula to increase reward going to states.

A7A2(s). Whether favors/opposes changing allocation formula to give a larger share of GRS funds to States and a smaller share to local units.

---

[3]Questions with "s" designation were asked "with respect to the *State* government."

186

A7A3(s). Whether favors/opposes changing allocation formula to give a smaller share of GRS funds to States and a larger share to local units.

A7A4(s). Whether favors/opposes changing allocation formula to give States and local governments shares of GRS proportional to their respective tax efforts.

A7A5(s). Whether favors/opposes changing allocation formula to provide incentives for regional cooperation.

A7A6(s). Whether favors/opposes changing allocation formula to make it easier to know GRS payments over next few years.

A7B(s). Whether favors/opposes adjusting GRS payments to keep up with inflation.

A7C(s). Whether favors/opposes allowing GRS funds to be used as matching share of Federal grants.

A7D(s). Whether favors/opposes imposing priority expenditure categories on state use of GRS funds.

A7E(s). Whether favors/opposes substantially increasing reporting and enforcement requirements for States.

A7A1(l).[4] Whether favors/opposes changing allocation formula to give more money to poorer communities.

A7A2(l). Whether favors/opposes changing allocation formula to omit very small local government units.

A7A3(l). Whether favors/opposes changing allocation formula to give more to big city areas.

A7A4(l). Whether favors/opposes changing allocation formula to discourage reduction in local tax rates.

A7A5(l). Whether favors/opposes changing allocation formula to encourage consolidation of small government units.

A7A6(l). Whether favors/opposes changing allocation formula to remove penalty against special districts by including local assessments as part of tax base.

A7A7(l). Whether favors/opposes changing allocation formula to make it easier for local governments to know their GRS payments over the next few years.

A7A8(l). Whether favors/opposes changing allocation formula to remove penalty against getting revenue from user charges by including them in the definition of local government tax effort.

A7B(l). Whether favors/opposes eliminating priority expenditure requirements for local governments.

A7C(l). Whether favors/opposes allowing local governments to use GRS money as matching share of Federal grants.

A7D(l). Whether favors/opposes developing more complete budget reporting categories for local governments.

A7E(l). Whether favors/opposes requiring formation of local citizen advisory committees to decide how to use GRS money.

A7F(l). Whether favors/opposes adjusting payments to local governments to keep up with inflation.

G1. Whether agrees/disagrees that concern about temporary nature of GRS may have led some governments to spend most GRS money on capital items.

G2. Whether agrees/disagrees that concern over continuation of GRS may discourage some governments from using GRS funds for experimental programs.

G3. Whether agrees/disagrees that increased public participation may make allocation of GRS funds different from that of other funds.

G4. Whether agrees/disagrees that best use of GRS funds may be to reduce taxes.

G5. Whether agrees/disagrees that GRS formula gives too much weight to tax effort and not enough to needs.

G6. Whether agrees/disagrees that fair share of GRS money goes to government services for poor people.

G7. Whether agrees/disagrees that, because local jurisdictions are not permitted to spend GRS funds on operating expenses for education, there is increased pressure on state governments to assist local units in financing education.

G8. Whether agrees/disagrees that GRS has undermined categorical grant-in-aid programs.

G9. Whether agrees/disagrees that active employee organizations mean that much of GRS money goes for salary increases.

G10. Whether agrees/disagrees that very small government units should get more GRS funds because they are closer to the people than bigger units.

G11. Whether agrees/disagrees that best system of GRS is one in which local governments may use GRS money for whatever they think best.

G12. Whether agrees/disagrees that administrative cost to states of GRS program is much less than cost associated with other Federal assistance programs.

G13. Whether agrees/disagrees that high rates of inflation mean that much of GRS money goes for salary increases.

G14. Whether agrees/disagrees that GRS funds will be used differently in future than in past.

G15. Whether agrees/disagrees that inflation has cut down on use of GRS funds for innovative programs.

G16. Whether agrees/disagrees that a goal of the GRS program should be equalization of financial capacities of the states.

G17. Whether agrees/disagrees that local governments should be given same freedom as States in spending GRS money.

G18. Whether agrees/disagrees that allocation formula for local governments should encourage them to reduce taxes.

G19. Whether GRS has strengthened State and local government.

G19A. Why GRS has/has not strengthened State and local government.

G20. Other general comments about GRS program.

SECTION 2. IMPACT OF REVENUE SHARING ON GOVERNMENT PROGRAMS

D1(1). Most important problem facing the State.
D1(2). Second most important problem facing the State.
D1(3). Third most important problem facing the State.
D2/2A. Whether/how GRS has made difference in ability to deal with first problem.
D3/3A. Whether/how GRS has made difference in ability to deal with second problem.
D4/5A. Whether/how GRS has made difference in ability to deal with third problem.
D5. Whether GRS is likely to make any difference in ability to deal with major problems in future.
D5A. Which future problems are likely to be affected by GRS.
D6. Whether would favor more or fewer Federal restrictions on use of GRS funds.
D7. Whether would allocate GRS funds same way or differently if could do so again.
D9. Whether GRS funds have been used *primarily* to finance ongoing activities or to start new ones.
D9(1). Whether *any* GRS funds have been used to start new activities.

---

[4]Questions with "l", were asked "with respect to *local governments* in this State."

SECTION 3. IMPACT OF REVENUE SHARING ON THE BUDGET PROCESS

E1. Whether GRS has made planning for future expenditures more or less difficult.

E1A. Why GRS has/has not affected planning for future expenditures.

E2. Whether GRS has made controlling expenditures more or less difficult.

E3. Whether GRS has made setting priorities for expenditures more or less difficult.

E4. Kinds of State-wide groups/organizations which have expressed interest in GRS.

E5. Kinds of things groups/organizations have done to show interest in GRS.

E6. Whether groups/organizations were as active before GRS as afterward.

E7. Whether particular groups have been critical about allocation of GRS funds.

E8. Whether respondent pays attention to different kinds of issues or problems because of GRS.

E9. Whether anyone has contacted State officials about civil rights enforcement in GRS program.

E10. Whether prohibitions against discrimination in GRS have been more or less restrictive than those in other Federal grant programs.

SECTION 4. IMPACT OF REVENUE SHARING ON INTERGOVERNMENTAL RELATIONSHIPS

F1A. Amount of contact with Federal administrators as a result of GRS.

F1B. Amount of contact with Congressmen and Senators as a result of GRS.

F1C. Amount of contact with (other) State officials as a result of GRS.

F2A. Amount of conflict over budget within departments or agencies of the State after vs. before GRS.

F2B. Amount of conflict over budget across State departments or agencies after vs. before GRS.

F2C. Amount of conflict over budget between executive and legislative branches of State government after vs. before GRS.

F2D. Amount of conflict over budget between State Government and local government units after vs. before GRS.

F2E. Amount of conflict over budget between State government and the general public after vs. before GRS.

F2F. Amount of conflict over budget between State government and local citizens' groups after vs. before GRS.

F2G. Amount of conflict over budget between State government and news media after vs. before GRS.

F3A. Whether GRS will/will not encourage cities and towns to annex outlying areas.

F3B. Whether GRS will/will not encourage municipalities and counties to take over some functions now being performed by special districts.

F3C. Whether GRS will/will not encourage less reliance on user charges by local governments.

F3D. Whether GRS will/will not encourage consolidation of existing governmental units such as cities and counties.

F3E. Whether GRS will/will not encourage some small governments to increase range of activities.

F3F. Whether GRS will/will not encourage the continued existence of inefficient units of local government.

F4. Whether State has changed taxing structure as result of GRS.

F4C. Whether State plans changes in taxing structure as result of GRS.

F5. Whether state has considered adjusting formula by which GRS funds are allocated to local governments.

F5C. Whether State plans to adjust formula by which GRS funds are allocated to local governments.

F6. Whether income tax factor in GRS formula has influenced tax policy in state.

F7/7A. Whether/how income tax provisions in GRS formula should be changed.

F8. Whether State has own program of sharing State funds with local governments.

F8A. Kind of State revenue-sharing program in existence.

F9. Whether State revenue-sharing program is more or less restrictive than Federal program.

F9A. In what ways State revenue-sharing program is more or less restrictive than Federal program.

F10. Whether State revenue-sharing program has become more or less restrictive in past 2-3 years.

F11A. Whether there should be minimum requirements for local government population size in order to be eligible for GRS money.

F11B. Whether there should be minimum requirements for local government range of functions in order to be eligible for GRS money.

F11C. Whether there should be minimum requirements for local government need in order to be eligible for GRS money.

F12. Whether State has felt pressure to expand local government functions in last 2-3 years.

F12B. What kinds of local governments have been exerting pressure to expand local government functions.

F12C. How State has responded to pressures to expand local government functions.

F12D. Extent to which pressure to expand local government functions is due to GRS.

F13. Whether GRS has affected State's willingness to expand local government functions.

F14. Whether, in last 2-3 years, State has felt pressure from local governments to provide additional direct services or funding to those units.

F14A. Kinds of services local governments have requested from State.

F14B. How State has responded to pressures to provide more services or money to local units.

F14C. Whether GRS has increased or decreased pressure to provide more services or money to local units.

F15. Whether GRS for local governments in state has increased or decreased pressure on State budget.

F16. Whether declining school expenditures and increasing revenues have reduced fiscal pressure on States.

F17. Whether feels that GRS should be continued for local governments.

F17A. Why feels that GRS should/should not be continued for local governments.

F18. Whether views GRS as supplement to or substitute for other forms of Federal support.

F19. Whether GRS has caused local government requests for changes in their tax structure.

F20. Whether GRS has resulted in requests by local governments to take over some special district functions.

F21. Whether GRS has resulted in less reliance on user charges by local governments.

F22. Whether there has been discussion in state about Federal offer to let State income tax be collected by Federal Government.

F23. What discussions about "piggy-back" collection of State income tax have involved.

SECTION 5. BACKGROUND INFORMATION ON RESPONDENTS

H1.   Age of respondent.

H3.   Length of residence in State where respondent now lives.

H4/4A.   Urbanicity of place in which respondent grew up.

H6.   Length of tenure in present governmental office.

H8.   Education of respondent.

(A)   Political characteristics of present administration of state (interviewer observation)

(B)   Sex of respondent (interviewer observation)

(C)   Apparent ethnic origin of respondent (interviewer observation)

Sample and
Survey Design

*Irene Hess, Amaury de Souza, F. Thomas Juster**

INTRODUCTION

This appendix is divided into four parts. The first describes the selection of governmental units to be studied; it deals with issues of sample design, examines the structure of U.S. general government jurisdictions at the local level, and documents the procedure for selecting a representative sample of general government jurisdictions. The second part describes the selection of respondents (officials) from the sample units. It discusses the criteria for respondent selection and presents results on response rates for the various categories of designated respondents. The third describes alternative weighting schemes for the data, indicating the weights appropriate for various types of analytical questions. The final part describes the specifics of the interview procedure and will be helpful to those concerned with the interpretation of some of the survey data.

SAMPLE DESIGN

General Design Considerations

Since revenue-sharing funds are distributed first to States and then to counties, municipalities and townships within States, interviews with officials at each of the four levels of government were desired. The States were altogether removed from sampling considerations, because it was decided

*Hess is Head, Sampling Section, Survey Research Center, The University of Michigan; de Souza is Assistant Study Director, Center for Political Studies, The University of Michigan.

that interviews were to be attempted with officials in each of the States. Local governments, however, presented some challenging sampling questions. In contrast to many other countries, the United States has an enormous variety of local governmental units. Counties range from those providing no services at all with only nominal existence, to those whose functions include the great bulk of public services provided below the Federal and State levels. Similarly, the township governmental unit shows a wide variation in functions throughout the country. Townships exist, for the most part, only in the Northeast and North Central regions of the United States. Finally, municipalities vary from very small governmental units within counties to large metropolises and independent cities. In addition to counties and townships, separate estimates were desired for five population size classes of municipalities: (a) 100,000 inhabitants and over; (2) 25,000 to 99,999; (3) 10,000 to 24,999; (4) 2,500 to 9,999; and (5) less than 2,500 inhabitants.

The study did not contain design specifications in the form of particular estimates to be made with stated precision. The final design was predicated upon several considerations. First, budgetary and time constraints set the desired sample of local governments at some 800 units. In addition to State governments, such constraints thus restricted total interviews to around 2,000 or between two and three interviews per governmental unit. Second, there was agreement to accept population as a base for sample selection. While there are alternative bases, e.g., a governmental unit's allocation of revenue-sharing dollars, population is the dominant factor in that formula. In addition, population is an appropriate base for almost any analytic purpose, while revenue-sharing dollars are not. Third, it was agreed that municipalities and townships chosen for the sample should be nested within sample counties.

Those several considerations led to the conclusion that the study objectives would be well served by exploiting an existing survey research organization with capabilities such as those of SRC, although it was recognized that satisfying sample requirements for townships and for five size classes of municipalities could be a problem if sample locations were limited to the current SRC sample of counties. The anticipated complication did arise and was resolved as described in subsequent sections of this report.

A final consideration had to do with the definition of the population to be sampled. A preliminary decision had to be reached regarding a minimum population size threshold for inclusion of municipal governmental units in the sample. Very small units would get too small a weight to justify costly interviews in any sample size decision subject to budgetary constraints. A threshold was therefore arbitrarily defined at a minimum population size of 100 inhabitants. Second, it seemed reasonable to exclude units with very special governmental structures, such as Indian tribes, some of' which had already failed to reach the minimum population size for inclusion in the sample. Finally, preliminary analysis of the association between population size and per capita tax effort (measured as an indicator of the relative complexity of local governmental functions) showed a standard deviation in per capita tax effort of five-fold the mean for places under 2,500 inhabitants, a relationship clearly out of line with that in other groups. This large deviation turned out to be due entirely to the presence of a dozen municipalities characterized by very high tax revenues, small population, and thus extremely high per capita tax effort. All but four of those municipalities had failed to meet one or both of the above restrictions for inclusion in the sample. These remaining cases were also eliminated by adopting a criterion that excluded places with per capita tax effort of $1,000 and above.

To sum up: The population from which to draw the sample of municipal units was defined as all the municipalities and townships in conterminous United States excluding (a) places with 100 inhabitants or less; (b) Indian tribes; and (c) places with per capita tax effort of $1,000 and above.

The SRC Sample of Primary Areas and the Selection of County Units

The importance of an adequate selection of county units is apparent. Most municipal governmental units are associated with counties. Further-

more, by design, the sample of local governments was to be selected from those in the SRC sample of 74 primary areas, which include 173 county areas, parts of eight other county areas, six independent cities, and the District of Columbia. The sample was subsequently expanded to 91 primary areas, including 204 counties, 10 part-counties, six independent cities and the District of Columbia.[1]

The classifications and definitions of local governments in this study followed closely those of the United States Census Bureau, Governments Division. Quoting from the Census publication: ''Organized county governments are found

---

[1]The 74 sample points located in 37 states and the District of Columbia include with certainty the New York-Northeastern New Jersey Standard Consolidated Area, the Chicago-Northwestern Indiana Standard Consolidated Area and the 10 largest Standard Metropolitan Statistical Areas (SMSA's) outside the consolidated areas. With the New York-Northeastern New Jersey area we include Monmouth County, New Jersey; and Orange County, California, is combined with Los Angeles County to form one primary area. Additionally there are 32 other SMSA's and 30 Non-SMSA's, generally single counties but occasionally part-counties or county groups to which an occasional independent city is attached; each of the 62 primary areas represents one stratum of two or more primary areas totaling around 2.25 million in population on the average. The SMSA definitions are those of February 1972, and no attempt is made to update for changes. Stratification criteria, applied independently within the four geographic regions include: SMSA classification, population of major city, population of primary area, rate of population change, geographic location, proportion of black population, median family income, proportion of seasonal housing units and vacancy rate. Controlled selection within regions is used to select one primary area, with probability proportional to size, to represent each stratum. With controls we can better approximate proportionate allocation of the sample by groups of states and degree of urbanization than could be achieved by chance alone. There are no controls by individual states.

Thus, by accepting the SRC sample of 74 primary areas, we had a probability selection of counties, municipalities, townships, and independent cities plus the District of Columbia distributed, in proportion to population, throughout the four geographical regions: Northeast, North Central, South and West. However, to reduce the range in weights for class 2 municipalities (see below) a decision was made to create two half-strata from each of 17 of the original SRC strata. An objective criterion was used to identify the 17 strata: any SMSA stratum in which one or more primary areas had a selection probability less than 0.13. That critical value gave an acceptable balance between precision of estimates and data collection costs.

When creating the half-strata, the initial stratification criteria were followed. Since each stratum was halved, it follows that 17 of the half-strata contained a primary area in the current SRC sample; those 17 areas were retained with their new selection probabilities. From the other 17 half-strata, independent selections of one primary area per half-stratum were made with probabilities proportionate to 1970 populations. The newly chosen 17 primary areas added 31 counties and two part-counties, bringing the grand total of geographical areas to 204 counties, 10 part-counties, six independent cities, and the District of Columbia. A consequence of the subdivision of strata was the expansion of the sample into two additional states, there now being 91 sample areas in 39 of the 48 states.

throughout the nation except for Connecticut, Rhode Island, the District of Columbia, and limited portions of other States.... Especially because these exceptional areas include New York City, Philadelphia, and several others of the most populous cities in the nation (where the municipality operates, in effect, as a composite city-county unit), nearly 12 percent of the total U.S. population is not served by any separately organized county government"[2] For sampling and other research purposes, therefore, the following operational definitions were established: (a) *county area* refers to a geographic area with recognized boundary, and (b) *county government unit* to a county area with an active county government as indicated by county tax effort.

Given the importance of the sample of counties as first-stage selections in sampling local governments, a number of sample estimates were derived for comparison with population values. Economic and demographic data for the SRC sample of counties was merged in from tapes prepared by the Office of Revenue Sharing (ORS). The data refer to the third entitlement period and include total population, per capita income, adjusted tax, and

revenue-sharing allotment. Due to the difficulties in extracting part-county data from the ORS tape, sample estimates in Table 1 were derived from 208 county areas, a number somewhat smaller than the total number of county and part-county areas in the 91-area sample. For purposes of comparison, the county share of revenue-sharing allocation to the county area was calculated as 100 times the revenue-sharing allotment to the county divided by the total allotment to the county area. The resulting percent estimates for all counties in the sample and in conterminous U.S. classified by population size and region are presented in Table 1.

These results clearly validate the use of the SRC sample of counties for the selection of local governmental units. Looking beyond the simple comparison of descriptive statistics of sample estimates and population values, Table 1 shows the inverse relationship between population size and the county's share of revenue-sharing area allocation. Typically, counties in the more rural areas of the United States tend to have a wider range of functions, and other local governmental units correspondingly smaller ranges of functions, than in the more urbanized and densely populated areas.

In selecting county governmental units a first inclination would be to include in the sample all county governments within the 204 county and 10

[2]U.S. Bureau of the Census, Census of Governments, 1972, Vol. I, *Governmental Organization*, U.S. Government Printing Office, Washington, D.C.: 1973, pp. 1-3.

Table 1

County Share as a Percent of the Revenue-Sharing Allocation to the County Area

Counties Classified by Population Size	SRC Sample of 91 Primary Areas[1]			Population[2]		
	Number of Units	Mean County Share[3]	Standard Deviation	Number of Units	Mean County Share[3]	Standard Deviation
100,000 Inhbts. or More .	122	36.4	21.6	331	37.3	19.4
25,000 to 99,999 inhbts .	68	46.1	16.5	889	49.1	17.3
10,000 to 24,999 inhbts .	9	66.5	17.6	998	64.7	16.3
2,500 to 9,999 inhbts . . .	7	82.7	14.0	741	75.3	14.9
Less than 2,500 Inhbts. . .	2	97.1	3.8	101	91.7	15.6
Counties Classified by Region						
Northeast	46	35.3	20.6	212	31.1	19.1
North Central	67	52.1	18.5	1,055	56.5	18.7
South	69	74.7	20.1	1,383	66.1	19.9
West	26	77.5	23.5	410	68.4	19.2
All Counties	208	. . . .	. . . .	3,060	. . . .	. . . .

[1]Sample estimates are derived from the Survey Research Center sample of 91 Primary Areas. Sample data are weighted by the reciprocal of the probability of selecting the Primary Area in which a given county is located. Due to the difficulties in extracting part-county data from the ORS tape, sample estimates were derived from 208 county areas, a number somewhat smaller than the total number of county and partcounty areas in the 91-area sample.

[2]Population data include all county areas in conterminous U.S., many of which do not have a county government and do not receive revenue sharing funds. Independent cities have been excluded from the data. By definition, the population excludes places with 100 inhabitants or less; places with per capita tax effort of $1,000 or more; and Indian tribes.

[3]The county share is calculated as the revenue sharing allotment to the county divided by the total allotment to the county area and multiplied by 100.

part-county areas, with some weight adjustment for part-counties. However, when multiple counties comprise a primary area and the estimation procedure weights responses of governmental officials in proportion to the populations represented, the majority of the primary area weight is allocated to the most populous county. Thus less populous counties may receive weights so low that they contribute negligibly to overall estimates but appreciably to costs. In such situations it is desirable to subsample counties that would otherwise receive low weights. By reducing the number of sample counties, we achieve about the same level of precision at lowered cost.

Still another consideration affected the county sample. To achieve the desired sample size from municipalities of 100,000 or more population, it was necessary to include all municipalities of that size within the 91 primary areas. The sampling of county areas proceeded through the following steps within the 91 primary areas:

Step 1. Accept for the sample all county and part-county areas containing one or more municipalities of 100,000 or more population;

Step 2. If a county area included only one additional county or part-county, add that county to the sample;

Step 3. If a county area included two or more additional counties or part-counties (that is, in addition to Step 1), subsample those counties in a manner to yield one county area for approximately 900,000 estimated population.

By summing populations over minor civil divisions, a part-county was assigned its proportionate share of the total county population.

County areas were selected at a rate of 1/900,000 applied to 1970 population. If a selected county area had an active local government, that governmental unit was accepted for the sample; when a county government was inactive (or nonexistent), there was no contribution to the sample of county governmental units.

Each sample county was assigned a weight in proportion to the population it represents in the sample, the weights being expressed in multiples of 900,000. A county of 900,000 population representing only itself in the sample would be assigned a weight of one. Likewise, a much smaller county that represents 900,000 population would also receive a weight of one. In short, counties representing larger populations receive larger weights, and vice-versa.

Weights were calculated according to the formula:

$$W_i = \frac{1970 \text{ county population}}{P_a \times P_c \times 900,000}$$

where

W_i = Weight for the ith county within a primary area
P_a = probability of selecting the primary area
P_c = probability of selecting the county area within the primary area.

The net result of the sampling was the choice of 149 county and part-county areas where predesignated officials were to be contacted by interviewers.

The Selection of Municipalities and Townships

Like counties, municipalities and townships were selected with probabilities proportional to size. However, two new issues had to be considered here. First, townships do not exist in all States and, where they do exist, they present a wide range in scope of government powers and functions. Second, the creation of population size classes for the selection and weighting of those governmental units should reflect some functional relationship between population size and the relative complexity of governmental functions as measured, say, by the local per capita tax effort. This rationale rests on the distinction between "need" and "incentive" factors in the basic formula for revenue-sharing allocation.

The definition of the population of local governmental units to be sampled had already eliminated from consideration those units most likely to distort any functional relationship between population size and complexity of local governmental functions. To reiterate, the population excludes: units serving very small populations, of 100 inhabitants or less; units with very special forms of government, as Indian tribes; and units which, by virtue of the local prominence of a few major economic enterprises, have a local tax effort highly disproportionate to their population. Those were the places with per capita tax effort of $1,000 or more.

The next task, therefore, was to establish a functional relationship between population size and local tax effort for different types of local governments. Aggregate data collected by the Office of Revenue Sharing (ORS) for the third entitlement period was merged in for the 4,606 municipalities and townships included in the SRC sample of 91 primary areas. Table 2-a shows the estimates of mean population by per capita tax effort groups and government type.

Inspection of Table 2-a suggests a strong positive association between population size and per capita tax effort for all 4,606 localities, but with a reversal at the lower per capita tax effort class. This association appears much more systematic when municipalities are analyzed separately, but hardly appears at all for townships. This finding led to a closer analysis of townships vis-a-vis municipalities, given the possibility of regional differences in townships' performance of governmental functions.

A detailed analysis of the association between population size and per capita tax effort for municipalities and townships for each one of the four major regions resulted in the classification of localities presented in Table 2-b.

Table 2-b shows that a strong positive association between population size and per capita tax effort holds for all municipalities and Northeast townships (or "towns") exclusive of New York State towns. The association is clearly negative for North Central region townships, and erratic for New York State towns. The explanation is relatively straightforward. In the Northeast region, excluding New York State, townships turn out to perform exactly the same functions and have the same relation to other governmental units as municipalities. In this region, townships do not encompass other general government jurisdictions. But in the North Central region and in New York State, townships typically will encompass other general government jurisdictions (villages, towns,

Table 2-a
Estimated Mean Population by Per Capita Tax Effort Groups and Government Type*

Per Capita Tax Effort Groups	All Municipalities, Towns and Townships			Only Municipalities			Only Towns and Townships		
	Number of Units	Mean	Standard Deviation	Number of Units	Mean	Standard Deviation	Number of Units	Mean	Standard Deviation
$100 or more....	453	36,100	276,750	325	65,220	386,680	128	6,210	10,390
$50 to $99	1,010	16,220	56,040	821	20,450	64,140	189	6,720	28,710
$25 to $49	1,307	3,730	8,740	982	3,590	7,070	325	4,330	13,620
$20 to $24	370	1,880	6,100	247	2,480	7,810	123	1,300	3,650
$15 to $19	405	1,670	4,160	218	1,990	4,840	187	1,270	3,040
$10 to $14	350	2,310	4,290	164	1,100	2,080	186	3,510	5,440
$5 to $9	354	1,750	5,950	108	1,020	1,750	246	2,100	7,130
Less than $5.....	357	3,170	14,510	98	440	460	259	5,300	19,110
All groups ...	4,606	5,630	59,730	2,963	7,190	76,760	1,643	3,360	13,100

*Estimates derived from the Survey Research Center sample of 91 Primary Areas. By definition, the population excludes places with 100 inhabitants or less; places with per capita tax effort of $1,000 or more; and Indian tribes. Sample data are weighted by the reciprocal of the probability of selecting the Primary Area in which a given municipality, town or township is located.

Table 2-b
Estimated Mean Population by Per Capita Tax Effort Groups and by Government Type*

Per Capita Tax Effort Groups	All Municipalities and Northeast Region Towns and Townships Exclusive of New York State Towns			North Central Region Townships			New York State Towns		
	Number of Units	Mean	Standard Deviation	Number of Units	Mean	Standard Deviation	Number of Units	Mean	Standard Deviation
$100 or more....	436	43,660	304,720	6	700	510	11	2,600	4,230
$50 to $99	964	17,640	57,430	16	890	3,360	30	22,420	88,150
$25 to $49	1,163	3,870	7,490	94	930	3,070	50	9,880	26,850
$20 to $24	324	2,420	6,920	39	570	2,660	7	8,500	14,280
$15 to $19	313	1,890	4,390	84	700	2,650	8	9,520	6,590
$10 to $14	210	1,300	2,110	137	3,580	5,820	3	5,570	1,040
$5 to $9	127	1,020	1,640	225	2,210	7,840	2	9,790	2,760
Less than $5.....	105	540	900	252	5,800	20,180	...	....	....
All groups ...	3,642	6,850	71,090	853	2,310	9,460	111	11,260	42,250

*See footnote to Table 2-a.

sometimes even cities) and these jurisdictions will provide functions in some or all of the township area. Thus North Central townships which are very large in population or area will generally tend to have quite limited functions, because other government jurisdictions will also be found in those areas and these are the ones that provide most of the services. But where townships are very small, they are apt to be the only general government jurisdictions in those areas and hence will provide a full range of governmental functions much like municipalities do. This classification by region and type of government is entirely consistent with the definitions employed by the Census of Governments. Moreover, for purposes of representing population it is clear that overlapping jurisdiction townships must be treated differently from townships which act like cities in their relation to other governmental units. If we were to represent municipal jurisdictions in the U.S. by a combination of towns and townships, populations

served by both would clearly be overrepresented in the sample.

These findings and considerations led to the creation of the sampling strata presented in Table 2-c. For purposes of sampling, a *municipality* was defined as any political subdivision meeting the census definition of municipality plus New England towns and New Jersey and Pennsylvania townships. Thus defined, municipalities were ordered by 1970 population within five size classes:

Class 1:   100,000 inhabitants or more
Class 2:   25,000 to 99,999 inhabitants
Class 3:   10,000 to 24,999 inhabitants
Class 4:   2,500 to 9,999 inhabitants
Class 5:   Less than 2,500

Townships were defined as any political subdivision in New York State or in the North Central region meeting the census definition of a township. Townships, irrespective of population size, form the sixth sampling stratum.

Table 2-c
Estimated Mean Population and Mean Per Capita Tax Effort by Government Type*

GOVERNMENT TYPE	Number of Units	Population Size		Per Capital Tax Effort (in dollars)	
		Mean	Standard Deviation	Mean	Standard Deviation
Municipalities and Northeast Townships Exclusive of New York State Towns	3,642	6,850	71,090	. . . . .	. . . .
100,000 inhbts. or more	70	396,050	791,020	$111.20	$57.30
25,000 to 99,999 inhbts.	374	46,650	19,810	76.10	40.90
10,000 to 24,999 inhbts.	598	15,420	3,930	60.80	37.10
2,500 to 9,999 inhbts.	1,115	5,330	2,100	47.90	40.20
Less than 2,500 inhbts.	1,485	800	590	29.20	36.00
North Central Townships and New York State Towns	964	2,890	14,240	19.80	23.20

*See footnote to Table 2-a.

Estimates of mean population and mean per capita tax effort are shown in Table 2-c for municipalities and townships. The results show a clearly positive association between population size and per capita tax effort for all municipalities.

Municipalities were selected as follows. It was previously established that some 100 units should be selected within each population size class, except for size class 2 where the larger class interval made 200 units a more appropriate sample size. For each county area of the 91 primary areas, a complete listing of municipalities ordered by 1970 population within five size classes was obtained. Independent cities, not a part of any county, appeared at the end of the listing for each primary area. A municipality in two or more counties was assigned to the county in which the major proportion of the municipal population was located.

All *class 1* municipalities, of which there were 70 in the 91 primary areas, were retained in the sample. Each place was selected at a rate of 1/90,000 and assigned a weight in multiples of 90,000, calculated as follows:

$$W_j = \frac{1970 \text{ municipal population}}{P_a \times P_c \times P_m \times 90,000}$$

where

W_j =   weight for the jth municipality within a primary area

P_a =   probability of selecting the primary area

P_c =   probability of selecting the county within the primary area

P_m =   probability of selecting the municipality within the county area

The denominator in the expression for W_j reduces to p_a (90,000) since p_c and p_m are one for class 1 municipalities. In many cases, p_a is one also, so that W_j varies from 88 for New York City to around one for a city of about 100,000 population in one of the 12 largest primary areas. However, many of these municipalities, assigned to the sample with certainty at all stages of sampling including the selection of respondents, contribute nothing to sampling variability—a reason why relatively precise estimates can be produced from a sample of 70 governmental units.

Class 2 municipalities, also selected at a rate of 1/90,000, presented the major sampling problem. By definition, SMSA's have central cities of 50,000 or more population. The source of the problem was the small SMSA's (with central cities in the range of 50,000 to 99,999 population), where the primary area has a relatively low selection probability and the central city has the majority of the population.

With a sample design that requires the selection of one municipality for every 90,000 population in class 2 municipalities, it was necessary to expand the sample of class 2 municipalities by increasing the number of primary areas in the sample; otherwise some of the municipalities would be heavily weighted. For example, consider a primary area of 114,000 population having a selection probability of .05 and a central city of 90,000 population. The primary area represents 20 x 114,000 or 2,280,000 population, while the city of 90,000 represents 20 x 90,000 or 1,8000,000. Consequently, that one municipality receives a weight of 20. The same size municipality around a major metropolitan area, such as Chicago or Los Angeles, would receive a weight closer to one.

One solution could have made the class 2 sample of municipalities self-weighting by adding a sufficient number of primary areas to the sample, but that would have increased costs beyond an acceptable figure. Or sampling rates of municipalities within the 74 primary areas could have been equalized, but that would have reduced the number of such municipalities in the sample to an unacceptable level. A compromise between these two extremes was to create two strata from each of 17 SMSA strata in which one or more primary areas had a selection probability less than .13, as described in the long footnote above. The immediate effects were increased selection probabilities and consequently reduced weights on 17 class 2 municipalities. Although disparity in weights was not removed completely, it was alleviated where the disparity had been greatest. The ultimate outcome was to accept for the sample every class 2 municipality in a sample county area with the 17 SMSA additional strata.

Class 3 and class 4 municipalities were sampled independently but at the same rate of 1/180,000. Generally, within each size class in each primary area one of two sampling techniques was used, whichever seemed to be advantageous:

1. Explicit groups, each representing about 180,000 estimated population, were formed and one municipality chosen with probability proportionate to size; departures from 180,000 were then corrected through weighting. In SMSA's where there were remaining municipalities unassigned to any group, or where the municipalities of a size class were insufficient to form a group approximating 180,000 estimated population, the group was assigned a measure which was some fraction of 180,000.

2. Within a size class, a sampling interval, as close to 180,000 as was practical, was calculated to yield an integral number of selections and applied after a random start, to the listed populations. Adjustments in weights compensate for sampling intervals that departed from 180,000.

Class 5 municipalities were sampled in the same manner as classes 3 and 4 with the qualification that selections were one for each 90,000 population represented by the sample municipality. Weights were calculated accordingly.

Townships, finally, were sampled the same way as municipalities in classes 3, 4, and 5, the only change being the selection rate of 1/360,000 population.

Table 3 shows the distribution of units included in the revenue-sharing sample by population size class and government type.

According to the definitions of local governmental units presented in this text, the revenue-sharing sample includes 149 county areas (of which 145 have county governments); 594 municipalities (including New England townships and New Jersey and Pennsylvania towns); and 74 townships in New York State and the North Central region of the United States.

Table 3
Distribution of the Revenue-Sharing Sample[1] by Population Size Class and Government Type

Population Size Class	All Types	County Areas[2]	Municipalities[3]	Northeast Towns and Townships Exclusive of New York State Towns	North Central Townships and New York State Towns
				Government Type	
100,000 Inhbts, or More	174	90	70	——	14
25,000 to 99,999 Inhbts.	275	41	193	26	15
10,000 to 24,999 Inhbts.	116	9	74	21	12
2,500 to 9,999 Inhbts.	113	7	66	22	18
Less than 2,500 Inhbts.	139	2	99	23	15
All classes	817	149	502	92	74

[1] The Revenue Sharing sample is a selection of counties, municipalities, towns and townships from the Survey Research Center sample of 91 Primary Areas.

[2] *County Areas* may include nongovernmental units, such as some counties in New England; counties coextensive with municipalities, as in the case of the cities of Philadelphia and New York, and part-counties.

[3] *Municipalities* include the independent cities.

Comparison of Sample Estimates and Population Values of Per Capita Measures

The first question about the sample of local governmental units is: how well does it estimate known population values? In order to answer that question, three per capita measures of income, tax effort, and revenue-sharing allocation were calculated for the sample and for the population of local governmental units in conterminous U.S. It is worth recalling that, by definition, the population excludes places with 100 inhabitants or less; Indian tribes, and places with per capita tax effort of $1,000 or more. Data originate from the Office of Revenue Sharing (ORS) and refer to the third entitlement period.

The first set of comparisons is that relative to government type, as presented in Table 4. It is important to emphasize that the results are shown by

Table 4
Comparison of Sample Estimates[1] and Populations Values[2] of Mean Per Capita Income, Revenue-Sharing Allocation, and Tax Effort By Government Type

Government Type	Revenue Sharing Sample			Population		
	Number of Units	Mean	Standard Deviation	Number of Units	Mean	Standard Deviation
Income						
Counties	149	$2,980	$ 920	3,060	$3,090	$ 690
Municipalities	502	3,180	990	17,783	3,230	830
Towns and Townships	166	3,310	1,150	15,248	3,290	1,000
Revenue-Sharing Allocation						
Counties	149	$ 4.20	$ 2.70	3,060	$ 4.00	$ 2.60
Municipalities	502	7.90	3.90	17,783	7.90	4.00
Towns and Townships	166	3.30	3.00	15,248	3.10	2.80
Tax Effort						
Counties	149	$39.60	$33.60	3,060	$38.30	$31.90
Municipalities	502	79.60	55.50	17,783	80.60	58.60
Towns and Townships	166	36.60	43.20	15,248	34.00	42.50

[1] Sample data are weighted in proportion to population represented, adjusted by multiplying size classes 1, 2 and 5 weights by 1; classes 3 and 4 by 2, and North Central townships and New York State towns weights by 4 before combining estimates across size classes. If estimates by population size class are desired, no further weighting is necessary.

[2] Population figures include all states in conterminous U.S. and originate from the Office of Revenue Sharing.

type of local governmental unit according to the census definition and not by definitions adopted in this report; that is, to say, the category "municipalities" includes only municipalities, and the category "towns and townships" includes all Northeast *and* North Central towns and townships. This table was constructed to show that the sample estimates can be derived for official governmental denominations. In order to do so, it was necessary to adjust sample weights such that sampling rates be reduced to the same scale.

Estimates of mean values of per capita income, tax effort, and revenue-sharing allocation by government type are indeed close to the true population values.

The relative accuracy of sample estimates was further tested by the addition of a second stratification factor to government type. Tables 5-a to 5-c show the comparison of estimated and observed mean per capita values by geographical region and government type. As in Table 4, government types refer to the official governmental denominations. Given the total size of the revenue-sharing sample, it is not surprising that the addition of a second

stratification factor results in somewhat more unstable estimates of mean per capita values. Yet estimated values remain remarkably close to the true population values.

The third and last set of comparisons is the most relevant one in judging the relative accuracy of sample estimates. Tables 6-a to 6-c show the comparison of sample estimates and population values of per capita measures for municipalities and townships as defined for the purposes of studying revenue sharing. Estimated and observed values for municipalities are accordingly presented for each of the five population size classes. Counties are left out from this set of comparisons because their estimated and observed values are already presented in Table 4.

The results shown in Tables 6-a to 6-c are self-explanatory and lend strong support to the adequacy of the revenue-sharing sample. It is also important to note that estimates of aggregate values, such as the total amount of revenue-sharing allocation, can be derived using ratio-type estimators and weights that are the inverses of selection probabilities.

Table 5-a
Comparison of Sample Estimates[1] and Population Values[2] of Mean Per Capita Income by Region and Government Type

Government Type By Region	Revenue-Sharing Sample			Population		
	Number of Units in Sample	Mean	Standard Deviation	Number of Units	Mean	Standard Deviation
Northeast						
Counties	32	$3,350	$ 900	212	$3,380	$ 620
Municipalities	106	3,420	760	2,126	3,400	790
Towns + Townships	108	3,450	950	4,047	3,520	1,020
North-Central						
Counties	45	3,030	930	1,055	3,180	540
Municipalities	188	3,180	1,310	7,915	3,290	830
Towns + Townships	58	3,170	1,290	11,163	3,090	930
South						
Counties	50	2,460	870	1,383	2,650	700
Municipalities	105	2,790	820	5,852	2,840	730
Towns + Townships	—	—	—	—	—	—
West						
Counties	22	3,380	460	410	3,380	560
Municipalities	103	3,450	580	1,890	3,500	820
Towns + Townships[3]	—	—	—	38	—	—

[1]See footnote 1 to Table 4.
[2]See footnote 2 to Table 4.
[3]There are only 39 townships in the West, none of which was included in the sample. One such township was excluded by virtue of the definition of the population.

Table 5-b

Comparison of Sample Estimates[1] and Population Values[2] of Mean Per Capita Revenue Sharing Allocation By Region and Government Type

Government Type By Region	Revenue Sharing Sample			Population		
	Number of Units in Sample	Mean	Standard Deviation	Number of Units	Mean	Standard Deviation
Northeast						
Counties	32	$ 2.70	$ 1.90	212	$ 2.60	$ 1.90
Municipalities	106	10.10	4.70	2,126	10.10	4.60
Towns + Townships	108	5.10	3.30	4,047	4.70	3.10
North-Central						
Counties	45	3.00	2.10	1,055	3.30	2.20
Municipalities	188	6.50	3.20	7,915	6.70	3.20
Towns + Townships	58	1.70	1.20	11,163	1.80	1.60
South						
Counties	50	5.40	2.40	1,383	4.60	2.60
Municipalities	105	8.70	3.50	5,852	8.60	3.80
Towns + Townships	—	—	—	—	—	—
West						
Counties	22	6.00	2.90	410	5.60	2.70
Municipalities	103	6.70	3.10	1,890	6.60	3.30
Towns + Townships[3]	—	—	—	38	—	—

[1]See footnote 1 to Table 4.
[2]See footnote 2 to Table 4.
[3]See footnote 3 to Table 5-a.

Table 5-c

Comparison of Sample Estimates[1] and Population Values[2] of Mean Per Capita Tax Effort By Region and Government Type

Government Type By Region	Revenue Sharing Sample			Population		
	Number of Units in Sample	Mean	Standard Deviation	Number of Units	Mean	Standard Deviation
Northeast						
Counties	32	$ 39.20	$ 37.30	212	$ 36.50	35.40
Municipalities	106	95.70	60.20	2,126	96.60	61.10
Towns + Townships	108	65.40	46.40	4,047	61.80	47.70
North-Central						
Counties	45	28.90	15.50	1,055	30.70	15.60
Municipalities	188	72.60	41.30	7,915	74.70	42.50
Towns + Townships	58	10.20	11.90	11,163	10.10	13.00
South						
Counties	50	29.60	18.10	1,383	28.60	21.90
Municipalities	105	72.90	65.40	5,852	73.30	59.80
Towns + Townships	—	—	—	—	—	—
West						
Counties	22	76.10	45.40	410	69.90	41.10
Municipalities	103	81.90	50.70	1,890	82.30	72.10
Towns + Townships[3]	—	—	—	38	—	—

[1]See footnote 1 to Table 4.
[2]See footnote 2 to Table 4.
[3]See footnote 3 to Table 5-a.

Table 6-a

Comparison of Sample Estimates[1] and Population Values[2] of Mean Per Capita Income by Population Size Class

Government Type Exclusive of Counties	Revenue-Sharing Sample			Population		
	Number of Units in Sample	Mean	Standard Deviation	Number of Units	Mean	Standard Deviation
Municipalities and Northeast Townships Exclusive of New York State Towns						
100,000 inhbts. or more	70	$3,360	$ 410	153	$3,320	$ 430
25,000 to 99,999 inhbts.	219	3,260	1,110	783	3,410	880
10,000 to 24,999 inhbts.	95	3,320	1,090	1,418	3,340	1,040
2,500 to 9,999 inhbts.	88	2,970	1,350	4,093	3,050	1,140
Less than 2,500 inhbts.	122	2,560	1,160	14,495	2,620	1,020
North-Central Townships and New York State Towns	74	3,270	1,240	12,089	3,120	980

[1]See footnote 1 to Table 4.
[2]See Footnote 2 to Table 4.

Table 6-b

Comparison of Sample Estimates[1] and Population Values[2] of Mean Per Capita Tax Effort By Population Size Class

Government Type Exclusive of Counties	Revenue Sharing Sample			Population		
	Number of Units in Sample	Mean	Standard Deviation	Number of Units	Mean	Standard Deviation
Municipalities and Northeast Townships Exclusive of New York State Towns						
100,000 inhbts. or more	70	$111.10	$61.70	153	$108.20	$59.20
25,000 to 99,999 inhbts.	219	74.90	40.80	783	77.00	41.90
10,000 to 24,999 inhbts.	95	58.60	32.50	1,418	62.00	38.10
2,500 to 9,999 inhbts.	88	50.50	38.30	4,093	48.60	37.60
Less than 2,500 inhbts.	122	32.70	29.00	14,495	34.70	39.50
North-Central Townships and New York State Towns	74	18.70	22.10	12,089	17.80	21.90

[1]See footnote 1 to Table 4.
[2]See footnote 2 to Table 4.

Table 6-c

Comparison of Sample Estimates[1] and Population Values[2] of Mean Per Capita Revenue Sharing Allocation by Population Size Class

Government Type Exclusive of Counties	Revenue Sharing Sample			Population		
	Number of Units in Sample	Mean	Standard Deviation	Number of Units	Mean	Standard Deviation
Municipalities and Northeast Townships Exclusive of New York State Towns						
100,000 inhbts. or more	70	$10.10	$3.60	153	$10.10	$3.60
25,000 to 99,999 inhbts.	219	6.60	3.40	783	6.70	3.50
10,000 to 24,999 inhbts.	95	5.90	3.40	1,418	6.20	3.40
2,500 to 9,999 inhbts.	88	6.60	3.50	4,093	5.90	3.50
Less than 2,500 inhbts.	122	5.10	3.10	14,495	5.40	3.50
North-Central Townships and New York State Towns	74	2.10	1.70	12,089	2.10	1.80

[1]See footnote 1 to table 4.
[2]See footnote 2 to table 4.

THE SELECTION OF RESPONDENTS AND THE DISTRIBUTION OF NONRESPONSES

For each of the sample jurisdictions, between two and four interviews were scheduled with government officials. The number of designated respondents was set constant within one class of governmental units, and no substitution was allowed when designated officials could not be contacted, refused, or for some other reason did not consent to be interviewed. Likewise, no changes in the sample of governmental units was made even though no interviews could be obtained from any designated official of a sample unit.

Four interviews were scheduled at the level of State governments: one with the State governor, one with the chief fiscal or budget officer, and one with the respective chairpersons of the appropriations committees in the upper and lower chambers of the legislature.

In all counties, and in municipalities with population of 25,000 and above, three interviews were scheduled: one with the chief executive officer of the jurisdiction, one with the chief fiscal or budget officer, and one with the chief executive officer. In municipalities with population below 25,000, only two interviews were to be taken: one with the chief executive officer and the other with the chief fiscal or budget officer.

The actual selection of respondents differs somewhat from the principles just described, since a great many special circumstances dictated either that a different number of interviews be conducted than originally scheduled, or in a few cases, that a different person be interviewed than originally designated.

The principal deviation from the regular format resulted from the fact that, in many jurisdictions, functions overlap and are handled by the same person. For example, in many small municipalities the chief executive officer also serves as his/her own chief budget or fiscal officer, and thus only one person was interviewed instead of the two originally scheduled. In other municipalities where three interviews were scheduled, the city manager was both the chief fiscal officer and the chief administrative officer, hence only two interviews were conducted. In a small number of cases, the chief executive officer appeared to be entirely ceremonial, and we interviewed both a city manager and a chief fiscal officer, with the city manager being regarded as the chief executive officer.

Table 7
Response Rates[1] of Selected Government Officials Classified by Jurisdiction

Jurisdictions	Selected Government Officials											
State Governments	Chief Executive Officer			Chief Finance Officer			Chairman of Upper House			Chairman of Lower House		
	S	C	S/C	S	C	S/C	S	C	S/C	S	C	S/C
All states	50	36	72%	50	50	100%	50	45	90%	50	48	96%
County Governments	Chief Executive Officer			Chief Functional Finance Officer			Chief Administrative Officer					
	S	C	S/C	S	C	S/C	S	C	S/C			
500,000 inhabitants or more	35[a]	29	83%	35	35	100%	32	32	100%			
100,000 to 499,999 inhabitants	50	47	94%	50	48	96%	30	30	100%			
Less than 100,000 inhabitants	60	57	95%	60	59	98%	29	29	100%			
All county government officials....	145	133	92%	145	142	98%	91	91	100%			
Municipal Governments	Chief Executive Officer			Chief Functional Finance Officer			Chief Administrative Officer					
Municipalities/Northeast Townships Exclusive of New York State Towns	S	C	S/C	S	C	S/C	S	C	S/C			
300,000 inhabitants or more	28	18	64%	28	27	96%	24	21	87%			
100,000 to 299,999 inhabitants ...	41	36	88%	41	40	98%	34	32	94%			
25,000 to 99,999 inhabitants......	219	208	95%	219	215	98%	174	174	100%			
10,000 to 24,999 inhabitants......	95	91	96%	95	92	97%	—	—	—			
2,500 to 9,999 inhabitants	88	87	99%	88	85	96%	—	—	—			
Less than 2,500 inhabitants...........	122	119	98%	122	120	98%	—	—	—			
North Central Townships and New York State Towns................	74	70	95%	74	72	97%	—	—	—			
All municipal government officials .	668	629	94%	668	651	97%	232	227	98%			

[1]Response rates equal completed interviews (C) divided by scheduled interviews (S).
[2]Four nongovernmental county areas selected for sample purposes were excluded from tabulations.

The data in Table 7 essentially depict a functional description of officials who were interviewed in the study. As indicated above, people who held one title but performed a function implied by a different title were reclassified into the proper functional category. For purposes of the study, we are primarily concerned with three functional positions: chief executive officer, chief finance officer, and chief administrative officer. The latter category was only relevant for interviews conducted in counties, or in municipalities with population greater than 25,000. A special file of functional executive and functional finance officers was therefore created. For the chief executive officer, this reclassification involved only a very small number of cases, e.g., those cases where ceremonial mayors with no real function were replaced by city managers or the equivalent. However, for the chief fiscal officer category, a substantial number of interviews were reclassified. The functional finance officer file includes respondents with titles like city manager, city clerk, etc., who were determined (by the field staff) to be the effective chief fiscal officer for the jurisdiction.

In addition, for municipalities where it was ascertained that the chief executive officer was also the chief fiscal officer (and hence only one interview was taken), the tabulations report the chief executive officer interview in both the chief executive category and the chief functional finance officer category. Thus the design of Table 7 is that every jurisdiction must have, by definition, a chief executive officer and a chief fiscal officer, and in a small number of municipalities these are the same person and the interviews are duplicated. The third category listed in Table 7—that of chief administrative officers—represent only those city managers or other chief administrative officers who had *not* been previously reclassified as chief functional finance officer. No duplicated interviews are involved here.

Finally, in order to emphasize the pattern of distribution of nonresponses, the sample of municipalities was reordered into six population size classes and the sample of counties reduced to three major population size classes.

As expected, response rates vary widely between sample jurisdictions; by type of governmental official scheduled for interview; and, in the case of local governments, by the population size of the governmental unit. Overall response rates for each of the sample jurisdictions range from 88 percent of scheduled interviews with State government officials, to 96 percent with county government officials, to 97 percent with municipal and township government officials. In all of the three sample jurisdictions, the lowest response rates are found among the chief executive officers. This is

especially true for two groups—governors and mayors of large cities. Finally, and as one would expect, response rates show a mildly negative association with population size in the sample of local governmental units.

It is apparent that a highly satisfactory overall response rate was obtained for the study. Evaluation of the field work should also take into account the fact that at least one interview was obtained from all but two of the 813 general government jurisdictions in the sample of local governments, and from every one of the State governments.

WEIGHTING AND ESTIMATION PROCEDURES

The revenue sharing survey data file of local governmental officials includes three series of weights, each prepared for a different purpose.

1. The 91 Primary Area Weights (or PSU WEIGHTS)

These weights are inverses of selection probabilities of the primary areas. A high level of agreement between sample estimates and complete counts can be obtained by appropriately weighting each primary area's population and financial data, from the data collected by the Office of Revenue Sharing, and then summing over the 91 areas. It is unlikely that the weights will be used for any other purpose.

2. Weights in proportion to the population represented (or PLACE WEIGHTS)

These weights have been described in the preceding sections of this report. They are the weights to use when data relate to opinions, attitudes, and other categorical data reported by local governmental officials. Thus the statistic "40% of the fiscal officers in the sample reported that..." should be interpreted as meaning "fiscal officers in localities representing 40% of the conterminous U.S. population reported that...". Weighting of this sort is clearly essential if we are to interpret results as being applicable to the overall allocation of revenue sharing dollars. Although the sample is not weighted by revenue sharing dollars, the population weights provide a very close approximation to the results that would have been obtained if weighting had been in accordance with revenue sharing allocation.

These weights may also be used with data on a per capita basis (e.g., per capita income, per capita tax effort, per capita revenue sharing allocation).

It must be emphasized that selection rates, and thus values of each unit of weight, vary with the type of government, as presented in Table 8.

When tabulations are restricted to one governmental type, weights are all of the same denomination. However, if tabulation *across* governmental types is desired, differences in denominations must be considered. If municipalities and townships are to be combined, townships are to receive an additional weight of 4; class 3 and class 4 municipalities get a weight factor of 2; and a weight factor of 1 applies for municipalities in classes 1, 2, and 5. The 4:2:1 relationship is a planned and not an accidental relationship.

Table 8
Selection Rates by Type of Local Government

Government Type	Population Represented by Each Unit of Weight
Counties	900,000
Municipalities and Northeast Townships Exclusive of New York State Towns	
Class 1	90,000
Class 2	90,000
Class 3	180,000
Class 4	180,000
Class 5	90,000
North Central Townships and New York State Towns	360,000

3. Weights that are the inverses of selection probabilities (or SAMPLE WEIGHTS)

These weights may be used with enumerative data to estimate total amounts or aggregate values. However, the researcher is warned that such estimates may be subject to substantial sampling error. Per capita estimates calculated with either weight series will be identical provided comparable data are used in the calculations.

It is worth examining the question of weights in more detail. Suppose we are interested in the question: do mayors think that the revenue-sharing allocation formula is fair? If we take individual responses from the mayors of a given type of local government, application of the place weights would tell us that mayors of, say, municipalities representing x percent of the population think the allocation formula is fair, while the mayors of $1-x$ represented people think it unfair. The calculation without using any weights would merely record the fraction of all mayors in the sample, regardless of the community size they represented, who thought the allocation formula was fair or not.

To take another illustration, suppose we are interested in examining the fiscal impact of revenue sharing on municipalities. Using the place weights,

we could say that x percent of the revenue-sharing allocation appeared to be used to reduce local taxes and $1-x$ percent to provide additional services. The calculation using place weights would involve, first, the computation of a weighted proportion of revenue-sharing dollars allocated to local tax reduction, calculated across all local communities, which would then be applied to an externally derived aggregate of revenue-sharing dollars. An alternative calculation would be to apply the sample weights to estimates of the amount of dollars in each community used for tax relief and simply aggregate directly. The differences in the two procedures is one of sampling variances, which would tend to be larger with the second procedure than with the first. In general, it is preferable to use the place weights and then create aggregates by multiplying the resulting variable by an externally derived figure for population, revenue-sharing allocation, and the like.

INTERVIEW PROCEDURES

Methods and procedures for obtaining the survey data from sample populations follow well developed guidelines within the Survey Research Center. Respondents are sent letters indicating the purpose of the survey, and the interviewer then attempts to conduct either a personal or telephone interview with the selected respondent. In the case of the Revenue Sharing Study, respondents were all officials of designated local governments or State government units. Thus there was no problem in locating designated respondents, as would often be the case in a conventional survey of households, and the only nonresponse problems are associated with the reluctance or refusal of designated officials to be interviewed.

As the response rate data suggests, the only response problems that we encountered were for the chief executive officers (mayors) of very large cities (those with over 300,000 population) and for the chief executive officers (governors) of States. In all other cases, response rates are in excess of 90 percent, and usually are well in excess of that figure.

The difficulties of obtaining interviews from big-city mayors and governors appeared to be attributed not so much to the reluctance of these officials to be interviewed, but to the barricade of administrative assistants of all sorts that inevitably surround the chief executive of a large city or State. Governors and big-city mayors are, after all, very busy people with many demands on their time. They are apt to have a variety of assistants for one area or another, and the typical response to a request for an interview from many such individuals (or more realistically, from the administrative assistant that our interviewer wound up contacting) was, "talk to so-and-so—he's our revenue sharing expert." Our response in all such cases was that we did not wish to talk to so-and-so, but to the governor or the mayor, and if that could not be arranged, we could not conduct an interview at all. The logic of this choice is simple. If one wishes to analyze the opinions, attitudes and perceptions of mayors or governors, it is essential to have the decision-maker and not the decision-maker's assistant for revenue sharing. Thus we systematically refused to talk with anyone other than the designated respondent, and ended up with moderately low response rates for governors and big-city mayors.

In an attempt to increase the response rate for governors and big-city mayors and to obtain at least some data of the sort that would be comparable to that obtained from other officials, we severely truncated the interview schedule shown in Appendix C. All of the fiscal impact questions were eliminated and substantial portions of the other part of the interview schedule were cut, in an attempt to reduce the length of the interview to more like 30 minutes than 1 hour. This did enable us to obtain additional interviews that would otherwise not have been obtained, but it resulted in the very heavy non-response observed in the chief executive responses [e.g. compare the chief executive estimates of fiscal impact with those obtained from finance officers for local governments in city size class 1 (data shown in the appendix to Chapter 2)]. The user of the basic data tapes will therefore find substantial numbers of governors and big city mayor responses missing even where an interview was obtained, due to the truncation of the basic interview schedule in an attempt to build up the response rate for these two categories of cases.

Basic Survey Instrument

REVENUE SHARING

OMB # 099S-74015

Project 466111
Summer, 1974

SURVEY RESEARCH CENTER
INSTITUTE FOR SOCIAL RESEARCH
THE UNIVERSITY OF MICHIGAN
ANN ARBOR, MICHIGAN 48106

(Do not write in above space .)

1. Interviewer's Label

2. P.S.U. _____

3. Your Interview No. _____

4. Date _____

5. Length of Interview _____
(Minutes)

INTRODUCTION:

In discussing general revenue sharing with you during this interview, we will be referring to "fiscal years." If we say "fiscal year 1974" we want your fiscal year. Will you tell me the beginning and ending dates of your fiscal year?

MO: _____ DAY: _____   MO: _____ DAY: _____
        BEGIN   END

IF R'S GOVERNMENT UNIT IS ON A CALENDAR YEAR (JAN. 1 - DEC. 31)

Since you use a calendar year, please give us information for the calendar year preceding the fiscal year asked about in the questions. (For example, if we ask for fiscal year 1974, give us information for calendar 1973.

207

time to the nearest minute _____

A1. Now that you have had some experience with general revenue sharing we would like
     to know how you feel about its impact. Are there particular features of general
     revenue sharing that you feel very favorable about? (IF YES) And what
     would those be?

     _____

     _____

     _____

     _____

     _____

     _____

     _____

A2. Are there particular features that you feel very unfavorable about?
     (And what would those be?)

     _____

     _____

     _____

     _____

     _____

     _____

     _____

2

A3. (CARD A, YELLOW) For each statement that I read, just tell me whether you agree strongly, agree somewhat, disagree somewhat, or disagree strongly. The first statement is: We have been able to develop some new programs. How do you feel about that? Just tell me the letter on the card.

	A AGREE STRONGLY (1)	B AGREE SOMEWHAT (2)	C DISAGREE SOMEWHAT (4)	D DISAGREE STRONGLY (5)
a. WE HAVE BEEN ABLE TO DEVELOP SOME NEW PROGRAMS.				
b. revenue sharing has been more trouble for us than it's worth				
c. we are now subject to less control by the federal government				
d. we are finally getting some of our tax money back				
e. we have been able to avoid tax increases				
f. we have been able to stay afloat, financially				
g. we are now subject to more control by the federal government				
h. revenue sharing has not made up for cutbacks in federal grants so we're getting less federal money than before				
j. revenue sharing does not amount to enough to make a real financial difference				

A4. When revenue sharing funds were received initially by this jurisdiction, did you look upon your revenue sharing money as being kept separate from local funds or as being merged with them?

| 1. KEPT SEPARATE | | 2. MERGED WITH LOCAL FUNDS |

A5. Do you look upon your revenue sharing money in the same way now?

| 1. YES | | 5. NO |

A5a. In what ways do you think about it differently?

_____

_____

_____

A6. Over the period that revenue sharing funds have been available, what would you say is the most satisfactory and productive use to which they have been put in your jurisdiction, either by actual spending or by allocation?

_____

_____

_____

_____

A7. What, in your judgment, is the least satisfactory or productive use to which these funds have been put?

_____

_____

_____

_____

_____

4

A8. As you know, federal revenue sharing will expire in 1976, unless it is extended. Do you think federal revenue sharing should continue?

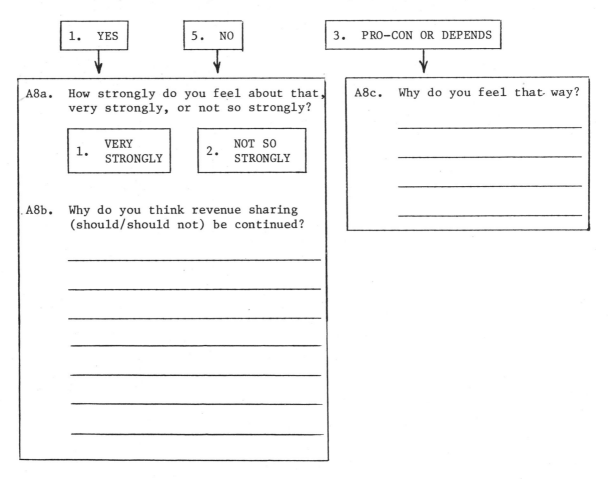

1. YES	5. NO		3. PRO-CON OR DEPENDS

A8a. How strongly do you feel about that, very strongly, or not so strongly?

1. VERY STRONGLY	2. NOT SO STRONGLY

A8b. Why do you think revenue sharing (should/should not) be continued?

_____

_____

_____

_____

_____

_____

_____

A8c. Why do you feel that way?

_____

_____

_____

_____

A9. If revenue sharing is extended, do you think the amounts should be increased a lot, increased a little, kept the same, decreased a little, or decreased a lot?

1. INCREASED A LOT	2. INCREASED A LITTLE	3. KEPT THE SAME	4. DECREASED A LITTLE	5. DECREASED A LOT

A10. (CARD B, ORANGE) *How would you feel about the following changes in the revenue sharing program?* For each <u>change</u> tell me whether you would be strongly in favor of it, somewhat in favor, or whether you would oppose it somewhat or oppose it strongly. Just tell me the letter on the card.

	A STRONGLY FAVOR (1)	B SOMEWHAT FAVOR (2)	C SOMEWHAT OPPOSE (4)	D STRONGLY OPPOSE (5)
a. eliminate priority expenditure requirements				
b. allow revenue sharing money to be used as the matching share of federal grants				
c. develop more complete budget reporting categories				
d. require the formation of citizen advisory committees to decide how to use revenue sharing money				
e. adjust payments to keep up with inflation				
f. change the allocation formula to...				
1. give more money to poorer communities				
2. omit very small government units				
3. give more to big city areas				
4. discourage reduction in local tax rates				
5. encourage the consolidation of small government units				
6. remove the penalty against special districts by including local assessments as part of the tax base				
7. make it easier to know your payments over the next few years				
8. remove the penalty against getting revenue from user charges by including them in the definition of tax effort				

A11. Are there any other changes that you would favor? (IF YES) What do you have in mind?

_____

_____

_____

SECTION B: REVENUE SHARING IMPACT--FISCAL YEAR 1974 BUDGET (CALENDAR 1973)

We are interested in your judgment about the budgetary impact in this (UNIT) of the general revenue sharing program during your fiscal year 1974. When we finish this series of questions we will also be asking you about fiscal year 1975 (calendar 1974).

B1.   What would have been different about the programs run by this (UNIT) without revenue sharing?

_____

_____

_____

_____

B2.   If there had been no revenue sharing money would you have reduced general <u>operating</u> expenditures for fiscal year 1974?

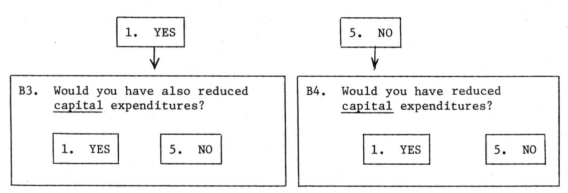

INTERVIEWER CHECKPOINT A

☐ 1.   IF YES ON B2 AND B3 ⟶ TURN TO P. 8, SEQUENCE I

☐ 2.   IF YES ON B2 AND NO ON B3 ⟶ TURN TO P. 11, SEQUENCE II

☐ 3.   IF NO ON B2 AND YES ON B4 ⟶ TURN TO P. 13, SEQUENCE III

☐ 4.   IF NO ON B2 AND NO ON B4 ⟶ TURN TO P. 15, SEQUENCE IV

SEQUENCE I

B5. Would the reduction in <u>operating</u> expenditures have been more than, the same as, or less than, the reduction in <u>capital</u> expenditures?

1. OPERATING EXPENDITURES WOULD BE REDUCED MORE	2. OPERATING EXPENDITURES WOULD BE REDUCED LESS	3. BOTH REDUCED SAME

B6. Would the reduction in operating and capital expenditures together have been equal to the amount of revenue sharing money you received or less than that amount or what?

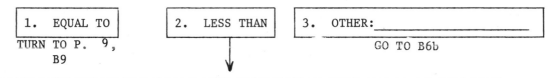

1. EQUAL TO

TURN TO P. 9, B9

2. LESS THAN

3. OTHER:_____

GO TO B6b

B6a. How much less? _____

B6b. Without revenue sharing would local taxes have been higher than they were?

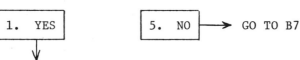

1. YES	5. NO	→ GO TO B7

B6c. Which taxes would have been higher? _____

B6d. How much higher? _____

B7. Would your level of borrowing have been higher than it was?

1. YES	5. NO	→ GO TO CHECKPOINT B

B7a. How much higher?

_____

INTERVIEWER CHECKPOINT B

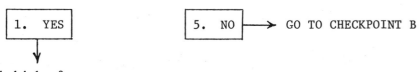

| ☐ 1. IF "YES" TO B6b & B7 ──────→ TURN TO P. 9, B8 |
| ☐ 2. ALL OTHERS ──────────────→ TURN TO P. 9, B9 |

B8. Would you have relied more on raising taxes or on increasing the level of borrowing?

| 1. RAISE TAXES | 2. INCREASE BORROWING | 3. BOTH EQUALLY |

B8a. Why is that?

_____

_____

_____

B9. Would your surplus or your reserve funds at the end of fiscal year 1974 have been lower than they were?

| 1. YES | | 5. NO | → GO TO B10 |

B9a. A little lower, somewhat lower or much lower?

| 1. LITTLE LOWER | 2. SOMEWHAT LOWER | 3. MUCH LOWER |

B10. You indicated earlier that general operating expenditures would have been lower during fiscal year 1974 if revenue sharing funds had not been available. Would this have involved...

1. ...less of an increase in salary rates? | 1. YES | 5. NO |

2. ...fewer personnel? | 1. YES | 5. NO |

3. ...less equipment and supplies? | 1. YES | 5. NO |

B11.   What specific programs would have been reduced or eliminated if
       revenue sharing funds had not been available?

       _____

       _____

       _____

       _____

       _____

B12.   What part of the public would have been most affected by this?

       _____

       _____

       _____

B13.   What kinds of capital expenditures would have been reduced or eliminated
       in fiscal year 1974 if revenue sharing funds had not been available?

       _____

       _____

       _____

       _____

       _____

B14.   What part of the public would have been most affected by this?

       _____

       _____

       _____

B15.   Thinking back to fiscal 1973, what specific programs, if any,
       would have been reduced or eliminated if revenue sharing funds had not
       been available?

       _____

       _____

       _____

TURN TO P. 16, SECTION C

B16. Would the reduction in operating expenditures have been equal to the amount of revenue sharing money you received or less than that amount?

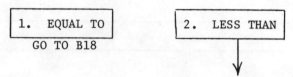

| 1. EQUAL TO | 2. LESS THAN |
| GO TO B18 | |

B17. Without revenue sharing would local taxes have been higher than they were?

| 1. YES | 5. NO → GO TO B18 |

B17a. Which taxes would have been higher?

_____

B17b. How much higher?

_____

B18. Would your surplus or your reserve funds at the end of fiscal year 1974 have been lower than they were?

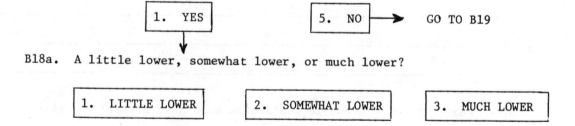

| 1. YES | 5. NO → GO TO B19 |

B18a. A little lower, somewhat lower, or much lower?

| 1. LITTLE LOWER | 2. SOMEWHAT LOWER | 3. MUCH LOWER |

B19. You indicated earlier that general operating expenditures would have been lower during fiscal year 1974 if revenue sharing funds had not been available. Would this have involved...

1. ...less of an increase in salary rates? | 1. YES | | 5. NO |

2. ...fewer personnel? | 1. YES | | 5. NO |

3. ...less equipment and supplies? | 1. YES | | 5. NO |

B20. What specific programs would have been reduced or eliminated if revenue sharing funds had not been available?

_____

_____

_____

_____

_____

B21. What part of the public would have been most affected by this?

_____

_____

_____

B22. Thinking back to fiscal <u>1973</u>, what specific programs, if any, would have been reduced or eliminated if revenue sharing funds had not been available?

_____

_____

_____

_____

TURN TO P. 16, SECTION C

B23. Would the reduction in capital expenditures have been equal to the amount of revenue sharing money you received or less than that amount?

1. EQUAL TO	2. LESS THAN

GO TO B25

B23a. How much less? _____

B24. Would you have made up the difference mostly by raising taxes, mostly by borrowing, or would you have used both equally?

1. RAISE TAXES	2. INCREASED BORROWING	3. BOTH EQUALLY

B25. Would your surplus or your reserve funds at the end of fiscal year 1974 have been lower than they were?

1. YES	5. NO	→ GO TO B26

B25a. A little lower, somewhat lower or much lower?

1. LITTLE LOWER	2. SOMEWHAT LOWER	3. MUCH LOWER

B26. What kind of capital expenditures would have been reduced or eliminated in fiscal year 1974 if revenue sharing funds had not been available?

_____

_____

_____

_____

_____

B27. What part of the public would have been most affected by this?

_____

_____

_____

B28. Thinking back to fiscal <u>1973</u>, what specific programs, if any, would have been reduced or eliminated if revenue sharing funds had not been available?

_____

_____

_____

_____

TURN TO P. 16, SECTION C

SEQUENCE IV

B29. You indicated that even without revenue sharing money you would have kept the same level of fiscal year 1974 <u>expenditures</u>. Without revenue sharing would local taxes have been higher than they were?

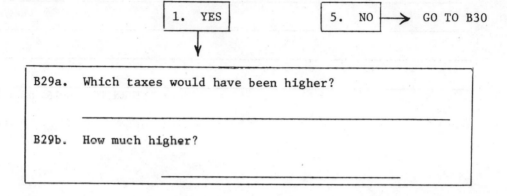

| 1. YES | 5. NO → GO TO B30 |

B29a. Which taxes would have been higher?

_____

B29b. How much higher?

_____

B30. Would your level of borrowing have been higher than it was?

| 1. YES | 5. NO → GO TO B31 |

B30a. How much higher?

_____

B31. Would your surplus or your reserve funds at the end of fiscal year 1974 have been lower than they were?

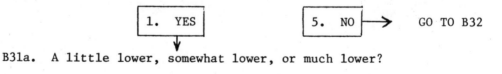

| 1. YES | 5. NO → GO TO B32 |

B31a. A little lower, somewhat lower, or much lower?

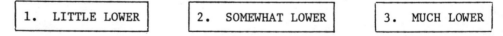

| 1. LITTLE LOWER | 2. SOMEWHAT LOWER | 3. MUCH LOWER |

B32. Thinking back to fiscal <u>1973</u>, what specific programs, if any, would have been reduced or eliminated if revenue sharing funds had not been available?

_____

_____

_____

_____

TURN TO P. 16, SECTION C

SECTION C: REVENUE SHARING IMPACT--FISCAL YEAR 1975 BUDGET

We are interested in your judgment about the budgetary impact in this (UNIT)
of the general revenue sharing program during your fiscal year 1975.

C1.   What would have been different about the programs run by this (UNIT)
       without revenue sharing?

_____

_____

_____

_____

C2.   If there were no revenue sharing money would you have reduced
       general _operating_ expenditures for fiscal year 1975?

        ┌─────────────┐   ┌─────────────┐
        │ 1.   YES   │   │ 5.   NO   │
        └─────────────┘   └─────────────┘

┌──────────────────────────────┐   ┌──────────────────────────────┐
│ C3. Would you also have reduced │   │ B4. Would you have reduced │
│ _capital_ expenditures?   │   │ _capital_ expenditures?   │
│   │   │   │
│ ┌─────────┐   ┌─────────┐   │   │ ┌─────────┐   ┌─────────┐   │
│ │ 1. YES │   │ 5. NO │   │   │ │ 1. YES │   │ 5. NO │   │
│ └─────────┘   └─────────┘   │   │ └─────────┘   └─────────┘   │
└──────────────────────────────┘   └──────────────────────────────┘

INTERVIEWER CHECKPOINT C

┌───┐
│ ☐ 1.   IF YES ON C2 AND C3 ───────▶ TURN TO P. 17, SEQUENCE I   │
│   │
│ ☐ 2.   IF YES ON C2 AND NO ON C3 ───▶ TURN TO P. 20, SEQUENCE II │
│   │
│ ☐ 3.   IF NO ON C2 AND YES ON C4 ───▶ TURN TO P. 22, SEQUENCE III │
│   │
│ ☐ 4.   IF NO ON C2 AND NO ON C4 ───▶ TURN TO P. 23, SEQUENCE IV   │
└───┘

SEQUENCE I

C5. Would the reduction in <u>operating</u> expenditures be more than, the same as, or less than, the reduction in <u>capital</u> expenditures?

| 1. | OPERATING EXPENDITURES WOULD BE REDUCED MORE | 2. | OPERATING EXPENDITURES WOULD BE REDUCED LESS | 3. | BOTH REDUCED SAME |

C6. Would the reduction in operating and capital expenditures together be equal to the amount of revenue sharing money you received or less than that amount or what?

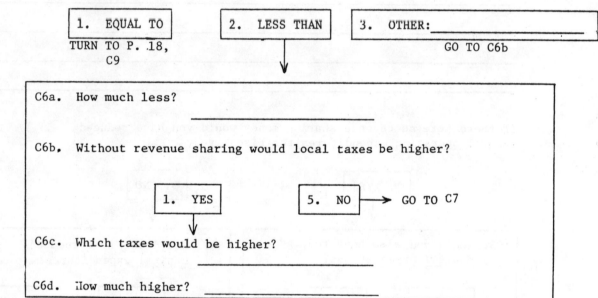

| 1. EQUAL TO | 2. LESS THAN | 3. OTHER:_____ |

TURN TO P. 18, C9

GO TO C6b

C6a. How much less?

_____

C6b. Without revenue sharing would local taxes be higher?

| 1. YES | | 5. NO | → GO TO C7

C6c. Which taxes would be higher?

_____

C6d. How much higher? _____

C7. Would your level of borrowing be higher?

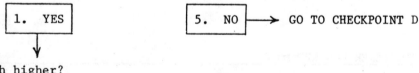

| 1. YES | | 5. NO | → GO TO CHECKPOINT D

C7a. How much higher?

_____

INTERVIEWER CHECKPOINT D

| ☐ | 1. IF "YES" TO C6b & C7 ————→ TURN TO P. 18, C8 |
| ☐ | 2. ALL OTHERS ————→ TURN TO P. 18, C9 |

C8. Would you have relied more on raising taxes or on increasing the·level
     of borrowing?

| 1. RAISE TAXES | 2. INCREASE BORROWING | 3. BOTH EQUALLY |

C8a. Why is that?

_____

_____

_____

C9. Without revenue sharing funds would your surplus or your reserve funds at
     the end of fiscal year 1975 be lower?

| 1. YES | | 5. NO | → GO TO C10

C9a. A little lower, somewhat lower or much lower?

| 1. LITTLE LOWER | 2. SOMEWHAT LOWER | 3. MUCH LOWER |

C10. You indicated earlier that general operating expenditures would be
      lower during fiscal year 1975 if revenue sharing funds had not been available.
      Would this have involved...

1. ...less of an increase in salary rates? | 1. YES | | 5. NO |

2. ...fewer personnel? | 1. YES | | 5. NO |

3. ...less equipment and supplies? | 1. YES | | 5. NO |

C11. What specific programs would have been reduced or eliminated if revenue sharing funds had not been available?

_____

_____

_____

_____

_____

C12. What part of the public would have been most affected by this?

_____

_____

_____

C13. What kinds of capital expenditures would have been reduced or eliminated in fiscal year 1975 if revenue sharing funds had not been available?

_____

_____

_____

_____

_____

C14. What part of the public would have been most affected by this?

_____

_____

_____

TURN TO P. 24, SECTION D

SEQUENCE II

C15. Would the reduction in operating expenditures be equal to the amount of revenue sharing money you received or less than that amount?

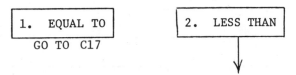

1. EQUAL TO	2. LESS THAN
GO TO C17	

C16. Without revenue sharing would local taxes be higher?

1. YES	5. NO → GO TO C17

C16a. Which taxes would be higher?

_____

C16b. How much higher?

_____

C17. Without revenue sharing funds would your surplus or your reserve funds at the end of fiscal year 1975 be lower?

1. YES	5. NO → GO TO C18

C17a. A little lower, somewhat lower, or much lower?

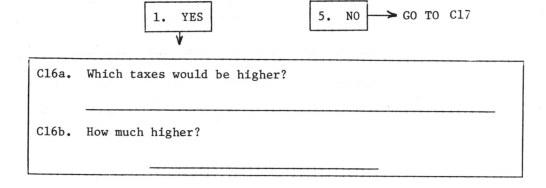

1. LITTLE LOWER	2. SOMEWHAT LOWER	3. MUCH LOWER

C18. You indicated earlier that general operating expenditures would be lower during fiscal year 1975 if revenue sharing funds had not been available. Would this have involved...

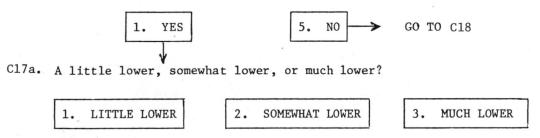

1. ...less of an increase in salary rates?	1. YES	5. NO
2. ...fewer personnel?	1. YES	5. NO
3. ...less equipment and supplies?	1. YES	5. NO

C19. What specific programs would be reduced or eliminated if revenue sharing funds had not been available?

_____

_____

_____

_____

_____

C20. What part of the public would be most affected by this?

_____

_____

_____

TURN TO P. 24, SECTION D

SEQUENCE III

C21. Would the reduction in capital expenditures be equal to the amount of revenue sharing money you received or less than that amount?

1. EQUAL TO	2. LESS THAN

GO TO C23

C21a. How much less? _____

C22. Would you make up the difference mostly by raising taxes, mostly by borrowing, or would you have used both equally?

1. RAISE TAXES	2. INCREASED BORROWING	3. BOTH EQUALLY

C23. Without revenue sharing funds would your surplus or your reserve funds at the end of fiscal year 1975 be lower?

1. YES	5. NO	→ GO TO C24

C23a. A little lower, somewhat lower or much lower?

1. LITTLE LOWER	2. SOMEWHAT LOWER	3. MUCH LOWER

C24. What kind of capital expenditures would have been reduced or eliminated in fiscal year 1975 if revenue sharing funds had not been available?

_____

_____

_____

_____

_____

C25. What part of the public would have been most affected by this?

_____

_____

_____

TURN TO P. 24, SECTION D

C26. You indicated that even without revenue sharing money you would keep the same level of fiscal year 1975 <u>expenditures</u>. Without revenue sharing would local taxes be higher than they are?

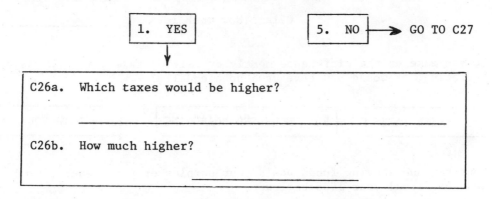

| 1. YES | 5. NO | → GO TO C27 |

C26a. Which taxes would be higher?

_____

C26b. How much higher?

_____

C27. Would your level of borrowing be higher?

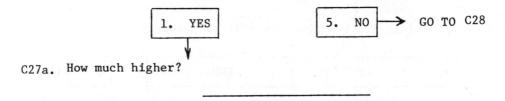

| 1. YES | 5. NO | → GO TO C28 |

C27a. How much higher?

_____

C28. Without revenue sharing funds would your surplus or your reserve funds at the end of fiscal year 1975 be lower?

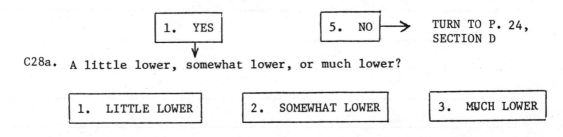

| 1. YES | 5. NO | → TURN TO P. 24, SECTION D |

C28a. A little lower, somewhat lower, or much lower?

| 1. LITTLE LOWER | 2. SOMEWHAT LOWER | 3. MUCH LOWER |

TURN TO P. 24, SECTION D

24

SECTION D: PROGRAM IMPACT

Now I have a few general questions about the area around here.

D1. What would you say are the three most important problems facing this (UNIT)?

1. _____

_____

2. _____

_____

3. _____

_____

D2. We're interested in whether revenue sharing has made any difference in your ability to deal with any of these problems. Let's take the first problem you mentioned (REPEAT FIRST PROBLEM). Has revenue sharing made any difference in dealing with that problem?

| 1. YES | | 5. NO |

D2a. Why is that?

_____

_____

_____

D3. What about the second problem (REPEAT SECOND PROBLEM). Has revenue sharing made a difference there?

| 1. YES | | 5. NO |

D3a. And why is that?

_____

_____

_____

231

D4. Finally, what about the third problem? (REPEAT THIRD PROBLEM.)

| 1. YES | | 5. NO |

D4a. And why is that?

_____

_____

_____

D5. Is revenue sharing likely to make any difference in your ability to deal with any of these major problems in the future?

| 1. YES | | 5. NO | → GO TO D6

D5a. In what ways and which problems?

_____

_____

_____

_____

D6. Would you say that the federal categories of "__priority__" expenditures have been very restrictive, moderately restrictive, or not restrictive at all?

| 1. VERY RESTRICTIVE | | 2. MODERATELY RESTRICTIVE | | 3. NOT RESTRICTIVE AT ALL |

TURN TO P. 26, D7

D6a. In what ways have they been restrictive?

_____

_____

_____

D7. Would you favor greater federal restrictions on the uses of revenue sharing funds?

| 1. YES | | 5. NO | → GO TO D8 |

D7a. What sorts of restrictions do you have in mind?

_____

_____

_____

D8. Would you favor the total elimination of federal "priority" categories?

| 1. YES | | 5. NO | → GO TO D9 |

D8a. And why do you feel that way?

_____

_____

_____

D9. If the use of priority expenditure categories is continued, are there any categories which you think should be added?

_____

_____

_____

D10. If you were free to allocate the revenue sharing funds for this (UNIT) all over again, would you do it the same way or do it differently?

| 1. DO IT THE SAME WAY | 2. DO IT DIFFERENTLY |

TURN TO P. 28, D12

D11. In what ways would you change the allocation of revenue sharing funds if you could do it all over again?

_____

_____

_____

D12. Overall, would you say that you have used revenue sharing dollars to finance continuing activities to start new ones?

1. NEW ACTIVITIES	2. CONTINUING ACTIVITIES	3. BOTH
GO TO D12a		GO TO D12a

Were any revenue sharing funds used to start new activities?

1. YES	5. NO
GO TO D12a	TURN TO P. 30, D13

D12a. Can you give me examples of the new activities you have begun with revenue sharing funds? (RECORD EACH ACTIVITY AT TOP OF COLUMN AND ASK D12b-D12g FOR EACH.)

ACTIVITY

1. _____

D12b. What was the approximate annual cost of the (ACTIVITY)?

$_____
ANNUAL COST

D12c. Would you have undertaken this new activity without revenue sharing?

YES 1. WOULD HAVE	NO 5. WOULD NOT

D12d. How would you best characterize these programs you have begun with revenue sharing funds. Is (ACTIVITY) an essential activity that you could not afford before, is it a useful activity or is it a luxury activity that you could not afford before?

1. ESSENTIAL
2. USEFUL
3. LUXURY

D12e. Would you describe (ACTIVITY) as an innovative addition to your programs?

1. YES	5. NO

D12f. Was (ACTIVITY) conducted by your (UNIT) alone or in cooperation with other government units or private agencies?

1. ALONE	OTHER 2. UNITS/ AGENCIES

D12g. (IF WITH OTHERS) What other units or agencies were involved?

(SPECIFY):_____

_____

_____

_____

235

ACTIVITIY

2. _____

$_____
ANNUAL COST

| 1. | YES WOULD HAVE |
| 5. | NO WOULD NOT |

| 1. | ESSENTIAL |

| 2. | USEFUL |

| 3. | LUXURY |

| 1. | YES |
| 5. | NO |

| 1. | ALONE |
| 2. | OTHER UNITS/ AGENCIES |

(SPECIFY): _____

_____

_____

_____

ACTIVITY

3. _____

$_____
ANNUAL COST

| 1. | YES WOULD HAVE |
| 5. | NO WOULD NOT |

| 1. | ESSENTIAL |

| 2. | USEFUL |

| 3. | LUXURY |

| 1. | YES |
| 5. | NO |

| 1. | ALONE |
| 2. | OTHER UNITS/ AGENCIES |

(SPECIFY): _____

_____

_____

_____

D13. Would the direct allocation of revenue sharing funds (for example those reported on the Actual Use reports) have been different if the law did not restrict expenditures to priority categories?

| 1. YES | | 5. NO | → GO TO D14 |

D13a. Which categories of expenditure might have received more revenue sharing funds?

_____

_____

D13b. Which categories might have received less revenue sharing funds?

_____

_____

D14. Would the direct uses of revenue sharing have been different if there were no prohibitions on the use of revenue sharing to match other Federal grants?

| 1. YES | | 5. NO | → GO TO D15 |

D14a. Which categories of expenditure might have received more revenue sharing funds?

_____

_____

D14b. Which categories might have received less revenue sharing funds?

_____

_____

D15. Have reductions, or the possibility of reductions, in federal categorical programs for local governments affected decisions regarding the uses of revenue sharing?

| 1. YES | | 5. NO | → TURN TO P. 31, SECTION E |

D15a. How was that? _____

_____

_____

SECTION E: IMPACT ON THE BUDGET PROCESS

E1. Has revenue sharing made it more difficult or less difficult or hasn't it made any difference in your planning for future expenditures?

1. MORE DIFFICULT	2. LESS DIFFICULT	3. HASN'T MADE ANY DIFFERENCE
↓	↓	GO TO E2

E1a. Why is that?

_____

_____

_____

E2. How about controlling expenditures? (Has revenue sharing made it more difficult, less difficult or hasn't it made any difference?)

1. MORE DIFFICULT	2. LESS DIFFICULT	3. HASN'T MADE ANY DIFFERENCE
↓	↓	GO TO E3

E2a. Why is that?

_____

_____

_____

E3. How about deciding on changes or reforms in the local tax structure? (Has revenue sharing made it more difficult, less difficult, or hasn't it made any difference?)

1. MORE DIFFICULT	2. LESS DIFFICULT	3. HASN'T MADE ANY DIFFERENCE
↓	↓	TURN TO P. 32, E4

E2a. Why is that?

_____

_____

_____

E4. How about setting priorities for local expenditures? (Has revenue sharing
made it more difficult, less difficult or hasn't it made any difference?)

1. MORE DIFFICULT	2. LESS DIFFICULT	3. HASN'T MADE ANY DIFFERENCE
		GO TO E5

E4a. Why is that?

_____

_____

_____

E5. How about finding out what the community wants? (Has revenue sharing made it
more difficult, less difficult, or hasn't it made any difference?)

1. MORE DIFFICULT	2. LESS DIFFICULT	3. HASN'T MADE ANY DIFFERENCE
		GO TO E6

E5a. Why is that?

_____

_____

_____

E6. If we think about your "normal" budget process _prior_ to revenue sharing, how
often did you hold public hearings on the budget? Would that be...

1. ____ Never ──────→ TURN TO P. 34 , E10

2. ____ At least once per budget period

3. ____ Two to four times per budget period or

4. ____ Five or more hearings per budget period.

E7. Did you hold public hearings on the disposition of your first revenue sharing
entitlement?

1. YES	5. NO	→ TURN TO P. 33, E8

E7a. Do you recall how many hearings were held?

_____(NUMBER)

E8. Did you hold public hearings during fiscal year 1974 specifically on your revenue sharing funds?

$$\boxed{1. \quad YES} \qquad \boxed{5. \quad NO} \longrightarrow GO\ TO\ E9$$

E8a. About how many hearings would that be?

_____(NUMBER)

E9. How would you compare attendance at public hearings before and after revenue sharing. First about how many people usually attended budget hearings <u>before</u> revenue sharing?

_____BEFORE

E9a. And about how many <u>after</u>?

_____AFTER

INTERVIEWER CHECKPOINT E

☐ IF AFTER LARGER THAN BEFORE ——→ GO TO E9b

☐ ALL OTHERS ——→ GO TO E9c

E9b. To what extent do you think this increase is due to revenue sharing--entirely, to some extent, or not at all?

$$\boxed{1. \quad ENTIRELY} \qquad \boxed{3. \quad TO\ SOME\ EXTENT} \qquad \boxed{5. \quad NOT\ AT\ ALL}$$

TURN TO P. 34, E10

E9c. Would you say, then, that revenue sharing has had no impact on the level of public interest in the budget?

$$\boxed{1. \quad YES} \qquad \boxed{5. \quad NO}$$

TURN TO P. 34, E10

E9d. In what ways has it had an impact?

_____

_____

_____

E10. Has this (UNIT) set up any citizen's groups or committees which advise you on budget, financial or program matters?

1. YES		5. NO → GO TO E13

E11. Were any of these groups formed because of the start of revenue sharing?

1. YES		5. NO → GO TO E13

E12. Which ones were formed because of revenue sharing?

_____

_____

_____

_____

E13. What kinds of community groups or organizations have expressed interest in revenue sharing?

_____

_____

_____

IF NONE ——————→ TURN TO P. 35, E16

E14. What kinds of things have they done to show their interest?

_____

_____

_____

_____

E15. Were all of these groups as active before revenue sharing as afterward?

$$\boxed{1. \quad YES} \qquad \boxed{5. \quad NO} \longrightarrow GO\ TO\ E16$$

E15a. Which ones became more active after revenue sharing was introduced?

_____

_____

_____

E16. Have any particular groups been critical because of the way revenue sharing funds have been handled?

$$\boxed{1. \quad YES} \qquad \boxed{5. \quad NO} \longrightarrow GO\ TO\ E17$$

E16a. Which ones would those be?

1. _____

2. _____

3. _____

E16b. What have they been critical about?

1. _____

2. _____

3. _____

E17. Do you find yourself paying attention to different kinds of issues or problems in this (UNIT) because of revenue sharing?

$$\boxed{1. \quad YES} \qquad \boxed{5. \quad NO} \longrightarrow TURN\ TO\ P.\ 36\ ,\ E18$$

E17a. What kinds of issues would those be in this (UNIT)?

_____

_____

_____

E18. Have you noticed any changes in newspaper coverage of local financial matters because of revenue sharing? First, what about the <u>amount</u> of attention or space devoted to the budget. Has this increased, decreased, or remained about the same? (CONTINUE WITH OTHERS.)

	INCREASED (1)	DECREASED (2)	REMAINED SAME (3)
a. AMOUNT OF ATTENTION (SPACE) IN NEWSPAPERS			
b. Adequacy of treatment			
c. Criticism of financial practices			
d. Support of financial practices			

E19. Let's think for a moment about other government officials in this (UNIT). Do you feel that revenue sharing has made any difference in their reaction to public criticism or support? (CONTINUE WITH OTHERS.)

E19a. (IF YES) Why do you think that has been true?

	5. NO	1. YES	WHY TRUE
a. THEIR REACTION TO PUBLIC CRITICISM OR SUPPORT?			
b. Their desire for better information?			
c. Their concern over fiscal problems?			
d. Their awareness of fiscal pressures?			

E20. Have federal or state officials communicated with you about civil rights enforcement in the revenue sharing program?

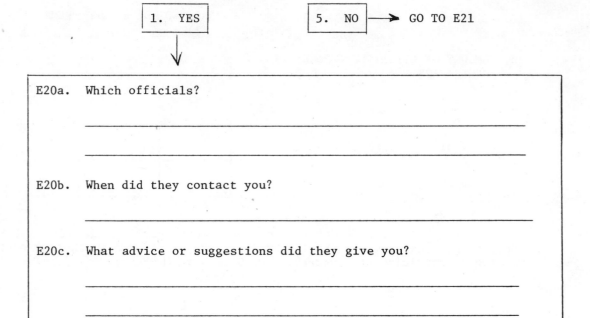

1. YES   5. NO → GO TO E21

E20a. Which officials?

_____

_____

E20b. When did they contact you?

_____

E20c. What advice or suggestions did they give you?

_____

_____

_____

E21. Have the prohibitions against discrimination in revenue sharing been more restrictive, less restrictive or about the same as those in other federal grants?

1. MORE RESTRICTIVE   5. LESS RESTRICTIVE   3. ABOUT THE SAME

SECTION F: INTERGOVERNMENTAL RELATIONSHIPS

F1.   (CARD C, WHITE) *We are also interested in the effect of revenue sharing on your relations with other government officials.*   For each type of official I mention, please tell me the amount of contact <u>of any kind</u> that you have with them as a result of revenue sharing. First, what about federal admini- strators, <u>other than</u> those in the Office of Revenue Sharing?

	A MUCH MORE CONTACT (1)	B SOMEWHAT MORE CONTACT (2)	C ABOUT THE SAME CONTACT (3)	D SOMEWHAT LESS CONTACT (4)	E MUCH LESS CONTACT (5)	
a. FEDERAL ADMINISTRATORS (OTHER THAN ORS OFFICIALS)						
b. Congressmen and Senators						
c. State Officials						
d. State legislators						
e. School district officials						
f. Officials in other special districts						
g. County officials (ASK IF R NOT COUNTY OFFICIAL)						
h. Municipal officials (ASK IF R NOT MUNICIPAL OFFICIAL)						
i. Township officials (ASK IF R NOT TOWNSHIP OFFICIAL)						

F1j. IF RESPONSE IS CATEGORY A, B, D OR E ASK: What is it about revenue sharing
      that causes you to have (more/less) contact with (OFFICIALS)?

_____

_____

_____

_____

_____

_____

_____

_____

F2. In general, *how would you judge the amount of disagreement over the local budget now as compared with what it was before revenue sharing?* First, how about <u>within</u> particular departments or agencies of this (UNIT)--is the conflict over the budget less, more, or about the same as it was before revenue sharing? (CONTINUE WITH REMAINDER.)

	A LESS CONFLICT THAN BEFORE (1)	B MORE CONFLICT THAN BEFORE (5)	C SAME AS BEFORE (3)
a. WITHIN DEPARTMENTS OR AGENCIES OF THIS (UNIT)?			
b. Across (UNIT) departments or agencies?			
c. Between administrators and the (UNIT GOV. BODY)?			
d. Between the (UNIT GOV. BODY) and the general public?			
e. Between the (UNIT GOV. BODY) and local citizens' groups?			
f. Between the (UNIT GOV. BODY) and the media?			
g. Between this (UNIT) and other governments?			

F3. If you had to judge what impact revenue sharing is likely to have on your willingness to work with officials from other local governments in the future, would you say that it will make you...

    1. _____ more willing

    5. _____ less willing, or that

    3. _____ it won't make any difference?

F4. Some people have argued that revenue sharing will encourage certain changes among local government jurisdictions. For each one I mention, *please indicate whether you think revenue sharing will or will not encourage certain changes.* First, do you think revenue sharing will encourage cities and towns to annex outlying areas?

	1. YES, WILL ENCOURAGE	5. NO, WILL NOT ENCOURAGE	8. DON'T KNOW
a. ENCOURAGE TOWNS AND CITIES TO ANNEX OUTLYING AREAS?			
b. Encourage municipalities and counties to take over some functions now being performed by special districts?			
c. Encourage less reliance on user charges by local governments?			
d. Encourage the consolidation of existing governmental units such as cities and counties?			
e. Encourage some small governments to increase the range of their activities?			
f. Encourage less cooperation across various units of local government?			

F5. As a result of revenue sharing has your (UNIT) undergone any changes in its taxing structure?

| 1. YES | | 5. NO |

F5a. Exactly what kinds of changes are you thinking of?

_____

_____

_____

F5b. What parts of the public are most likely to be affected by these changes?

_____

_____

_____

GO TO F6

F5c. Are there any plans for such changes?

| 1. YES | | 5. NO |
GO TO F6

F5d. What kinds of changes?

_____

_____

_____

F5e. What parts of the public are most likely to be affected by these changes?

_____

_____

_____

GO TO F6

F6. As a result of revenue sharing has your (UNIT) taken on any of the functions ordinarily performed by special districts?

| 1. YES | | 5. NO |

F6a. What functions do you have in mind?

_____

_____

_____

_____

GO TO F7

F6b. Do you think it is likely to happen?

_____

_____

_____

_____

GO TO F7

F7. Currently, there is no minimum population size in order to be eligible for revenue sharing money. Do you think there should be a minimum size for eligibility?

| 1. YES | | 5. NO | → TURN TO P. 43, SECTION G

F7a. What do you think that minimum figure should be? _____

SECTION G: OPINIONS ABOUT REVENUE SHARING

(CARD A) People have expressed many different opinions about revenue sharing. I will read a number of such opinions, and for each one I'd like you to tell me whether you agree strongly, agree somewhat, disagree somewhat or disagree strongly. If you aren't sure or don't know, please indicate that.

	A AGREE STRONGLY (1)	B AGREE SOMEWHAT (2)	C DISAGREE SOMEWHAT (4)	D DISAGREE STRONGLY (5)	DON'T KNOW (8)
G1. Concern about the temporary nature of revenue sharing funds may have led some governments to spend most of their revenue sharing money on capital items.					
G2. Concern over the continuation of general revenue sharing may discourage some governments from using revenue sharing funds for experimental programs.					
G3. Increased public participation may make the allocation of revenue sharing funds different from other funds.					
G4. Revenue sharing may not be worth its cost because of the expense involved in meeting the administrative requirements.					
G5. The best use of revenue sharing funds may be to reduce taxes.					
G6. The revenue sharing formula gives too much weight to tax effort and not enough to needs.					
G7. A fair share of revenue sharing money goes to government services for poor people.					

44

	A AGREE STRONGLY (1)	B AGREE SOMEWHAT (2)	C DISAGREE SOMEWHAT (4)	D DISAGREE STRONGLY (5)	DON'T KNOW (8)
G8. Active employee organizations mean that much of the revenue sharing money goes for salary increases.					
G9. Very small government units should get more revenue sharing funds because they are closer to the people than bigger units.					
G10. The best system of revenue sharing is one in which local governments are allowed to use the money for whatever they think best.					
G11. The administrative cost of the general revenue sharing program is much less than the cost associated with other federal assistance programs.					
G12. High rates of inflation mean that much of revenue sharing goes for salary increases.					
G13. Revenue sharing funds will be used differently in the future than they have been in the past.					
G14. Inflation has cut down the use of revenue sharing funds for innovative programs.					

G15. As you know, one of the announced aims of revenue sharing was to strengthen the role of local government. Now that the plan has been in operation for a while, how well do you think that intention has been met over all -- has revenue sharing strengthened local government or has it not made much difference?

1. STRENGTHENED LOCAL GOVERNMENT	3. STRENGTHENED IN SOME WAYS, NO DIFFERENCE IN OTHERS	5. NOT MADE MUCH DIFFERENCE

G15a. And could you tell me why you feel that way? (PROBE FOR AS MUCH DETAIL AND REFLECTION AS POSSIBLE.)

_____

_____

_____

_____

_____

_____

_____

_____

G16. Are there any other general comments you would like to make about the General Revenue Sharing program, either relating to questions that I have asked or to aspects that were not mentioned?

_____

_____

_____

_____

_____

SECTION H: BACKGROUND INFORMATION

Our last, short series of questions deal with background data about yourself. We usually find that these questions help explain why people have different sorts of attitudes and perceptions. However, you may decide you would prefer not to answer some of these questions, even though your name will <u>never</u> be associated with your answers. If that is the case, just tell me and we'll go on to the next question.

H1.   In what year were you born?   _____
                                        YEAR

H2.   Where was it that you grew up? (IF UNITED STATES) Which state or states?

_____

_____

(IF R GREW UP IN STATE DIFFERENT   H2a. How old were you when
   FROM CURRENT RESIDENCE - ASK H2a)   you came to this state?

                                              _____
                                                        YEARS

H3.   How long have you lived in the (NAME OF COMMUNITY) area?   _____
                                                                  YEARS

H4.   Were you brought up mostly in the country, in a town, in a small city or in a large city?

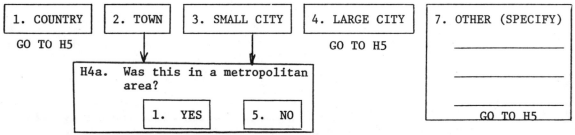

H5.   How long have you held your present position as (TITLE)?

      _____
        YEARS

      H5a. (ASK UNLESS OBVIOUS) Is being (TITLE) a paid or unpaid position?

            | PAID | | UNPAID |

H6.   Did you have a previous official position in this jurisdiction?

_____

H7. Is being (TITLE) of this community regarded as a parttime or a full time position?

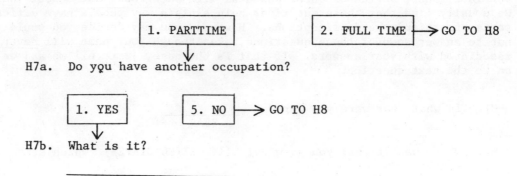

┌─────────────┐   ┌─────────────┐
│ 1. PARTTIME │   │ 2. FULL TIME │ ──→ GO TO H8
└─────────────┘   └─────────────┘

H7a. Do you have another occupation?

┌─────────┐   ┌───────┐
│ 1. YES │   │ 5. NO │ ──→ GO TO H8
└─────────┘   └───────┘

H7b. What is it?

_____

H8. What is the highest grade of school or year of college you completed?

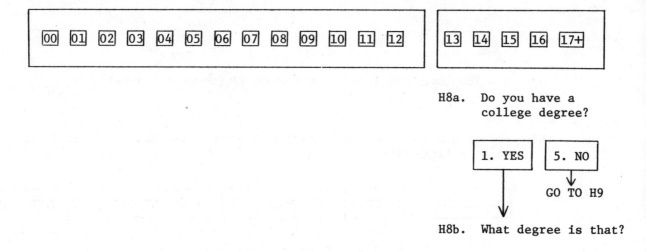

┌──┐   ┌────────────────────────────┐
│ 00 01 02 03 04 05 06 07 08 09 10 11 12 │   │ 13 14 15 16 17+ │
└──┘   └────────────────────────────┘

H8a. Do you have a college degree?

┌─────────┐   ┌───────┐
│ 1. YES │   │ 5. NO │
└─────────┘   └───────┘
                  │
                  ↓
              GO TO H9

H8b. What degree is that?

_____

H9. How about your father's main occupation while you were growing up? What sort of work did he do?

_____

COMPLETE FOLLOWING QUESTIONS BY OBSERVATION

(A) Political characteristics of the present administration in the jurisdiction.

| PREDOMINANTLY DEMOCRAT | MAJORITY DEMOCRATIC | PREDOMINANTLY REPUBLICAN | MAJORITY REPUBLICAN | NONPARTISAN |

(B) Sex of respondent:

| 1. MALE | 2. FEMALE |

(C) Apparent ethnic origin:

| 1. WHITE | 2. BLACK | 3. SPANISH | 7. OTHER (SPECIFY) _____ _____ | 8. DK |

(D) Persons besides R present during interview:

| 1. NO ONE | 7. OTHER OFFICIAL (SPECIFY):_____ |

(E) (IF OTHERS PRESENT DURING INTERVIEW) How often did this person speak up during the interview?

| 1. CONSTANTLY | 2. OFTEN | 3. OCCASIONALLY | 4. RARELY | 5. NEVER |

(F) Length of interview [EXACTLY, PLEASE]

_____(minutes)

time to the nearest minute _____

THUMBNAIL SKETCH:

SURVEY RESEARCH CENTER
INSTITUTE FOR SOCIAL RESEARCH
THE UNIVERSITY OF MICHIGAN
ANN ARBOR, MICHIGAN 48106

(Do not write in above space .)

1. Interviewer's Label

2. STATE:_____

3. Your Interview No. _____

4. Date _____

5. Length of Interview _____
            (Minutes)

STATE OFFICIALS

INTRODUCTION:

In discussing general revenue sharing with you during this interview, we will be referring to "fiscal years." If we say "fiscal year 1974" we want <u>your state's</u> fiscal year. Will you tell me the beginning and ending dates of your fiscal year?

MO:_____ DAY:_____   MO:_____ DAY:_____
        BEGIN   END

IF R'S STATE IS ON A CALENDAR YEAR (JAN. 1 - DEC. 31):

WHERE THE QUESTIONS CONTAIN THE PHRASE FISCAL YEAR 1974 SUBSTITUTE THE PHRASE CALENDAR YEAR 1973; WHERE THE QUESTIONS SAY FISCAL YEAR 1975 OR FISCAL YEAR 1973 SUBSTITUTE CALENDAR YEAR 1974 or 1972.

THESE APPEAR IN THE HEADING FOR SECTION B, B2, B5, THE INTRODUCTION TO B6, B11, B12, B14, B15.

ALSO, THE PHRASES APPEAR IN THE INTRODUCTION TO C1 (PAGE 12), C2, C5, THE INTRODUCTION TO C6, C11 AND C12.

257

time to the nearest minute _____

A1. Now that you have had some experience with general revenue sharing we would like to know how you feel about its impact. Are there particular features of general revenue sharing that you feel very favorable about? (IF YES) And what would those be?

_____

_____

_____

_____

_____

_____

_____

A2. Are there particular features that you feel very unfavorable about? (And what would those be?)

_____

_____

_____

_____

_____

_____

_____

A3. (CARD A, YELLOW) For each statement that I read, just tell me whether you agree strongly, agree somewhat, disagree somewhat, or disagree strongly. The first statement is: Because of revenue sharing we have been able to develop some new programs at the state level. How do you feel about that? Just tell me the letter on the card.

	A AGREE STRONGLY (1)	B AGREE SOMEWHAT (2)	C DISAGREE SOMEWHAT (4)	D DISAGREE STRONGLY (5)	NO IDEA, DON'T KNOW (8)
a. BECAUSE OF REVENUE SHARING WE HAVE BEEN ABLE TO DEVELOP SOME NEW PROGRAMS AT THE STATE LEVEL					
b. The state as a whole is finally getting some of its tax money back					
c. State governments have been able to avoid tax increases					
d. Local governments have been able to develop some new programs					
e. Local governments are now subject to less control by the _federal_ government					
f. Local governments are now subject to less control by the _state_ government					
g. Local governments have been able to avoid tax increases					

A4. Over the period that revenue sharing funds have been available, what do you think is the most satisfactory and productive use to which this state has put its share of these funds?

_____

_____

_____

_____

A4a. And what do you think is the most satisfactory and productive use to which the local governments in this state have put their revenue sharing money?

_____

_____

_____

_____

A5. What, in your judgment, is the least satisfactory or productive use to which this state has put its revenue sharing money?

_____

_____

_____

_____

A5a. And what would you say is the least satisfactory use to which local governments in this state have put their revenue sharing money?

_____

_____

_____

_____

4

A6. As you know, federal revenue sharing will expire in 1976, unless it is extended. Do you think federal revenue sharing should continue?

1. YES	5. NO		3. PRO-CON OR DEPENDS

A6a. How strongly do you feel about that, very strongly, or not so strongly?

1. VERY STRONGLY	2. NOT SO STRONGLY

A6b. Why do you think revenue sharing (should/should not) be continued?

_____

_____

_____

_____

_____

_____

_____

A6c. Why do you feel that way?

_____

_____

_____

_____

A7. (CARD B, ORANGE) How would you feel about the following changes in the revenue sharing program? For each <u>change</u> tell me whether you would be strongly in favor of it, somewhat in favor, or whether you would oppose it somewhat or oppose it strongly. Just tell me the letter on the card.

First with respect to the <u>state</u> government, how do you feel about:

	A STRONGLY FAVOR (1)	B SOMEWHAT FAVOR (2)	C SOMEWHAT OPPOSE (4)	D STRONGLY OPPOSE (5)
a. Changing the allocation formula to				
1. increase the reward going to the states which have their own income taxes				
2. give a larger share of the funds to states and a smaller share to local units				
3. give a smaller share of the funds to states and a larger share to local units				
4. give the states and local governments shares proportional to their respective tax efforts				
5. provide incentives for regional cooperation				
6. make it easier to know your payments over the next few years				
b. How do you feel about adjusting payments to keep up with inflation				
c. Allowing revenue sharing money to be used as the matching share of federal grants				
d. Imposing priority expenditure categories on state use of revenue sharing funds				
e. Substantially increasing the reporting and enforcement requirements				
With respect to <u>local governments</u> in this state, how do you feel about...				
a. Changing the allocation formula to				
1. give more money to poorer communities				
2. omit very small government units				
3. give more to big city areas				

6

	A STRONGLY FAVOR (1)	B SOMEWHAT FAVOR (2)	C SOMEWHAT OPPOSE (4)	D STRONGLY OPPOSE (5)
4. discourage reduction in local tax rates				
5. encourage the consolidation of small government units				
6. remove the penalty against special districts by including local assessments as part of the tax base				
7. make it easier for them to know their payments over the next few years				
8. remove the penalty against getting revenue from user charges by including them in the definition of tax effort				
b. Again with respect to local governments how do you feel about eliminating priority expenditure requirements?				
c. Allowing revenue sharing money to be used as the matching share of federal grants?				
d. Developing more complete budget reporting categories?				
e. Requiring the formation of citizen advisory committees to decide how to use revenue sharing money?				
f. Adjusting payments to keep up with inflation?				

A8. Are there any other changes that you would favor either at the state or local level? (IF YES) What do you have in mind? (INTERVIEWER--INDICATE WHETHER STATE OR LOCAL.)

_____

_____

_____

_____

SECTION B: REVENUE SHARING IMPACT--FISCAL YEAR 1974 BUDGET (CALENDAR 1973)

We are interested in your judgment about the budgetary impact in this state of the general revenue sharing program during your fiscal year 1974. When we finish this series of questions we will also be asking you about fiscal year 1975 (calendar 1974).

B1.   What would have been different about the programs run by this state without revenue sharing?

_____

_____

_____

_____

_____

B2.   Thinking of total expenditures at the state level, including state transfers to local governments, would you have reduced total spending for fiscal year 1974 if there had been no revenue sharing money?

| 1.   YES |
| 5.   NO |

TURN TO P. 8,   TURN TO P. 11,
SEQUENCE I   SEQUENCE II

SEQUENCE I

B3. Would the reduction in total spending, including transfers to local governments, have been equal to the amount of revenue sharing money you received or less than that amount or what?

1. EQUAL TO	2. LESS THAN	3. OTHER: _____
GO TO B5		GO TO B3b

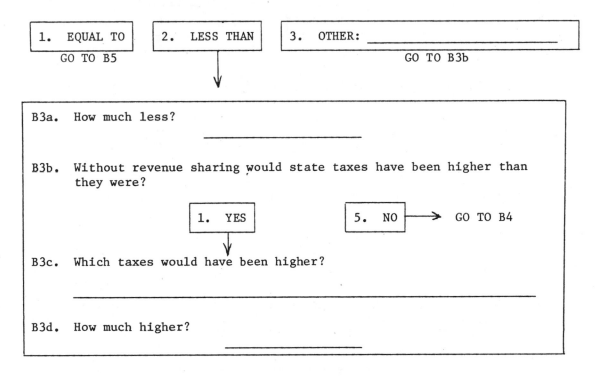

B3a. How much less?

_____

B3b. Without revenue sharing would state taxes have been higher than they were?

| 1. YES | 5. NO | → GO TO B4 |

B3c. Which taxes would have been higher?

_____

B3d. How much higher?

_____

B4. Would your level of borrowing have been higher than it was?

| 1. YES | 5. NO | → GO TO B5 |

B4a. How much higher?

_____

B5. Would your surplus or your reserve funds at the end of fiscal year 1974 have been lower than they were?

| 1. YES | 5. NO | → TURN TO P. 9 , B6 |

B5a. A little lower, somewhat lower or much lower?

1. LITTLE LOWER	2. SOMEWHAT LOWER	3. MUCH LOWER

You indicated earlier that total spending would have been lower during fiscal year 1974 if revenue sharing funds had not been available.

B6. Would this reduction have involved direct <u>operating</u> expenditures at the state level?

| 1. YES | 5. NO |

B7. Would capital expenditures at the state level have been lower?

| 1. YES | 5. NO |

B8. Would transfers to local governments have been lower?

| 1. YES | 5. NO |

B9. What specific state programs would have been reduced or eliminated if revenue sharing funds had not been available? (ASK FOR RANKINGS IF SEVERAL PROGRAMS ARE GIVEN--WHICH PROGRAM WOULD HAVE BEEN CUT FIRST, SECOND, ETC.)

_____

_____

_____

_____

B10. What part of the public would have been most affected by this?

_____

_____

_____

_____

B11. Thinking back to fiscal <u>1973</u>, what specific programs in this state, if any, would have been reduced or eliminated if revenue sharing funds had not been available?

_____

_____

_____

_____

TURN TO P. 12 , SECTION C

SEQUENCE II

B12. You indicated that even without revenue sharing money you would have kept the same level of fiscal year 1974 <u>spending</u>, including transfers to local government. Without revenue sharing would state taxes have been higher than they were?

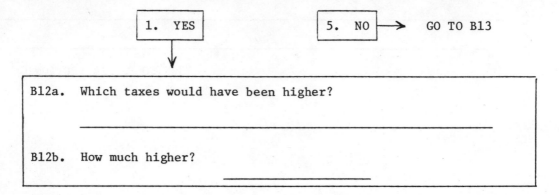

1. YES

| 5. NO | → GO TO B13 |

B12a. Which taxes would have been higher?

_____

B12b. How much higher?

_____

B13. Would your level of borrowing have been higher than it was?

1. YES

| 5. NO | → GO TO B14 |

B13a. How much higher?

_____

B14. Would your surplus or your reserve funds at the end of fiscal year 1974 have been lower than they were?

1. YES

| 5. NO | → GO TO B15 |

B14a. A little lower, somewhat lower, or much lower?

1. LITTLE LOWER	2. SOMEWHAT LOWER	3. MUCH LOWER

B15. Thinking back to fiscal <u>1973</u>, what specific programs, if any, would have been reduced or eliminated in this state if revenue sharing funds had not been available?

_____

_____

_____

SECTION C: REVENUE SHARING IMPACT--FISCAL YEAR 1975 BUDGET

We are interested in your judgment about the budgetary impact in this state of the general revenue sharing program during your fiscal year 1975.

C1. What would have been different about the programs run by this state without revenue sharing?

_____

_____

_____

_____

_____

C2. Thinking of total expenditures at the state level, including state transfers to local governments, would you have reduced total spending for fiscal year 1975 if there had been no revenue sharing money?

1. YES		5. NO
TURN TO P. 13,		TURN TO P. 16,
SEQUENCE I		SEQUENCE II

SEQUENCE I

C3. Would the reduction in total spending, including transfers to local governments, be equal to the amount of revenue sharing money you received or less than that amount or what?

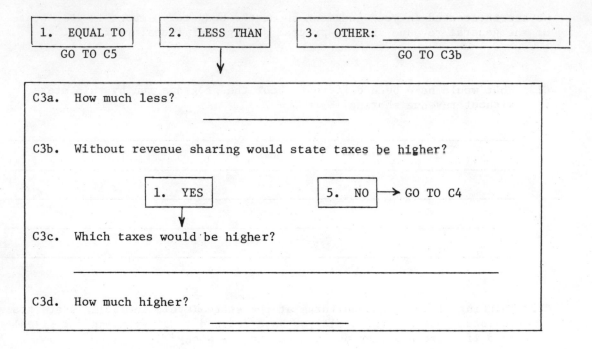

1. EQUAL TO	2. LESS THAN	3. OTHER: _____
GO TO C5		GO TO C3b

C3a. How much less?

_____

C3b. Without revenue sharing would state taxes be higher?

| 1. YES | 5. NO | → GO TO C4 |

C3c. Which taxes would be higher?

_____

C3d. How much higher?

_____

C4. Would your level of borrowing be higher?

| 1. YES | 5. NO | → GO TO C5 |

C4a. How much higher?

_____

C5. Without revenue sharing funds would your surplus or reserve funds at the end of fiscal year 1975 be lower?

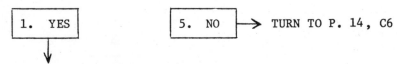

| 1. YES | 5. NO | → TURN TO P. 14, C6 |

C5a. A little lower, somewhat lower or much lower?

| 1. LITTLE LOWER | 2. SOMEWHAT LOWER | 3. MUCH LOWER |

14

You indicated earlier that total spending would be lower during fiscal year 1975 if revenue sharing funds were not available.

C6. Would this reduction involve direct <u>operating</u> expenditures at the state level?

| 1. YES | 5. NO |

C7. Would <u>capital</u> expenditures at the state level be lower?

| 1. YES | 5. NO |

C8. Would transfers to local governments be lower?

| 1. YES | 5. NO |

C9. What specific state programs would be reduced or eliminated if revenue sharing funds were not available?

_____

_____

_____

_____

_____

C10. What part of the public would be most affected by this?

_____

_____

_____

_____

C11. At the end of fiscal year 1974, about how large was your general fund surplus?

$_____

C12. Will your general fund surplus at the end of fiscal year 1975 be larger or smaller than that?

1. LARGER		2. SMALLER		3. ABOUT THE SAME
				GO TO C13

C12a. About how much?

$_____

C13. In general what types of factors are responsible for the present surplus in your general fund?

_____

_____

_____

_____

C14. Do you think these factors will continue to produce general fund surpluses in the future, or are they temporary, or what?

_____

_____

_____

_____

TURN TO P. 18, SECTION D

SEQUENCE II

C15. You indicated that even without revenue sharing money you would keep the same level of fiscal year 1975 <u>spending</u>, including transfers to local governments. Without revenue sharing would state taxes be higher than they are?

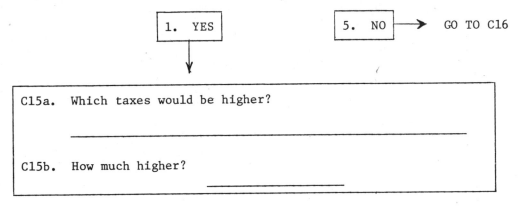

| 1. YES | 5. NO → GO TO C16 |

> C15a. Which taxes would be higher?
>
> _____
>
> C15b. How much higher?
>
> _____

C16. Would your level of borrowing be higher?

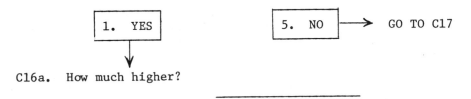

| 1. YES | 5. NO → GO TO C17 |

C16a. How much higher?   _____

C17. Without revenue sharing funds would your surplus or reserve funds at the end of fiscal year 1975 be lower?

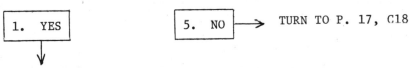

| 1. YES | 5. NO → TURN TO P. 17, C18 |

C17a. A little lower, somewhat lower, or much lower?

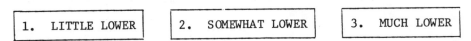

| 1. LITTLE LOWER | 2. SOMEWHAT LOWER | 3. MUCH LOWER |

C18. At the end of fiscal year 1974, about how large was your general fund surplus?

$_____

C19. Will your general fund surplus at the end of fiscal year 1975 be larger or smaller than that?

1. LARGER	2. SMALLER	3. ABOUT THE SAME
		GO TO C20

C19a. About how much?

$_____

C20. In general what types of factors are responsible for the present surplus in your general fund?

_____

_____

_____

_____

_____

C21. Do you think these factors will continue to produce general fund surpluses in the future, or are they temporary, or what?

_____

_____

_____

_____

TURN TO P. 18, SECTION D

SECTION D: PROGRAM IMPACT

Now I have a few general questions about (STATE NAME).

D1. What would you say are the three most important problems facing (STATE NAME)?

1. _____

_____

2. _____

_____

3. _____

_____

D2. We're interested in whether revenue sharing has made any difference in your ability to deal with any of these problems. Let's take the first problem you mentioned (REPEAT FIRST PROBLEM). Has revenue sharing made any difference in dealing with that problem?

| 1. YES | 5. NO |

D2a. Why is that?

_____

_____

_____

_____

D3. What about the second problem (REPEAT SECOND PROBLEM). Has revenue sharing made a difference there?

| 1. YES | | 5. NO |

D3a. And why is that?

_____

_____

_____

_____

D4. Finally, what about the third problem? (REPEAT THIRD PROBLEM).

| 1. YES | | 5. NO |

D4a. And why is that?

_____

_____

_____

D5. Is revenue sharing likely to make any difference in your ability to deal with any of these major problems in the future?

| 1. YES | | 5. NO | → TURN TO P. 20, D6

D5a. Which problems? _____

_____

_____

D5b. In what ways will revenue sharing make a difference?

_____

_____

D6. Would you favor more or fewer   federal restrictions on the use of revenue sharing funds?

1. MORE	2. ABOUT THE SAME	3. FEWER
	GO TO D7	

D6a. What sort of restrictions do you have in mind?

_____

_____

_____

_____

GO TO D7

D6b. What sort of restrictions would you like to see eliminated?

_____

_____

_____

_____

GO TO D7

D7. If you were free to allocate your state revenue sharing funds all over again, would you do it the same way or do it differently?

1. DO IT THE SAME WAY	2. DO IT DIFFERENTLY
TURN TO P. 22, D9	

D8. In what ways would you change the allocation of revenue sharing funds if you could do it all over again?

_____

_____

_____

_____

D9. Overall, would you say that your state government has used revenue sharing dollars to finance ongoing activities or to start new ones?

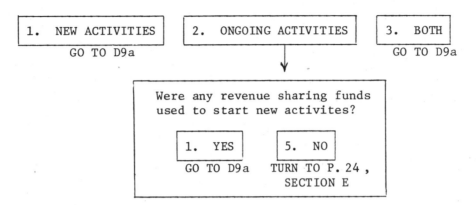

1. NEW ACTIVITIES	2. ONGOING ACTIVITIES	3. BOTH
GO TO D9a		GO TO D9a

Were any revenue sharing funds used to start new activites?

1. YES	5. NO
GO TO D9a	TURN TO P. 24, SECTION E

D9a. Can you give me examples of the new activities you have begun with revenue sharing funds? (RECORD EACH ACTIVITY AT TOP OF COLUMN AND ASK D9b-D9f FOR EACH.)

D9b. What was the approximate annual cost of the (ACTIVITY)?

D9c. Would you have undertaken this new activity without revenue sharing?

D9d. Would you describe (ACTIVITY) as an innovative addition to your programs?

D9e. Was (ACTIVITY) conducted by your state alone or in cooperation with other government units or private agencies?

D9f. (IF WITH OTHERS) What other units or agencies were involved?

ACTIVITY

1. _____

$_____
   ANNUAL COST

YES 1. WOULD HAVE	NO 5. WOULD NOT

1. YES	5. NO

1. ALONE	OTHER 2. UNITS/ AGENCIES

(SPECIFY):_____

_____

_____

_____

ACTIVITIY

2. _____

$_____
ANNUAL COST

| 1. | YES WOULD HAVE | | 5. | NO WOULD NOT |

| 1. YES | | 5. NO |

| 1. ALONE | | 2. | OTHER UNITS/ AGENCIES |

(SPECIFY): _____

_____

_____

_____

ACTIVITY

3. _____

$_____
ANNUAL COST

| 1. | YES WOULD HAVE | | 5. | NO WOULD NOT |

| 1. YES | | 5. NO |

| 1. ALONE | | 2. | OTHER UNITS/ AGENCIES |

(SPECIFY): _____

_____

_____

_____

SECTION E: IMPACT ON THE BUDGET PROCESS

E1. Has revenue sharing made it more difficult or less difficult or hasn't it made any difference in your planning for future expenditures?

1. MORE DIFFICULT	2. LESS DIFFICULT	3. HASN'T MADE ANY DIFFERENCE
		GO TO E2

E1a. Why is that?

_____

_____

_____

E2. How about controlling expenditures? (Has revenue sharing made it more difficult, less difficult or hasn't it made any difference?)

1. MORE DIFFICULT	2. LESS DIFFICULT	3. HASN'T MADE ANY DIFFERENCE
		GO TO E3

E2a. Why is that?

_____

_____

_____

E3. How about setting priorities for expenditures? (Has revenue sharing made it more difficult, less difficult or hasn't it made any difference?)

1. MORE DIFFICULT	2. LESS DIFFICULT	3. HASN'T MADE ANY DIFFERENCE
		TURN TO P. 25 , E4

E3a. Why is that?

_____

_____

_____

E4. What kinds of state-wide groups or organizations have expressed interest in revenue sharing?

_____

_____

_____

IF NONE ⎯⎯⎯⎯⎯⎯→ GO TO E7

E5. What kinds of things have they done to show their interest?

_____

_____

_____

_____

E6. Were all of these groups as active before revenue sharing as afterward?

| 1. YES | | 5. NO |
GO TO E7

E6a. Which ones became more active after revenue sharing was introduced?

_____

_____

E7. Have any particular groups been critical because of the way revenue sharing funds have been handled?

| 1. YES | | 5. NO | → TURN TO P. 26 , E8

E7a. Which ones would those be?

1. _____

2. _____

3. _____

E7b. What have they been critical about?

1. _____

2. _____

3. _____

E8. Do you find yourself paying attention to different kinds of issues or problems in this state because of revenue sharing?

| 1. YES | | 5. NO | → GO TO E9 |

E8a. What kinds of issues would those be? _____

_____

_____

_____

E9. Have state officials been contacted by anyone about civil rights enforcement in the revenue sharing program?

| 1. YES | | 5. NO | → GO TO E10 |

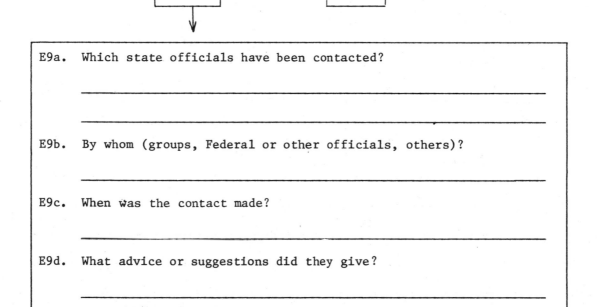

E9a. Which state officials have been contacted?

_____

_____

E9b. By whom (groups, Federal or other officials, others)?

_____

E9c. When was the contact made?

_____

E9d. What advice or suggestions did they give?

_____

_____

_____

E10. Have the prohibitions against discrimination in revenue sharing been more restrictive, less restrictive or about the same as those in other federal grants?

| 1. MORE RESTRICTIVE | 5. LESS RESTRICTIVE | 3. ABOUT THE SAME |

SECTION F: INTERGOVERNMENTAL RELATIONSHIPS

F1. (CARD C, WHITE) *We are also interested in the effect of revenue sharing on your relations with other government officials.* For each type of official I mention, please tell me the amount of contact of any kind that you have with them as a result of revenue sharing. First, what about federal admini-strators, other than those in the Office of Revenue Sharing?

	A MUCH MORE CONTACT (1)	B SOMEWHAT MORE CONTACT (2)	C ABOUT THE SAME CONTACT (3)	D SOMEWHAT LESS CONTACT (4)	E MUCH LESS CONTACT (5)
a. FEDERAL ADMINISTRATORS (OTHER THAN ORS OFFICIALS)					
b. Congressmen and Senators					
c. State Officials					

d. (IF RESPONSE IS CATEGORY A, B, D OR E ASK): What is it about revenue sharing that causes you to have (more/less) contact with (OFFICIALS)?

_____

_____

_____

_____

_____

_____

F2. In general, *how would you judge the amount of disagreement over the state budget now as compared with what it was before revenue sharing?* First, how about <u>within</u> particular departments or agencies of this state--is the conflict over the budget less, more, or about the same as it was before revenue sharing? (CONTINUE WITH REMAINDER.)

	A LESS CONFLICT THAN BEFORE (1)	B MORE CONFLICT THAN BEFORE (5)	C SAME AS BEFORE (3)
a. WITHIN DEPARTMENTS OR AGENCIES OF THIS STATE			
b. Across state departments or agencies?			
c. Between the executive and legislative branches of the state government?			
d. Between the state government and local government units?			
e. Between the state government and the general public?			
f. Between this state government and local citizens' groups?			
g. Between the state government and the media?			

F3. Some people have argued that revenue sharing will encourage certain changes among local government jurisdictions. For each one I mention, *please indicate whether you think revenue sharing will or will not encourage certain changes.* First, do you think revenue sharing will encourage cities and towns to annex outlying areas?

	1. YES, WILL ENCOURAGE	5. NO, WILL NOT ENCOURAGE	8. DON'T KNOW
a. ENCOURAGE CITIES AND TOWNS TO ANNEX OUTLYING AREAS?			
b. Encourage municipalities and counties to take over some functions now being performed by special districts?			
c. Encourage less reliance on user charges by local governments?			
d. Encourage the consolidation of existing governmental units such as cities and counties?			
e. Encourage some small governments to increase the range of their activities?			
f. Encourage the continued existence of inefficient units of local government.			

F4. As a result of revenue sharing has your state undergone any changes in its taxing structure?

| 1. YES | 5. NO |

F4a. Exactly what kinds of changes have occured?

_____

_____

_____

F4b. What do you think will be the effect of these changes?

_____

_____

_____

F4c. Are there any plans for such changes?

| 1. YES | 5. NO |
GO TO F5

F4d. What kinds of changes?

_____

_____

_____

F4e. What do you think will be the effect of these changes?

_____

_____

_____

F5. Has your state considered adjusting the formula by which revenue sharing funds are allocated to local governments?

| 1. YES | 5. NO |

F5a. What kinds of adjustments are you thinking of?

_____

_____

_____

F5b. What types of local government are most likely to be affected by these adjustments?

_____

_____

_____

F5c. Are there any plans for such adjustments?

| 1. YES | 5. NO |
GO TO F6

F5d. What kinds of adjustments?

_____

_____

_____

F5e. What types of local government are most likely to be affected by these adjustments?

_____

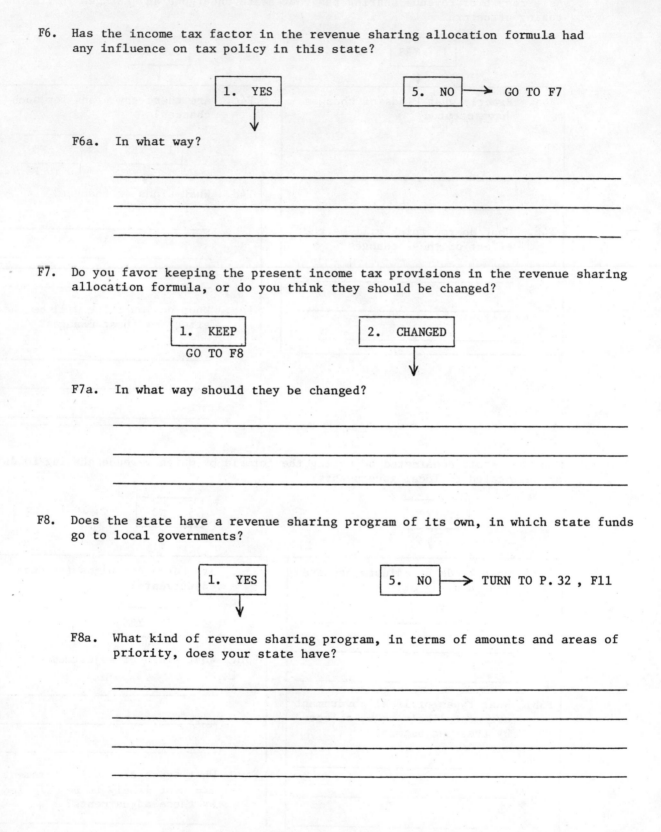

F6. Has the income tax factor in the revenue sharing allocation formula had any influence on tax policy in this state?

1. YES   5. NO → GO TO F7

F6a. In what way?

_____

_____

_____

F7. Do you favor keeping the present income tax provisions in the revenue sharing allocation formula, or do you think they should be changed?

1. KEEP   2. CHANGED
GO TO F8

F7a. In what way should they be changed?

_____

_____

_____

F8. Does the state have a revenue sharing program of its own, in which state funds go to local governments?

1. YES   5. NO → TURN TO P. 32 , F11

F8a. What kind of revenue sharing program, in terms of amounts and areas of priority, does your state have?

_____

_____

_____

_____

F9. Is your state revenue sharing program generally more restrictive, less restrictive, or about the same as the federal revenue sharing program?

| 1. MORE RESTRICTIVE | 2. LESS RESTRICTIVE | 3. ABOUT THE SAME | 4. DEPENDS |

GO TO F10

F9a. In what ways? _____

_____

_____

_____

_____

F9b. Could you tell me more about this?

_____

_____

_____

_____

F10. In the past two or three years, have your state revenue sharing programs to localities become more restrictive, less restrictive, or remained about the same?

| 1. MORE RESTRICTIVE | 2. LESS RESTRICTIVE | 3. ABOUT THE SAME |

F11. Currently, there are no requirements that general purpose local governments must meet in order to be eligible for revenue sharing money. Do you think there should be minimum requirements for...

F11a. Why do you feel that way?

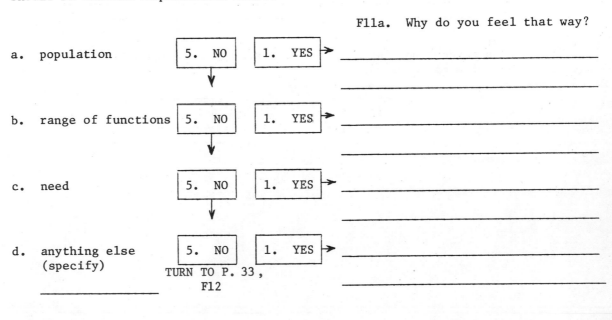

a. population | 5. NO | 1. YES → _____

b. range of functions | 5. NO | 1. YES → _____

_____

c. need | 5. NO | 1. YES → _____

_____

d. anything else (specify) | 5. NO | 1. YES → _____

TURN TO P. 33, F12

_____

_____

F12. In the last two or three years has your state government felt any pressure to expand local government functions?

| 1. YES | | 5. NO | → GO TO F13 |

F12a. What kind of functions? _____

_____

_____

F12b. What kind of local governments have been exerting this pressure?

_____

_____

F12c. How has your state responded? _____

_____

_____

F12d. To what extent is this pressure due to general revenue sharing-- entirely, to some extent, or not at all?

| 1. ENTIRELY | 2. TO SOME EXTENT | 3. NOT AT ALL |

F13. Has revenue sharing affected your state's willingness to expand local government functions?

| 1. YES | 5. NO |

F14. In the last two or three years has your state government felt any pressure from local governments to provide additional direct services or additional funding for locally provided services?

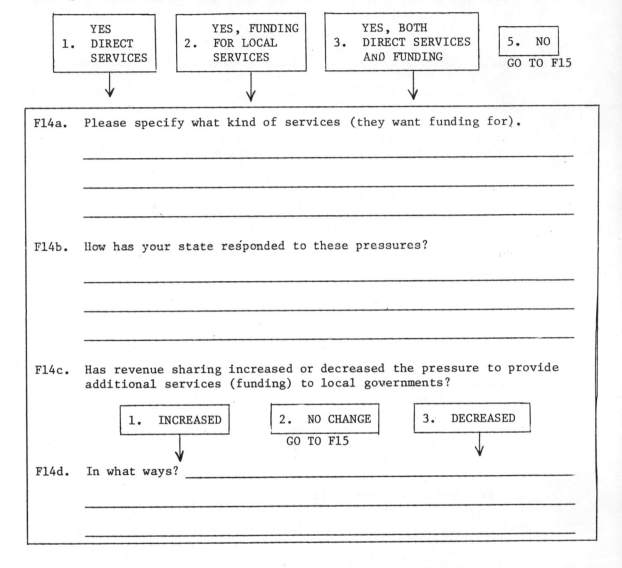

| 1. YES DIRECT SERVICES | 2. YES, FUNDING FOR LOCAL SERVICES | 3. YES, BOTH DIRECT SERVICES AND FUNDING | 5. NO GO TO F15 |

F14a. Please specify what kind of services (they want funding for).

_____

_____

_____

F14b. How has your state responded to these pressures?

_____

_____

_____

F14c. Has revenue sharing increased or decreased the pressure to provide additional services (funding) to local governments?

| 1. INCREASED | 2. NO CHANGE GO TO F15 | 3. DECREASED |

F14d. In what ways? _____

_____

_____

F15. Would you say that federal revenue sharing for local governments in your state has increased or decreased the pressure on your state budget?

| 1. INCREASED | 2. DECREASED | 5. NO CHANGE TURN TO P. 35, F16 |

F15a. In what specific way has your state budget been affected?

_____

_____

_____

F16. It has been suggested that because of such things as declining school expenditures and increasing revenues, state governments are experiencing less fiscal pressure. How do you feel about that?

_____

_____

_____

F17. It has been suggested that general revenue sharing be continued for local governments but not for state governments. Do you see any merit in this idea?

| 1. YES | | 5. NO |

F17a. Why do you feel this way? _____

_____

_____

_____

F18. Do you view revenue sharing as a supplement or as a substitute to other forms of federal support to state and local governments?

| 1. SUPPLEMENT | | 2. SUBSTITUTE |

F18a. Why do you feel this way? _____

_____

_____

_____

F19. Has general revenue sharing resulted in local government requests for changes in their tax structure regarding millage limitations, types of taxes that they can levy, and so forth?

| 1. YES | | 5. NO | → TURN TO P. 36 , F20

F19a. What kinds of requests? _____

_____

_____

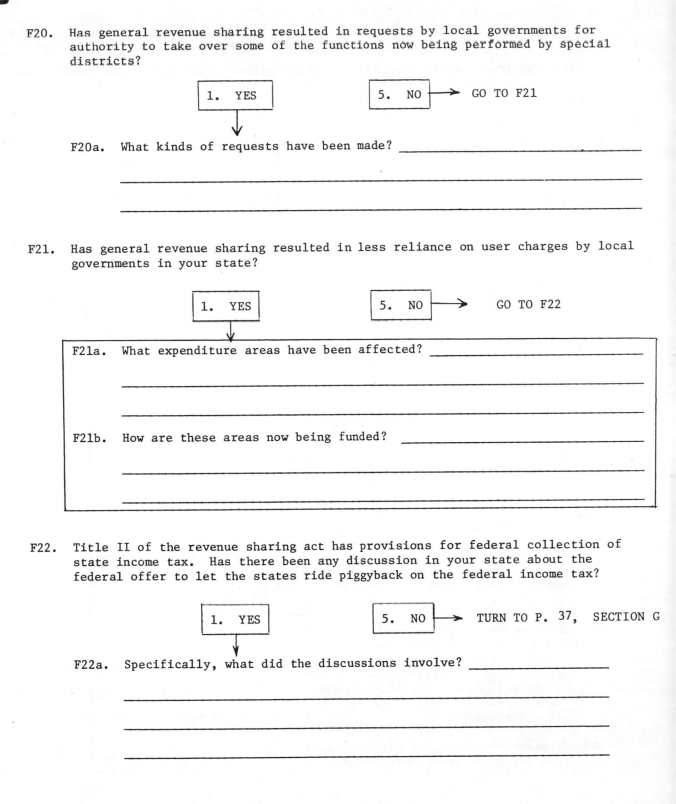

F20. Has general revenue sharing resulted in requests by local governments for authority to take over some of the functions now being performed by special districts?

| 1. YES | | 5. NO | → GO TO F21 |

F20a. What kinds of requests have been made? _____

_____

_____

F21. Has general revenue sharing resulted in less reliance on user charges by local governments in your state?

| 1. YES | | 5. NO | → GO TO F22 |

> F21a. What expenditure areas have been affected? _____
>
> _____
>
> _____
>
> F21b. How are these areas now being funded? _____
>
> _____
>
> _____

F22. Title II of the revenue sharing act has provisions for federal collection of state income tax. Has there been any discussion in your state about the federal offer to let the states ride piggyback on the federal income tax?

| 1. YES | | 5. NO | → TURN TO P. 37, SECTION G |

F22a. Specifically, what did the discussions involve? _____

_____

_____

_____

SECTION G: OPINIONS ABOUT REVENUE SHARING

(CARD A, YELLOW) People have expressed many different opinions about revenue sharing. I will read a number of such opinions, and for each one I'd like you to tell me whether you agree strongly, agree somewhat, disagree somewhat or disagree strongly. If you aren't sure or don't know, please indicate that.

	A AGREE STRONGLY (1)	B AGREE SOMEWHAT (2)	C DISAGREE SOMEWHAT (4)	D DISAGREE STRONGLY (5)	DON'T KNOW (8)
G1. Concern about the temporary nature of revenue sharing funds may have led some governments to spend most of their revenue sharing money on capital items.					
G2. Concern over the continuation of general revenue sharing may discourage some governments from using revenue sharing funds for experimental programs.					
G3. Increased public participation may make the allocation of revenue sharing funds different from other funds.					
G4. The best use of revenue sharing funds may be to reduce taxes.					
G5. The revenue sharing formula gives too much weight to tax effort and not enough to needs.					
G6. A fair share of revenue sharing money goes to government services for poor people.					
G7. Because the local jurisdictions are not permitted to spend their revenue sharing funds on operating expenses for education, there is increased pressure on state government to assist local units in financing education.					
G8. Revenue sharing has undermined categorical grant-in-aid programs.					

38

	A AGREE STRONGLY (1)	B AGREE SOMEWHAT (2)	C DISAGREE SOMEWHAT (4)	D DISAGREE STRONGLY (5)	DON'T KNOW (8)
G9. Active employee organizations mean that much of the revenue sharing money goes for salary increases.					
G10. Very small government units should get more revenue sharing funds because they are closer to the people than bigger units.					
G11. The best system of revenue sharing is one in which local governments are allowed to use the money for whatever they think best.					
G12. The administrative costs to the states of the general revenue sharing program is much less than the cost associated with other federal assistance programs.					
G13. High rates of inflation mean that much of revenue sharing goes for salary increases.					
G14. Revenue sharing funds will be used differently in the future than they have been in the past.					
G15. Inflation has cut down the use of revenue sharing funds for innovative programs.					
G16. One of the goals of the federal revenue sharing program should be equalization of the financial capacities of the state.					
G17. Local governments should be given the same freedom as the states in spending revenue sharing money.					
G18. The allocation formula for local governments should encourage them to reduce taxes.					

G19. As you know, one of the announced aims of revenue sharing was to strengthen the role of state and local governments. Now that the plan has been in operation for a while, how well do you think that intention has been met overall--has revenue sharing strengthened state and local government or has it not made much difference?

STRENGTHENED	STRENGTHENED IN SOME	NOT MADE MUCH
1. STATE & LOCAL GOVERNMENT	3. WAYS, NO DIFFERENCE IN OTHERS	5. DIFFERENCE

G19a. And could you tell me why you feel that way? (PROBE FOR AS MUCH DETAIL AND REFLECTION AS POSSIBLE.)

_____

_____

_____

_____

_____

_____

_____

_____

G20. Are there any other general comments you would like to make about the General Revenue Sharing program, either relating to questions that I have asked or to aspects that were not mentioned?

_____

_____

_____

_____

_____

INTERVIEWER INSTRUCTION WHEN INTERVIEWING GOVERNOR OF THE STATE:

SKIP SECTION H--FILL OUT OBSERVATION SECTION, P. 42, AND WRITE THUMBNAIL SKETCH.

TIME NOW: _____

SECTION H: BACKGROUND INFORMATION

Our last, short series of questions deal with background data about yourself.
We usually find that these questions help explain why people have different
sorts of attitudes and perceptions. However, you may decide you would prefer
not to answer some of these questions, even though your name will <u>never</u> be
associated with your answers. If that is the case, just tell me and we'll go
on to the next question.

H1.   In what year were you born?   _____
                                          YEAR

H2.   Where was it that you grew up? (IF UNITED STATES) Which state or
      states?

      _____

      _____

         (IF R GREW UP IN STATE DIFFERENT   H2a.   How old were you when
          FROM CURRENT RESIDENCE - ASK H2a)   you came to this state?

                                                          _____
                                                                YEARS

H3.   How long have you lived in the (NAME OF COMMUNITY) area?   _____
                                                                    YEARS

H4.   Were you brought up mostly in the country, in a town, in a small city
      or in a large city?

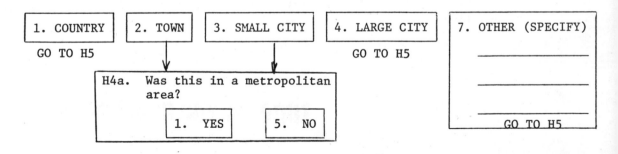

H5.   How about your father's main occupation while you were growing up? What
      sort of work did he do?

      _____

H6. How long have you held your present position as (TITLE)?

_____(YEARS)

H7. Did you have a previous official position in the state government?

_____

H8. What is the highest grade of school or year of college you completed?

| 00 | 01 | 02 | 03 | 04 | 05 | 06 | 07 | 08 | 09 | 10 | 11 | 12 |

| 13 | 14 | 15 | 16 | 17+ |

H8a. Do you have a
college degree?

1. YES   5. NO

H8b. What degree is that?

_____

These are all the questions I have. Thank you very much for all your time and cooperation.

time to the nearest minute _____

42 COMPLETE FOLLOWING QUESTIONS
BY OBSERVATION

(A) Political characteristics of the present administration in this state.

| PREDOMINANTLY DEMOCRAT | MAJORITY DEMOCRATIC | PREDOMINANTLY REPUBLICAN | MAJORITY REPUBLICAN |

(B) Sex of respondent:

| 1. MALE | 2. FEMALE |

(C) Apparent ethnic origin:

| 1. WHITE | 2. BLACK | 3. SPANISH | 7. OTHER (SPECIFY) _____ _____ | 8. DK |

(D) Persons besides R present during interview:

| 1. NO ONE | 7. OTHER OFFICIAL (SPECIFY): _____ |

(E) (IF OTHERS PRESENT DURING INTERVIEW) How often did this person speak up during the interview?

| 1. CONSTANTLY | 2. OFTEN | 3. OCCASIONALLY | 4. RARELY | 5. NEVER |

THUMBNAIL SKETCH:

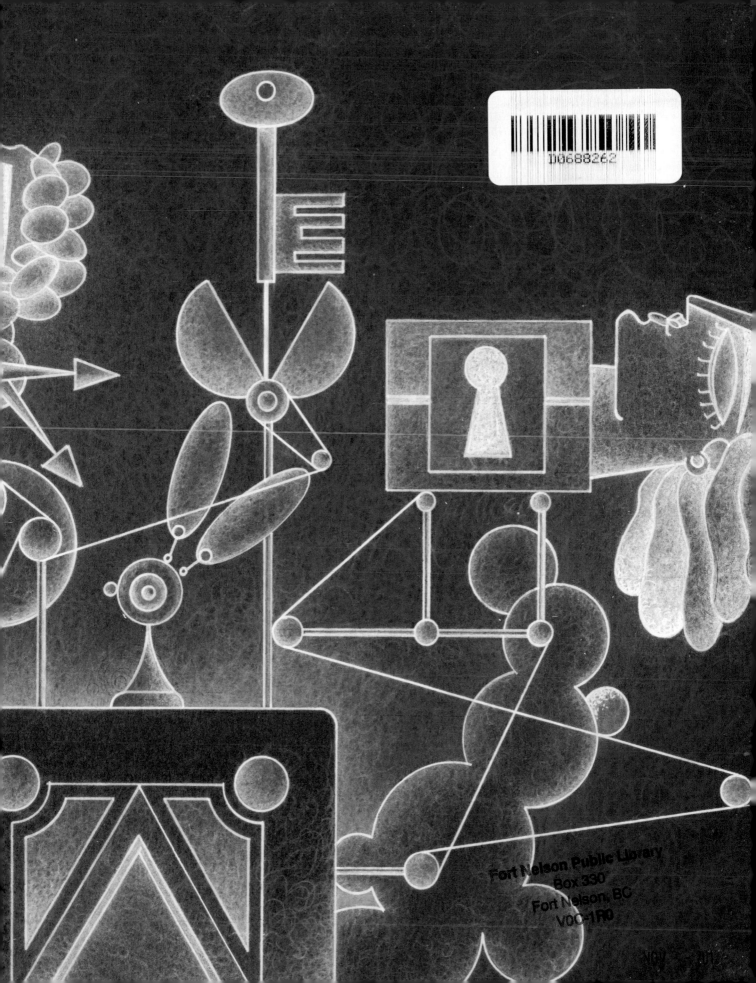

CUENTO DE LUZ

"Magic is as real as the magic of reality."
- Anonymous

To my parents, Manuel and Rosario, for everything.
To my sister, Nati, for everything.

- Fran Nuño

To Carmen, Julia, Pablo and Marta,
For the gift of the magic of your childhood.

To my parents and brothers.
To Mabel, Paco and Miguel.
To Luz, and of course, to my FRIEND Francisco Morilla.
For everything you've ever given me.

- Enrique Quevedo

The Great Magician of the World

Text © 2012 Fran Nuño
Illustrations © 2012 Enrique Quevedo
This edition © 2012 Cuento de Luz SL
Calle Claveles 10 | Urb Monteclaro | Pozuelo de Alarcón | 28223 Madrid | Spain | www.cuentodeluz.com
Original title in Spanish: El Gran Mago del Mundo
English translation by Jon Brokenbrow

ISBN: 978-84-15241-11-9

Printed by Shanghai Chenxi Printing Co., Ltd. in PRC, January 2012, print number 1256-06

FSC
www.fsc.org
MIX
Paper from
responsible sourc
FSC® C00792

The Great
Magician
of the
World

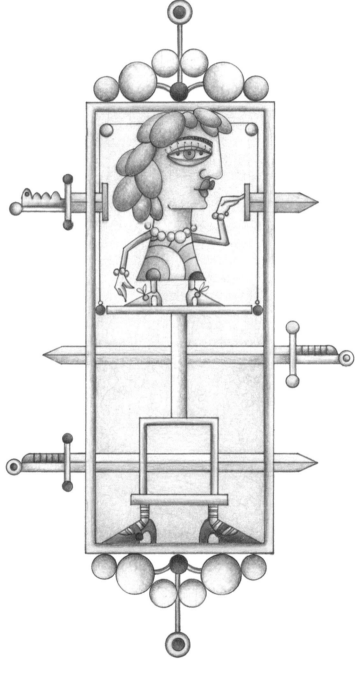

Fran Nuño
Illustrated by Enrique Quevedo

I like magic so much that sometimes I pretend I'm a great magician and that I can do the most beautiful, amazing tricks in the world.

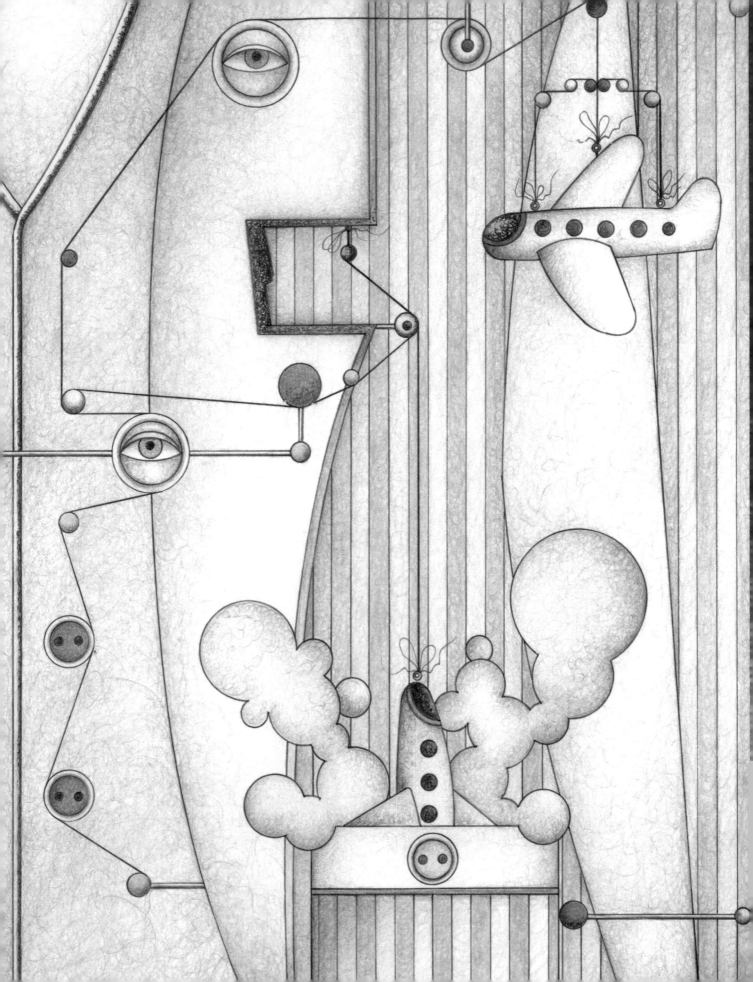

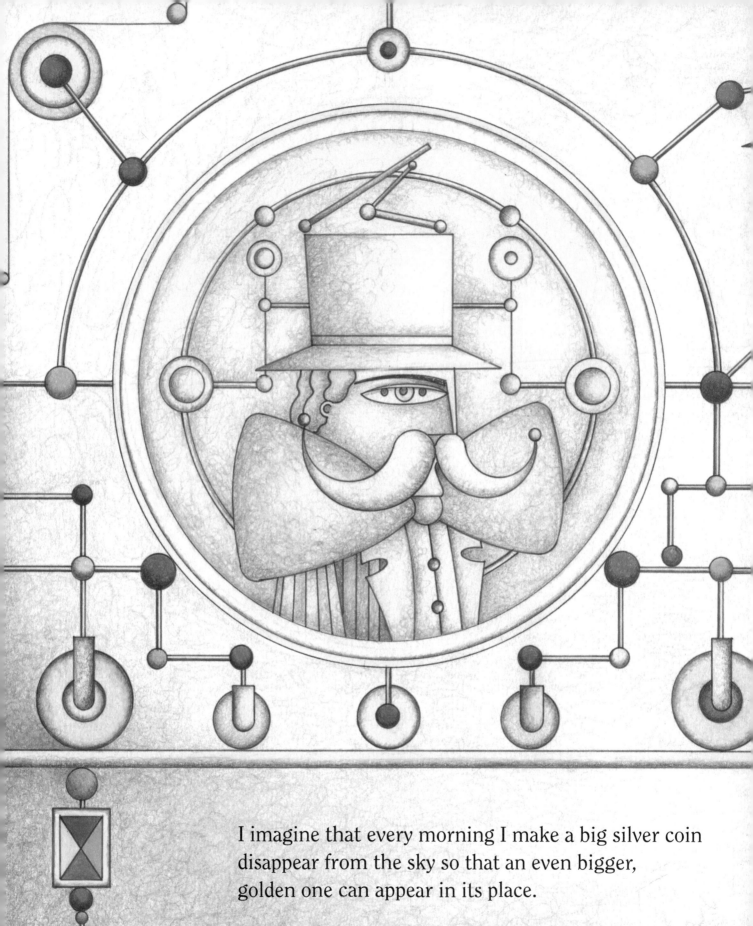

I imagine that every morning I make a big silver coin disappear from the sky so that an even bigger, golden one can appear in its place.

I think that sometimes I fill the same sky with huge white and gray doves, which appear with a wave of my hands...

And that all of these birds have cards in their beaks, which they release to flutter gently down on us.

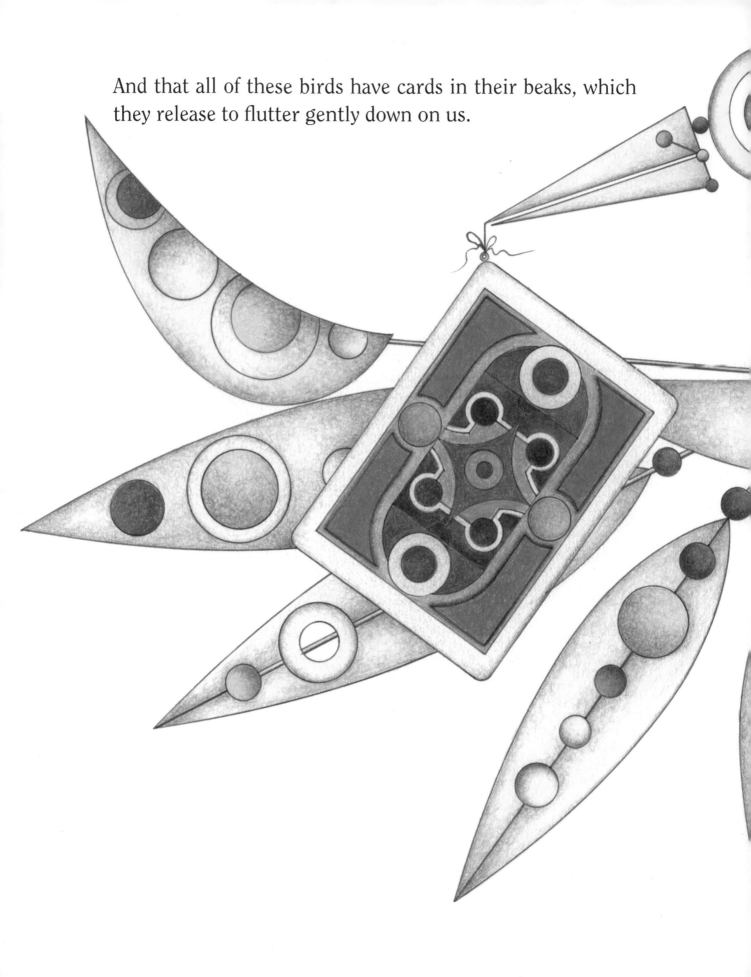

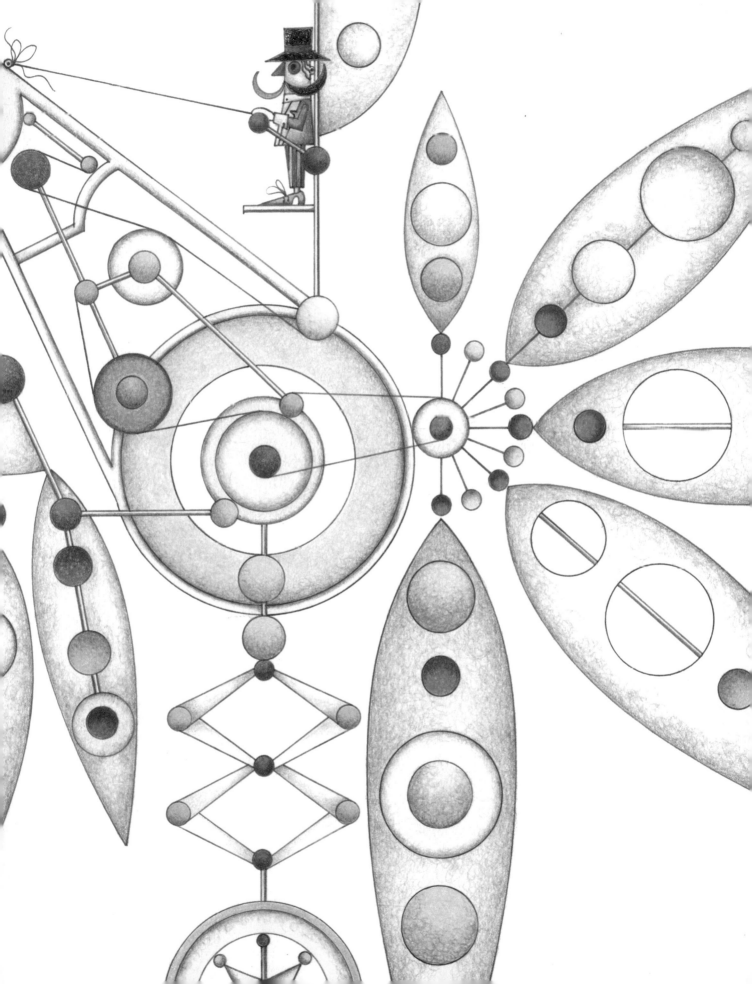

Sometimes the cards reach the ground cold,
with their drawings, letters or numbers faded away,
and sometimes they've turned into drops of water.

I dream that in the afternoons I make a perfect, extraordinary rainbow with seven handkerchiefs in different colors: red, orange, yellow…

And, from time to time, I wave my magic wand to make millions of beautiful flowers, which I scatter all around me.

I daydream that by blowing gently, I can make the tops of the trees wave, blowing away their dry leaves to make a magic, crispy carpet on the ground...

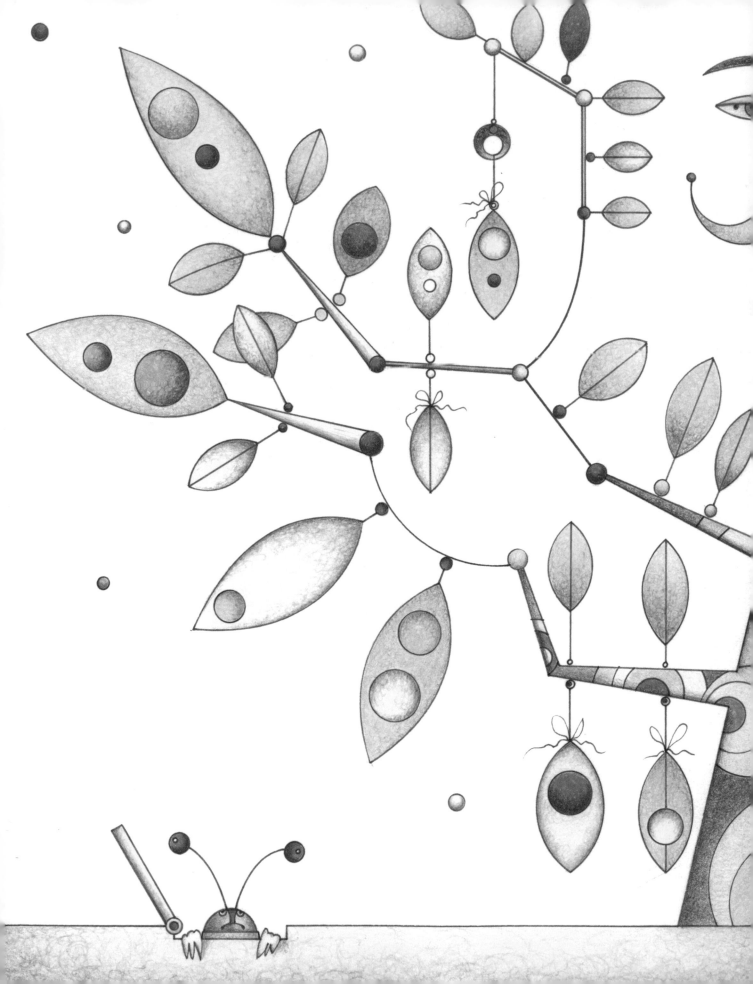

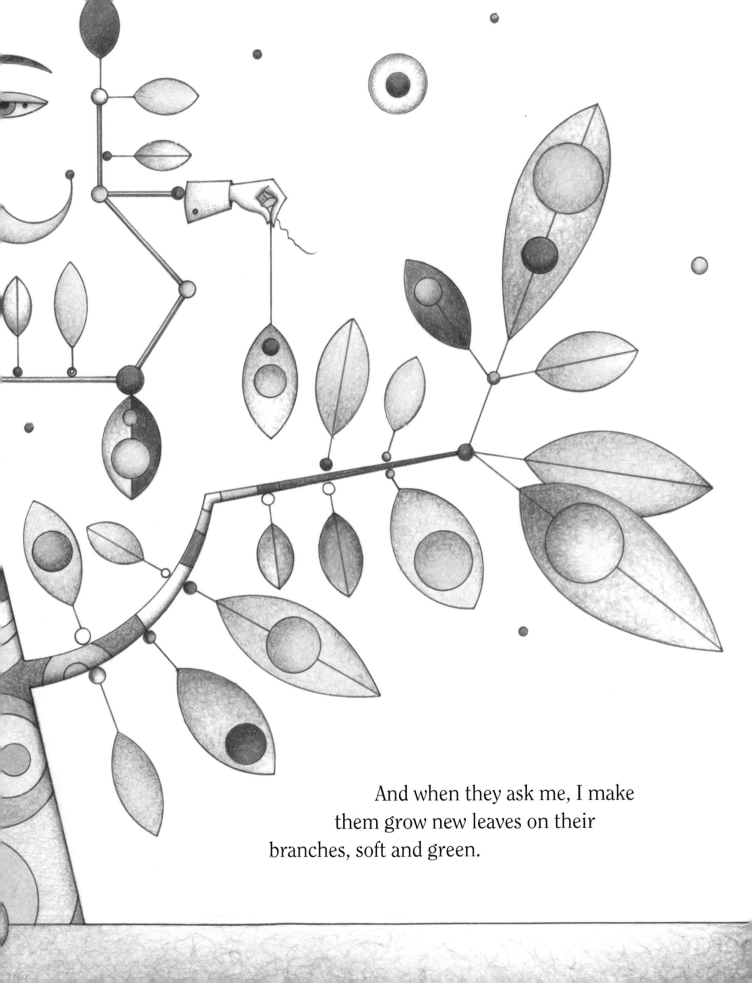

And when they ask me, I make
them grow new leaves on their
branches, soft and green.

I pretend that every day I perform in a great theater and I leave the stage raising my top hat, which I can use to darken half of the earth for a few hours, allowing me to rest.

I like magic so much that there are mornings when I wake up imagining things, thinking, dreaming and fantasizing…

...enchanted by the idea
that I can do all of these
wonderful things...

And that's why I'm known as…

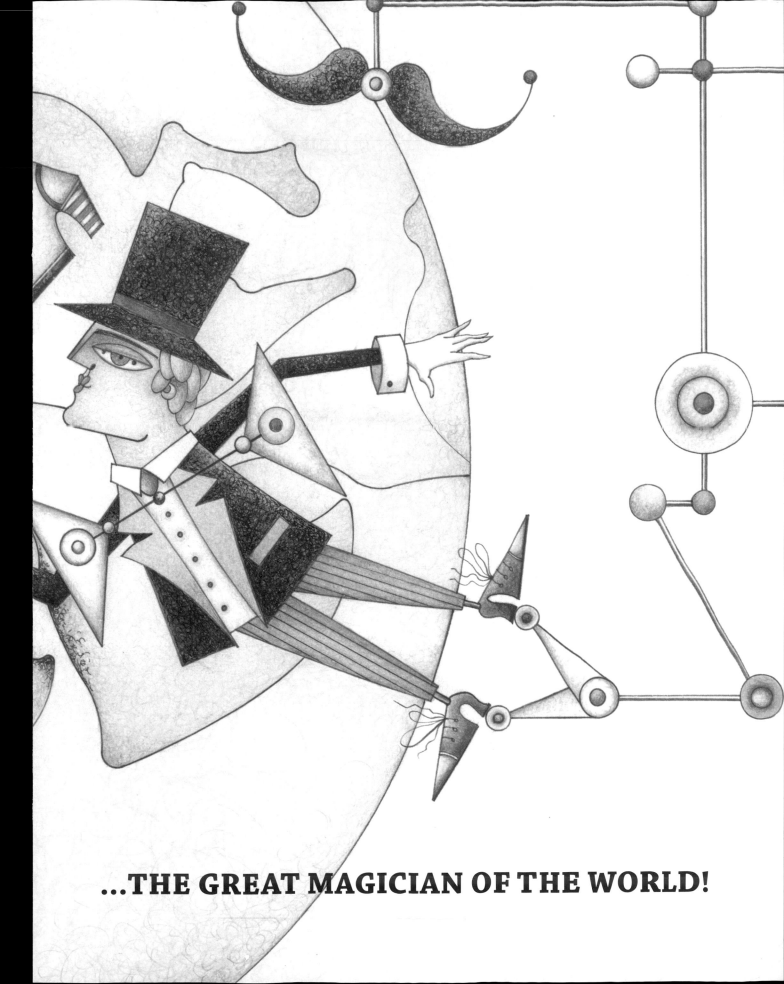

...THE GREAT MAGICIAN OF THE WORLD!